ACCIDENTAL
INDIA
• • •

ACCIDENTAL INDIA

A

HISTORY OF THE NATION'S

PASSAGE THROUGH CRISIS

AND CHANGE

SHANKKAR AIYAR

ALEPH

ALEPH BOOK COMPANY
An independent publishing firm
promoted by *Rupa Publications India*

First published in India in 2012 by
Aleph Book Company
7/16 Ansari Road, Daryaganj
New Delhi 110002

Copyright © Shankkar Aiyar 2012

All rights reserved.

No part of this publication may be reproduced, transmitted, or stored in a retrieval system, in any form or by any means, without permission in writing from Aleph Book Company.

ISBN: 978-81-923280-8-9

1 3 5 7 9 10 8 6 4 2

For sale in the Indian subcontinent only.

This book is sold subject to the condition that it shall not, by way of trade or otherwise, be lent, resold, hired out, or otherwise circulated without the publisher's prior consent in any form of binding or cover other than that in which it is published.

ACCIDENTAL INDIA

A
HISTORY OF THE NATION'S
PASSAGE THROUGH CRISIS
AND CHANGE

SHANKKAR AIYAR

ALEPH

ALEPH BOOK COMPANY
An independent publishing firm
promoted by *Rupa Publications India*

First published in India in 2012 by
Aleph Book Company
7/16 Ansari Road, Daryaganj
New Delhi 110002

Copyright © Shankkar Aiyar 2012

All rights reserved.

No part of this publication may be reproduced, transmitted, or stored in a retrieval system, in any form or by any means, without permission in writing from Aleph Book Company.

ISBN: 978-81-923280-8-9

1 3 5 7 9 10 8 6 4 2

For sale in the Indian subcontinent only.

This book is sold subject to the condition that it shall not, by way of trade or otherwise, be lent, resold, hired out, or otherwise circulated without the publisher's prior consent in any form of binding or cover other than that in which it is published.

Prathamesh Sri Siddhi Vinayaka
Sri Saraswati, the Goddess of Learning
and all who taught me to learn

...

CONTENTS

PREFACE 9
Why is crisis the stimulus for positive change in India? Is the flaw cultural or political? The country seems to dwell permanently in the domain between celebrated potential and frustrating failure. Will the nation's leaders only act when spurred on by shame or fear?

THE BONFIRE OF THE VANITIES 21
THE LIBERALIZATION OF THE ECONOMY 1991
For four decades India's leaders believed they could manage the economy according to preconceived political ideas. Their instrument of regulation was the licence-permit-quota raj. It throttled growth. Yet, evidence of failure was used to further tighten control. Change was compelled by circumstance and propelled by crisis.

THE HUNGER GAMES 74
THE GREEN REVOLUTION 1964
India suffered the worst famines in world history during British rule. When the country achieved independence it was clear that its rulers had learned little from the past because there was no attempt to become agriculturally self-sufficient. Instead, India depended on food aid and pretended it could feed itself. Salvation came via shame, the christening of the country as a 'ship-to-mouth' economy, and the Malthusian threat of annihilation by famine.

DAS KAPITAL 118
THE NATIONALIZATION OF BANKS 1969
Since 1947 banking was largely controlled by industrial houses. Access to capital was virtually a privilege and the spread of banking was dictated by profitability. Socialists and leftists agitated for the nationalization of banks but successive governments skirted the issue. Then, Indira Gandhi discovered the political capital that could be released through democratizing capital.

THE MILKY WAY 157
OPERATION FLOOD 1970
The idea of milk cooperatives, and the Amul model created by Verghese Kurien—these have been around since the fifties. These innovative ideas should have been adopted at

the national level to end the shortage of milk and improve rural incomes but they were ignored and even actively opposed for decades. India would have still been dependent on imports had it not been for Kurien's creative intervention in converting free butter and powder into venture capital to fund the national milk grid.

SOUP KITCHEN FOR THE SOUL   188

THE MID-DAY MEAL SCHEME 1982

This was an idea first mooted in 1923. The mid-day meal scheme addresses malnutrition, curbs population rise and pushes up literacy by encouraging enrolment in schools. Despite such obvious positives India's children were denied a fair shot at a future for forty years. The adoption of the programme was contested relentlessly as populist and resisted by the Centre till the new millennium.

THE BLACK SWAN   219

THE SOFTWARE REVOLUTION 1990

India's talent pool and geographical advantage, based on its location on the time zone, gives it an edge in certain sectors of the software industry. Software delivers high employment with low capital investment. By the late seventies the ability of India's engineers was already known. The sector also had the potential to earn badly needed foreign exchange. Shackled by controls on the import of computers, crippled by poor connectivity and denied travel dollars the revolution awaited a saviour.

THE DA VINCI CODE   257

THE RIGHT TO INFORMATION 2005

The Constitution recognizes freedom of speech as a fundamental right. The right to access information is implicit in this recognition without which this fundamental right is essentially toothless. But freedom of information was systematically denied to the country's citizens for decades despite efforts by pressure groups and activists. And then, the Supreme Court stepped in to enable the right.

EPILOGUE   288

Not every crisis catalyses action. The state of poverty and human deprivation in the country is shameful. Agriculture needs a second revolution. Water scarcity is a silent crisis. The lack of energy security threatens growth. National security is compromised by political compulsions. The relationship between the Centre and the states is barely functional. India must formulate cogent responses to the myriad problems that threaten its well-being and not await a crisis to initiate change.

Author's Note   315
Acknowledgements   316
Selected Interviews and Sources   318
Notes   321
Index   339

PREFACE

Five out of ten middle-class Indians born in the nineties scarcely know of an India that languished in want. Where millions waited years for a telephone. When members of parliament were implored for a cooking gas connection from their quota. Where you waited for the better part of a decade, after booking it, to ride a Bajaj scooter. When choice was limited to the colour of the car, not fifty brands and one hundred and fifty variants. These post-91ers probably couldn't conceive of a scenario where their countrymen queued up at the crack of dawn at ration shops to collect Punjab wheat instead of the dirt-brown 'PL 480 wheat'.

The 'Hindu rate of growth' was but a reflection of, well, the Indian rate of change.

Today, the economy that was left ravaged and broken by the departing colonial power is regularly touted as one of breathtaking promise. And although much remains to be done, some of the country's achievements are definitely worth celebrating.

Accidental India is a quest to reconstruct the architecture and ancestry of the change that has taken place in the country, after it became independent on 15 August 1947.

The transformation of India is most apparent in the neon-lit pace of growth in certain sectors of the economy. Every second, mobile telecom companies log in three new subscribers; every minute, twenty Indians ride off on new motorbikes and 200 new passenger cars hit the roads every hour. To the casual observer, the country's lift-off from pathos to the promise of prosperity might seem ordained, orderly and guided by vision. The transformation might even appear spectacular if one shrinks the axis of time. This is a country that has gone from dependence on food aid to an annual harvest of 250 million tons in 2012 with a surplus of nearly 70 million tons; from queuing before donors at the Aid Consortium to being projected as among the top three economies in the world by 2050 by Goldman Sachs.

In reality, change has been slow, sore, stalked by sloth and incompetence; and, as we shall see, it has been driven by neither ideology nor institutional vision. An accident, normally, is an event that has unfortunate consequences. In this political economy, though, an accident can also be fortuitous. India's ascent has been fuelled by serendipity; change has come about as a consequence of circumstance and crisis, and has always been a result of an exogenous force. Most often, that force has been a crisis.

◆

The genesis of this book can be traced back to an afternoon in July 1991 when crates of gold were being furtively unloaded from the dull-grey vans of the Reserve Bank of India (RBI) into the loading bays of a heavy-bellied cargo aircraft. The country had only enough foreign exchange to pay for seven days of imports and had therefore secretly pledged 47 tons of gold from its reserves to the Bank of England to borrow $400 million to pay its creditors. I scooped the news of the emergency gold lift for *The Indian Express*. The news shocked a nation which traditionally reveres gold as uber-Lakshmi, the pawning of which was seen as public humiliation and woke people up to the enormity of the crisis.

Even as I filed follow-up reports, I thought subconsciously: was this the best the country could do—pledge its gold to pay creditors? Why did we wait for a crisis to act?

I have, since, been studying the evolution of the country's economy and my research reveals that every major change in modern India has come about in the wake of a crisis.

It is not as if India has not been blessed with iconic political leadership. Whatever their failings—and many of them were responsible for, at the very least, flagrant sins of omission—it is indisputable that our leaders were forces for lasting and beneficial change. Mahatma

Gandhi united a fractious country under the idea of freedom. India owes every shred of modernity it now boasts, be it democratic tradition or scientific outlook, to Jawaharlal Nehru. The diminutive Lal Bahadur Shastri was uncommonly courageous during the 1965 war with Pakistan; he displayed equal strength and shrewdness in his decision to support C. Subramaniam's idea of the Green Revolution. Indira Gandhi democratized capital by nationalizing banks and capitalized nationalism by creating Bangladesh. Rajiv Gandhi put technology on the map in the eighties. P. V. Narasimha Rao presided over the repair of a broken polity and a broken economy, Atal Bihari Vajpayee worked to bring various strands of the economy together.

Yet, India falters. It often teeters on the brink of catastrophe. Why should this be so? Why do Indian leaders not anticipate adversity and act before being engulfed by catastrophe? What prevents them from operating with foresight—the exigencies of their term; the mindset of their peers or perhaps even their subjects; the compromises of politics? The answer is a combination of all these factors.

The chasm between what a country is and what it should be, we are told, is located in its culture. What, then, is culture? Culture, says historian Philip Bagby, is mostly regularities or irregularities in the behaviour—internal, external—of members of a society. If so, is India's failure to respond with alacrity to challenges dictated by the peculiarities of its culture? Celebrated historian Arnold Toynbee wrestled with the context of culture while studying challenge and response in his *A Study of History*. He rejected it as a factor, citing 'inconstancy and variability' in the results he obtained. To apportion blame on culture one needs the predictability of success in response to challenges, and the evidence doesn't support any such conclusion. It doesn't stand to reason globally, it doesn't stand to reason in India.

Pop sociologists trot out theories about the slow rhythm of river-valley civilizations, bountiful geography and the somnolent climate to explain most Indians' tolerance of the dysfunctions in their society. This is just as flawed as the theory of uniformity in nature. The context of geography is relative to the approach of a people. The truth is, this very culture and this very river-valley civilization, commanded over

20 per cent of the global GDP in the 1700s.

One theory to explain the Indian way of dealing with crisis has some traction. It is the belief in karma, or destiny, which lends an air of fatalism to our response to everything that goes wrong. But surely, while karma could serve to explain fatalism at an individual level, it cannot be an alibi for institutional inertia. Besides, subscription to fate over free will is hardly unique to Indians.

Other theories abound. A radical opinion finds currency among development economists in seminar discourses and academic discussions. It is often opined that India chose universal suffrage too early, at the birth of the republic, as a result of which democracy itself has been the biggest millstone around the necks of its teeming millions. Certainly, the grant of voting rights was subject to qualifications and came in tranches in several of the more vibrant democracies. Political scientist Francis Fukuyama, discussing the origins of political order, observes that in the West, the rule of law was established first, followed by state-building, and, finally, the installation of democracy. India, in stark contrast, chose to do all this simultaneously. This did enlarge the magnitude of complexity in planning the country's evolution but a rich idea cannot be held responsible for poor execution.

Does the multiplicity of languages lead to a loss in translation of goals? Singapore's Lee Kuan Yew once remarked, 'India is not one nation, it is many nations with over thirty-two languages. No prime minister can speak in a language that will be understood across the country.' If this was the case, the seven 'mini miracles' discussed in this book would not have come to be, the revolutions would not have percolated.

What, then, explains the inability of Indian leaders to act decisively and imaginatively? What explains their repeated failures? The fatal flaw, it would appear, is primarily located in the very nature of the Indian political beast, which dictates its peculiar approach to development. Economists Daron Acemoğlu of MIT and James Robinson of Harvard University, authors of *Why Nations Fail: The Origins of Power, Prosperity and Poverty*, provide an insight. The destiny of a country, they say, is largely determined by its choice of political and economic systems.

The countries that have succeeded chose inclusive politics and inclusive economics. Indian politicians—influenced less by pride and more by prejudice and paranoia—chose a combination of incompatible ideas. That is, inclusive politics and extractive economics. In other words, political freedom was granted and economic freedom denied.

The members of the Constituent Assembly chose to make suffrage universal in the Constitution of India, thereby enshrining the principle of political freedom. This enlightened approach did not extend to economic freedom; the first government in its economic policy chose a closed economy. This, despite the fact that until 1914, India was among the world's most globalized economies with a share of over 2.5 per cent in world trade. The choice was driven by the collective perception that a country ravaged by colonization would need to be a nanny nation in which the state necessarily knew what was best for the individual.

And so it came to pass. A closed economy with its infamous process of granting licences and reserving quotas crippled the principal factors of production—technology, capital and labour. The closed economy precluded the adoption of better technology. Licensing constrained the deployment of capital as it was the government and not the market that decided what you could produce, how much you could produce and at what price you could sell. As a result, labour lost its right to price its services competitively, given that it operated in a buyers' market. Industrial labour could only get a part of what it was due, as returns on output were determined not by the market but by the government. Farmers were no better off, the policy of price suppression through the import of food grains to meet demand rendered agriculture virtually unviable.

One prescient observer predicted this nightmare-in-the-making. Shortly after India adopted the Constitution, its principal architect B. R. Ambedkar asked, 'On 26 January 1950, we are going to enter into a life of contradictions. In politics, we will have equality and in social and economic life we will have inequality. In politics, we will be recognizing the principle of one man one vote and one vote one value. In our social and economic life, we shall by reason of our social and economic structure, continue to deny the principle of one man one value. How long shall we continue to live this life of contradictions?'

For decades, as it turned out. The state reigned, though it didn't really care to serve.

◆

To its initial grave misstep, India's political and planning establishment added more. To promote economic growth, especially in the nascent stages of development of a country like India, common sense dictates that resources be allocated to agriculture for the upliftment of the largest mass of people. To grasp what 'mass' means in the Indian context, some figures are necessary. In 1951, India's population was 361 million, of which, half were below the poverty line; eight out of ten, or 82.7 per cent of its citizens lived in rural areas.

Although it was amply evident that the country was an agrarian economy, political compulsions dictated the need to shackle the feudal zamindars who owned vast rural tracts. In order to do this, resources had to be denied to agriculture for it was believed that the transfer of resources to agriculture would further enrich the rural rich. There was, in fact, an attempt in the thirties to bring land and agricultural markets under state control. But Mahatma Gandhi intervened, fearing class conflict and violence. Political scientist Francine Frankel observes in *India's Political Economy, 1947-2004* that a class-based nationalist organization 'would have splintered the independence movement'. There was also a fear that the land-owning kulaks would join forces with the British against the Congress.

For two decades after it gained independence, instead of trying to radically reinvent and support its agricultural sector, India sustained its food economy by increasing imports. Change was finally triggered by the fear of mortgaging national security at the altar of foreign food aid. It created the impulse for the Green Revolution.

The economy is not the only aspect of the country to have been hit hard by the deadly combination of political compromise, ineptitude and misgovernance. As we will see, by way of the seven 'accidents' discussed in the book, the economic history of modern India is littered with instances of missed opportunities in every sector, in every decade. Any change has come about in the wake of institutional failure and individual courage.

The India story we witness and celebrate today would have scarcely been visible had it not been for the cascading sequence of crises and change. Prime Minister Manmohan Singh has admitted candidly that the 1991 crisis was 'a blessing in disguise' and it helped 'liberalize the economy; there would have been difficulties in making changes without a crisis'.

◆

Crisis is universally known to be a change agent. United States President Barack Obama used the 2008 financial crisis to redraw the path for his country's economy. He engineered a stimulus package that aimed to stabilize housing markets, create room for consumption through tax cuts and expansion of employment through new projects—$46 billion for transportation, $31 billion to modernize federal buildings, $17 billion for renewable energy. He was doing what President Franklin Delano Roosevelt had done before him in 1932—use a crisis to push an agenda. The Depression of the thirties resulted in the crafting of the 'New Deal'. In the first 100 days of his tenure, President Roosevelt enacted legislation to cover a slew of political and economic issues that confronted the US. While some of the measures were later contested, many of those initiatives survive even today, including deposit insurance, housing administration and the social security system. When the Berlin Wall came down, Germany was confronted by a political challenge that could have triggered a crisis in the economy. It engineered the reunification plan and converted the challenge into an opportunity for political reconciliation and economic resurgence.

So, viewed through that particular filter, the experience of India is not unique. What sets the history of change in India apart from other nations is the fact that recurring failures and crises have not led to a systematic plan to fix the country's endemic problems once and for all. Why is this so?

We will examine aspects of this question in depth throughout *Accidental India*, but certain broad themes are immediately apparent.

Crisis does trigger change though not every crisis results in change, as the Epilogue will amply prove. C. Rangarajan, former RBI governor and now chief of the Prime Minister's Economic Advisory Council points out, 'The response to crisis and the trajectory of change can vary depending on conditions. The 1991 crisis resulted in a turn in the correct direction, the dismantling of the licence raj.'

Change is also limited by the force of the crisis. The 1991 crisis did force the political class to liberalize the economy but it was not followed through to a logical conclusion or its best outcome.

Change is halted, stalled or extinguished once the crisis retreats. The momentum afforded by the crisis is frittered away. Post the Green Revolution there has been no impetus to improve agricultural productivity. Post liberalization, once the economy was kick-started, the government not only retained discretionary clearances to maintain control but also brought in new ones. India has migrated from permit raj to what economist Kaushik Basu calls 'permission-ism'.

Twenty-one years after the 1991 reforms, the World Bank ranks India 132nd among 183 economies for 'ease of doing business'. It is ranked 181 for enforcing contracts—which can take as much as 1,420 days—and 182 for construction permits. Setting up a hotel can take ninety clearances, setting up a factory needs fifty-seven. And each clearance requires a 're-clearance' if the owner re-jigs a number, even for upping the total number of labourers. Once a business is operational it is subject to inspections under twelve different Acts of Parliament. At any given time, any official from any one of the departments implementing the laws can bring the enterprise to a grinding halt unless the gears of the bureaucracy are adequately greased. In theory, the dread system of licensing has been abolished. In practice the system has mutated. Every clearance has been converted into an opportunity to delay and demand. This new permissions raj forces corporate chieftains to fly to Delhi on Wednesdays to get a laundry list of clearances and then try to influence policy decided at the Thursday cabinet meetings.

'Resistance to change is both exogenous—enforced by vested

interests which profit from the status quo—and endogenous—enabled by sloth and those seeking the preservation of pelf,' points out G. V. Ramakrishna, veteran bureaucrat and former chairman of the Disinvestment Commission. Bimal Jalan, former governor of the RBI, recounts a telling anecdote. Sometime in the seventies, as he was about to announce a major liberalization in import licensing, he was approached by a senior official. Don't do it now, pleaded the officer. Asked why, he told Jalan to wait till after the marriage of his daughter as nobody would turn up with gifts!

As with the bureaucrats so with the politicians. For the people, change is usually a good thing; for the country's rulers, change is often a threat. Creative destruction not only reallocates economic power but also political power as it wrenches away rent from the entrenched. Not surprising, then, that politicians resist change, regardless of the criminal cost of neglect. They don't seem to care that every second Indian child suffers from malnutrition or that over 800 million people defecate in the open.

India is often described as a democracy of the poor in which governments voted in by the silent majority work for the vocal minority. Surely the political class should be worried about alienating the poor—the country's largest segment of voters? And why haven't the poor arraigned the political class for their neglect? What explains their infinite tolerance of repeated failure by political leaders? The truth is in the finite ability of the poor to come together, to not be able to leverage their numerical strength to form a political or social coalition.

As early as 1952, economist John Kenneth Galbraith educated 'small consumers' on the power of collective bargaining. The theory is applicable in politics too except that many impediments have been set up as hurdles to collective bargaining. Not only has the lack of education been a barrier, but also till 2005 the citizen was denied access to information by government. Add to this the ingrained fear of facing authority and the costs and institutional structures that inhibit the poor from engaging with the government. Above all is the navigation of complex loyalties based on caste and identity politics.

Political independence in 1947 brought with it many changes.

But beneath the surface power is still wielded by the edifice of social structures resting on community and caste that feed the political hierarchy. To capitalize on this state of affairs, political parties have successfully engineered divisions based on caste to overcome the threat of class action. Indians are justifiably proud of the unity that prevails across its diverse peoples. However, while this may hold true where the national spirit is concerned, this diversity has been exploited by successive regimes to divide and rule.

History has proven repeatedly that vested interests can overcome numerical interests. Political scientist and historian Gaetano Mosca notes in *The Ruling Class* that the people never rule as democrats think. Whatever the form of dispensation, 'the domination of an organized minority, obeying a single impulse, over the unorganized majority is inevitable'. The Indian experience bears out this truth.

◆

The competition is now between coalitions of interests. Idealism is rapidly dying, ideology is all but paralysed. Politics has become a family enterprise. Political parties no longer seek to be accepted by all, they just need to win a fractional vote share to enjoy derivative power. Leverage is the new morality and the quest for power is the new individual ideology. This has led to the emergence of the coalition era. Unsurprisingly, politicians have learnt to opportunistically blame coalition politics and the lack of an absolute majority for their failure to effect positive, enduring change.

And yet the truth, as we will see in the course of this book, is that the big game changers arrived in India not amidst the stability of a majority rule but despite volatility and political instability. This is true of the 1991 liberalization, the Green Revolution, bank nationalization and the enactment of the Right to Information Act.

Typically, for successive Indian governments, the unstated principle objective is to address the optics of the situation. This frustrates even well-meaning leaders and bureaucrats who are forced to choose the status quo. As a result, incrementalism reigns. As does the classic Indian antidote—studied indecision. Meleveetil Damodaran, former chairman of the Securities Exchange Board of India, recalls how a former boss told him rather wryly, 'Some decisions are taken, most others simply come into being.'

India is a complex landscape—culturally, demographically, geographically and politically—on such a vast scale that any political excuse will always be vaguely right because it will never be absolutely wrong. Politicians tend to choose a solution that is electorally profitable, bureaucrats choose that which is convenient and the public accepts that which is morally satisfying. The received wisdom in India, sponsored by those with vested interests, is that engineering wide or deep systemic change is too dangerous. It is argued that in a political economy as intricate and volatile as India's, change has to be gradual, calibrated. This has become one of the alibis for inertia.

However, those awaiting succour will eventually try and force change. As world-renowned author and epistemologist Nassim Nicholas Taleb observes, 'Suppressing volatility makes the world less predictable and more dangerous.' It is the very instinct to preserve the status quo that triggers the crisis. A blow-up, he says, will occur. The longer it takes for the blow-up to occur, the more damaging it will be for both economic and political systems.

The legacy of neglect is now mounting. India is faced with competing crises and conflicting compulsions. The country can scarcely be proud of the fact that development has missed millions by miles. It is imperative that this state of affairs not be allowed to continue.

What we will look at in this book are the crises that prompted the most far-reaching positive change, but, equally, we will see how our people need never have undergone the trauma they were forced to undergo. If India is to forever escape its reality as an inequitable, problem-ridden country with delusions of power and glory, it must change its way of thinking and doing.

Sixty-five years after independence, the lament about India is not so much about what it could not do but what it could but did not do. Crisis cannot be a permanent prefix for change.

> Once among the world's most globalized economies, India was ravaged by war and colonialism before it achieved freedom in 1947. After independence, it should have opted for an open economy, but pride and paranoia prevailed. Economic freedom was mortgaged to state control. The economy worsened with every passing decade and the nation grew more indebted. Its rulers lived in denial, until matters arrived at the inevitable tipping point...

THE BONFIRE OF THE VANITIES

6 P.M., 20 JUNE 1991
12, WILLINGDON CRESCENT ROAD

It was a typical Delhi summer day with the temperature hovering in the forties. The rasp of starched khadi blended with the rustle of raw silk, the thud of car doors bounced off the walls of the colonial mansion. Nervous laughter mingled with faux bonhomie and the air was heavy with the obsequiousness unique to the Delhi Durbar.

P. V. Narasimha Rao had been anointed prime minister just a few hours earlier and the pilgrims lined up to pay obeisance. Ironically, just a few weeks earlier, the wily hermit of the Congress party had been nudged into retirement to write his memoirs, through which he hoped to relive his days of political glory. Tragedy and fate willed otherwise.

As India lurched from turmoil to trauma following the assassination of Rajiv Gandhi on 21 May 1991, Rao returned to centre stage. In less than a fortnight, he engineered his resurrection, outwitting Sharad Pawar, a much younger challenger, through a combination of guile and intellect. Patiently, Rao allowed the aggression and disruption that Pawar represented to threaten the Congressmen. Arguably the most experienced practitioner of Congress politics, the polyglot managed to communicate to members of parliament and loyalists of the First Family—the Gandhis—that it was in their best interest to persist with a tried and tired status quo. The dictates of the moment, though, left no room for any sort of status quo. India may have emerged from its worst political crisis in recent history but it was trapped in an economic crisis that compelled an agenda for disruption.

Rao was to take oath in less than twenty-four hours and had to select a team that was acceptable to the First Family and the fragile coalition of interests he had forged. After sundown that day, all hangers-on at his official residence were shooed away, and Rao asked for his soup. In a quiet chamber, along with another wily old campaigner, Sitaram Kesri, he awaited the return of P. C. Alexander, his aide de campaign.

Just then, an usher walked in to inform Rao that an important visitor had arrived and was waiting to see him. It was Cabinet Secretary Naresh Chandra, an accomplished bureaucrat. As chief of the bureaucracy, Chandra had witnessed the most tumultuous period of his career since he took over in December 1990. India would swear in its third prime minister in eighteen months. Its economy had already been downgraded twice in six months from stable to speculative by the rating agencies. Its foreign exchange reserves were enough to cover just seven days of imports. Inflation was rising and the government was on the edge of bankruptcy.

Rao called him in. After the usual pleasantries, Chandra discussed the plans for the swearing in. Everything seemed in order—inasmuch as the chaos that defines politics would allow. The list of forty-five ministers was yet to be finalized and it would, as always, be a last-minute affair. Chandra then pulled out the file he had brought with him and handed it over to the prime minister-in-waiting. It included two notes: one was a detailed account of the economic crisis, the second laid out the blueprint for the revival of the country's economy.

Rao recognized the fait accompli he had been presented with. The draft for economic revival was the New Delhi Consensus, a promissory note India had committed to while seeking financial assistance from the Bretton Woods twins, the International Monetary Fund (IMF) and the World Bank. The Government of India had already availed of two tranches of loans as emergency funding to prevent a financial meltdown but it needed to do much more. On the verge of default, India had committed, in principle, to mend its ways of managing the economy.

To effectively defuse a crisis of this magnitude, Rao needed both political empowerment, ideally through a parliamentary majority, and the room to manoeuvre, but he had neither. He owed his crown to a covenant of loyalty to the Gandhis and he didn't have the freedom to act without let or hindrance. But not for nothing was Rao legendary for his political acumen and his ability to turn perilous situations to his advantage. He sensed this was the opportunity to dismantle not just the apparatus of state control, but an entrenched political class.

However, in order to put his plan into action, he would need an effective firefighter. Even before the final word on his coronation was out, Rao had approached the famous economist and former governor of the RBI, I. G. Patel, to join his team. Patel, ever the pragmatist, had begged off and suggested another career bureaucrat, Manmohan Singh, as a possible choice. Rao's need was for someone who was an acceptable face to the IMF and the World Bank, who knew the economy and understood the web of levers that controlled political decision-making. Singh qualified on all counts. He had served on every rung of hierarchy in the bureaucracy and was familiar with the interlocutors in the Fund-Bank dispensation. As secretary general of the South Commission—an institution set up to boost cooperation between poor and developing economies—he had interacted closely with Bank officials and IMF Managing Director Michel Camdessus. He was also known to harbour political ambitions.

Singh was on a flight back from Japan. The next day, at 5 a.m., Alexander rang him to say he wanted to see him. Alexander turned up at Singh's house at 7 a.m. and offered him the post of finance minister. Singh, says Alexander in his memoirs, *Through the Corridors of Power: An Insider's Story*, replied with a classic bureaucratic poser: 'What do you think?' His concern: would Rao and he get the political backing they needed? It was more a rhetorical poser than a real concern. After all, Singh had survived every political turn—from the nationalization of banks to partial liberalization—of successive governments for over two decades. He owed his survival to his ability to make a distinction between his opinion and the expediency his political masters expected of him. An economist as ambidextrous as any, he knew his 'on the one hand and on the other hand' arguments well. And, as adviser to the preceding prime minister, Chandra Shekhar, he knew the lie of the land, metaphorically and literally.

THE SEEDS OF STATE CONTROL

Since it became independent in 1947, India had believed in the mythological power of the State to deliver prosperity. The cult of nationalism was replaced by the church of socialism. To consolidate their hold on their parish, the evangelists of socialism used every crisis as an opportunity. Each time the economy stalled, these pundits argued that more control was needed, whereas the need was for an open economy. The country had always needed foreign exchange for imports and to sustain its economy. The strategy of import substitution—through, among other things, the licence-permit-quota raj—precluded competition, promoted inefficiency, stifled exports and aggravated the country's dependence on aid. As a result, every external shock or internal failure produced an economic crisis. India ended up a regular visitor to the soup kitchens of multilateral institutions, often on the verge of bankruptcy. Each visit to the lenders of foreign aid was greeted with the same prescription: remove the controls on the economy. Each time the rulers, living in denial, refused reform.

The seeds of state control were sown in the run-up to independence. The question of what an appropriate economic policy for independent India would be was debated from as early as the thirties. Within the Congress there were three lines of thought. Gandhian thought emphasized self-sufficient village economies in which goods would be produced in decentralized village and cottage cooperatives that would be protected from large industry. Adherents to this way of thinking felt it would raise the standard of living in rural areas, reduce unemployment and preserve the traditional Indian way of life. The second stream of thought was the preserve of Congress leaders like Rajendra Prasad and Sardar Vallabhbhai Patel who envisaged a mixed economy—a sort of private-public partnership—in which the private sector would play a major role in the rebuilding of the economy. The third, dominant stream of thought was led by Congress leaders like Jawaharlal Nehru who had had the benefit of Western education. This group was influenced by socialist doctrines and was convinced that wealth would need to be redistributed through the nationalization of industrial assets; they were convinced that the State should have a dominant role in the rebuilding of the economy.

By the end of the thirties, it was becoming clear that after independence some form of state-controlled socialism would be imposed on the country. The revolution that had established the Soviet Union and caused regime change in China swayed thinking within the Congress. The Indian National Congress, at its Working Committee meeting at Wardha in 1937, debated the need for national planning, and a year later at Haripura, resolved that Jawaharlal Nehru would head the National Planning Committee. The business community sensed the bias towards state control and pressure to enforce populist redistributive politics.

In late 1942, one of the country's leading industrialists, G. D. Birla, drove the initiative to design a new economic model for the politicians to consider. By January 1944, the Bombay Plan, formally titled *A Brief Memorandum Outlining a Plan of Economic Development of India,* authored by a group of entrepreneurs and technocrats including Purushottamdas Thakurdas, G. D. Birla, J. R. D. Tata, A. D. Shroff, Lala Shri Ram, Ardeshir Dalal, Kasturbhai Lalbhai and John Mathai was released and presented to the Congress. The Plan was received with great enthusiasm and, in a first, even published as a book in March 1944. For its time it was a far-sighted, well-articulated blueprint for independent India. The Plan listed the priorities that lay ahead of the new country and suggested how the new government could go about dealing with them. Ambitious and broad in its sweep, it sought to achieve a host of objectives, including a strategy to double per capita income within fifteen years. The stated objective of the Plan was to make the country aware of the issues that faced it and to aid in the process of creating a new India. In the words of the authors, the Bombay Plan 'was put forward as a basis of discussion, a statement in as concrete form as possible, of the objectives to be kept in mind in economic planning in India, the general lines on which the development should proceed and the demands which planning is likely to make on the country's resources.'

War and colonization had left vast segments of the economy and industry in tatters. First the East India Company, then the British government had rearranged rules and taxes to promote commercial crops, thereby virtually destroying the livelihood of farmers growing food grains. India had been reduced to a supplier of raw materials, be it ore or cotton. In fact, the American Mission led by Henry F. Grady that visited India in 1942 as part of the effort amidst World War II to scout for resources and capabilities, captured the pathetic state of affairs that existed in the country at the time when it described the industrial landscape as comprising mostly 'jobbing shops producing a wide variety of articles'.

The erstwhile colonial masters had frowned upon the ambitions of Indian entrepreneurs and used all manner of controls to thwart them from setting up independent businesses. The economy had been open in theory but was, in practice, heavily loaded in favour of British companies who used the open policy to source materials and raise resources from India. For instance, when Jamsetji Tata sought permission in the 1890s to raise funds to set up a steel plant in eastern India, the British government not only turned down his request but even questioned the competence of Indians to set up large industrial plants. Undeterred, Tata raised funds at home with help from various notables like Motilal Nehru and Mohammed Ali Jinnah to set up Tata Steel in 1907. But not everyone could be a Jamsetji Tata and the country was reduced to a market for British goods. The great economic damage caused to the country by colonization is well established by the statistical work of the Cambridge historian Angus Maddison. India's share of world income collapsed from 22.6 per cent in 1700, almost equal to Europe's share of 23.3 per cent at that time, to as low as 3.8 per cent in 1952. Indeed, at the beginning of the twentieth century, 'the brightest jewel in the British Crown' had become the poorest country in the world in terms of per capita income.

It was in these circumstances that the Bombay Plan was authored and disseminated. It was meant to convey to everyone who was interested that the business community sought a role in the rebuilding of India. The ideas mooted by the Plan resonated positively with the masses at large who had hitherto viewed most Indian industrialists as lenders to the British and partners in the exercise of colonization. Of course, it was not pure altruism that drove the effort. At the heart of the Plan lay the simple impetus of survival. And the Plan did succeed to a fair degree by creating a platform for reconciliation between the dominant political group and the business class, between Nehru's aim to design a state-controlled economy and the entrepreneurs' desire to stay relevant.

To make the Bombay Plan acceptable to the State, its architects declared that, 'no development of the kind we have proposed will be feasible except on the basis of a central directing authority, which enjoys sufficient popular support and possesses the requisite powers and jurisdiction'. Pleading the need for managing the environment and inflation, the Plan argued that when the country achieved independence, the State should seize all levers of economic freedom. It said: 'Every aspect of economic life will have to be so rigorously controlled by government that individual liberty and freedom of enterprise will suffer a temporary eclipse.'

In hindsight, it is clear that the surrender of economic freedom—as India attained political freedom—was intended to be a tactical retreat. The deafening cry for nationalization from within the Congress and the Left was a threat that couldn't be overlooked. So the authors of the Bombay Plan went short on freedom and long on survival. True to their entrepreneurial genes, they bought insurance by selling a peace pact to the political class. Not only did the Plan pre-empt the nationalization of business, it also sought to protect its existing interests from any new competitors. Building on the theme of nationalism, the Plan corralled business opportunities for domestic players and shut the door on foreign companies.

In its detailing of how development in the newly independent nation would be funded, the Plan listed as resources foreign borrowings or aid, hoarded wealth such as gold, sterling securities, savings and deficit financing or created money. There was no reference to foreign investment and, consequently, there was no role for foreign companies in post-1947 India. The implicit quest of the Bombay Plan soon found explicit political articulation, albeit clothed in nationalistic garb. Import substitution and self-reliance were declared as the cornerstones of government policy.

In the first week of April 1948, some six years after the Bombay Plan was first presented to the Congress, Syama Prasad Mookerjee, the minister for industry and supplies, moved the Industrial Policy Resolution. The Resolution paid obeisance to Gandhian thought, was socialist in tone and business-friendly in content. It was mostly what Indian business wanted. Thanks to the influence of Deputy Prime Minister Sardar Vallabhbhai Patel, hardline socialists were reined in. The Resolution provided for a role for the private sector and restricted the role of the State to just three sectors: munitions, atomic energy and railways, although it did reserve provisions for government investment in new capacities.

The political class did not rush to take over the space yielded by the business class but it was clear they intended to do so fairly quickly. Nehru set the tone in a debate on the Industrial Policy Resolution in the Constituent Assembly on 7 April 1948. He declared: 'Inevitably, the trend of events is to make the State more and more the organizer of construction and industry, and not the private capitalist or anybody else. This is inevitable as far I can see objectively. I do not entirely rule out the profit motive; I do not know how long it will last in a limited sense but in the larger sense of the term it will come more and more in conflict with the new idea of the socialist state. That conflict will go on and it is clear that it is the State which will survive, not that group which represents the profit motive in industry in its pure essence. This is an inevitable development.'

Decisive action followed. The Constitution of India was adopted in January 1950. In March 1950 the Planning Commission was constituted. In July 1950, the prime minister was appointed chairman of the Planning Commission. Within a year, in 1951, the government enacted the Industries Development and Regulation Act (IDRA). In December 1951, the First Five Year Plan was presented to Parliament and unveiled by 1952. The First Plan was mostly an accounts statement, a projection of the expenditure plan of the government. The IDRA served as the principle instrument of state control over industry and the economy. Although it did not deviate from the promise of 1948 to allow the private sector to participate in the evolution of the country's economy, the political rabble in the Congress left no one in any doubt about how the country would develop in the future. The theme of the chorus was redistribution and a greater role for government.

In 1955, the ruling Congress passed a resolution at its Avadi Session establishing a socialist pattern of society. The push for socialism was accompanied by the emergence of the economist P. C. Mahalanobis as the high priest of planning in government. The Mahalanobis model emphasized the need for government to take a leading role in investment to create capacity that would eventually lead to consumption. Just months before he passed away, Sardar Patel had rather ominously stated that a government which engaged itself in trade would come to grief. The Congress heard him but did not listen, and the clamour for state control became deafening.

The consequence was the Second Five Year Plan (1956-61) and the Industrial Policy Resolution of 1956, which comprehensively articulated the strategy for industrial development in India. The government was designated the biggest business house. The areas from which the private enterprise was barred went up from three in the First Plan to fifteen. The State acquired a monopoly over all big, capital-intensive businesses. The private sector was only allowed to operate in 'open areas' and was subject to clearances and controls. Flanking the new Industrial Policy Resolution were the Essential Commodities Act 1955, and the Companies Act 1956. The Essential Commodities Act gave the government the authority to regulate or prohibit the production and control of supply and distribution and absolute control over the pricing of anything declared essential. The Companies Act, widely viewed as one of the most detailed and stringent codes enacted by the new government, enabled it to virtually dictate terms to private corporations. Adding firepower to its arsenal was the Capital Issues Control Act 1956, which governed the pricing of capital and the archaic apparatus of import and export controls.

The government was now in full control. It decided where you could set up your business, what you could produce, how much you could produce, who you could sell to, how much you could sell, and at what price. The government decided on scale and even if the potential existed, it was subjected to the test of socialism. Moreover, the government had the first charge on every rupee that could be invested and enjoyed complete control of resources. The ramping up of controls on capacity and output threatened the very existence of private industry.

It wasn't long before industry found its voice. In a stringent critique, G. D. Birla described the Second Plan as unimaginative and Mahalanobis as a 'statistician devoid of a sense of economic organization'. He went on to characterize the Plan as a 'theoretical shibboleth which if enforced will in one sweep endanger India's future industrialization'.

C. Rajagopalachari, popularly known as Rajaji, who quit the Congress in 1954 and founded the Swatantra Party in 1959, brilliantly defined the proposed dispensation as the licence-permit-quota raj, and was among the first to oppose it. The denunciation by Rajaji was scathing. At a policy meeting of the newly formed Swatantra Party, he said, 'The policies of government should be founded on faith in the people and not on state compulsion and the encouragement of hatred and conflict between class and class, expropriation, repudiation of obligations and the conferment of more and more powers on the officials of government at the expense of the freedom of the citizens.'

Economists like B. R. Shenoy, P. R. Brahmananda and C. N. Vakil too disagreed with the approach. Their contention was that instead of focusing on government-led growth, policy should focus on empowering sectors in which India had inherent competitive strengths—like steel and textiles in which it was a global leader—and rely on market forces to achieve industrial development. This, they argued, would create employment, consumption, investment and growth.

Curiously, the concept of a planned economy, archaic as it sounds today, had quite a few takers in that era. The idea that a nation could plan to meet its citizens' demands for food, goods, employment, health, infrastructure, poverty alleviation and progress in general had the support of intellectuals within the country as well as abroad. Successive regimes in the US—which was keen to engage with India—were sympathetic to the idea of a planned economy. Nehru invited the best and the brightest international economists to come to India to study, assist and be convinced by the idea. I. G. Patel recalls in his memoir, *Glimpses of Indian Economy: An Insider's View*, how a parade of economists—Ragnar Frisch, Gunnar Myrdal, Jan Tinbergen, Richard Goodwin and Oskar Lange—visited India, romanced by the idea that development could be plotted and planned to the last mile.

The Nehruvian approach was by no means unique, nor was India the only country captivated by the idea of state control of capital and development. The Harrod-Domar model of economic development, crafted by economists Roy F. Harrod and Evsey Domar, was the reigning template of the era. The model emphasized the role of capital and preached that investment would drive growth. It was believed to be most suitable for the post-colonial, post-War world, given the availability of surplus labour, the lack of demand and the scarcity of capital prevalent in parts of the world at the time. Nehru and Mahalanobis injected it with ideology and believed that it was best if the State led the industrialization process. Private investment, which was dictated by opportunity, would necessarily wait for and follow demand and that would delay growth. The nation could not afford to postpone development. Adding ballast to this thesis was the nation's need for self-reliance after its experience of the deleterious effects of colonialism. It could be argued that the choice of state-led industrialization to develop the newly independent country's economy was not entirely erroneous. The mistake was in foreclosing the option of private-sector participation and persisting with the model in the face of inefficiency and failure.

As a result of the over-involvement of the State in planning, independent India lost many opportunities. The most glaring instance was steel production. Sir Arthur Lewis, the renowned economist, identified the competitive advantage India possessed in manufacturing steel given the availability of natural resources and surplus labour. He suggested that India should ramp up production from 1 million tons to 10 million tons and begin to export steel. This would boost investment and employment at home and enable the country to earn scarce foreign exchange. I. G. Patel recalls that T.T. Krishnamachari (also known as TTK), who was minister for steel, was impressed by the idea but was overruled by the then minister for finance, C. D. Deshmukh. Deshmukh rejected the thesis that there would be a growing demand for steel in India and elsewhere. India's opportunity to become one of the steel capitals of the world was thus frittered away; the Koreans, who visited Indian plants to observe steel-making, and the Japanese captured the market.

By the mid-sixties, the thesis of 'government knows best' and the idea of planned development came under increasing criticism. Among those who visited India to study the idea of planning was the economist Milton Friedman. His criticism, documented in 1963, was prescient and clinically dispassionate. 'Time and again one will hear as an article of faith that India must develop at a faster rate than Western countries did. A standard cliché is that India must compress into decades what took other countries centuries. There is, of course, much merit to this position. The scope for improvement is tremendous and the desirability of improvement is unquestioned; and it should be easier and faster to imitate than to initiate.' Friedman then predicted that at the rate of growth estimated by the Indian authorities it would take over a century for the country to reach the then current level of per capita income in Japan, and well over three centuries to reach the current level of per capita income in the US. He noted wryly: 'The current danger is that India will stretch into centuries what took other countries decades.'

The problem was not that the Plans were achieving too little, but that they were trying to do too much. Consider the objectives that the State was trying to achieve with its model of planned industrialization: the equitable distribution of income, the raising of employment, the balancing of investment and growth across geographies, the prevention of concentration of economic power, the protection of the balance of payments and the promotion of industrial and economic growth. Six objectives in all! The loading of all these objectives on to industrialization made the policy counter-productive and contradictory.

The Five Year Plans decided the what, where, when, how and why of industrialization. The licensing and control of capacity was achieved through the IDRA. Growth was to be achieved through the deployment of an array of instruments: import and export controls, control of capital issues, control of foreign exchange, laws to control the distribution of raw materials, price controls on industrial commodities and control over the allocation of credit. Every aspect of output and input was controlled and so was distribution and pricing.

The apparatus for control and regulation was based on a war-time fiat (the Defence of India Rules, issued by the British in 1939 and subsequently adapted in 1946). It enabled blanket provisions for the regulation or prohibition of production, treatment, storage, movement, transport, distribution, disposal, acquisition, use or consumption of articles or things of any description whatsoever. It was designed in the context of war to manage scarcity, not to promote development in times of peace.

In terms of operation, the process was extraordinarily confusing and opened the doors to corruption. Licensing was controlled by the ministry of industry; the ministry of commerce controlled imports and exports; tariffs and duties were set by the ministry of finance; and guidelines on the allocation of credit were prepared by the ministry of industry and implemented by the ministry of finance. Any entrepreneur who wanted to set up a unit in India required central government approval at every step. Licences were classified into three kinds: there was a free list for categories in which licences were granted without any scrutiny, there was a merit list in which the issue of licences required scrutiny and study of capacity, and a rejection list in which the government parked applications seeking to add capacity.

To appreciate the nightmare the system was, one need only consider the clearances necessary. The entrepreneur would first have to go to the ministry of industry to get an 'in-principle approval'. Once granted, this approval would result in the issuance of a Letter of Intent. This Letter was the basic document for further clearances. To set up a factory and import machinery one went to the chief controller of imports and exports in the ministry of commerce. If you had a foreign collaborator or wanted one, you went to a committee of the ministry of industry chaired by a secretary from the ministry of finance. If funds were required and equity was to be raised, the clearance of the controller of capital issues in the ministry of finance was mandatory. If raw material was to be imported, the import would have to be cleared by the chief controller of imports and exports in the ministry of commerce and that required a non-availability clearance from the directorate general of technical development in the ministry of industry. Once everything was tied up, the entrepreneur would have to return to the ministry of industry to obtain a formal licence.

Every industrial enterprise had to follow this procedure involving an astonishing amount of red tape. In his interim report on licensing, Bombay-based economist Rabindra Kishen Hazari pointed out that the Birla group of companies had, between 1964 and 1966, applied for 325 licences. The licences covered every industrial domain barring steel and power. If one extrapolates the number of applications over a twenty-four-month period, it means that every third day, an executive of the corporate house was knocking on the doors of the government for permissions, clearances and sanctions.

The situation was, if anything, worse for businesses reserved for the small-scale sector. To start with, the reservation of certain sectors for small-scale industry was based on the dubious 'low capital, high employment' theory. The government defined small-scale industries by turnover. The sectors were often those in which technology upgrades and scale were critical for efficiency. For instance, until the early eighties, the business of manufacturing video cassettes was reserved for the small-scale sector while in the rest of the industrialized world it was a sector in which margins were driven by scale and automation.

Now consider the contradictions state policy had imposed, which in turn led to corruption. By definition, a small-scale enterprise could not install machinery worth more than ₹10 lakh whereas the cheapest import cost ₹12 lakh. So the first step the entrepreneur had to take was to under-invoice his imports. The second challenge was to manage the problem of scale. The number of cassettes that a small-scale unit could produce was capped at 20,000 a year while the machine actually produced 20,000 in a week. So what did one do with the machine for the rest of the year or fifty-one weeks?

The way around the problem was tedious, explains Mumbai-based Shravan Kumar Sharma, financial consultant and auditor. The entrepreneur would lease licences, under various names, to put his installed capacity to full use. He would approach the regulatory authority that issued the permit—in this case the Department of Electronics in Delhi—and choose a place designated as a destination by the State for small-scale electronics, say Chiplun in Maharashtra. He would then obtain a Small Scale Industries (SSI) licence. The next steps would entail renting a place in Chiplun, which is near Ratnagiri, driving to Ratnagiri, and registering the business to get a provisional SSI certificate. This would then be stamped by officials in Chiplun, following which the stamped copy would be sent to Delhi with a fee of ₹100.

The entire process would take from six weeks to three months. He would then have to repeat the process fifty-one times, under different names, even though the address for the manufacturing unit would remain the same in order to acquire licences to produce 20,000 cassettes every week. A very high duty—330 per cent—was imposed on imported video cassettes. So if the entrepreneur could work the system, he could make a lot of money very quickly. In fact, the accumulation of SSI licences in itself became a small-scale industry.

This convoluted process of industrialization engendered a fascinating ecosystem. In the initial years following the First Plan, private enterprise was gripped by a version of Stockholm Syndrome. It went along with the politics of state control, partially because it sympathized with the nationalist fervour that accompanied independence, and partially because it had no real option. After the Second Plan, when entrepreneurs found their businesses floundering, they switched gears and deployed manpower to find a way through the maze of controls. By the mid-sixties, businessmen had figured out how to work the system through the use of lobbies and bribes.

This is well illustrated by the procedure of licensing. Once issued by the ministry of industry, a Letter of Intent remained valid for a period of six months till all clearances were secured. And in the period the Letter of Intent remained valid, no further applications in that specific area of operation were entertained. Hazari reveals in his report that one group had applied for and secured 375 licences, of which only a third were finally deployed for the creation of capacity. The rest were allowed to lapse. In short, the applications for licences were used to block new or competing players from creating new capacity. The result: supply was constrained, allowing existing players to enforce cartel prices. Milton Friedman observed, 'One gets the impression, depending on whom one talks with, either that the government runs business, or that two or three large businesses run the government.' Through the sixties, economists and foreign collaborators alike marvelled at the navigational skills of Indian entrepreneurs as they found ways to turn the system to their advantage.

The system of licences and permits was meant to ensure the control of the State over resources and promote growth. The policy of import substitution was justified by the quest for self-reliance and import controls were deemed necessary to protect fragile Indian industries that had been ravaged by colonization. The irony is that state controls retarded growth, import controls were used to thwart competition by price cartels which thrived on scarcity. The failure of state-led industrialization and the idea of the planned economy was obvious to all yet it was persisted with because by then it was a joint venture of the political class and the business class.

By the time Lal Bahadur Shastri took charge as prime minister, it was clear that the economy was floundering. Bernard Bell, the economist who led the team that produced the fourteen Bell Reports detailing the state of the Indian economy, summarized the failure of planning and state-led economic development succinctly. He observed that India was experiencing increasing difficulty in feeding its enormously increased population and in providing productive work opportunities. He said, 'There was only modest improvement in average living levels in the last 15 years and virtually none in the Third Five Year Plan.'

A HARD LEFT TURN

The policy of controls, which were deemed necessary for the country to achieve self-reliance, had resulted in India becoming dependent on foreign aid. India faced one foreign exchange crisis in 1957 and was approaching another by the mid-sixties. If India had invested in industrial sectors, in which the country had a comparative advantage, and opened up trade to enhance the efficiency of domestic industry, it could have added value to the economy and added to individual incomes. An open economy would have enabled it to fund industrialization and deploy scarce resources better. But that was not to be.

A quick summary of the prevailing conditions will put into perspective the odds the economy operated under. Growth depended on a model that was inherently flawed and inefficient. There was the omnipresent threat of natural or man-made disasters which could easily trigger a crisis. There were wars as well, which ravaged the economy. In 1962 and 1965, India had to fight China and Pakistan respectively. To make matters worse, India suffered droughts in 1965 and 1966. The US had suspended food aid and India desperately needed monetary aid to cover imports and keep the economy chugging along. It also needed resources to finance the Fourth Plan. India therefore approached the US government for food grains and the IMF and the World Bank for long-term assistance.

The Fund-Bank twins were willing to help but first wanted India to devalue its currency to reflect the true value of the rupee, restructure its policies and move away from state control. This meant doing away with the Nehru-Mahalanobis model. Veterans in the Congress roared their disapproval. Unlike Nehru, Prime Minister Shastri was not wedded to state control and, in fact, preferred an open economy. Pragmatist that he was, Shastri decided to use the window of opportunity provided by the crisis to push ahead with the restructuring of the economy. The first step that needed to be taken was the devaluation of the currency but the finance minister, TTK, was dead set against it. Shastri eased him out and brought in the largely unknown Sachin Chaudhuri as finance minister. A team was set up to sequence the process of restructuring. Tragically, Shastri passed away soon after he okayed the decision to proceed with the devaluation of the rupee and Indira Gandhi took charge as prime minister.

As we will see in greater detail in the chapter 'Das Kapital', Indira Gandhi's passage to power was by no means without strife. But she was more than equal to the challenges she had to deal with and even as she took stock of the political challenges facing her, she got cracking on the economic front. The immediate need was to overcome the foreign exchange crisis and secure supplies of food grains. India had always been dependent on food imports but the need, this time, was critical. Along with credit, India expected—and desperately needed—a special package of a billion dollars in non-project aid (essentially, aid with no strings attached). Indira battled her party and the Opposition to devalue the rupee and agreed to consider opening up sections of the economy.

In June 1966, India devalued the rupee by 36.5 per cent, imposed export duties and liberalized imports but the much needed non-project aid didn't materialize. The Americans and the IMF didn't think that Indira Gandhi's government had done enough. Their contention was that import controls on virtually all consumer goods were intact and that the whole exercise was negated by the government's focus on not letting imports fuel inflation. I. G. Patel, who—along with RBI Governor P. C. Bhattacharya and senior government officials L. K. Jha and Dharam Vira—worked on the process, characterized the episode as the 'great betrayal'.

What made Indira Gandhi a formidable politician was that she never worked just on Plan A. Confronted by the twin challenges of a sputtering economy and a fragile political majority, she put into place Plan B. Although she had gone ahead with the currency devaluation and engaged actively with the US, Indira Gandhi had never been quite convinced about the integrity of the Lyndon Baines Johnson administration that was in power at the time. She met LBJ in the US in 1966 and returned to India via Moscow where she met with Soviet premier, Alexei Kosygin. The meeting led to close trade ties with the Soviet Union and, internally, helped her enlist the support of the left parties to ensure her political survival.

A year later, the Congress went to the polls and lost ground both at the Centre and in the states. It won 283 out of 520 seats, the lowest it had recorded until then. In 1969, faced with a challenge from party stalwarts like K. Kamaraj and the Syndicate he led, Indira split the party by opposing the Congress candidate N. Sanjiva Reddy and supporting V. V. Giri for president (who was backed by the Left). Giri won, the Congress split and Indira partnered with the Left for survival. Moving to the left helped procure political backing in Parliament and the support of the Soviets as a bulwark against the US.

Naturally, economic policy also turned left. Indira Gandhi brought home to business the real power of the State. On 19 July 1969 the government nationalized fourteen major banks and brought them under state control. Mrs Gandhi justified this step by arguing that critical levers of economic growth were being monopolized by the big businesses which dominated the banking sector—as a result banks had not reached out to the masses. They were, she held, denying credit to agriculture and small- and medium-scale entrepreneurs. The political justification to democratize capital overrode any criticism that the move would lead to the politicization of the banking sector and loss of efficiency.

But she didn't stop at that. Deploying socialist sloganeering, a few months later, Indira Gandhi promulgated the Monopolies and Restrictive Trade Practices (MRTP) Act to monitor and control the expansion of business houses. Ostensibly, this was to prevent the concentration of wealth and protect consumers against monopolistic pricing and practice, but the real objective was to enforce the monopoly of politics over economics. The provisions of the MRTP were used to bring recalcitrant big business to heel.

Business, naturally, was upset. J. R. D. Tata, the chairman of the Tata Group, lamented that the expansion of government ownership and controls on the means of production and distribution eroded opportunity for the private sector. He described it as 'unprecedented in any country other than those under totalitarian rule'. Indira Gandhi was unconcerned. In a move to appease powerful trade unions and win political brownie points, her government nationalized the coal industry, troubled textile mills and steel units. In 1973, Indira Gandhi also pushed through the Foreign Exchange Regulation Act (FERA). Under this Act, foreign companies were obliged to bring down their stake in Indian operations from 51 per cent to 40 per cent.

Despite mounting criticism of her actions within the country and abroad, Indira Gandhi pressed on undeterred. The promulgation of MRTP, FERA and the nationalization of banks delivered the optics she desired. However, Indira Gandhi was shrewd in her management of the new laws she had pushed through. She kept foreign banks out of the nationalization net to prevent a global uproar. The criteria for MRTP left enough loopholes to let big conglomerates escape the purge on a case-by-case basis. The FERA had built-in escape clauses with provisions for companies using specific types of technology; for producers of goods defined as essential; plantation owners and those who fulfilled export quotas to claim exemption. Even as she achieved her political objectives, she ensured niche interests were afforded some sort of refuge.

Nevertheless, Mrs Gandhi's actions had a debilitating effect on industry and the economy. Government and independent studies reflect the harsh truth of failure. In the first-ever comprehensive review of the licence raj, R. K. Hazari declared that industrial licensing 'failed to fulfil its principal purpose which is to channel private investment into industries whose development on a priority basis was required by the Five Year Plans'. The report advocated a restructuring of policy.

Indira Gandhi enjoyed total control over the party and government after the 1971 polls; India had drubbed Pakistan and she enjoyed mass adulation. Theoretically, she could have resumed the policies of 1966 and changed the course of history by restructuring the economy. However, the reality on the ground made such moves difficult to implement. At home, she couldn't have wrested control of the government and party in 1969 from the Syndicate without the Left who were now dictating policy. Abroad, she had to contend with hostile American regimes under LBJ and Richard Nixon who were wooing Yahya Khan and Pakistan to open the door to China.

Indeed, it could be argued that the US pushed India and Indira towards the Soviet Union. Kosygin, whom Indira had met in 1966, offered her the Friendship Treaty as early as September 1969. India didn't sign it for over twenty months. Indira sent D. P. Dhar, ambassador to the Soviet Union and her confidant, to Moscow to sign it on 9 August 1971 only when Secretary of State Henry Kissinger, after his visit to China in July, signalled to India the formation of a new alliance and made it clear that India could not expect the US to intervene if China interceded in a war between Pakistan and India. As it turned out, it was not China but the US which jumped into fraught waters. In the Indo-Pak war of December 1971, the US sent the USS *Enterprise* to the mouth of the Bay of Bengal only to be countered by the Soviets. Admiral Sergey Gorshkov, naval chief of the USSR, ordered Soviet submarines in the area to surface, sending a clear signal to the Americans. It is amply clear that the left turn in policy and politics was dictated by the desperate exigencies of survival.

THE EMERGENCY

The Congress came to power after the general elections of 1971 on the promise of eradicating poverty—'*Garibi Hatao*' was its slogan. On the ground, however, high inflation was squeezing the poor and the middle class. Indira Gandhi's tenure began well—the victory over Pakistan had capitalized nationalism. But the triumph, and the creation of Bangladesh, came with a price. India had to take care of over ten million refugees who poured across the border. The euphoria of victory in the elections and in the war was soon overwhelmed by angst and anger. The cost of war had enlarged the gap between the inflow of revenue and government expenditure, pushing up inflation and prices. This was aggravated by drought, which affected both the availability and affordability of all manner of goods. As agricultural production dropped, food prices shot up by 25 per cent between 1972 and 1973. In September 1973, crude oil prices shot up from $2.50 a barrel to over $11 per barrel. This left the country without enough funds to pay for its imports and foreign debt spiralled to 14.5 per cent of the Gross Domestic Product (GDP). Theoretically, India should have been able to export enough to pay for its imports but India's export performance was abysmal at the time and its share in global trade had in fact slid from 2.6 per cent in 1948 to 0.72 per cent in 1973.

Indira Gandhi may have secured political brownie points for her left turn, but nationalization transferred the onus of managing expectations from private business to the government. The nationalization of large sectors of the economy spawned the growth of trade unionism. Unions, mostly affiliated to political parties, battled to expand their footprint of influence. The stage was thus set for a political agitation.

The fire started in two corners of India—in Gujarat, where protestors wanted the ouster of a corrupt regime led by Chimanbhai Patel of the Congress, and in Bihar, where students' unions made common cause with the Communist Party of India (CPI) against another corrupt Congress regime, led by former freedom fighter Kedar Pandey, to demand food and jobs.

The agitation went national when the students in Bihar asked septuagenarian leader Jayaprakash Narayan to lead the movement. JP, as he was affectionately known, was a young hero of the Quit India movement, and was once described by Nehru as one of the best leaders in the Opposition. He abandoned politics in 1952, campaigned for a free Tibet, worked to resolve the Kashmir issue with Sheikh Abdullah, intervened in the Naga Movement and enabled the surrender of dacoits from the ravines of Chambal. JP was angered by the neglect of the poor and the rise of corruption.

As Indira Gandhi challenged his authority to question the government and its policies, JP upped the ante and invited political parties and trade unions to come together. He also asked senior ministers in government to resign and for all parties to merge and oppose the Congress. In May 1974, two million employees of the Railways threatened to go on strike for higher wages and bonus and this was, in many ways, the flash point. The government declared the call to strike illegal, invoked the Defence of India Rules, and in a brutal wave, arrested over 20,000 workers. The government's action backfired and—to borrow a phrase from the cyber age—the movement went viral, with many uniting under the slogan '*Andhere mein ek prakash, Jayaprakash, Jayaprakash.*'

Amidst all this tumult, Raj Narain, a follower of socialist leader Ram Manohar Lohia, who had lost the elections in 1971 against Indira Gandhi, filed a case in the Allahabad High Court, accusing her of election malpractice. The Opposition quickly sensed an opening and parties ranging from the Jan Sangh to estranged factions of the Congress, even the old warhorse Morarji Desai, began pushing for the ouster of the government. On 12 June, the High Court acquitted Indira Gandhi of most of the charges but declared her election to Parliament to be null and void. Indira Gandhi appealed the High Court judgement in the Supreme Court. She received a stay but was disallowed from voting in Parliament. Some ministers advised her to step down and re-contest; others asked her to continue in the interest of the nation.

She decided to continue. On 25 June 1975, an internal Emergency was declared. All fundamental rights stood suspended, press censorship was introduced and in a nationwide swoop, the police arrested leaders from across the political spectrum and lodged them in jails all over the country. That single action brought over to JP's side all politicians and political parties who had hitherto been unconvinced by his call. Even as the government sought to lull the populace with twenty-point and five-point programmes, even as Indira's son Sanjay Gandhi emerged as the heir apparent, JP's movement continued in covert and overt ways. The Emergency was lifted in January 1977 and Parliament dissolved to hold fresh elections. The Jan Sangh, Bharatiya Lok Dal, Socialist Party and Congress (O) came together to form the Janata Party. Indira Gandhi was ousted from power and Morarji Desai became prime minister.

The economy, meanwhile, showed signs of improvement. The improvement is cited as a consequence of the Emergency. The fact is that eighteen months is too short a period to right historic wrongs. More fundamentally, two good monsoons, improved food grain production and the calming of international crude oil prices delivered stability. By the end of 1975, inflation had ebbed, food prices had fallen thanks to higher agricultural output and manufacturing had picked up pace. On the external front, the pressure on the balance of payments was eased by a unique combination of events. In 1971, the US dollar delinked from the gold standard. India delinked its currency from the US dollar—for obviously political reasons—and aligned it to the pound. The pound was a weak currency and the rupee devalued alongside, which enabled higher exports. Increased exports, coupled with higher remittances from Indian workers in the Middle East, resulted in a better foreign exchange position. Yet the economy was clearly operating below its potential and wasn't doing enough for the upliftment of the huge mass of people still living in poverty.

The period between 1966 and 1977, though trying for India and Indira, was not devoid of positive change. The crisis on the external front had resulted in some reforms. In an effort to boost value-added exports, the government eased both qualitative and quantitative import controls. But these steps were hardly enough to make an impact on the legacy of failure. The Janata Party government, despite the supposedly business-friendly leadership of Morarji Desai, could not dismantle the licence-permit-quota raj. Indeed, thanks to the chaos in the coalition, the Janata Party exacerbated the damage already caused by the spree of legislation introduced by Indira Gandhi in the early seventies. For instance, George Fernandes, as minister for industries, chased IBM and Coca-Cola out of India when he enforced the FERA requirement to dilute equity to 40 per cent.

Around the world, newly industrialized countries like South Korea that had embraced private-sector-led growth and chosen to focus on competencies were growing at between 5.5 to 6.5 per cent and their per capita incomes had trebled. India, however, was growing at a snail's pace. Even Malawi, a country wracked by poverty and underdevelopment, grew faster than India. Between 1960 and 1979, the per capita income of Malawi grew by 2.9 per cent while that of India grew by an abysmal 1.4 per cent.

The perfect pictogram for the economy would be the Ambassador car, the chosen chariot of the country's rulers for decades. A superannuated avatar of the 1950s Morris, it reflected the state of the economy most eloquently. It was outdated in its design, it owed its etymology to a bygone era, it consumed too much fuel, delivered poor efficiency and was overweight and sluggish.

Vijay Joshi and Ian Malcolm David Little describe the mess most succinctly in their book *India: Macroeconomics and Political Economy 1964–1991*: 'A fashionable view of Indian economic policy is that it was unsound micro-economically but was sound macro-economically. In contrast, one of our central conclusions is that India's control system was not only micro-economically inefficient but also macro-economically perverse.' In 1994, at a World Bank lecture, I. G. Patel observed rather tellingly, 'Our cardinal sin in India was that we sought to be self-reliant, even in such areas as machinery and capital goods—and that too on the basis of imports under tied aid and a technology prescribed by donors. It was like injecting the virus of inefficiency at the very root, from which it would spread to all branches of the economy. It would have been wiser, in an area at the cutting edge of efficiency, to rely on the best equipment, technology and management that money could buy.'

Between 1960 and 1990, over a dozen committees were set up to examine every aspect of the controlled economy. Each committee found glaring faults in the system and concluded that it was the licence-permit-quota raj that was the cause of failure. What is worse is that even the system of controls failed. Haribhau K. Paranjape, a member of the Industrial Licensing Policy Inquiry Committee of 1969, said, 'In respect of licensing, the committee had firmly concluded that the system had failed practically on all counts whether it was regional dispersal, import substitution, or preventing concentration of economic power. Licensing could not even ensure the development of industries.'

The most significant observation that can be made about the prevailing climate on economic policy is that through the sixties and seventies, all committees focused solely on issues of process. No one actually recommended that the licence-permit-quota raj be dismantled or even questioned it at all. But outside government, those who recognized that the system was failing were raising their voices. Among the first were economists T. Nilkanta Srinivasan and Jagdish Bhagwati who had initially proved the link between the policy of controls and low growth. Brahmananda and Vakil critiqued the failure of the economy to create jobs. The thesis of state-led industrialization was that it would shift the underemployed in agriculture to factory floors and deliver incomes. However, the neglect of agriculture kept a vast section of the populace poor, resulting in a shallow economy which limited industrial growth. Like car manufacturers, policymakers in India indulged in cosmetic tinkering every few years to convey the illusion of motion while retaining all the levers of control. There was no great pull or push to open up the economy; any initiatives that did take place were the result of individual effort at the margins rather than institutional consensus.

By July 1979, the Janata Party government collapsed under its many internal contradictions, making way for a rent-and-lease regime installed by Congress. The government, led by Charan Singh, didn't last more than a few weeks. The economy was yet again in the throes of another crisis. A combination of severe drought in 1979, reckless profligacy, and the rise of crude oil prices pushed up inflation and the deficit. Wholesale prices shot up an incredible 17 per cent in 1979 and 18 per cent in 1980. A large portion of India's imports was not covered by available foreign currency reserves. The country was back at the doors of international multilateral lending institutions.

THE RAJIV GANDHI YEARS

In the run-up to the general elections of 1980, Indira Gandhi accused the ragtag coalition in power of gross economic mismanagement. People, tired of the bickering parties, voted her back to power. At the beginning of 1980, she sent a team led by Finance Minister R. Venkataraman to negotiate with the IMF. India drew $530 million under the Special Drawing Rights and $266 million from the Compensatory Financing Facility. Mindful that any acceptance of conditions would trigger criticism from the Opposition, Indira Gandhi pre-empted the IMF by pushing through a tough budget which raised taxes and the prices of crude oil, power and fertilizers. In November 1981, India secured a $5 billion loan from the IMF. The crisis of 1980 led to incremental steps in opening up imports but did not provoke any great rethink on new ways to manage the economy. Even if there were thoughts about ramping up exports and India's potential to earn foreign exchange, they were drowned in the euphoria of discovering oil in Bombay High. Indeed, after it drew $3.9 billion from the $5 billion sanctioned, India terminated the programme as the offshore oil platform, Sagar Samrat, became operational and added to India's oil, cutting down the outflow of foreign exchange.

As Indira Gandhi was preoccupied with the political turmoil in Punjab, the opportunity to restructure the economy was neither a priority nor a compulsion. Also, the economic crisis had passed. Faced with rising militancy she deployed the army and even ordered the storming of the Golden Temple in Amritsar to flush out militants. In a violent reaction to the storming, Indira Gandhi was gunned down by her own guards on 31 October 1984. Her son Rajiv Gandhi took over and immediately called for general elections in which the Congress won 408 seats, riding a huge sympathy wave.

When Rajiv Gandhi came to power he inherited a healthy economy—low inflation, a current account surplus and rising GDP growth rates. There was also a legion of reports as well as intellectual support for the need to reform, free and restructure the economy. These included the P. C. Alexander Committee Report on Import and Export Policies of 1978, the Vadilal Dagli Report of the Committee on Controls and Subsidies of 1978, the Abid Hussain Committee Report on Trade Policy of 1984 and the M. Narasimham Report on Industrial Licensing of 1985. In fact, the Narasimham Report virtually recommended the dismantling of the superstructure of the licence raj. It concluded that 'the licensing system has tended to obstruct the play of competitive forces in our industrial economy'.

Along with a relatively healthy economy, Rajiv also inherited a public mood for change. It was the perfect window of opportunity for him to dismantle the business model of politics and end the politicized control of the economy. Rajiv Gandhi recognized the misalignment between his party's interests and its business model. He understood that his mother's triumph in 1980 was a vote against the hotchpotch politics of the Janata brigade and the victory in 1984 didn't actually reflect the popularity of the Congress—the victory was fuelled by sympathy. To him, the reasons were obvious—the party had ceased to serve the people and the prevailing model of economic management had been hijacked by vested interests and was therefore incapable of delivering public services or growth in the economy.

In his famous speech of December 1985, delivered at the Congress Centenary Session in Bombay, he spoke about the nefarious nexus between big businesses and politicians and chose to confront the power-brokers within his party and their external beneficiaries. He said that business had a glorious heritage of nationalism and of socially relevant radicalism. However, he went on to say, big business was oblivious to the concerns of millions. 'They feel little concern for the creation of national wealth, only for a larger and larger share in it. Nothing is considered illegitimate if one marches under the right flag. Power without responsibility, rights without duties have come to be their prerogative. Will productivity arise from such stony soil? Let us not forget that the poor and the unemployed have to sacrifice their development programmes to subsidise inefficient industry.'

Turning his attention to the power-brokers, he observed, 'Millions of ordinary Congress workers throughout the country are full of enthusiasm for Congress's policies and programmes. But they are handicapped, for on their backs ride the brokers of power and influence who dispense patronage to convert a mass movement into a feudal oligarchy. They are self-perpetuating cliques who thrive by invoking the slogans of caste and religion and by enmeshing the living body of the Congress in their net of avarice.' His speech was recognition that the Congress was a prisoner of its own economic policy, the coalition of vested interests nurtured by the licence-permit-quota raj.

The first step forward was to break the stranglehold of industrial empires on the funding of the party. This would enable government to ignore the pressures brought to bear by the industrial lobby and go ahead with the reforms necessary to restructure the economy. If insiders are to be believed, alternate sources for political venture capital included the burgeoning sectors of real estate and defence procurements. This would enable the party to bypass the entrenched interests responsible for policy sclerosis.

In the eighties it was speculated that the Congress party had switched its funding model from internal to external, from domestic industry to overseas procurement. Some even believe that the model was very much in place by the time Rajiv Gandhi spoke at the Congress Centenary Session; that the candour was born out of confidence in a new source of funding. In his autobiography *My Presidential Years*, in a comment on the Bofors scandal in which alleged pay-offs were made to many powerful politicians by an arms dealer, former President of India R. Venkataraman, writes about a courtesy call made by J. R. D. Tata. Tata, who knew Venkataraman from the latter's days as minister for industries and, later, as minister for finance, told the president that 'it would be difficult to deny the receipt of commissions by the Congress party. He felt that, since 1980, industrialists had not been approached for political contributions and that the general feeling amongst them was that the party was financed by commissions on deals'. There is, of course, no independent corroboration or evidence of a change in the funding model. Much of the speculation revolves around the circumstance of change, the fact that India had moved away from the Soviet Union and diversified its arms purchases; that its defence expenditure had shot up and, of course, allegations of commissions paid on arms deals.

It cannot be denied, though, that the Rajiv Gandhi administration did initiate the process of creative disruption. A series of decisions taken by Rajiv Gandhi as prime minister indicate a shift in stance in both the business of politics and the politics of economics. The first step was to inject internal or domestic competition into the economy, threatening the profits of the entrenched. The government abolished licensing in thirty industries. In the wake of the Asian Games, Rajiv Gandhi opened up imports and allowed joint ventures and laid down the foundation for the establishment of a home-grown consumer electronics sector. Entrepreneurs were allowed to be efficient and produce at 133 per cent of capacity. Rules which restricted groups with assets of ₹20 crore from expanding were eased, allowing expansion up to ₹100 crore. This was accompanied by external competition. Restrictions on imports were eased, allowing new technology into manufacturing. Tax rates were reduced in the Budget of 1985 and a White Paper entitled Long Term Fiscal Policy authored by Bimal Jalan, who was then the chief economic adviser, promised long-term predictability in policy.

After the carrots came the stick. The move to open up the economy was accompanied by a drive to clean up the corporate sector of tax and duty evasion. Finance Minister V. P. Singh, who initiated the move to cut tax rates, launched a programme to hunt tax evaders across the country. Every department—Income Tax, Excise, Customs and the Enforcement Directorate which probed foreign-exchange violations—was involved in tracking down tax evaders. Those raided included some of the biggest names in business, including the legendary business icon and well regarded octogenarian, S. L. Kirloskar. Such was the ferocity of the drive that in the six months between August 1985 and January 1986, the income-tax department alone conducted 3,563 raids—almost twenty a day. Soon enough, V. P. Singh, the scion of a minor principality, earned the sobriquet 'Raid Raja'.

The opening up of various industrial sectors was good economics. For the Congress, it was also good politics—the entry of new players, incentives for efficient industries and the opening up of imports all translated into competition and diluted the protection granted to industry. The terms of trade—in the engagement between business and politicians—was tilted against entrenched business and in favour of the Congress. Policies aimed at efficiency were also pro-people.

Predictably, the coalition of vested interests ganged up to throttle reforms. It wasn't so much the business lobby but the procurers of pelf within Rajiv's own party who arrested his drive to change the way things worked. The sequence of events that followed is unclear but these facts are undeniable. V. P. Singh grew over-ambitious, Rajiv's friends grew nervous and conspiracy theorists planted the seeds of suspicion that led to a split.

Harvard professor, politician, and master of intrigue Subramanian Swamy recalls a conversation he had with Rajiv Gandhi that should give some idea of the distrust that had permeated the government at the time. In September 1986, Swamy met Rajiv before his visit to

Pakistan. Rajiv asked him about India's stance at the Uruguay rounds of the Conference on GATT—General Agreement on Tariffs and Trade, which was the earlier avatar of the World Trade Organization—held that month. Swamy told him that V. P. Singh had surrendered on all points in the proposed new GATT agreement with the United States and had, hence, become very popular with the American government and media. In fact, he was being projected as the next prime minister by the Americans. Swamy says, 'Rajiv Gandhi nodded in a manner which suggested all was not well.'

The interest groups most affected by the nascent reforms had succeeded in their attempt to portray V. P. Singh as challenger and had managed to widen the rift between the minister for finance and the prime minister. Soon enough, V. P. Singh was pushed out of the ministry of finance to the ministry of defence. A flurry of scandals followed, including the suspicious purchase of submarines from the German manufacturer Howaldtswerke-Deutsche Werft. The equation between Gandhi and Singh worsened and political repercussions followed. By March 1987, V. P. Singh was thrown out of government. He retaliated by charging the government with corruption in the purchase of Bofors guns from Sweden.

As he began to battle for his own survival, Rajiv Gandhi, the man with the largest ever political majority in Parliament—414 seats—lost his will to restructure the Indian economy. The vested interests within the party gained the upper hand and Rajiv's initiative collapsed. This demonstrates that a majority in Parliament does not necessarily result in change.

EARLY ALARM BELLS

In March 1989, IMF Managing Director Michel Camdessus visited India and met with Prime Minister Rajiv Gandhi soon after the budget was presented. The meeting focused on the impending crisis and offered aid if India agreed to take up structural reforms. The IMF alerted the Indian government to the spectre of a balance-of-payments crisis and offered a safety net. While the reformer in Rajiv Gandhi recognized the goodwill that accompanied the offer, his coterie brought up the flip side of such a move—the damaging political fallout of seeking foreign aid just before elections. The politician in Rajiv Gandhi saw merit in their argument and postponed the inevitable. However, he didn't give up on the idea of systemic change. In his last weeks in government, Rajiv Gandhi told different sets of people to draft a policy that would unshackle the potential of India. One of the people he spoke with was B. G. Deshmukh, then cabinet secretary. He told Deshmukh that if India was to make it to the twenty-first century, systems had to change. Simultaneously, he also asked S. Venkitaramanan—who had by then moved from the ministry of finance and was adviser to the government of Karnataka—and Vijay Kelkar—who was heading the Bureau of Industrial Costs and Prices, a body tasked with advising government on costs, prices and industrial efficiency—to draft a paper which would provide advice on clearing the layers of red tape that clogged the system and slowed down growth. Deshmukh asked Montek Singh Ahluwalia to work on it. Ahluwalia, now the deputy chairman of the Planning Commission, was then in the Prime Minister's Office (PMO). He recalls putting together 'a broad sweep of ideas beginning with opening up some sectors, dismantling physical controls, freer currency to lead into further reforms'.

The crisis in the economy was worsening and was flagged again at a board meeting of the IMF on 17 July 1989. Executive Director K. Yamazaki warned that India was faced with 'a deteriorating external position and a high poverty level' requiring 'far-reaching structural adjustment' and advised that the country carefully monitor the low level of official reserves. Between 1980-81 and 1990-91, India lived beyond its means. The overall deficit—expenditure over earnings—of the central government increased from 5.4 per cent to 8.4 per cent of the GDP. Close to 20 per cent of the expenditure went towards paying interest and repaying debt.

The country's finances may have been in a dire state, but everything would have to wait as there was grave turmoil on the political front. The Rajiv Gandhi government was on its last legs. V. P. Singh's movement against corruption was approaching a crescendo. Initially a lone warrior, Singh was joined by Arun Nehru—who was once part of the corporate sector, and had joined politics having won from Rae Bareli, the pocket constituency of the Gandhi family—and Arif Mohammed Khan, both ministers in the Rajiv Gandhi government. Ever the consummate politician, Singh had also wooed Ramakrishna Hegde; ageing Turk, Chandra Shekhar; Ajit Singh; Devi Lal and many others to come on board and oppose Rajiv Gandhi. Soon enough, V. P. Singh's Jan Morcha merged with factions of the Janata Party and the Devi Lal-led Lok Dal to become the Janata Dal.

Elections were announced on 17 October 1989 and it soon became a bitterly fought campaign between one-time friends. The Janata Dal was a hotchpotch of parties united only in their hatred of Congress. However, that didn't matter for the public mood was against the Congress. When the results rolled in, the Congress had won 197 seats, the Janata Dal 143. The Congress polled 30.53 per cent of the votes while the Janata Dal polled just 17.79 per cent. Rajiv Gandhi and the Congress had been defeated but a government wouldn't be formed.

The Janata Dal didn't have the numbers but, uniquely, both the left parties, which had won forty-eight seats, and the BJP, which had won eighty-five, decided to back the newly formed National Front. In the history of India this was perhaps the only time a formation was supported by both the extremes, the Left and the Right. The battle for the top job was far from settled, though. V. P. Singh and Chandra Shekhar were both contenders for the prime ministership. V. P. Singh played his cards shrewdly by first nominating Devi Lal for prime minister. Devi Lal refused, stating that he would much rather be the Tau, or elder uncle, of the Front and nominated Singh instead. Chandra Shekhar was thus thwarted.

On 2 December 1989, V. P. Singh was sworn in as India's seventh prime minister. As a former finance minister, V. P. Singh knew his numbers as well as his politics. On 3 December, in his first address to the nation on national television, V. P. Singh declared, 'The government's coffers are empty, there is a fire raging in our hearts, the earth is stained with blood and high prices have made human lives cheap'; thereby buying popularity with a speech that was a melodramatic rendition of the truth.

Bitter evidence in support of the speech was produced by Finance Minister Madhu Dandavate when he presented the 1990-91 Budget on 19 March 1990. The fiscal deficit was double what had been projected by the previous government. Dollar reserves were down to half of what they were in 1985 as the government had borrowed heavily in dollars to fund domestic consumption. Dandavate warned that continuing along that trajectory 'risked mortgaging hard won economic independence'. Of course, he did not care to heed his own warning.

Dandavate, an austere, homespun socialist and V. P. Singh, who introduced the first tranche of tax reforms in 1986, could have initiated a course correction. But the 1990 Budget paid mere lip service to very real concerns and nothing in its 13,500 words spread across twenty-eight pages suggested a change of ways. Indeed, Dandavate aggravated the crisis by announcing a loan waiver for farmers that cost the exchequer an additional ₹10,000 crore. Economists aver that just that one step alone shaved nearly 1 per cent off GDP growth. Neither the Left nor the BJP, who formed the crutches of this splintered coalition, opposed the profligacy. The Congress, the principal opposition party led by Rajiv Gandhi, didn't object either. The reasons behind the silence were obvious—no party wanted to risk the wrath of the ryot class.

Having been the finance minister who initiated the big reforms of 1985, expectations of V. P. Singh were naturally high. His circumstances in 1989 were, however, completely different. The National Front owed its existence to the external support of parties who viewed it as a convenience, an unavoidable stopgap till their own plans fructified. There was little room for experimentation or, indeed, for a revolutionary change.

When the V. P. Singh regime came to power, a large number of pro-Rajiv Gandhi officials were moved out and loyalists brought in. Montek Singh Ahluwalia, although closely identified with Rajiv Gandhi, survived and continued as special secretary in the PMO. On a trip to Malaysia, Singh observed how the small country had prospered despite its size and other handicaps. The discussion offered a window of opportunity for Ahluwalia to mention the report he had prepared at the behest of Rajiv Gandhi. Singh called for a presentation and listened with interest but his core team shot it down. One senior mandarin told the prime minister, 'We can't just allow this kind of liberalization. Rupee resources are scarce. People will set up units to produce wasteful stuff, like stockings for women.'

V. P. Singh also shot down the ideas of Venkitaramanan and Kelkar, and the committee proposed by the outgoing government of Rajiv Gandhi was disbanded before it came into being. Whether V. P. Singh, the reformer of 1985, had changed his stand, or not, is debatable. However, one thing is certain: the decisions taken by him were driven solely by politics. The idea of change and the committees set up to facilitate it were seen to be those of the previous government. Venkitaramanan, Ahluwalia and the team were identified with Rajiv Gandhi's regime and there was no way V. P. Singh was willing to accept or consider any idea or draft that had been conceived of by a regime that his government had replaced. V. P. Singh was also weighed down by a coterie of officers who would not countenance any idea from what they called the 'Bofors Club'.

There was, however, the realization that the current system had been hijacked by vested interests and wasn't delivering results. Younger politicians with a stake in the future, and who were free of political baggage, were willing to advocate reform. One of them was Ajit Singh, minister for industries in the V. P. Singh-led National Front regime. Ajit Singh was the son of Jat leader, Chaudhary Charan Singh, who had a huge following among farmers and was the founder of the Lok Dal. Ajit Singh had quit his job at IBM and returned home to take over his father's legacy. Like Rajiv Gandhi, Ajit Singh found the systems bewildering and, having come from a corporate culture, understood that layers retard speed and growth. He also understood that the licence-permit-quota raj was the business model of Congress politics.

Within days of taking charge Ajit Singh set up a team led by Amar Nath Verma, who was then secretary in the ministry of commerce and industries and Rakesh Mohan who was chief economic adviser. Verma and Mohan were to put together the first draft of a comprehensive policy to dismantle the licence-permit-quota raj.

Interestingly, this was not a project that was pushed through with secrecy and stealth. Ajit Singh held many meetings with economists, entrepreneurs and industry chambers for their suggestions. Ajit Singh recalls that he had several discussions with the prime minister on the new industrial policy and remembers that his boss did not give an opinion or any assurance. The draft was released on 1 June 1990 and promptly bundled into the freezer. The government depended on the Left and the BJP for survival. Neither the Left, which wanted more control to be exerted by the State, nor the BJP, which swore allegiance to a Swadeshi philosophy, would let a minority government go ahead with such substantive reforms. Ajit Singh's valiant efforts to push for a discussion in Parliament too were shot down.

However, in an interesting turn of events, the idea which was rejected by the government in Delhi was bestowed with legitimacy in Washington. It was presented as a plan, a highlight of India's reforms agenda, at the IMF board meeting on 13 June 1990 and finds mention in the minutes of the meeting held at the IMF where India was represented by Executive Director Gopi Arora. The orphaned idea was adopted and offered as a promissory note to the IMF by those managing the economy. The draft, which was also tabled in the Rajya Sabha as a White Paper, reveals that some of the reforms being mooted included the abolition of the foreign equity participation limit, automatic licensing, build-operate-transfer systems for infrastructure projects like power, and permission to set up offices overseas.

Authored by Verma and Mohan, the paper was a first attempt at a revolution that was waiting to be made. Ajit Singh recalls the enthusiasm of the team and the team's excitement over the idea in a regime that was otherwise obsessed with the politics of identity. 'It was effectively the first draft of the industrial policy unveiled in 1991 by P. V. Narasimha Rao. We had sequenced it differently. We had planned to institute regulatory systems ahead of liberalization. The Rao regime came to power when the economy was in deep crisis and many of the points were left out, resulting in a decade of scams.' Did V. P. Singh favour the idea? Ajit Singh quips, 'He was neither for nor against but he did know this was on my agenda.' In September 1990, Ajit Singh once again sought to present the finalized draft to Parliament but the plan was torpedoed by the BJP, the Left and Chandra Shekhar.

It didn't matter that the existing economic model was crumbling; it didn't matter that the country was being pushed towards bankruptcy. It didn't matter that the world was changing and that India was getting left behind. It didn't matter that even the Chinese had begun to shift away from their faith in Marxism as early as 1978 and were moving towards modernism. Faced with persistent poverty and low growth, Chinese reformist leader, Deng Xiaoping had opened up the economy to implement his theory that 'it doesn't matter what colour the cat is as long as it catches mice'. It didn't matter that by the end of 1989 the Berlin Wall had come down. It didn't matter that the political tactic of netting economic gains from non-alignment had run its course with the end of the Cold War. The looming crisis, the pressure on the financial architecture, the changing geopolitics of the neighbourhood and the emerging spectre of a unipolar ideology were all subjugated by the expediency of politics.

By the early nineties, the inherent contradictions of the V. P. Singh government began to surface. And as the contradictions gathered momentum, they began to pull the government apart. In an attempt to stall the inevitable breakdown, V. P. Singh unveiled his plan to implement the recommendations made by the Mandal Commission on reservations for the lower castes. His effort was to deploy caste politics to split the support base of the BJP even as it pursued its agenda of consolidating Hindu votes with the campaign for a Ram temple in Ayodhya. The country was thus buffeted between 'Mandal' and 'kamandal'. In October 1990, BJP leader Lal Krishna Advani, the charioteer of the movement for the Ram Temple, was arrested during the course of his rath yatra in Bihar by V. P. Singh acolyte Lalu Prasad Yadav. The BJP had sensed it could make a pitch for power and was waiting for the V. P. Singh government to give it a reason. Following the arrest, the BJP withdrew its support, pulling the government down. V. P. Singh went out and a splinter group, sponsored by the Congress and led by Chandra Shekhar, took charge on 10 November 1990.

The Chandra Shekhar government was conceived of long before

the V. P. Singh government was toppled. It was born, so to speak, the day V. P. Singh, with Devi Lal, outwitted Chandra Shekhar for the top job. By the summer of 1990, it was clear that the V. P. Singh regime would crumble. Subramanian Swamy reveals that sometime in September 1990, he had convinced Rajiv Gandhi that over fifty MPs would walk out of the Janata Dal with Chandra Shekhar if the Congress agreed to support him as prime minister. Swamy claims, 'Rajiv Gandhi wasn't comfortable with Chandra Shekhar. He suggested that I become the prime minister which I refused.'

Eventually, as it turned out, the sequence of events left no room for discussion. By October, the final countdown for the V. P. Singh government began but the Congress was not ready for the polls nor was it willing to form the next government. It was looking for a stopgap arrangement and the arrangement suggested by Swamy suited it fine. The arrest of Advani triggered a cascade of events that ended with Rajiv Gandhi accepting Chandra Shekhar as prime minister.

THE TIPPING POINT

The coming into power of the new government coincided with the invasion of Kuwait by Iraq in 1990. Consequently, India's oil import bill shot up, bringing foreign exchange reserves down, yet again, to precarious levels. Soon after taking over, in the third week of November 1990, Chandra Shekhar asked Kamal Morarka—a businessman and a minister in the PMO—to arrange for a meeting with the nation's top industrialists. Also present were Finance Minister Yashwant Sinha and Manmohan Singh.

Blunt and lucid, the new prime minister told his guests at Race Course Road that India was neck deep in trouble. However, if the purpose of the meeting was to find answers to a vexing problem, the prime minister was disappointed. In theory this group was best placed to advocate reforms and liberalization akin to what had led to the success of countries like Singapore, Taiwan, South Korea and Malaysia—the Asian Tigers—who had opened up their economy, adopted technology, accepted investment and recorded high growth. They would also have been aware of the voluminous literature dating back to the sixties and seventies by leading economists like T. N. Srinivasan and Jagdish Bhagwati which had repeatedly established the failure of the 'planned economic model'. They could have chorused for the dismantling of the licence-permit-quota raj and pressed for the opening up of the economy to push investment and growth. But disrupting a settled system they had specialized in working around was not something they wanted. The entrepreneurs were as much part of the status quo as was the political regime.

This explains to a great extent why, even on the brink of the biggest crisis the country had faced, change was not on the agenda. When Chandra Shekhar asked the assembled businessmen for possible solutions to the crisis, it was not change but survival that influenced their responses. Chandra Shekhar, a seasoned observer of the way things worked, knew better than to expect any blueprint for creative disruption. He had no expectations, but consultation—even if fruitless—is an established aspect of governance in India and Chandra Shekhar went through the motions.

A few days later, Finance Minister Sinha initiated measures to stave off disaster. With foreign exchange reserves dipping to just a billion dollars, the possibility of a default loomed large. Sinha asked the RBI to keep a 24x7 tab on all foreign exchange transactions to avert any mischief and ensure availability of credit for 'must pay' transactions for institutions like Indian Oil. He cut expenditure by 10 per cent across all ministries. Sinha also hiked duties, and austerity measures were imposed on all government departments. Harsh as they were in a slowing economy, the severity of the crisis was such that the measures amounted to rearranging the deck chairs on the sinking *Titanic*.

The pressure to approach the IMF was growing within the government. Former RBI Governor Bimal Jalan recalls the efforts made to prevail upon Chandra Shekhar to loosen controls and approach the IMF. A survivor of the Indira Gandhi era, Chandra Shekhar knew the political risks such a move involved. The fact that the ideas proposed by Jalan had not been taken up by the previous regime further fuelled the prime minister's suspicions. Steeped in conspiracy theories, he suspected Jalan of being a Trojan horse left behind by the V. P. Singh regime. After all, Jalan had been appointed finance secretary by Singh. Jalan's ideas were turned down, but, ironically, he was promoted to head the Economic Advisory Council to the prime minister.

The war in the Gulf had global economic repercussions and worsened the crisis in India. India's oil import bill shot up from $280 million to $671 million a month and rating agencies downgraded India's economy to speculative. The previous regime of V. P. Singh had already withdrawn $660 million from the reserve tranche available with the IMF and spent most of it. International banks were reluctant to extend additional lines of credit. India was on the brink of a balance-of-payments crisis. The choice was clear—India could default or seek contingency financing from the IMF.

No Indian government ever admits to talking to the IMF or the World Bank till it is undeniable. Indeed, the V. P. Singh-led regime had never publicly admitted to having borrowed the $660 million available to the country from the IMF. The Chandra Shekhar regime continued with the tradition of denial but understood it had run out of options.

Practitioners of voodoo economics though, were convinced that India had options and presented them to Chandra Shekhar. Some solutions suggested were invitations to scandal. For instance, even as the non-resident Indians (NRIs) were withdrawing their deposits from Indian accounts, a few audaciously suggested to the prime minister that there was no need to beg the IMF for money and that wealthy NRIs could bridge the gap. All that the vulture capitalists needed was an authorization letter from the government indicating they were collecting funds abroad on behalf of the Government of India. The idea had all the makings of a scam. It is a measure of the desperation prevailing then that Chandra Shekhar wasn't totally averse to the idea. He, fortunately, drew the line—on good advice—at issuing authorization letters. In his inimitable style, he asked the NRIs if it wasn't time they did something for the motherland without ulterior motives.

Simultaneously, some influential bureaucrats and members of Chandra Shekhar's coterie began to strongly suggest that default was not a bad option and cited the example of some Latin American countries who had resorted to that course of action. Another option suggested was to freeze the accounts of NRIs so that foreign-exchange balances were maintained. India had been a frequent borrower from aid agencies since 1948 and had an impeccable record when it came to repaying loans. This time, however, the possibility that the country would default was strong. There was also a very real fear that a government on shaky footing could inflict irreversible damage on the country. A group of concerned bureaucrats informally briefed President Venkataraman about the consequences of ill-considered action. Venkataraman, who had dealt with a similar crisis in 1980 when he was finance minister, subtly conveyed the collective concern to the prime minister. Mercifully, Chandra Shekhar was a man who understood the importance and value of not going back on one's word.

The prime minister sent Foreign Secretary Muchkund Dubey to Washington to persuade the US to tell Japan and Germany to come to India's rescue. But there was no getting away from seeking the help of the IMF. In mid-December, C. Rangarajan, who was then deputy governor of the RBI, and Deepak Nayyar, who was chief economic adviser, headed to Washington where they caught up with Gopi Arora, then executive director at the IMF. India's impeccable record as a borrower helped. What didn't help was India's stubborn persistence with the licence-permit-quota raj and its political slant away from the US—a hangover of the Cold War. It would take more than just goodwill and good economists to convince the US and the IMF to come to the country's aid.

Although rustic in every way, Chandra Shekhar understood the tectonic shift that had taken place in the world following the collapse of the Berlin Wall and the Soviet Union. Realizing that India would have to reconcile itself to the emergence of a unipolar world and that it would have to do business with America and the institutions it underwrote, he announced on 17 December that the country would approach the IMF for assistance. 'I told our officials that they should initiate a dialogue with the IMF because in the present situation, we need the help,' the prime minister said. 'India will not hesitate to make an appeal, a request to help us in the present situation.' In the

US, policymakers were alive to the opportunity for a trade-off. It was clear India's soft approach to Iraq—though implicit—would need to be recast and India's position on the occupation of Kuwait would need explicit articulation.

History shows us that India's response to invasions and occupations has always been dictated by its own relations vis-à-vis the aggressor, be it Hungary, Vietnam or Afghanistan. When Iraq occupied Kuwait, the whole world was horrified, and, of course, the V. P. Singh-led regime which was in power at that time responded too, but ambivalently. Perhaps V. P. Singh's immediate concern was the safe repatriation of the 180,000 Indians trapped in the war zone. Perhaps the domestic response to the geopolitical situation was tempered by the exigencies of domestic vote-bloc politics. There was also the historic relationship with Iraq that had to be taken into account.

This time around, given the crisis he faced, Chandra Shekhar's actions were radically different from those of his predecessors. He urged Iraq to quit Kuwait immediately. He went further and condemned Iraqi attacks on Israel. This was India's first departure from its pro-Palestinian stance and its first step away from the policy of non-alignment it had subscribed to for decades. More daringly, it went against the line Congress was taking at the time, even though Chandra Shekhar's government depended on the Congress for support. The Congress linked the invasion to the Palestine issue and wanted a UN force and not one led by the US to initiate action. Chandra Shekhar rejected the idea.

In Washington, Indian officials were struggling to find support for their pitch to the IMF for aid. It was clear that India would need the influence of the US which had a vote of over 80 per cent in the IMF. But the US state department was not biting. Chandra Shekhar deployed Swamy, then minister for commerce and known for his deep links in the American establishment, for a breakthrough. Swamy achieved this on 3 January. He says, 'They wanted US war planes flying from the bases in Philippines to Saudi Arabia to be allowed to refuel in India. We had never allowed this.' Swamy asked what India would get in return and the Americans offered three times the regular landing charges. Swamy laughed and put his counter offer on the table—support India's request for a loan in the IMF.

The sequence of events that followed provides a fascinating insight into the world of geopolitics. On Friday, 4 January, the deal was more or less tied up. On 6 January, Swamy declared that the IMF had agreed to give India a loan. On 9 January, the Government of India agreed to allow US war planes to refuel in Bombay. On 17 January 1991, while America bombed Iraqi forces, Prime Minister Chandra Shekhar declared that the US decision to attack Iraq was right and the US state department, almost on cue, welcomed the Indian stand. A day later, the IMF cleared a loan of $1.03 billion under the Compensatory and Contingency Financing Facility to meet India's immediate needs and earmarked $789 million as the first tranche of a standby arrangement.

The arrangement between the US and India may have been a quid pro quo, but it did not obviate the imposition of conditions. The minutes of the 18 January 1991 meeting of the IMF to discuss India's bailout plan are revealing. Speaker after speaker questioned India's persistent romance with controls. The most scathing review came from Executive Director K. Yamazaki. He observed that 'India has been confronted with economic difficulties on almost every front—fiscal, monetary, exchange rate and industrial. These problems are deeply embedded in the economy.' It was an indictment of four decades of planning.

The presentation made by Gopi Arora appealing for aid was virtually a promissory note on reforms. The Indian pitch for aid included the statement of Finance Minister Yashwant Sinha in Parliament as evidence of 'prior steps' taken by India. And most significantly, the draft Industrial Policy of 1990 authored by A. N. Verma and Rakesh Mohan was presented as an 'article of intent'. Thomas C. Dawson, the US executive director of the IMF, who was sympathetic to the Indian cause, observed, 'The industrial policy of May 1990 was a step in the right direction and I would urge the authorities to recommit themselves to the broad implementation of that policy.'

Arora told the IMF board that the government was aware that stabilization was not the only priority on the national agenda and that 'more enduring solutions to the problems that confront the Indian economy have to be found in policies aimed at raising the efficiency of the national economy'. He assured them that 'government intends to implement a wide range of policies that would enhance efficiency and the competitiveness of industrial production'. The meeting ended with the IMF clearing a first tranche of $551 million with the implicit promise of further aid when certain long overdue measures were implemented in the budget of 1991. Sure enough, on 27 August 1991, Finance Minister Manmohan Singh sent a Letter of Intent outlining, across sixteen pages, the steps that had been taken and those that still needed to be taken for the next tranche of the $1.656 billion loan to be released.

CONTEXTUAL AUTISM

It might suit present-day Indian politicians to aver that India voluntarily took a strategic right turn in 1991 to dismantle controls and open up the economy. However, the truth is that liberalization was compelled by an unprecedented crisis. And the proof for that is furnished by the Project Completion Report (Structural Adjustment Loan/Credit of June 1995) of the World Bank. It states that 'of the twenty-five specific agreed actions contained in the SAL/SAC loan agreement, twenty-two had by the time of second tranche release (May 1992) been fully and three substantially complied with.' The latter related, specifically, to: (i) removal of administrative export controls on selected agricultural products; (ii) formulation of satisfactory policy measures for adjustment by industrial firms; and (iii) initiation of measures for restructuring/closure of patently unviable sick central public enterprises. Ten years after the 1991 turnaround, Deepak Nayyar, then finance secretary, confirmed that 'a blueprint for the change that in fact came in June–July 1991 was not a bolt from the blue; the plans were laid out in detail during Mr [Yashwant] Sinha's tenure. The first step towards some fiscal adjustment was taken in December 1990 after consultations with the IMF when a supplementary budget was presented to raise revenues.' Which is why Yashwant Sinha claims paternity for the liberalization of 1991, although unfortunately for him the government he was part of couldn't pull it off.

With just fifty-two MPs, Chandra Shekhar needed the support of the Congress to survive. Within the Congress, there was considerable disquiet over the moves being made by the Chandra Shekhar government. By the end of January 1991 Congress began distancing itself from a regime it supported from the outside, using the permission granted to US war planes to refuel in India as a possible deal-breaker. What the Congress was actually afraid of was Chandra Shekhar's ability to turn disastrous situations to his advantage. First, he had overturned the policy of non-alignment by permitting the refuelling of US warplanes. Next, he had claimed that he was close to a breakthrough in the Ayodhya dispute. Although details of this breakthrough are fuzzy, his reputation with regard to bringing two warring sides to the discussion table was formidable. Further, there was considerable speculation at the time that his long-time friend Sharad Pawar was attempting to split the Congress from within. And now he was all set to dismantle the licence-permit-quota raj and disrupt the business model of the Congress. As *The Financial Times* of London observed, the Congress was trying to pull the rug out from under Chandra Shekhar because he was turning out to be an 'uncomfortably successful' prime minister.

In the second week of February, Rajiv Gandhi met with President Venkataraman. In his discussions, the president of the Congress expressed his party's sense of disquiet about the government's actions. Venkataraman recognized the severity of the crisis and told Rajiv Gandhi that urgent steps to stabilize the situation were needed in the forthcoming budget. Rajiv Gandhi was not totally convinced about the ideas proposed. He met the president again, the very next day, along with Pranab Mukherjee who had succeeded Venkataraman as finance minister. They discussed the conditions imposed by the lenders and the serious cutbacks in government expenditure that were being proposed. Chandra Shekhar wanted to balance the political fallout of seeking assistance from the IMF by levying higher taxes on the rich and corporates. The thesis had political benefits and economic merit. However, the Congress did not want Chandra Shekhar to move any further; the party said it was not convinced by his ideas and opposed the need for a budget full of austerity measures.

By mid-February it was clear that the days of the Chandra Shekhar regime were numbered. The spin doctors of the Congress had zeroed in on the issue of foreign policy to stoke public anger. On 16 February, the Congress Party threatened to withdraw its support and topple the Chandra Shekhar regime unless it withdrew the refuelling rights granted to US warplanes. Ghulam Nabi Azad, then general secretary, announced that the Congress would move a no-confidence motion against the Chandra Shekhar government unless refuelling was halted. Those who knew Chandra Shekhar understood that he couldn't be blackmailed into changing his mind. Also, there was no guarantee that one threat wouldn't be followed by another very soon. The Congress wanted to be back in power and began readying itself for a midterm election.

It appeared that India was, yet again, about to be denied the change it so badly needed. It was clear that the Congress would not allow a budget—especially one that delivered change—to be presented by the puppet regime. Congress now needed an excuse to topple the government. And it was duly provided on 2 March. Prem Singh and Raj Singh, two constables of the Haryana Police, were arrested outside 10 Janpath, the residence of Rajiv Gandhi. The Congress preferred to assume the worst—the two constables had been spying on Rajiv Gandhi at the behest of Om Prakash Chautala, then chief minister of Haryana and, more importantly, son of Devi Lal, who was deputy prime minister in the Chandra Shekhar government. On 3 March, Congress demanded the ouster of the Haryana government.

On 4 March, Finance Minister Sinha wanted to present an interim budget but the Congress refused to let him. That marked the end of the Chandra Shekhar regime. The budget which remained unpresented distilled the crisis well. It said, 'The burden of servicing the accumulated internal and external debt has now become onerous. Neither the government nor the economy can live beyond its means for long. The room for manoeuvre, to live on borrowed money or time, has been used up completely. The soft options have been exhausted.' However, an interim budget could be tabled. The country would have to wait for a regular budget until after elections were held in May.

The economy was starved of money and credit was not just hard to come by but was also expensive. Interest rates had shot up and government was borrowing abroad at a shocking 2 per cent over the London Inter-Bank Offered Rate, the benchmark to pay creditors. NRIs were pulling out their deposits, adding pressure to the foreign exchange balance. India continued to beg for aid from the US, Japan and Germany. Muchkund Dubey was knocking on the doors of donors in Washington and Yashwant Sinha went all the way to Tokyo. Japan extended a soft loan of $150 million with a further commitment of $350 million and Germany granted a loan of $400 million. Then the negotiations with the IMF and the World Bank were put on hold as the country went to the polls.

Foreign exchange reserves—despite the booster shot from the IMF in January 1991—were down and barely enough to fund seven days of imports. There was a growing feeling among investors and lenders that while India was seeking assistance on the strength of an impeccable track record, it was not doing enough with the resources available to it. The idea of putting the nation's gold to use was suggested to Chandra Shekhar by Venkitaramanan and Manmohan Singh. The RBI governor explained to the prime minister the statute that allowed reserves to be deployed at times of crisis. India could raise money from international banks by offering gold as collateral. Chandra Shekhar agreed that it was a practical step. When his colleagues flinched at the political impact of pledging the country's gold, Chandra Shekhar roared at them in chaste Hindustani: 'When your reputation is at stake, what is more important? A piece of metal or your credibility?' Chandra Shekhar also knew the political consequences of his pragmatism. He knew that Rajiv Gandhi and his coterie in the Congress would attack him.

Yashwant Sinha writes in his memoirs, *Confessions of a Swadeshi Reformer: My Years as Finance Minister*, that he was getting ready for campaigning when he noticed a very senior official of the finance ministry amidst his party workers and the crowd. He had some documents for the finance minister to sign and from his grim demeanour it was clear that the prime minister had cleared the pledging of gold. Sinha signed. The operational details, though, were left to Venkitaramanan and Rangarajan who was then deputy governor of the RBI. The pawning of the nation's gold reserves still remained a hugely contentious issue and the government didn't want to access the reserves unless absolutely necessary. So, in May 1991, smuggled gold confiscated by Customs was leased to the State Bank of India which, in turn, sold it to a Swiss bank to raise $200 million.

The RBI then negotiated with the Bank of England and the Bank of Japan for an additional loan of $400 million, which would be secured by the gold collateral. But there was a hitch. The gold had to be of a particular grade—London Standard Pure—for the Bank of England to accept it. It wasn't. So the gold was first sent as it was to the Bank of England for a proximate assessment. An advance payment was made based on this. Thereafter, the Bank of England arranged for the gold to be converted to the required grade, assessed it again, and made the final payment to India.

India bought itself time to deal with the crisis in the economy but disaster struck on the political front. On 21 May, Rajiv Gandhi, while campaigning in Sriperumbudur near Chennai in Tamil Nadu, was assassinated by terrorists of the Liberation Tigers of Tamil Eelam (LTTE). When he was prime minister, Rajiv Gandhi had chosen to intervene in the ethnic conflict between the Sinhalese and Tamil people in Sri Lanka and had despatched Indian armed forces to the island nation in a disastrous attempt to impose peace. The move boomeranged politically and also cost Rajiv Gandhi his life. It was a tragic event made all the more so by its suddenness. India was shocked and the Congress party, left without a successor, grief-stricken. The objective of the terrorists was not only to seek revenge but also trigger chaos. However, the political class rallied to ensure that the election process was not interrupted. It is a tribute to India that the attempt to disrupt democracy was countered with courage and equanimity.

When the results were declared, it became clear that Congress had barely scraped through. Political instability fuelled economic uncertainty. Between April and June 1991, NRIs withdrew over $900 million from their bank accounts. The imperative for action was never more urgent. The installation of P. V. Narasimha Rao on 20 June 1991 as prime minister brought some order to the chaos.

Rao was sworn in at around noon on 21 June. He was heading a government that did not have a majority. It would have been daunting for any politician to deal with a crisis of the magnitude of the 1991 economic meltdown without the power and legitimacy of a majority. However, the situation was tailor-made for Rao's kind of politics. The lack of a majority afforded him an instrument to deal with the party high command. The government survived on outside support and Rao frequently engineered dissent to counter the diktat of the high command and ensure his suzerainty. The fragility imposed by the crisis gave him a lever to unsettle the power centres entrenched in the system. Rao clearly saw the opportunities embedded in the challenging circumstance of political instability and economic crisis. And, for a man who was making a comeback from retirement, there were no downsides.

At 9.50 p.m. on 22 June, in a late night televised address, Rao presented the plan to revive the economy. 'There is no time to lose. The government and the country cannot keep living beyond their means year after year. There are no soft options left. We are determined to address the problems of the economy in a decisive manner. This government is committed to removing the cobwebs that come in the way of rapid industrialization. We will work towards making India internationally competitive.' He declared that foreign direct investment would be welcome to accelerate development, upgrade technologies and promote exports. 'A time-bound programme will be worked out to streamline our industrial policies and programmes to achieve the goal of a vibrant economy that rewards creativity, enterprise and innovativeness.'

There is no question that the credit for the reforms of 1991 goes to Rao. Among the first decisions he took as prime minister was to retain the ministry of industries portfolio. Having chosen Manmohan Singh as minister for finance, Rao brought in P. Chidambaram as minister for commerce. His choice of people was dictated by the need to protect executive decisions from political baggage and influence. Simultaneously, he brought in as his principal secretary A. N. Verma from the Planning Commission and asked him to get Rakesh Mohan to create a presentation of the new industrial policy. Rao also instituted a steering group within the PMO which met every week to discuss and debate the architecture of what would eventually be defined as the liberalization of 1991. It was decided that the budget would be presented on 24 July, which left the team less than a month to get everything ready.

In Bombay, the RBI was faced with the twin challenges of managing the foreign exchange balance and restructuring exchange rates. Having been associated with virtually every important ministry including being finance secretary, RBI Governor Venkitaramanan was able to locate, analyse and resolve complex issues while simultaneously managing his political masters. His partner at the time was Deputy Governor C. Rangarajan, one of the top Indian economists. For almost a year Rangarajan had been part of a core team which included Deepak Nayyar, Gopi Arora, Venkitaramanan and Y. Venugopal Reddy, then joint secretary in the ministry of finance.

This team had been tasked with the infinitely delicate and complex task of restructuring the economy. Among other things, it required the exchange rate of the rupee to be devalued further, to reflect both the fragility of the balance-of-payments situation as also the real value of the rupee. Together, they pushed through a devaluation of 18 per cent between 1 July and 3 July. The core team knew that waiting for legislative sanction would delay relief. So Rangarajan, Venkitaramanan and Verma advised Rao and Manmohan Singh to use administrative powers wherever possible to prevent political opposition from within the Congress or from the Opposition. The two-step devaluation of the rupee, for instance, was not only hastened but also pushed through by executive fiat. It was agreed that Rao would manage the uproar after the deed was done.

Even as all this was going on, the RBI had to manage a unique logistical challenge. It had to ship 47 tons of gold to the Bank of England. The earlier shipment of confiscated gold had been sent in tranches on commercial flights. However, the airlines, worried about the risk, objected. So the RBI chartered Heavy Lift Cargo Airlines for four flights to ship the gold in stages. The gold had to be shifted from the vaults of the RBI in South Bombay and first transported 35 kilometres by road to the airport before being loaded on to the aircraft. Needless to say, all this required the utmost secrecy because of the security and political backlash that would ensue if the news leaked out.

As it happened, the operation could not be kept secret. In their anxiety, the RBI had reached an agreement with the Customs Department that the consignment would not be specified but it was precisely this which was the giveaway. Working on a tip-off, on 6 July 1991, I reached the Sahar International Airport in Bombay with photographers Mukesh Parpiani and Sudharak Olwe. All I had to work with was a chit that said '21,000 kilograms of precious metal being shipped to England'. Six hours of probing at the airport and the cordoned off Customs' enclosure resulted in a national scoop, published in sixteen editions of the then unified *Indian Express*. The story, accompanied by an eight-column picture of the aircraft being loaded with gold, brought home the magnitude of the crisis to Indians. Expectedly, the news triggered public outrage, for nothing is more humiliating in this country than pawning family gold. The day after, there was a furore in and outside Parliament. The government was forced to own up—India was broke.

In Delhi, work on the budget was proceeding at a furious pace. The package was ready in terms of the commitments to the lenders but it had to be made politically palatable. To start with, this was not a regime with a majority in Parliament. Worse, there was tremendous resistance to the budget even within the Congress party as well as in the cabinet and in the bureaucracy. Entrenched interests—both politicians on pelf row and big businesses nurtured on the licence-permit-quota raj—were concerned, and marshalled all their resources to prevent long-term damage to their interests. However, the options for derailing the process were limited by the circumstance. Providence provided me with a follow-up scoop and the government with exogenous support. A consignment of 14 tons of gold made its way from the RBI to the airport and on to the front pages again. Everybody recognized and accepted that defaulting would be a recipe for long-term disaster.

To make the plan politically palatable, Rao and the managers of the process presented to the stakeholders the strategic shift in the country's economic policy as a temporary tactic. The policy change would result in the dismantling of the Nehruvian way that the Congress had worshipped for decades. So Rao advised the team to present the package to the public and to the high priests of socialism in the Congress as a minor detour and not as game-changing disruption. In the final days, before the policy was presented the steering committee met many times every day to fine-tune the language.

Once a final version was ready, Rao and Chidambaram—who simultaneously spearheaded the liberalization of the country's trade policies—went over it one more time, injecting a political message. Obeisance was paid to the entire pantheon of the Congress leadership—from Jawaharlal Nehru to Indira and Rajiv Gandhi—in the new industrial policy and in the budget. Six new paragraphs were added to the policy in which encomiums were paid to the vision of Nehru and Indira Gandhi. Audaciously, the liberalization of the economy of 1991 was portrayed as a tribute to the aspirations of Rajiv Gandhi; further, it was represented as being built on the foundations laid by Nehru and Indira Gandhi. Homage was also paid to India's socialist past. It said: 'Thanks to the efforts of Pandit Jawaharlal Nehru, Indira Gandhi and Rajiv Gandhi, we have developed a well-diversified industrial structure. This constitutes a great asset as we begin to implement reforms.' Despite all efforts there was no dearth of protests. The Opposition even alleged that the budget had been written in Washington. Undeterred, helped by the enormity of the crisis, Rao carried the day.

On 24 July 1991, India finally honoured the promissory note it had presented to the lenders who had bailed the country out. The new industrial policy was unveiled by Prime Minister Rao, dismantling the licence-permit-quota raj of four decades. The Indian economy was finally unshackled. As Finance Minister Manmohan Singh said in his budget speech, quoting Victor Hugo, 'No power on earth can stop an idea whose time has come.'

CHANGE INTERRUPTED

Two decades later, it would seem that the lessons of 1991 have scarcely been learnt. The licence-permit-quota raj has been replaced by the clearance raj. It takes between three to five years before the scissor meets the ribbon for any industry to start. Survival still requires navigational skills of the political kind—getting clearance for land; approvals for environmental safeguards; permission for power and water; and to keep the inspector raj well fed. Industry accounted for 25 per cent of the GDP in 1991. Two decades later, it continued to lag at 27 per cent of the GDP in 2011. Employment in the organized sector in manufacturing—which was supposed to absorb surplus labour after liberalization—is, in 2012, stagnant at around 6 million, the same as it was in 1991. The next strategic steps on the agenda of reforms have been sacrificed at the altar of tactical politics.

Even under the watch of the Congress, coalition allies and the 'reformist' Sangh Parivar, the economy ails from political sclerosis. As in 1991, government expenditure is far in excess of its income. Driven by profligacy, borrowings in 2012 have burgeoned to over ₹1,300 crore a day from ₹200 crore in 2004. Foreign exchange outflow is far in excess of inflow, placing the deficit in the current account at a higher level than it was in 1991. Policy paralysis is driving Indian investment abroad; sliding growth has forced rating agencies to review their outlook on India. The economy is yet again poised at the brink of a crisis. The India Story, it would seem, awaits a sequel to 1991.

Victor Hugo would be baffled.

For a country periodically devastated by famine, the revival of agriculture should have been uppermost on the government's agenda. Yet, in the years following independence, the State shut out the largest number of people and the biggest part of the economy from growth. India suffered repeated droughts, food shortages and the shame of being tagged as a ship-to-mouth nation before the end of...

THE HUNGER GAMES

JULY 1964
PALAM AIRPORT, DELHI

It would have been difficult not to notice him. His attire was incongruous for a passenger arriving in a city wilting from heat and humidity. On a hot summer morning he was dressed in a suit and had an overcoat slung over his arm. The Pan Am flight, which landed at Delhi's Palam Airport, was coming from Manila, not exactly a cold place either. When Customs officials stopped him for questioning, he explained that he was on his way back from a conference in Christchurch, New Zealand, which, like all countries in the southern hemisphere, experiences its winter between June and August. Following the conference on seed-testing, he explained, he had stopped en route in Manila to visit the International Rice Research Institute in Los Banos.

Asked if he had anything to declare, the traveller said that while there was nothing in his luggage that would be of interest to the officials, he was carrying some seeds in his overcoat pockets. When asked what kind of seeds he was carrying and in what quantity, the man replied that he had about a kilogram of paddy seeds called Taichung Native-1.

Under the Livestock Importation Act 1898 and the Destructive Insects and Pests Act 1914, officers of the Customs department are obliged to stop and quarantine anybody carrying plant or animal material from a foreign country. These laws are aimed at preventing imports that could adversely affect the health of the nation's plant, human and animal population. The officers told the man they would have to impound the seeds.

The passenger protested. He declared that he was carrying the seeds for government use and under instructions from the minister for agriculture. But he had no documents or papers to back his claim. The passenger then asked the officers to call the office of the minister to check. After about an hour of back and forth, a senior officer called up the office of the minister. On the other end of the line was an IAS officer, private secretary to the minister for agriculture. The IAS officer confirmed that the seeds were indeed being brought for the minister and told the officials to let the passenger through. Not wishing to take on the office of a senior minister, the Customs officials reluctantly documented the consignment and let the passenger go.

The passenger was Dr Guduru Venkata Chalam. The IAS officer who took the call was S. Venkitaramanan, who would go on to win renown as the eighteenth governor of the Reserve Bank of India, but who was at the time of this story, private secretary to Subramaniam, who had recently taken over as minister for agriculture. Subramaniam, of course, had not asked for the seeds and was perhaps not even aware of Chalam's travels. Indeed, conventional wisdom within the government at that time was ranged against the introduction and use of high-yield hybrid seeds and was heavily in favour of indigenous seeds and cultivation methods. Fortunately, Venkitaramanan knew of Chalam and his rather unconventional methods. He knew he could trust Chalam and had thrown his weight, or rather the weight of his minister, behind the man, confident that the minister would support his decision. This was a decisive moment as Chalam had—in a sense, with the active connivance of Venkitaramanan—smuggled in the seeds of a revolution.

A HISTORY OF WANT

The scourge of colonial rule in India began with the famine of 1769 in Bengal and ended with the famine of 1943. Between 1860 and 1909, famines struck various parts of India twenty-two times, claiming millions of lives. In one year alone, 1897, famine affected eight provinces where three million people were—to borrow the phraseology used by the British in their reports—'relieved' of their lives. Famines are, of course, about scarcity but, even more than that, they are about unaffordability engineered by corrupt and insensitive regimes. Warren Hastings, the first governor-general of British India, who witnessed the effects of the Bihar famine in 1784, observed that although drought contributed heavily to the distress caused to the population, 'the cause existed principally in a defective, if not corrupt and oppressive, administration'. Such was the devastation of the 1784 famine that by 1788, one-third of arable land in India had gone out of cultivation. Left without food to eat, the populace used up all the seeds reserved for the following year's sowing. The fear of hunger drove people to migrate, leaving lands untenanted.

For the East India Company, the recurrence of famine in India was a problem that did not exist. The Company's sole objective was the maximization of revenue from the land, not the health of the colony. The profit it made was based on the rent it was able to extract from farmers. And as the rent itself was calculated not on actual produce but on an estimate of future harvests, it didn't matter what the eventual production would be. This callous system paid scant attention to the welfare of farmers. A survey conducted by the Congress on agrarian distress in the thirties revealed that the worst impact of the usurious taxation was on tenant farmers. The zamindar himself retained a tenth of the holdings for personal cultivation and rented the rest to cultivators. After the cultivator bought seeds, paid rent and spent money on other operating costs, he still needed to work on other farms just to stay alive. And although rent rates hadn't changed since Mughal times, the ruthlessness with which revenue was collected drove many into penury and perpetual debt. As Malcolm Darling wrote in his classic, *The Punjab Peasant in Prosperity and Debt*, the eponymous peasant of the title 'is born in debt, lives in debt and dies in debt', and after death, bequeaths debt.

In the early days of its tenure, the Company bartered goods imported from England for Indian spices, crafts and commodities which were then sold for a profit. However, once it had acquired the right to collect revenue, as happened in Bengal, the Company converted the right to collect tax into a zero-capital, high-profit business model. It collected revenue and then used the same money to buy commodities to export to Europe. Or to put it differently, it took money from the farmers and then used a part of it to pay them for commodities. It was a brilliant business model from the Company's point of view, but grievously exploited Indian farmers.

The British government could have—had it chosen to—made reparation when it took control of the country after the Sepoy Uprising in 1857. It could have dealt with zamindars charging usurious rent from tenant farmers and restructured the revenue system to accommodate the cost of seeds and inputs while fixing rent. However, the primary focus of the colonial masters was on national politics and not on the economics of agriculture. The British had adopted the strategy of classes-against-the-masses to deal with, and disrupt, the Civil Disobedience Movement, and the zamindars were among those the British wooed to splinter the movement for independence. Intervention in the messy rent system would have led to a confrontation with the zamindars and the loss of their support against the agitators. The economics of agriculture was handcuffed to the politics of the colonial raj.

The crisis in Indian agriculture was apparent to anyone who cared to look as early as in the twenties. Everybody in government, from colonial times onwards, as well as every economist who had studied India's economy, had warned of the human and economic costs imposed on society by perpetual scarcity. In 1928, the Royal Commission on Agriculture headed by Lord Victor Alexander Linlithgow highlighted the huge gap between consumption and production that existed in India and emphasized the need to boost output. The commission said: 'India has long been a very large producer of rice; the annual quantity harvested being about 25,000,000 tons. Although India accounts for 2/5th of the world's output it consumes all of this and so large quantities ranging between 15 to 25 lakh tons are imported from Burma, Thailand and the French Indo-China.' It added that supplies from these regions would dry up and 'therefore production in India must be increased to meet at least the basic requirement'.

The commission's recommendations to address the problem of low output, scarcity and the need for a blueprint to map the revival of the agricultural economy were ignored even though the report appeared in the wake of many famines and a state of perpetual food scarcity. The neglect happened because the British were more interested in the potential for research to complement research back home. It was to this end that the Imperial Council of Agricultural Research was established. However, the question of the British sharing the fruits of their research with their subjects was never on the agenda.

For decades, India's human narrative was punctuated by food scarcity, famine and appeals for food aid. Through the forties, particularly during World War II, there were severe restrictions on the movement of grains, and rice was rationed to about 30 grams per person per day. Indeed, it was commonplace for wedding invitations to mention 'please carry your ration card with you', almost like liquor permits. The Americans—once they emerged on the global scene after World War II—were quick to recognize the nature and seriousness of the food crisis in India. In the summer of 1946, President Herbert Hoover's Famine Emergency Committee visited India. Having reviewed the impact of the war on the economy in general, the committee declared that the food situation in the country was extremely poor. The US then led from the front and immediately sent 800,000 tons of food grains to India. It said that the 'lives of 225 million people [would be] at risk if other countries didn't pitch in with food aid'.

The British, when they left, put the onus of the resolution of the food crisis on India's new rulers. The partition of the country added a new dimension to the problem. After the split, India was left with 82 per cent of the total pre-Partition population and 75 per cent of the total pre-Partition land mass, introducing a new arithmetic in terms of per capita output and demand. The surplus-producing provinces of Sind and west Punjab, which had well-integrated irrigation systems, went to Pakistan, further handicapping food security. The Congress was alive to the need to do something but, as always, political compulsions delayed effective decision-making. The party was split between two ideological positions—Gandhiji advocated the concept of fasting, sacrifice, self-restraint and food conservation to ensure that there was enough food to go around. The modernists, led by Nehru, didn't quite agree. They believed that conservation was not enough and that India would need to fund agriculture and find ways to grow more food to meet the burgeoning demand.

This was easier said than done; the scale of the problem was staggering. Only 15 per cent of farming was based on irrigation and over 80 per cent was rain-fed. Nitrogen- and potash-based fertilizers—internationally recognized as an effective means of improving yield and in use in Europe for nearly half a century—was very frugally used across India—less than one kilogram per acre. Groundwater could be drawn and used as a substitute for canal-based irrigation but that required power. India at independence had little access to power and barely 4 per cent of the total power generated was used to draw water from the ground, and that too not necessarily for agriculture.

Nobody was more acutely aware of the difficult situation than Pandit Jawaharlal Nehru. At a civic reception in New York in 1949, during an official visit, he was asked what India's biggest problem was. He answered candidly, 'Poverty. We must have food for our people,' and openly campaigned for food aid. He said, 'America could be most helpful to India by making available a large quantity of wheat of which I understand you have a surplus.' On his way back, at a meeting with Indians in London, he lobbied again. 'It is true that we are anxious to get wheat as cheap as possible—if possible free or on a deferred payment system so that we can pay in parts for five years.'

Ideally, the prime minister's persistent campaign for food aid and supplies should have led to a push for the transformation of the agricultural sector, but efforts in this direction continued to be halting. Like the British before them, the new Government of India preferred to set up committees and fact-finding missions rather than actually take concrete steps to fix the crisis. In 1947, a Food Grains Policy Commission headed by Purushottamdas Thakurdas was set up. In its report, submitted in April 1948, the commission emphasized that 'dependence on food imports should be phased out and India's food problem should be solved by increasing domestic food grain production'. The commission recommended that the government take steps to ensure food security and that indigenous food grains production be increased by at least 10 million tons per year until self-sufficiency was achieved. Even though little was done to implement the findings of the 1947 commission, another panel, the Food Grains Investigation Commission of 1949, was appointed. It recommended that government invest in irrigation and improve the distribution of seeds and fertilizers to increase production so that demand could be met.

THE POLITICS OF ECONOMICS

It is commonly held that growth is the outcome of a virtuous cycle in which investment in industry fuels employment, incomes, consumption and savings to once again drive investment. In India, however, the threat of famine and the urgent need for poverty alleviation demanded as much investment of resources in agriculture as was happening in industry. The government needed to invest in irrigation, seeds, technology and fertilizers. Annual budgets were required to create room for investments to set up seed farms, fertilizer plants, and, of course, to provide price incentives for farmers. What was also needed, on a priority basis, was the adoption of technology to boost per-acre yield.

Almost a decade before independence, the Congress party had decided that its political objectives would dictate its approach to economic development. The goal was not merely the achievement of a numerical target and the maximization of growth, but rather, complete self-reliance and an end to the dependence on Western industrial powers. This was to be achieved by focusing on an industrial policy that emphasized massive investment in core industries and import substitution.

However, the objective of self-reliance and industrialization led to a bias in the allocation of resources. Given the limitation of resources, agriculture was not granted the priority it deserved. And what complicated matters was the Congress party's conviction that any initiative to improve agricultural growth should not lead to the enrichment of the rural rich. Even though technology is supposed to be scale neutral, it was felt that the introduction of high-yield varieties of crops and added investment in agriculture would benefit big farmers more than the small farmers. It was widely felt that the yawning gap between the zamindars who owned the land and the farmers who tilled the soil should be addressed through the redistribution of wealth.

Historically, land in India belonged to local communities and the local communities recognized the rights of those who worked their land. The Mughals, and the British who followed them, altered this structure so that the collection of levies became easier. The Mughals appointed favoured gentry to collect levies for them in return for the right to retain a fixed proportion of the levy as fee. Over a period of time, as the Mughal Empire went into decline, rent collectors converted the territories assigned to them into personal fiefdoms. The tenure and rights of the farmers, thus far guaranteed by the monarch, were thus diluted and taken away from them. The farmers became tenants at the mercy of the zamindars. This system suited the British, used as they were to the idea of a monarch owning all land and distributing it to favoured gentry. The zamindars became the new aristocracy of the country and aligned themselves with the new rulers in return for all manner of favours.

This injustice of the relationship between the feudal and the ruling class found resonance in popular cinema. The silent movie *Savkari Pash* (a.k.a. the Indian Shylock) of 1925 starring V. Shantaram told the story of exploitation by landlords and moneylenders. The 1936 Franz Osten-directed Bombay Talkies production *Janmabhoomi*, starring Ashok Kumar and Devika Rani, explored the ideal of converting class conflict into class collaboration. Nitin Bose's *Desher Mati*, and K. A. Abbas's *Dharti Ke Lal*, starring Sombhu Mitra and Balraj Sahni, romanced the idea of sharecroppers coming together to practise Soviet-style collective farming to take on the zamindar.

Throughout the independence movement, both retribution and redistribution were a constant refrain. The All India Kisan Sabha demanded 'the abolition of zamindari tenures without compensation, abolition of all debts and redistribution of all cultivable waste lands with government to subsistence farmers and landless labourers'. At the Faizpur Session of 1937, the Congress, aligning itself with popular sentiment, called for immediate action in all manner of problems afflicting the rural poor, ranging from a reduction in rent to exemption from land tax, the abolition of feudal dues, the liquidation of unconscionable debts and occupancy rights for all tenants. Nehru was convinced that the problem of agriculture could not be solved piecemeal. The land system, he said, 'cannot endure and an obvious step is to remove the intermediaries between the cultivator and the State. Cooperative or collective farming must follow'.

Mahatma Gandhi, however, recognized the potential for violence embedded in the quest for radical change. He realized that the radicalization of the movement could result in the alienation of the landed class—carefully cultivated for their support—from the movement for independence. Worse, a ham-handed attempt at revolution would end his idea of a non-violent struggle for independence. Gandhiji stepped in to counter those within the Congress intent on revolution.

By the time the country attained independence, Congress had toned down its rhetoric of radical change. However, despite the efforts of the Mahatma, the votaries of radical change and the communists sensed an opportunity to push through their agenda soon after independence and indulged in adventurism in their strongholds in Telangana and Bengal to uproot the zamindars and restore land to tillers. The murders, the bloodshed and loot that followed muddied the morality of the cause. Further, the communal carnage that followed Partition and the assassination of Gandhiji prompted a new mood of conciliation within the nation. Change continued to be on the agenda of Congress and others who were wedded to the idea but the pace at which it would occur was slowed down, and the means through which it would take place were changed.

The left-leaning members of Congress, though, continued to insist that for total independence, the restoration of ownership and title of land to the community was necessary. While Nehru favoured the idea, he also realized that it entailed the risk of disruption and class conflagration that could potentially derail democracy in the young republic. Nehru, a true democrat, then chose to locate his policy in the area of convergence between capitalism and communism, or what he described as 'a third way which takes the best of all existing systems—the Russian, the American and the others—and seeks to create something suited to one's history and philosophy'.

SEEDING OF BIAS

By 1950, Congress was ready with the ideas on development that were to be enshrined in the First Five Year Plan. India was to focus on both industry and agriculture. Even though the logic of economics dictated that attention be first paid to the large majority of people and to agriculture, the government decided to proceed with the plan to modernize industry, a move that was to be funded by domestic savings, foreign aid and growth in agricultural output.

The scale of the ambition was astounding. India, a nation that up until independence was forced to import even pins, aspired to become a nation that built world-class industries in metals, power and heavy machinery. These goals demanded monetary and technical resources far in excess of what the country possessed. But Nehru was not deterred. He rejected the premise that endemic poverty required an absolute focus on agricultural development and placed his faith on a model in which import substitution and investment in heavy industry would lead to growth.

The faith in this model may be criticized today but then, it was the dominant idea among scholars working on development economics. It is critical to understand the context in which the choice was made. At the end of World War II, thinking was very clearly influenced by the Depression of the thirties, the collapse of international trading and financial systems and, most importantly, the success of Soviet central planning in transforming an agrarian economy into an industrial state that could muster enough strength to defeat Germany.

The approach to reviving agriculture was based on community development programmes. The idea was plausible. Agriculture, like industry, requires scale and technology to drive output. Farmers in Australia, the US and the Soviet Union were able to push up crop yields, at least in part, due to scale, that is, the size of their holdings. The idea was that in India, land held by zamindars would be redistributed to tillers who would form cooperatives. These cooperatives would be advised by knowledge workers—on not just farming but activities like dairy farming or keeping poultry, which would augment income—who had been trained and developed by the government. This would result, it was hoped, in the development of the human and material resources of the rural community. Economic development was to be achieved through social transformation, not the other way around.

Economists, industrialists and commentators from Britain and the United States worried that the focus on creating a modern industrial complex would leave little in terms of resources for agriculture. Nehru didn't take kindly to unsolicited, even if well-intentioned, advice on how India should proceed on the path to economic development. As early as 1946, in a style inimitable for its blend of passion and lucidity, he stated: 'Ever since the demand for the development of modern industry arose in India, we have been told that India is pre-eminently an agricultural country and it is in her interest to stick to agriculture. Industrial development may upset the balance and prove harmful to her main business—agriculture. The solicitude that the British industrialist and economist have shown for the Indian peasant is very gratifying ... as if any Indian with an iota of intelligence could forget the peasants. The Indian peasant is our main focus and it is on his progress that India's progress depends. But crisis in agriculture, grave as it is, is interlinked with crisis in industry, out of which it arose. The two cannot be disconnected and dealt with separately, and it is essential for the disproportion between the two to be remedied.'

In that one breathless burst, Nehru made clear that his mind was set on the middle path. The First Plan outlined this in words and rupees. Agriculture received a substantial allocation, but did not command the entire focus of government. Nonetheless, the Plan did make significant provisions for spending on power and irrigation. It was also a testament to Nehru's vision that he could conceive of a large irrigation-cum-power project like the Bhakra Nangal complex as early as in 1948. Indeed, while in the US, the one place Nehru spent considerable time was at the Tennessee River Valley project. He obviously understood the critical need for energy for growth and the multiplier effect of large-scale projects.

Even as the First Plan was being debated vigorously, India was hit by scarcity. The pre- and post-war price controls mechanism—which was withdrawn in 1947 in deference to Gandhiji's antipathy to controls—was reinstated by the end of 1948 but it didn't help narrow the gap between supply and demand. Many messages were sent through diplomatic channels for food aid. At first, the US administration did not respond to the requests. Their concern was that India was drawing more aid than needed and using it as an instrument of price control. This meant the interests of private landowners were being hurt and that was politically unpalatable to the US—they felt that this could foment Communism.

Soon enough, though, India's plea for food aid received a fillip because of a fortunate turn of events. After World War II, the US had begun to engage more vigorously with the world at large as it grew accustomed to its new role as a global superpower. Following the war, the US put together the Marshall Plan—worth $25 billion—to fund the reconstruction of Japan and Germany. In the 1948 elections, Harry Truman outlined a four-point programme that was essentially conceived around using American resources to influence the course of global politics. When Chiang Kai Shek was chased out of China into Taiwan by Mao's mob, it deeply worried Western democracies. The US grew concerned about the growth of Communism in Asia as two large blocs, the Soviet Union and China, were ruled by Marxist regimes. In many ways this period marked the beginning of Cold War politics and Nehru was quick to realize this. He saw that India, having vowed to stick to the idea of non-alignment, could prove to be the bulwark in preventing the spread of Communism and made sure the US saw the country in this light.

In June 1951, the Harry Truman regime passed a special law—the India Emergency Food Aid Act. Signing the act with his characteristic flourish, Truman said: 'I am delighted to be able to sign this act of Congress which will make it possible for the United States to send to the people of India up to 2 million tons of food grains. These shipments of food from the United States will supply nearly two-thirds of all the food which India is buying abroad to meet its emergency.'

The aid delivered a reprieve to the hard-pressed Nehru government but the concern about food scarcity and low output in India's agricultural economy persisted. The World Bank, in its assessment of the Indian economy, also found reason to emphasize the need to upgrade agriculture. It stated that 'India has long been a food-deficit region. The food problem has been aggravated in the post-war period by transfer of surplus grain areas to Pakistan, by a series of poor monsoons, by increased consumption and by steady growth of population.' The import of grains resulted in widening trade deficits between 1949 and 1952. Indeed, while processing its first loan for India, the World Bank warned that India's economic development could be maintained 'only if further financial aid [was] forthcoming'.

Meanwhile, the ideas that held the First Plan together ran into roadblocks. Even a modest renaissance in agriculture depended on the abolition of zamindari through the introduction of reforms that improved the contractual terms of tillers and placed a ceiling on landholdings. To achieve this the government introduced the Zamindari (Abolition) Act. Immediately, feudal landlords across various states challenged the act in court, arguing that it violated their basic rights as the Constitution guaranteed the right to property. In the landmark *Kameshwar vs State of Bihar* (1951) case, the Patna High Court held the Bihar Land Reforms Act unconstitutional. However, many courts—Allahabad and Nagpur, for instance—upheld land reforms. The zamindars then knocked on the doors of the Supreme Court. But even as the appeals were pending, the government decided to amend the Constitution.

The wording of the amendment speaks volumes. 'During the last fifteen months of the working of the Constitution, certain difficulties have been brought to light by judicial decisions and pronouncements especially in regard to the chapter on fundamental rights.' The citizen's right, it stated, was subject to reasonable restrictions in the interests of the general public. The amendment then went on to 'insert provisions fully securing the constitutional validity of zamindari abolition laws in general and certain specified State Acts in particular'.

The amendment didn't help beyond a point. The Congress, through the struggle for independence, had carefully nurtured zamindars as important cogs in the movement for freedom. Typically, the basic unit was built at the local level with members of the dominant caste and the land-owning gentry making up the foundation of political mobilization. A collection of these units, from village to district to state, made up the national party pyramid in which every unit was intricately linked to the other by various alliances on issues and votes. Loyalty was dictated by allegiance to causes and consequences. Any decision in the policy sphere naturally had implications for party members with vested interests and, therefore, on the electoral fortunes of both the state and central leaders. The landed class saw the cooperative movement and land reforms as a direct attack on their property interests and held the political system to ransom. Ergo, barring Kerala and West Bengal, land reforms floundered everywhere else. The success of land reforms in Kerala and West Bengal is largely explained first by its acceptance by civil society and the influence of competitive socialism between the Left and the Congress.

The impasse in reforms was frustrating for the ideologues in the party. Nehru and the other planners repeatedly held out the example of China to push through land reforms. However, what they ignored was that revolution drove change in China. The country's administration was authoritarian and, therefore, the transfer of land automatic. More importantly, land ownership and revenue collection was streamlined from the bottom up while, in contrast, India had a multiplicity of systems and patterns of revenue collection.

The moral suasion of the Bhoodan Movement did prick the collective conscience but didn't translate into action beyond a point. The Bhoodan Movement derived legitimacy from the presence of Acharya Vinoba Bhave and his commitment to ensure the distribution of land and the redistribution of wealth. A Gandhian, Bhave succeeded in getting people across many states to relinquish control over large tracts of land so that they could be redistributed among the tillers.

The idea of land reforms could not be driven by philanthropy; it demanded political acceptance.

Undeterred, the Congress and Nehru continued with their faith in community plans to address the goals that needed to be met in agriculture. The juggernaut of planned development kept rolling. The Second Five Year Plan placed greater emphasis on industrialization. We have examined in the chapter 'The Bonfire of the Vanities' how the planners, led by P. C. Mahalanobis, brought all but three sectors of industry under state control and rendered the Government of India the largest industrial house in the country. Despite valuable advice from economists to the contrary—that a better way to industrialize India would be to open up the economy to competition, invite foreign investment, allow imports to induct technology and cost efficiency—Mahalanobis and his group stuck to their guns.

Mahalanobis believed that only industrialization, as opposed to an emphasis on agriculture, would enable developing countries to have stable relations with foreign powers; any country dominated by agriculture could be bullied. The counter that food aid from the US and other countries could also be converted into an instrument to subjugate national interests had no currency at that point.

Out of a total sum of ₹4,800 crore in the Plan, just ₹568 crore was allocated for agriculture and community development. The spending on agricultural programmes was slashed from ₹196 crore to ₹170 crore. The planners contended that low and static standards of living, underemployment and unemployment were all manifestations of an economy dependent on agriculture. The planners pointed out that the proportion of population employed in the agricultural sector in the US had dropped from 54 to 23 per cent and in Japan from 80 to 48 per cent. From the precedents set by these countries, they concluded that the diversification of industry and speedy industrialization were the only ways in which development could occur.

As an aspiration it was laudable, but as a plan it was divorced from the reality of sustained food scarcity which needed to be addressed. Worse, the Plan assumed and demanded the continuation of food aid, cheap imports and food grains from the US. Not only was food aid to be used to bridge the demand gap, it was also expected to suppress domestic prices to ensure higher household savings that would, in turn, fund planned industrialization. There was also the political diktat: prices needed to be kept low for any government to be re-elected. It is unlikely that the planners failed to understand that the suppression of domestic prices with imports would kill any incentive for Indian farmers to produce more food. It is entirely possible that political logic prevailed over economic rationale.

By the mid-fifties, food shortage was a common headline in India's newspapers. And although the continuing Cold War provided India the necessary leverage to ask the US for aid, the benefactor country was concerned that continuing inequalities within India could lead to social conflict which, in turn, could provide a breeding ground for Communism. Such concerns notwithstanding, on 10 July 1954, President Dwight D. Eisenhower signed the Agricultural Trade Development Assistance Act or Public Law 480 (PL 480) into law. Enacted to support American farmers and the export of American agricultural products, PL 480 was also an instrument of geopolitics to keep Communism at bay. Non-aligned India was among its biggest beneficiaries. Between 1955 and 1971, India received over 50 million tons of grain—almost half of all food grains given under the PL 480 programme.

The financing of the PL 480 purchases was unique. The price was discounted and payments were made in rupees through the issue of government bonds so there was no outflow of precious foreign exchange. These monies were for the use of the US government within India and for it to fund development activities in India. John Perkins estimates in his book, *Geopolitics and the Green Revolution*, that these monies amounted to a third of the total money in circulation within the country. While this contention cannot be validated, what is known for sure is that in 1971, the US government placed this amount at $3 billion and during the Nixon regime Indian officials negotiated with Ambassador Daniel Moynihan and got interest payments due to the US—to the tune of over $4 billion—written off. This creation of money, studies by economist B. R. Shenoy have revealed, fuelled inflation and amounted to 35 per cent of the deficit financing between 1962 and 1971.

The impact of the PL 480 purchases was more damaging on agriculture. Nehru's two-pronged strategy of investment in industrialization, backed by a revival of agriculture driven by community effort, had stalled. By the end of 1956 it was clear that the template for agricultural revival was a failure. Yet another committee was appointed, headed by Balwant Rai Mehta, to suggest ways to improve community development programmes. The Mehta Committee suggested decentralization of political power to the panchayats in the hope that a bottom-up initiative might defeat the vested interests that had blocked the top-down revolution. But the idea was soon buried under the weight of caste considerations that sustained the hierarchy of political power.

On his part, Nehru wouldn't give up on his idea of collective cooperation. In 1956, in his fortnightly letters to chief ministers, he repeatedly brought up the issue of agricultural growth and drew comparisons with the progress China claimed to have made in collective farming. Indeed, in 1956, a seven-member delegation led by R. K. Patil, a Gandhian, travelled to China to study how that country had propelled agricultural growth—40 per cent as compared to India's 15 per cent. Following the report, the Planning Commission increased the target of expected growth in agricultural output to 40 per cent over the objections of the minister for agriculture, A. P. Jain.

While the politicians debated and planners squabbled, the economy went into a tailspin. India's export performance continued to be poor, it didn't earn enough dollars. The Plan hadn't budgeted adequately for foreign exchange requirements and the import bill commanded by industrialization drove India to the brink of a balance-of-payments crisis in 1957. It was the first in the series of balance-of-payments crises India faced till 1991. The crisis forced the government to impose import controls and seek help from the IMF and the US to remain creditworthy. The US and the World Bank were critical of the Second Plan which obviated the scope for private and foreign enterprise. Eventually, after a year of deliberations—during which many concessions for multinationals were extracted by the US—a resident mission of the World Bank was installed in Delhi and an Aid Consortium of Developed Nations set up to help India. It marked the beginning of the aid raj.

1957 was also an election year. A rise in prices is usually fatal for ruling parties and to the dismay of Nehru's Congress, inflation drove prices up; the government was forced to procure higher quantities of grain at lower-than-market prices thereby pushing farmers already hit by drought deeper into distress. Although Nehru's personal standing was not affected by the drought or inflation, the party lost Kerala to the Communist party.

EARLY GREEN SHOOTS

By the late fifties, foreign lenders and economists were openly critical of the economic model India was planning to put in place. They were vociferous in their view that India should move its focus from rapid industrialization towards reviving agriculture. Douglas Ensminger of the Ford Foundation, who was touring India at that time, met with the prime minister for discussions. Nehru accepted the Foundation's suggestion to set up a team to study the crisis in agriculture. The team, headed by Sherman Johnson of the US Department of Agriculture, would submit its report by 1959.

Simultaneously, Nehru appointed another committee, the Food Grains Enquiry Committee, headed by Asoka Mehta, to look into the problems of availability of food grains and price management. This committee was the first to recommend a system of incentives for farmers and laid the foundation for the current model of agricultural management. It suggested that the government create an institution that would directly procure from farmers when prices were falling. This would provide the price support necessary to keep agriculture viable. If and when prices shot up, the body could offload grains on to the market to subdue prices and inflation. The committee also suggested the creation of buffer stocks for emergencies.

Even as these measures were being contemplated, the National Development Council (NDC) came up with some voodoo to manage scarcity. The NDC resolved that the government should take over the wholesale food grain trade. The idea was to procure from both surplus and deficit states at a minimum support price. The move boomeranged. Inflation worsened as the wholesale dealers manipulated the policy. The dealers used the minimum support price meant to help farmers as the minimum sale price. And since there was never enough production, the government couldn't reverse the practice by selling food grain in the open market to bring prices down.

The cause of failure through two decades was located in production. The fundamental issue facing agriculture was the need for an exponential growth in the indigenous production of food grains to meet the needs of a rising population. That was the elephant in the room Indian policy wonks appeared reluctant to deal with. In 1959, the Ford Foundation team submitted a report entitled 'India's Food Crisis and Steps to Meet It'. Mincing no words, the team declared that India was facing a crisis in food production. In a body blow to the romantics in the Congress party, the team advised a paradigm shift from a social to a technological revolution.

India was urged to deliver improved seeds, fertilizers, better irrigation equipment, credit, technical advice and ensure a guaranteed price that would serve as an incentive to farmers to take risks and grow more crops. It also stressed that although many plans and programmes had been initiated for population control, there wasn't any appreciable slowing of population growth. The report stated bluntly, 'This means that food will have to be provided for eighty million more people by the end of the Third Plan...the present population places severe pressure on food supplies and unfavourable crop conditions create an immediate crisis.' The 259-page report anticipated that India would need an additional 20 million tons of food grains every year by the end of 1970—a quantity so large that it couldn't be imported.

The Planning Commission, though, was not ready to accept the diagnosis. The planners were still convinced that India's demand for food grains could be met by a combination of a marginal increase in domestic production and imports. This contention was completely rubbished by H. S. Rao, one of the analysts of the Ford Foundation.

Rao proved through forensic analysis that India was at the doors of a crisis. Assuming that India would have a shortfall of 10 million tons per annum; even if half of it, or 5 million tons, was imported free of cost, the country would still have to come up with ₹170 crore in foreign exchange, or 22 per cent of its export earnings. If the shortfall was 15 million tons per year, then the cost, after free imports of 5 million tons, would be ₹340 crore or 44 per cent of exports. Rao estimated the gap between demand and supply of food grains to be 20 million tons and concluded that there was no way India could fund its food grain imports. Even if the country did find the funds, there was no guarantee that world markets would have a surplus of 20 million tons for India to tap into.

These calculations prompted Nehru to accept the characterization of the situation as a crisis. The labours of the Ford Foundation had an impact. At the request of Nehru, Ensminger created another group headed by Johnson for a specific programme that India could initiate. The group drafted a programme which recommended a focused approach to the problem. It was suggested that as a pilot project, seven districts should be chosen and provided with all necessary inputs, from fertilizers to seeds to pesticides, to enable higher crop yield. These districts would be the foundation of the Intensive Agricultural District Programme (IADP). The seven districts—Thanjavur in Tamil Nadu, West Godavari in Andhra Pradesh, Shahabad in Bihar, Raipur in Madhya Pradesh, Aligarh in Uttar Pradesh, Ludhiana in Punjab and Pali in Rajasthan—were chosen for their history of high crop yields.

The idea met with serious opposition within the Congress. Opponents to the plan felt the country was moving away from the idea of social revolution to a more technical, focused approach and feared that this would lead to the betterment of rich farmers, the bullock capitalists. Nehru himself was not against the idea but was disheartened by the failure of the community to come together. By then he had been at the helm for nearly seventeen years and he was beginning to feel the effects of age and fatigue.

At around the same time, in 1959, M. S. Swaminathan, then an assistant cytogeneticist at the Indian Agricultural Research Institute, who would in time come to be regarded as one of the fathers of the Indian Green Revolution, met with Orville Vogel, American agronomist, wheat breeder and pioneer in hybridization. Vogel put him in touch with Norman Borlaug, the Nobel laureate who is credited with saving millions from famine. Swaminathan knew that the Rockefeller Foundation in Mexico had successfully developed a dwarf variety of wheat seeds which were capable of tripling wheat yields. He wanted the government to adopt these practices in India to improve productivity.

Swaminathan was among the few who questioned the efficacy of the many theories of the Planning Commission, including the Intensive Agricultural Development Programme (IADP), announced in 1960. Swaminathan recalls pointing out that the planners were ignoring two critical inputs for improving output—the availability of high-yield seeds and a price guarantee that would encourage the farmer to take the necessary financial risk to obtain higher yields. Swaminathan advocated that India approach Borlaug at the Rockefeller Foundation and obtain the new hybrid seeds, while at the same time instituting a procurement mechanism to assure farmers that they would be guaranteed a fixed return on their investment. This meant that the ministry of finance would first have to release foreign exchange for the purchase of seeds and then budget for procurement at a remunerative price. The government chose to ignore Swaminathan's ideas, primarily because he had argued for foreign exchange investment in the project. The IADP meandered along and eight more districts were added to the pilot project.

Elsewhere, it was business as usual. The price of food grains spiralled upwards and this was offset through the increased offloading of PL 480 stocks. The focus on the crisis was diluted as national politics grew increasingly fractious and divided. The nationalist fervour, which had achieved independence and which had held a disparate group of politicians together, was weakening and the cracks beginning to show. As a result, many of the high-minded initiatives that had been promulgated soon after independence began to falter. The measures to abolish the rapacious zamindar class were the first casualty. Despite the abolition of the zamindari system, many landlords managed to retain their landholdings. Similarly, the panchayati raj initiative was hijacked by the dominant castes, the propertied class and thus the oppression of disadvantaged caste groups and tenant farmers continued unabated.

By the time the Third Plan was to be drafted in 1961, the nation was drifting and the Congress was in disarray. In the run-up to the 1962 polls, Nehru took up the challenge of restoring people's faith in the party. He campaigned relentlessly, travelling over 20,000 kilometres by rail and road, addressing election meetings in hundreds of constituencies. Congress won, but by fewer seats. Worryingly, these elections saw the emergence of sectarian interests for the first time in the history of the new nation. The Akali Dal wanted a Sikh state within Punjab. In the south the DMK planted the idea of a Dravidistan, encompassing the four southern states of Tamil Nadu, Kerala, Andhra Pradesh and Mysore. Marxist ideology was on the rise in Kerala and West Bengal. In the Hindi hinterland, the right-wing Jan Sangh was finding growing support for its cause. And everywhere, vested groups—the zamindars, rajas, maharajas and nawabs—angry with the Congress, fearing dispossession and loss of wealth, aligned themselves to different splinter groups to try and buy political insurance.

Analysts described the poll verdict as a reflection of the failure of the Congress brand of socialism. The economy (principally, agriculture) was floundering. Even as Nehru battled the Opposition and the Congress struggled with internal strife, a larger threat temporarily stopped all squabbles. In October 1962, India was attacked by China on its northeast frontier and in Ladakh. The Chinese occupied over 14,000 square miles of Indian territory, inflicting on post-independence India its most humiliating defeat. Nehru was shocked by the treachery of the Chinese whom he had gone out of the way to befriend and the nation was dismayed by the inadequacy of its basic defences.

The attack on Nehru and his government, within Parliament and outside, was immediate and without precedent. Atal Bihari Vajpayee, a future prime minister and a rising star in Parliament at the time, reflected public anger when he asked: 'Wars are fought over *zar*, *zevar* and *zameen* (women, wealth and territory). We have lost *zameen*. What else is the government planning to give away?' Nehru calmly explained the series of events that had led to the war, and said, 'If this House thinks that the way our government has carried out this work is not satisfactory, it is open to this House to choose more competent men...' But there was no doubt that Nehru was hurt, personally and politically, by the defeat. His ideas and, indeed, even his voice as the final arbiter on national policy were beginning to be challenged.

As the Congress reeled from these setbacks, a brilliant political gambit, the Kamaraj Plan, was created to counter perceptions. The author of the strategy, K. Kamaraj, was easily the tallest of the Congress leaders of the era after Nehru. Although a high school dropout, he was a thinker and a reformer—for instance, when he was chief minister of Tamil Nadu from 1954 to 1963, he introduced free education for millions of the rural poor and experimented with a mid-day meal scheme. With an uncannily accurate finger on the political pulse of the nation, Kamaraj proposed that the party and the government needed what modern spin doctors call a makeover.

In the summer of 1963, Kamaraj mentioned to C. Subramaniam, whom many thought was Nehru's favourite, that he was considering resigning as chief minister and devoting his time to the party. He thought that if others too sacrificed power, public anger towards the party could be neutralized. Subramaniam instantly recognized the idea's potential and mentioned it to Nehru. On his part, Nehru was concerned about the unending parade of Congressmen wanting to be in government rather than the party. This was weakening the organization just when he wanted the support of the party to take the initiatives of the government to the people. Nehru caught on to the potential of Kamaraj's idea as well. Quite in keeping with his character, he declared he would be the first to tender his resignation. He was instantly dissuaded from doing so but no one denied the power of the idea.

The Plan was tabled within weeks at the working committee of the party then headed by D. Sanjivaiya. On 10 August 1963, it was decided that all the central ministers and chief ministers would quit. Nehru was authorized to decide who would remain in government and who would shift to the party. Nehru accepted the resignations of Morarji Desai, Jagjivan Ram, Lal Bahadur Shastri, S. K. Patil, B. Gopala Reddy and K. L. Shrimali. At the state level the party accepted the resignations of six chief ministers: K. Kamaraj (Tamil Nadu), Biju Patnaik (Orissa), Bakshi Ghulam Mohammed (Jammu and Kashmir), M. B. Jha (Bihar), C. B. Gupta (Uttar Pradesh) and B. A. Mandloi (Madhya Pradesh). They were asked to take up the task of strengthening the organization.

The Kamaraj Plan may have helped stabilize the party and government, but the reality on the ground, especially when it came to agriculture, remained grim. In 1963, a study conducted by the Food and Agricultural Organization (FAO) brought more bad news. Agriculture, the study declared, was going nowhere. Despite ten years of planning, there had been little change in the situation. About 83 per cent of the population lived in rural areas—unchanged in two Plan periods—and about 68 per cent of the people were dependent on agriculture. India, it said, was struggling to supply food to a rising population that had shot up from 361 million in 1951 to 438 million in 1961.

In 1964, the Bell Mission sent by the World Bank said that while industrial capacity had been expanded and modernized, 'no comparable modernization of agriculture [had] occurred', and that agricultural output grew by barely 3 per cent, leaving India vulnerable to hunger. In a damning review, the Bell Report said that Indian yields per acre were the lowest in the world. In 1959-60, the average yield in India of rice was barely 1,256 pounds per acre compared to 5,000 for Australia, 4,238 for Japan, 3,162 for the US and 3,033 for Turkey. Quoting agri-economist Theodore Schultz, it said the failure was best reflected in the comparison between Japan and India. In Japan, agricultural production had been increasing at 4.6 per cent per annum while in India the growth rate was just 2.1 per cent. 'If difference in farmland had been a strong factor, the ratio of agricultural growth should have been the other way around. On a per capita basis India has six times as much agricultural land as Japan, the land is of better quality; in terms of irrigated area India has three times as much as Japan on per-capita basis. Yet, the per-acre output in Japan is eight times that in India.' The study, which examined ten years of policy and development initiatives, concluded that of all the impediments, the biggest failure had been making available to sixty million farmers the necessary incentives and spreading the knowledge of improved farming methods.

The Kamaraj Plan restored the Congress's image to an extent, but Nehru's health began to fail. On 10 January 1964 Kamaraj assumed the presidentship of the party at the Bhubaneswar Session; Nehru was present but didn't participate in the deliberations. His blood pressure was high and he was tired and weak. Shortly afterwards, he suffered a stroke. Doctors were flown in to attend to him and he was shifted from Bhubaneswar to Delhi to rest and recuperate. It was clear that Congress would have to find a new leader.

Typically, Nehru's response to those who pestered him to nominate a successor was that it should be left to the people to decide. The persuaders, including Kamaraj, C. Subramaniam and Indira Gandhi, then convinced him to accept the idea of having a senior minister in his office to help him with his workload. It would also be a way of knowing his mind on his successor. For a while Nehru resisted the idea but then eventually saw the wisdom of what his colleagues were suggesting. He asked Lal Bahadur Shastri to join the cabinet as a minister without portfolio and help him. The induction of Shastri was not without its problems. Gulzarilal Nanda and T. T. Krishnamachari, who were number two and three in the cabinet, were upset at being superseded. But it was certain that Shastri would be Nehru's successor.

Those opposed to Shastri's appointment were eventually persuaded but there was a delay in Shastri's appointment owing, of all things, to an astrological prediction. Even in the cabinet of that arch rationalist, Nehru, there were those who believed in the powers of the occult. Subramaniam recalls in his memoirs that Nanda, who was a neighbour, introduced him to an astrologer called Haveli Ram who apparently divined the future by reading palm leaves. The readings 'warned of an untoward event' if a short man was inducted into the Nehru cabinet. When Nehru was informed about the prediction he was enraged but also amused. Subramaniam was worried about the 'what-if' factor. However, Nehru shrugged off the prediction and the melodrama and appointed Shastri a week later.

In the third week of May 1964, Nehru took a break and headed for Dehradun. He aimed to spend a week to try and recuperate from the debilitating stroke he had suffered in January but, instead, he spent much of his time ruminating over strategy with Pitamber Pant, a close confidant as well as his secretary whom Nehru had hand-picked to head the Perspective Planning Division in the Planning Commission. On Tuesday, 26 May, a day before Parliament was to reconvene, Nehru returned to Delhi. He was to attend the opening session the next day but took ill that night. The next morning he woke up at around 6 a.m., complained of pain in his shoulders, and collapsed. A clot in his heart is believed to have triggered an attack. A team of doctors and medical experts were in attendance but couldn't help. Indira was by his side; Shastri, Nanda and Subramaniam soon rushed to his residence. A little before 2 p.m., on 27 May 1964, Nehru, prime minister for seventeen years and the architect of modern India, was declared dead. He was seventy-four. At about 2 p.m., Subramaniam walked into Parliament and said, 'The light is out.'

JAI KISAN, JAI JAWAN

The coronation of Lal Bahadur Shastri was a foregone conclusion for most except for some old Congressmen, including Nanda—who was interim prime minister—and Morarji Desai, who hoped to contest and win. There were some obsequious Congressmen too, who tried to promote the idea of Indira for prime minister. Kamaraj, who had personally known of Nehru's choice, marshalled support by getting the seniors in the party to endorse Shastri's candidature and ensured the challengers' defeat.

Lal Bahadur Shastri defied the stereotype of a political leader. Soft-spoken, unimpressive in physical stature and humble to a fault, he was born in a small railway town, Mughalsarai, near Varanasi, better known for once being home to the longest railway yard in the country. Having lost his father before he was two, Shastri was reared, along with his siblings, by his maternal grandparents. Nanhe, as he was known, was sent to an uncle in Varanasi so that he could attend high school.

Influenced at a very early age by Gandhiji, Nanhe quit his studies to plunge into the freedom movement. He later joined Kashi Vidyapeeth, which was set up in defiance of British laws, and was honoured at graduation with the title of Shastri. Renowned for his integrity, Shastri would not budge from any stance he took. In Nehru's cabinet, he quit as railway minister following a railway accident, despite Nehru appealing to him to withdraw his resignation. Shastri may not have looked imposing but was certainly strong-willed.

Everything about Shastri was different from Nehru—his personality, his style, his politics and his vision of economic development. In contrast to Nehru, Shastri was not burdened by dogma or high expectation. Shastri did more than most to move the country out of the crisis it was mired in. Among his greatest achievements were his roles in setting the country free from famine and scarcity and restoring national pride after the humiliation the country had suffered in 1962 at the hands of the Chinese.

Shastri believed in a very personal style of engagement. Officers who took files to him would often be asked to summarize the matter at hand and he would ask for their opinion on it. At the end of the discussion, he would ask the officers to leave the file behind, obviously to consult with colleagues. Democratic in approach yet decisive in thought, Shastri rarely ever left anyone with any doubt about what needed to be done or who was in charge.

A couple of days before the members of the cabinet were to be sworn in, Shastri paid a personal visit to each of the ministers he wanted on his team. He requested each to join him to help build India. Soon after it was confirmed that he would be the new prime minister, Shastri called on C. Subramaniam who was both surprised and touched. After congratulating him, Subramaniam protested and said he could have simply called. Typically, Shastri just laughed and in his soft, humble style requested Subramaniam to join his team. There was no discussion about portfolios.

That night Shastri made perhaps one of the most important

decisions to affect India's political economy. He rang up Subramaniam at around 10 p.m. and asked him to be minister for food and agriculture. Surprised, Subramaniam said that he assumed he had done well as minister for industry under Nehru. Shastri did not disagree but said that he wanted Subramaniam to restructure the agriculture sector, especially as many other senior ministers had declined the portfolio. Subramaniam didn't protest further and accepted the decision.

Senior leaders phoned Subramaniam the next day to say that he had made a mistake. He was told that the agriculture ministry was where ministers whose political shine was fading were shunted off to. None of Subramaniam's predecessors—Rajen Babu, J. D. Ram, Kanaiyalal Maneklal Munshi and Rafi Ahmed Kidwai—had had stellar political careers, it was pointed out. Others sought to pin the blame on Kamaraj; there was no dearth of other conspiracy theories. To his credit, Subramaniam did not waver. Shastri's decision to choose Subramaniam and the latter's acceptance of his fate would later prove to be one of the biggest fortuitous accidents in Indian political history. It is unclear why Shastri chose Subramaniam as minister for food and agriculture, especially when he had done so well as minister for industries. Subramaniam, in his memoirs, explains accepting the appointment as bowing to the hand of destiny. Indeed, all three volumes of his memoirs are titled *Hand of Destiny*.

Born in Senguttaipalayam, a small village near Pollachi in Tamil Nadu, Subramaniam graduated in physics from Presidency College and later took a degree in law. Soon after he graduated in 1930, he was all set to travel to the United Kingdom to study electrical engineering or textile technology at Manchester University—when destiny called. His uncle, Swami Chidbhavananda, was not in favour of his going abroad to study. Swami Chidbhavananda wanted Subramaniam to take up leadership which, in those days, was a euphemism for public service or politics. Subramaniam was torn between his desire to study and the call of the motherland.

The turning point was the resolution of the Congress on 2 January 1930 to observe 26 January as Purna Swaraj day. He plunged into the freedom movement and from there gravitated towards a career in politics.

Few politicians in India can boast a legacy as rich as his. Subramaniam drew up the blueprint for the steel sector, built steel complexes like the one in Bokaro, revived agriculture, played a part in the milk revolution and created the concept of holistic rural development by designing the Integrated Rural Development Programme.

Despite his many successes in government, Subramaniam was more a technocrat and student of science than a politician, which probably explains his success as an administrator as minister of steel and heavy industries, as also agriculture. A scientific approach to every situation defined Subramaniam and helped, ultimately, to make the Green Revolution a reality.

While running the ministry of steel, mines and heavy engineering, Subramaniam had understood that a sustainable industrial revolution would need to be profitable to all stakeholders. He brought the same approach to agriculture. After studying the viability of farming activities he concluded that it was a losing concern. Since independence, it had been posited that the rural economy would need to be fixed so that farmers could be helped. Subramaniam inverted the formula and argued that it was only by helping farmers grow more produce and make a profit from it that India would be able to fix the rural economy.

Subramaniam drew up his blueprint for the revival of the agricultural sector like he would for a profitable public sector steel plant. He assessed the need for inputs, investment in infrastructure and a pricing policy that would define viability. Subramaniam's formula factored in the import of seeds, the import of fertilizers, investment in public infrastructure and an expansion in extension services where government officials would be available across rural areas to advise farmers on new techniques to improve yield. But, most importantly, the blueprint guaranteed remunerative pricing and procurement policies.

The fundamentalists in the Congress saw this as a cop-out, an overturning of the Nehruvian idea of transformation. Many saw it as a conspiracy and a consequence of the influence of C. Rajagopalachari. Subramaniam, who was a minister in Rajaji's cabinet in Madras State in 1952, was often viewed as Rajaji's protégé. Rajaji, known for his distaste of the Congress's brand of socialism, had opposed the focus on state-led industrialization and quit to launch the Swatantra Party. The conjecture was that in overturning the Nehruvian idea, Subramaniam was following the thinking of his one-time mentor. There was also the historic antipathy to bullock capitalists which came to the fore. Opponents of his plan argued that the use of public money to import seeds and provide price guarantees was aimed at benefitting the big farmer. It didn't matter that technology was neutral in terms of scale—big and small farmers would both benefit in proportion to their holdings.

Within the government, Finance Minister T. T. Krishnamachari shot down the idea of price guarantees. For years, industrialization had been fuelled by the systematic suppression of food grain prices. The adoption of price incentives, he said, would result in higher prices and lower savings, hurting the investment plans of industry. The attack by the Planning Commission was led by V. K. R. V. Rao who pointed out that the import of seeds, fertilizers and pesticides would entail a huge outflow of foreign exchange—he labelled the Subramaniam formula as being inflationary and anti-Plan.

Curiously enough, while there was strong opposition to investment in fertilizers, there was no opposition to increasing expenditure on irrigation projects. The argument is not about choosing one and not the other. The choice is not competitive but complementary; one was not a substitute for the other. But given the Indian circumstance of scarce resources it would have made sense for the government to study the cost-benefit analysis of capital-output ratios. R. N. Poduval, an economist from Sudan with the Food and Agriculture Organization (FAO), pointed out that the capital cost of producing fertilizers was lower than the capital cost of delivering irrigation and it made sense for India to balance its investments and spend more to produce fertilizers. He argued that it cost ₹350 to irrigate an acre of land; this delivered an additional output of 0.25 tons, which meant irrigation cost ₹1,400 for every additional ton of food grain. In contrast, an investment of ₹4,000 in production of one additional ton of nitrogenous fertilizer delivered ten additional tons of food grain bringing the investment per ton of food grains to ₹400. Yet the opposition to fertilizers was severe. There were suggestions to initiate studies to assess how the output of cow dung manure could be raised. The rush for irrigation projects, which persists to this day, was connected to the economics of politics—it helped generate kickbacks to fund the party.

Subramaniam tackled the political opposition first. 'There is nothing derogatory to the prestige of our ancestors or of our present day farmers if we emphasize the need to discard outdated ideas and outdated tools in agriculture,' he said in his note on agriculture to the cabinet. In conclusion, he presented the cabinet with an ultimatum: 'If the cabinet is not in a position to accept this agricultural policy based on price incentives, then they should find somebody else to take charge of the agriculture ministry.' For good measure he added that since he had just taken over, it should not be too difficult. Subramaniam knew that there were not many takers for the ministry and that Shastri would back him. Also, interestingly, the hand of destiny worked again for Subramaniam. The high priests of socialistic thinking, V. K. Krishna Menon and K. D. Malaviya, were no longer in government and several ministers who entered the cabinet after the departure of Nehru were not enamoured with the socialist ideology even though they mouthed it. Maharashtra strongman S. K. Patil was a critic of the Planning Commission and though Y. B. Chavan was left of centre, he was pro-farmer. However, the most significant of all was the support of Shastri.

Shastri recognized the need to revive agriculture to deliver growth in the rural economy even if it came at the expense of industrialization. It didn't matter to Shastri that the Subramaniam formula would overturn the Nehruvian idea of agricultural growth through social transformation. But he was a democrat and allowed dissent to be aired. In true Indian tradition, a decision was put off and a committee headed by the all-powerful L. K. Jha, who was the prime minister's principal secretary and virtually ran the bureaucracy, looked at the pros and cons of the situation. The Jha Committee observed that augmenting agricultural production was one of the biggest priorities facing the nation. It suggested the adoption of technology, additional investment and a price incentive policy to achieve it. It was a virtual endorsement of Subramaniam's plan.

But the battle had only just begun. Outside government, the leftists, perpetually on the wrong side, protested. Their contention was that the whole idea was sponsored by the US-based Ford and Rockefeller Foundations. The Communists felt that this would make India increasingly dependent on imports from the US and Western economies. Within government, TTK rejected proposals from foreign investors willing to set up five large fertilizer factories in collaboration with the Government of India arguing that this would dent the nation's quest for self-sufficiency. That this forced the government to procure fertilizers from abroad was a moot point! It didn't seem to occur to the leftists, or the Congressmen, that dependence on foreign food aid was far worse than a temporary dependence on imports for inputs.

The opposition intensified. At the annual session of the Congress held in January 1965 in Durgapur, the leftists in the Congress, and those aligned to Nehruvian socialism, attacked the new ideas. A group of Congressmen organized under the Congress Forum for Socialist Action (CFSA) led the attack. They argued that in January 1964, under Nehru, the party had reaffirmed its faith in the ideals of socialism. And now, within a year, that faith was being overturned. What was surprising was that Kamaraj aligned himself with the dissenters, questioned the size of the Fourth Plan and suggested that the proposal be re-evaluated. Eventually, Congress did what it does best: it camouflaged change. Shastri and his team articulated the goals of socialist progress even as they kept intact the action plan for change.

However, the idea had some distance to travel before it could become a revolution. It was yet to get the clearance of the ministry of finance and the Planning Commission and was yet to be passed by the cabinet. Subramaniam didn't wait for a conclusive outcome to the various debates that were raging. He went ahead with discussions to execute the blueprint he had drawn up. His first meetings were with scientists, and he took steps to ensure their efforts were not hampered by bureaucrats. He brought in B. Sivaraman, an Orissa cadre officer—who had made a great impression with his work in rural development as secretary, agriculture—to implement his plan.

The switch from a social to a technological orientation in

agriculture required the creation of a knowledge base. The Land Grant Universities in the US had sent a team headed by Ralph Cummings, director of the Rockefeller Foundation's agriculture programme, to explore the possibility of setting up agricultural universities in India. Subramaniam understood the potential of the idea and enabled the setting up of the first institutions—the Punjab Agricultural University in Ludhiana and the Govind Ballabh Pant University in Pantnagar in Uttar Pradesh followed by a third in Bhubaneswar in Orissa. He also pushed the respective state governments to hand over state research outfits to the universities to build scale. Cummings also briefed Subramaniam about the potential of new hybrid seeds but lamented the fact that there was systemic resistance to their introduction. He pointed out that Swaminathan had proposed the use of high-yield seeds as early as in 1961; he had also obtained and successfully tried out semi-dwarf wheat seeds in Indian conditions. Yet, no decision could be taken on the need for a seeds programme, critical for the success of an agricultural strategy aiming at high yields, for over a year. After the meeting with Cummings, Subramaniam quickly set up three panels—comprising scientists, economists and administrators—to assess the introduction of new seeds and farming techniques. He was to encounter resistance, strange superstitions and prejudices.

Scientists claimed that Indian farmers were illiterate and doubted their ability to execute the complex plan that amalgamated seeds, fertilizers and pesticides. Economists once again brought up the issue of the import of fertilizers and wondered if the output would justify the expenditure. They pointed out that the country would need to spend the foreign exchange equivalent of over ₹1,146 crore—six times the sum allocated in the budget—on fertilizers and pesticides alone. They also suggested that India should use organic manure. An incensed Subramaniam explained that the new seeds needed between 60 to 100 kilograms of nitrogenous fertilizers per hectare. Organic manure contains barely 3-5 per cent nitrogen which meant tons of manure would be needed to fertilize each hectare. However, the worst piece of logic was presented by the bureaucracy. The administrators cited sociologists who declared that the new technological methods would aggravate inequality in society. Subramaniam took them head on. He asked: 'Should we stop industrial development just because some categories of workers will get better salaries than the masses? Should industrialization be banned because managers would get better emoluments than farmers, nurses and teachers?'

Along with the formal resistance there was a very active, informal group opposing the new initiative. A conclave of agricultural economists led by Bagicha Singh Minhas and A. Vaidyanathan produced a series of papers disputing the efficacy of hybrids. B. Sivaraman was worried and was all set to respond in detail but Subramaniam and the officials of the Rockefeller Foundation suggested a better alternative—simply ignore the naysayers.

All this didn't go down well with the Planning Commission which was the final arbiter of all development in India. More than principles, it was a case of hurt egos. In his book, *Bitter Sweet*, Sivaraman recalls how a slighted V. K. R. V. Rao (who was member, agriculture, in the Planning Commission and the clearing authority for agriculture programmes) took issue with him for moving ahead with the initiative without obtaining his clearance. Rao threatened to take the matter up with the prime minister. Sivaraman tried to apologize even though it was Asoka Mehta, deputy chairman of the Planning Commission, who had given the go ahead after a meeting with Shastri and Subramaniam. In the end Sivaraman went ahead with Subramaniam's backing although the Planning Commission denied clearance.

Along with systemic resistance, funding was a major hurdle. The agriculture ministry used a multi-pronged approach to create resources. When a large seed farm in Suratgarh in Rajasthan needed tractors and mechanical harvesters, Subramaniam got it from the Soviet Union for free under the guise of trials. When Swaminathan needed to import 18,000 tons of Mexican wheat seeds, seed money came from American foundations. When there was an urgent need for fertilizers, $50 million was extracted from the United States with the help of Orville Freeman, then US secretary for agriculture.

Then, of course, there were some typically Indian problems. It was clear that every available official would have to travel to the districts to promote the programme but the budget for travel for the entire department was just ₹1 lakh. Sivaraman got it raised to ₹6 lakh. State governments could, potentially, profiteer from funds meant for farm loans. Typically, they would divert money meant for agriculture to other schemes. If they did lend money, they would do so only for a single crop or for six months. The money, when repaid, would be diverted to other uses. Sivaraman forced state agricultural departments to lend money for two crops in a year wherever possible, doubling the availability of credit to farmers.

G.V. Chalam, meanwhile, was working hard to ready the seeds he had half-smuggled in. Initial trials had shown that the seeds were vulnerable to browning or pests. Adept at sidestepping red tape, Chalam did not bother with official clearances and travelled to Hindustan Antibiotics Limited, obtained a large quantity of tetracycline, and spread it on the seeds on the terrace of his residence in Delhi. The seeds were thus eventually readied for propagation. After clearing the initial hurdles, Chalam managed to get select seed farms in West Godavari and Vijayawada districts to propagate the Taichung Native-1 seeds and achieved returns of up to 300 per cent. Such was his success that observers from the Rockefeller and Ford foundations were astonished at the yield.

Chalam travelled incessantly to meet the farmers and get them to participate in his initiative. As expected, there was no dearth of gobbledygook in the articulation of opposition. It was alleged, for instance, that since the hybrid crop took only 110 days instead of five months to grow, the end product would be bereft of nutrition. Undeterred, Chalam sought to answer every irrational claim rationally. He got his friend Venkateswara Rao, editor of *Andhra Jyoti*, to run a weekly column 'Ask Chalam' in which he answered any questions from the farming community.

Meanwhile, as part of his relentless drive to get his opponents to buy in to his idea, Subramaniam decided to engage in some trials himself. One morning, in 1965, his son Rajasekhar found the cricket pitch in the garden of their 8, Hastings Road residence in New Delhi completely dug up. Subramaniam had ploughed up his garden and planted Taichung Native-1 paddy seeds and Sonora 64 and Lerma

Rojo wheat seeds. Every afternoon Subramaniam would monitor the progress of the plants and record the growth rates on a chart which would be shown to anyone who visited him. While Indian politicians may have been reluctant converts, a battery of scientists, economists and officials from the US foundations visited his home, more to applaud his commitment than to examine the plants.

One afternoon, a lanky man turned up at his house and wanted to photograph him. Subramaniam was known to be serious about his afternoon nap and the staff refused to wake him up. When the visitor insisted they woke up a rather irritated minister. The visitor was Lord Snowdon. The icon of portrait photography was in Delhi to photograph the man leading the Green Revolution. Subramaniam agreed on the condition that his plants too were shot. After the shoot, Subramaniam told Lord Snowdon, 'Send me a copy.' Snowdon, tongue firmly in cheek, replied, 'It will cost you five pounds.' Subramaniam shot back, 'You can deduct it from the 100 pounds you owe the Government of India for photographing my hybrid plants.'

Subramaniam was tireless in propagating his message through the media and influential people around him. But he knew nothing would work as well as a large-scale demonstration of the new methods so that farmers could see for themselves the efficacy of the new farming techniques.

M. S. Swaminathan suggested that 1,000 demonstration farms be set up across India for the education of the farming community as a whole. It was decided that the government would select farmers who had access to good irrigation to plant the hybrids and prove their potential. Typically, the bureaucracy raised objections. If the experiment failed, who would pay? Exasperated, Subramaniam declared that the central government would pay the farmer compensation equal to whatever he had earned from his last harvest. There was no allocation but Subramaniam was confident the need would not arise. An assurance would suffice. The trials were a huge success and there was demand for the wheat seeds from across Punjab and Haryana and for paddy from all parts of India.

The irony was that despite the success of the experimental seeds, stubborn politicians heading many states—including Subramaniam's own Tamil Nadu—had banned the use of hybrid seeds. However, since the government had no control over what farmers planted, the ban was only a toothless administrative threat. The seeds were available for whoever was interested and there were many. Sivaraman recalls in his memoirs that despite the ban, farmers embraced new technology. On a tour in Thanjavur, Sivaraman saw acres of farms growing hybrids. He stopped and asked a farmer: 'Isn't this seed banned by the government?' The farmer retorted, 'Should I be stupid just because the government is?' Across the country, farmers queued up to see the demonstrations and demand the new seeds. The demonstrations put up by Swaminathan were easily the biggest experiment in the history of agricultural research.

The full implementation of the idea called for funding and this—as for all long-term programmes—would be decided by the Planning Commission. Even as the trials were on, Shastri, Subramaniam, other ministers and the Planning Commission got down to finalize the Fourth Five Year Plan. This was critical, as allocations would be altered in favour of agriculture. Soon after he took over, Shastri had decided to address the veto power over ministries that the Planning Commission enjoyed. He set up the elite Prime Minister's Secretariat with astute officers to advise him. He also brought into play the National Planning Council in which chief ministers and ministers had a weightier say.

Yet there was no stopping the Commission from erecting roadblocks. The Commission found the proposal of the ministry of agriculture, to promote the Green Revolution, unacceptable. Their contention—economic and ideological—was that the new initiative would cramp industrial investment and hurt the import substitution strategy. They then proposed that the ministry of agriculture revert to the Nehruvian model. Shastri knew he had a fight on his hands.

Luckily, fate played a decisive part in events. The fear of hunger and famine had returned to haunt academics and governments around the world. The theory Thomas Malthus had first propounded in 1798 had made a comeback. Malthus concluded that growth in population would eventually outstrip the increase in production of food grains, leading to scarcity, famine and conflict. By a strange coincidence, even as India debated the way forward, the mid-sixties saw a series of books by disciples of Malthus rock the world. They predicted that famine was almost upon them all.

Most strident in its tone was *Hungry Nations* authored by the Paddock brothers, William and Paul. Based on a set of arithmetic postulates, the Paddock brothers forecast that there would soon be a global food scarcity and food riots. In the dramatic *Famine 1975! America's Decision: Who Will Survive?* they declared that famines would begin by 1975. More ominous was their prescription which proscribed food aid to countries beyond help. Using the concept of triage, in which the priority of treatment of patients in an emergency room is decided based on the severity of their condition, the brothers suggested that the US should determine which countries could be saved, which were the walking wounded and which were those that couldn't be saved. They declared that India fit the 'couldn't be saved' category. Their argument ran as follows: 'India is the example that cuts across all political and economic guide rules. More than any country, if the US should cut off food aid or curtail it, immediate turmoil and catastrophe would result. Today India absorbs, like a blotter, 25 per cent of the entire wheat crop.' The Paddocks believed that no matter how one adjusted statistics to allow for future increases in US aid and Indian agricultural growth, 'today's trends show it will be beyond the resources of the United States' to keep famine out of India. The Paddocks declared that 'of all the national leaderships the Indian [came closest] to being the most childish, inefficient, perversely determined to cut the country's economic throat'. They added geopolitics to arithmetic and pointed out that despite $6.5 billion in aid, India, in articulation and stance, was against everything American. In conclusion they recommended, 'If we cut off the food aid to India we are not losing a reliable friend, nor do we gain an enemy able to do us serious hurt.'

Events in India seemed to support this doom-laden prophecy. The monsoon had failed first in 1965 and again in 1966. In Maharashtra, each of the twenty-eight districts was affected by drought. So were many other parts of the country. Agricultural output had dropped sharply from 88 million tons to 72 million tons, necessitating imports. Inflation had shot up by 17 per cent and food prices by over 22 per cent. Some analysts pegged the 1965 drought to be as bad as the one that had resulted in the famine of 1899, triggering a further scare. The government had already imported 7.5 million tons of food grains in 1965 and was petitioning for 11 million tons for the next year. Imports cost money and India's foreign exchange reserves had dipped from over $655 million to less than $500 million. In desperation, India approached the IMF for standby credit of $200 million of which $150 million was immediately withdrawn. To bring home the problem of scarcity and to prevent famine, Shastri, ever the Gandhian, fasted every Monday and advised others to do the same. India's economic health was clearly deteriorating. The IMF was putting pressure on India to restructure its economy. It pointed out that India's currency, pegged at 4.76 to the dollar since 1949, was overvalued.

The geopolitical report was no better. Lyndon B. Johnson, who took over as president of the United States in 1963 from President John F. Kennedy, did not have a particularly good equation with the Indian administration. His meeting with Nehru, in May 1961, when he had visited India as vice president hadn't gone too well. In his narration of the oral history of the Johnson regime for the LBJ Library, George E. Reedy, his aide, dubs it a 'mystical meeting' while in contrast Johnson and Ayub Khan became 'blood brothers inside of three minutes of their meeting'. Johnson always had trouble with the prime ministers of India because, in his view, Indians looked upon their relations with the US as a one-way street. Also, India's harsh opposition to America's war in Vietnam—which by the mid-sixties had escalated to alarming proportions—did not help matters at all. It was Johnson who in December 1963 issued a National Security Memorandum on the distribution of foreign aid and called for a review, as it had implications on foreign policy.

The conflict in Vietnam had other repercussions for India. In April 1965, President Johnson cancelled an invitation issued to Prime Minister Lal Bahadur Shastri. The cancellation was part of a statement he had issued declaring he would not travel anywhere and that visits of all dignitaries—Indian and others—stood postponed. India had been petitioning for additional food aid under the PL 480 programme; this was one of the many issues that were to be discussed at the Shastri-Johnson meeting.

Dean Rusk, who was secretary of state in the Johnson administration, reveals that at the policy level the LBJ administration grew resistant to the idea that the US would simply stand by and make up the difference of whatever India needed regardless of what India did about its problems. Johnson, in a scathing attack, told Orville Freeman, the agriculture secretary, and Rusk that the president of the United States could not be more interested in feeding Indians than the prime minister of India. He forced Freeman to get India to commit to a programme of restructuring. Freeman recalls Johnson saying, 'You can't give all this [food aid] away and run around dewy-eyed. You've got to be a little practical as to what it does and what India builds and we can't keep doing it forever.'

Even as India lobbied for food security elsewhere, at home national security was threatened by the hostility of its neighbours. Since taking over, Shastri had made efforts to improve relations with Pakistan and China. His efforts didn't bear much fruit. Indeed, Pakistan, emboldened by India's China debacle, was openly hostile. On 1 September 1965, India's worst fears came true—Pakistan launched an offensive in the Chhamb sector while the Chinese threatened an offensive in the eastern sector. The US suspended all aid and food shipments to India, worsening the crisis. However, in its soft-spoken prime minister, India found a leader who could lead from the front. Shastri warned that if the Chinese intervened, India would fight to the last man and ordered the troops to mount an offensive in the western sector against Pakistan. The Indian forces—despite being ill-equipped—brought the Pakistani army to its knees in twenty-two days. In victory, Shastri found confidence and a winning slogan: '*Jai Jawan, Jai Kisan*'. In October 1965, Shastri, in an address to the nation on All India Radio, said, 'I consider self-sufficiency in food to be no less important than an impregnable defence system for the preservation of our freedom and independence. In the present emergency...every bit of land should be cultivated.'

Notwithstanding the victory and the immense sense of achievement, war had aggravated the stress on the economy and worsened food scarcity. In November 1965, Subramaniam went to Rome to attend a meeting of the FAO. There he met with Orville Freeman. Subramaniam told him that India would need at least 10 million tons of wheat under the PL 480 programme. Freeman told Subramaniam rather bluntly that this could happen only with the authorization of the president. He also suggested that Subramaniam visit Washington and meet with Johnson.

The US wanted India to commit to a programme and furnish evidence of what it was prepared to do about its agricultural crisis. On the sidelines of the FAO summit in Rome, Freeman and Subramaniam agreed on a detailed programme on what India would do. Freeman reveals in his narration of the history of the LBJ regime, 'We had them over a barrel and we squeezed them.' And they did. On 26 November 1965, India signed an agreement with the US agreeing to increase investment in agriculture to improve productivity.

In January 1966, Shastri passed away in Tashkent and Indira Gandhi took charge. India was reeling under the effects of one the worst droughts in its history and over 1.5 million lives were feared to have been lost. With a full-blown, scarcity-driven famine threatening India, Indira Gandhi asked officials to push for food aid from the US.

The LBJ administration, which had promised 3.5 million tons of food aid, had placed all shipments under despatch control, shipping only just enough food every month which led to the coining of the term 'ship to mouth'—a policy where food would be released just in time to reach consumers and couldn't be stored or used as a buffer. At one point in December 1966, Indira Gandhi had to personally call President Johnson to push for food aid. At the end of the conversation, she clenched her fist and angrily told Subramaniam, who was present at the time, that she never wanted India to ever have to beg for food again.

The humiliation inflicted by the US and the lessons of the war finally brought home to politicians the imperative of food security. Subramaniam's plan was fast-tracked. Indira Gandhi backed Subramaniam on the revival of agriculture even though it meant the end of the road for the Nehruvian dream of economic transformation through social revolution.

The revolution was seeded in the 1966 sowing season across millions of hectares. The logistics of the operation boggle the mind even today. Hundreds of closed wagons had to be requisitioned across India to transport the improved hybrid seeds—they had to be carried in closed containers to retain moisture. Fertilizer and pesticides, along with credit, had to be made readily available. And all of this had to be organized, in sequence, within a time frame of 100 days as that is the slim window of opportunity available to ensure a rich harvest.

In 1967, as the first reports on that year's harvest came in, they stunned the world. India had produced 17 million tons of wheat, 5 million tons more than the previous highest yield. In the state of Punjab, schools were closed down and classrooms were used to stock the grain. India's farmers had shamed the scientists who had doubted their ability to pull it off, and Subramaniam had silenced his opponents in the cabinet.

The gory consequences of war and the spectre of famine ensured the revival of agriculture. After the bumper harvest of 1967, India went from strength to strength, harvesting over 100 million tons in 1971. Not having to worry about food security meant that India could face the intimidation of the US and adverse global opinion in the war against Pakistan in 1971 and in going ahead with nuclear tests in 1974. That the quest for national security could not be achieved without food security came to be accepted as an indisputable fact by the political class.

LESSONS FORGOTTEN

By the beginning of the eighties, however, the momentum built up in the seventies had died down. This retardation validates the theory that India acts only at the cusp of a crisis, and often not vigorously enough. From the eighties onwards, successive governments took food security—and therefore agriculture—for granted. Investment in irrigation dropped and commitment to new technology petered out.

Post-1991, and the liberalization of the economy, the renewed focus on industrial revival should have brought back attention to agriculture. After all, rapid industrial growth can only take place on the foundation of a robust rural economy. India only had to look at China, which revived agriculture before it opened up the economy under Deng Xiaoping in 1978. That, however, was not to be.

Investment in agriculture dropped to barely 3 per cent of the GDP between 1980 and 2005. The average holding of 70 per cent of the farmers was less than a hectare and nearly 70 per cent of cultivable land—over 100 million hectares—was still rain-fed, vulnerable to the vagaries of weather. As the twenty-first century advanced, 571 irrigation projects were running behind schedule, over 150 dating back to the seventies. Of the 253 projects sanctioned under the Accelerated Irrigation Benefits Programme between October 1996 and March 2008, only 100 projects were reported as complete, of which twelve were eventually found to be incomplete.

M. S. Swaminathan, internationally recognized as one of the founding fathers of the Green Revolution, voiced his concern to this author in a conversation in 2004. 'India has missed many steps in its reforms dance. Agriculture and industry have to tango for growth.' India denied its farmers the technology needed for the upgradation of seeds and the infrastructure to irrigate. Nearly two-thirds of farmers have no access to credit from banks and depend on moneylenders. The impact of neglect is most visible in its human aspect. India has the largest number of farmers committing suicide—between 2004 and 2010 over 120,000 farmers committed suicide. It is also visible in the scale of deprivation. Between 1991 and 2011, India's GDP grew at 7.5 per cent but agriculture grew at less than 3 per cent and now accounts for less than 15 per cent of the GDP. What this means is that six out of ten Indians living off agriculture are living on less than a sixth of the national income.

Since 2004, the government has raised agricultural credit from ₹69,000 crore to over ₹4 lakh crore, enrolled farmers in a Kisan Credit Card scheme to help them access funds, hiked support prices for crops, and promoted crop insurance. While it is difficult to prove a direct correlation of the steps taken and the output, the fact is that in 2012, India harvested over 257 million tons of food grains.

Yet these are but drops in the ocean and India still misses the big picture. By 2050—or even earlier—it is estimated that India's population will touch 1,500 million, which means that the demand for food will touch 450 million tons as against the current output of 257 million tons. If a large number of Indians in the rural sector are living below the poverty line, it is simply because too many people are living off land that is producing too little. India is the world's largest producer of fruits and vegetables but 40 per cent of the produce rots in the fields due to inadequate post-harvest storage and transportation facilities, and only about 2 per cent of the total production is commercially processed. Low output aggravates poverty and is responsible for high prices. The average per-hectare yield of Indian farms is poor and has been stagnant for decades; the best Indian farmers produce half of what farmers in China produce. India urgently needs to introduce high-yield varieties of crops and improve rural infrastructure. While this would seem to be common sense, governments appear immune to this need. This neglect not only defies the logic of economics but also that of politics. The headcount of farmers and the mass of consumers impacted by the crisis in agriculture, directly or indirectly, constitute the single largest political constituency in Indian democracy.

Yet India's politicians—a third of whom claim to be farmers—continue to wilfully neglect the cause of agriculture.

Politics demands that its practitioners deliver on electoral promises. But this needs ample funding, so it follows that politicians will seek control of resources. Yet, till 1969, material resources were corralled by a few business houses, development programmes were starved of funds, and access to banking was a luxury. The politicians' quest for power led to the nationalization of banks and the democratization of...

DAS KAPITAL

4 OCTOBER 1963

TIRUPATI

Some forty-eight hours after the Congress pushed through the Kamaraj Plan, the biggest makeover of the party since 1947, an odd quintet of pilgrims descended on the holy abode of Lord Venkateswara. Pilgrims usually visit the Lord of the Seven Hills to pray for peace and prosperity—not necessarily in that order. Led by K. Kamaraj, the group included Atulya Ghosh, member of parliament from West Bengal, Andhra Pradesh Chief Minister N. Sanjiva Reddy, S. Nijalingappa from Mysore and Srinivas Mallya from Mangalore. Like everyone else who visits Tirupati, this group too came with prayers, but of a higher order—they were looking for political sainthood.

The next day the pilgrims moved on to Mahabalipuram, originally known as Mamallapuram or kingdom of the great wrestler. Here they debated their own strength and the weaknesses of their opponents. Their objective was to wrest control of the party. On 5 October 1963, Kamaraj, along with the members of his newly formed parish, concluded their deliberations and declared that the next Congress president 'should be a leader most acceptable to all sections of the party, commanding influence not only in the organization but also in the legislature wing'.

The statement sounded the death knell for the ambitions Morarji Desai, then minister of finance, harboured for high office. The phrase 'most acceptable' effectively shut out Desai who, to many, represented the voice of free market policies. Jagjivan Ram, a Dalit leader favoured by Nehru, too was excluded from the race by the fiat issued by

Kamaraj. Further, to ensure that there would be no ambiguity, the statement called for unanimity in the choice of the next president so that party unity could be preserved. This was the first step of a purge to ensure the succession of a chosen one.

The group had shrewdly estimated that Lal Bahadur Shastri would be the candidate most acceptable to all and hence the front runner for the presidency. They also estimated that Shastri would be loath to push himself forward for the position. Therefore, by first promoting Shastri's cause, they could neutralize everyone else. And once Shastri had declined, Kamaraj would be the automatic choice for presidentship of the Congress.

Interestingly, many of Kamaraj's supporters entertained the fond hope that he could push for the prime ministership after Nehru. Kamaraj, though, knew his limitation—language. He was once asked by the media in Delhi why he did not desire to be PM. Normally, Kamaraj would have deployed his favourite phrase, the all-encompassing Tamil term 'paarkalam', essentially a sophisticated articulation of procrastination which means, literally, 'let's see'. But on this occasion he quipped in heavily accented English, 'No Hindi, no English, how can be PM?' Indira Gandhi, when she was president of the Congress in the fifties, had delectably described Kamaraj as a 'rustic', possibly the first time anyone had called him that. But beneath that rustic countenance was a hard core of ambition. Kamaraj knew he couldn't be king but there was nothing to stop him from becoming king-maker.

On 9 October 1963, the Kamaraj caucus hijacked the agenda of the Congress Working Committee (CWC). Atulya Ghosh presented the fait accompli by proposing the name of Kamaraj. Nehru, grateful for Kamaraj's makeover idea, saw no reason to oppose it. On 9 December 1963, the party voted on the matter and on 15 December 1963 Kamaraj was declared winner. He was to take over on 10 January 1964. In just over nine weeks since the Tirupati conclave, Kamaraj and his cohorts had seized the levers of power.

The quintet had laid the foundation of the Syndicate for the party to be effectively hijacked. The Syndicate ruled unchallenged for nearly six years before it was destroyed by Indira Gandhi. She used power and policy, namely, the nationalization of banks, to woo the masses and split the party.

THE IDEA OF SOCIALISM

In 1933, Jawaharlal Nehru defined socialism in a letter to his daughter Indira. This was the time when Mahatma Gandhi and Nehru were debating the approach to development that needed to be taken for independent India and what socialism meant for the country. He said to Indira: 'Socialism is of many kinds but there is general agreement that it aims at control by the State of the means of production, that is, land and mines and factories and the like, and the means of distribution like railways and also banks and similar institutions. The idea is that individuals should not be allowed to exploit any of these methods or institutions or the labour of others to their own personal advantage.' Indeed, the Congress party, in 1948, through resolutions passed in Bombay in April and again in Jaipur in December, advocated the nationalization of banks and financial institutions, including insurance, as part of a package to establish a just order.

Like with agrarian reforms, the tussle in this case too was to ensure the redistribution of wealth without triggering class conflict. The first two Plans made it amply clear that the goal of socialism would be attained by using all the levers available in the economic system. And the Planning Commission bluntly declared in 1953 that banks would have to reboot their operations to suit the 'priorities for development indicated in the Plan and less and less in terms of returns on capital'. It also added that the banking systems and financial institutions would have to fit into the scheme of development 'visualized for the economy as a whole'.

Whatever the intentions, there was never any doubt that India didn't have the resources to fund its ambitions. From the Bombay Plan of 1944 to the initial draft of the First Five Year Plan, it was clear that all the savings, foreign aid and export earnings of the country wouldn't be enough and India would have to fill the gap between expenditure and resources by creating money. The planners were also aware that there was a limit to deficit financing.

As early as 1954, it was quite apparent that the country could not continue to live beyond its means. That year, the National Development Council (NDC) called for a special meeting on 9 November at the ornate Hyderabad House in New Delhi. The Council was informed by Vangal T. Krishnamachari, deputy chairman of the Planning Commission, that the government was running out of money. He said that 'the anticipated gap between revenue and spending in the first Five Year Plan first estimated at ₹811 crore shot up by ₹400 crore to ₹1,200 crore in a plan size of ₹2,290 crore'. Simply put, the government had reached the limits of money-creation. If the government was spending a rupee, half of it was funded by debt that was to be repaid by future earnings of the government; indeed, by the next generation. This again was not surprising. The savings rate at the time was barely 11 per cent and the tax to GDP ratio, which, roughly translated, is total tax as a percentage of national income, was worse. To illustrate, if India's domestic output was ₹100, central taxes accounted for barely ₹4 and state taxes a measly 58 paise. The mismatch between India's capacity and government's ambitions was clear. The conclusion drawn by the political class, though, was that money was not available because private banks owned by business houses were cornering funds and were not falling in line with the government's vision for development.

Initially, the managers of the banks were cajoled and persuaded by the RBI and the Planning Commission to expand their reach and tap savings in the hinterland to raise resources. By 1955, the cajoling was replaced by intimidation. In the famous Avadi Session of the Congress in 1955, in which the party resolved to adopt a socialistic pattern of society, hardening inalterably the course of economic thinking, Congress President U. N. Dhebar stated without ambiguity that 'a vast country like India cannot hope to secure orderly development unless there is a central agency charged with the responsibility of mobilizing resources under central direction'. The rhetoric was a veiled warning to private bankers—fall in line with political thinking or your bank will be taken over.

The political class believed that to achieve the goal of socialism, the government needed to control productive assets. However, the quest to seize and control banks, among other things, was in direct conflict with the protection afforded to individuals by the Constitution. Even though the Directive Principles of State Policy required government to deliver on the promise of equitable distribution of resources—and the prevention of concentration of wealth—the same could not be interpreted as a right to seize wealth. We have already seen in the chapter 'The Hunger Games' how, in 1952, when zamindari was sought to be abolished, the government was pushed to amend the Constitution. Besides the legislative runaround and litigation any takeover of the banks would involve, the issue of large-scale compensation—ensured by provisions in the Constitution—also daunted the government.

Nevertheless, letting things slide wasn't an option for the simple reason that government needed to find the resources to keep the country going. By 1960, in a rising chorus, the leftist elements in Congress declared that if the government was to achieve the goals of planning, it would need control of the flow of funds. Congress President Dhebar warned the government that while the First Plan had, in fact, created three million jobs, the rapid increase in population had resulted in almost nine million people continuing to be unemployed. More jobs meant more investment and more money, which was hard to come by. Dhebar then went on to quote Nobel Prize-winning economist Gunnar Myrdal who, while addressing Parliament on 22 April 1958, had said: 'The danger is not, as I see it, that you are going too rapidly but is, on the contrary, that you will be tempted to try to advance too slowly.' To Dhebar and many Congressmen, this translated into finding the right instruments to accelerate the acquisition of resources.

Till the beginning of the sixties, banking was concentrated in cities and major towns. In 1960 India's population touched 420 million of which 340 million people lived in rural India. The ruling perception amongst planners and ministers in Nehru's cabinet was that savings among people living in rural areas, which they believed would have gone up since independence, by whatever small measure, were not being tapped by the banking system. This was because the bank owners' quest for profits dictated where new branches should be set up. Not only were the banks not branching out to rural areas, they were shying away from providing credit to agriculture as well. Since banks were mostly owned by industrial houses, the political class felt that bank managements, in dancing to the tune of the shareholders, were becoming insensitive to the needs of society and the goals of national development. Simultaneously, there was another concern—numerous private banks were failing. In 1951, there were 566 banks in operation but by the early sixties barely 100 were left standing. The regular failure and closure of banks—nearly forty a year—led to suspicions of malfeasance, that banks were not only not contributing to the common public good but were perhaps actually defrauding society at large. The demand for state intervention was but a natural corollary.

When the eighteenth NDC met in 1961, the chief ministers of various states made public their demand for the nationalization of private banks. Rajasthan Chief Minister Mohanlal Sukhadia, who was known to speak his mind, asked Nehru and the planners how they expected to fund the Third Plan when public savings were being hijacked by private interests. Sukhadia bluntly told the NDC that 'the resources with the commercial banks were being diverted more and more to the private sector and unless some definite policy was laid down it would be difficult to obtain resources for the public sector.' Y. B. Chavan, the chief minister of Maharashtra, echoed Sukhadia. He said that there was no real reason for the lack of resources. Quoting from the report of the Savings Committee, he said that there was no gap in resources and that ₹8,300 crore could be raised for the Plan. He made the damning observation that it was the commercial banks which hadn't contributed towards resources. His assessment was that private banks contributed barely ₹40 crore to the First Plan and just ₹10 crore to the Second Plan. Chavan, a veritable giant among Congressmen by then, advised the NDC that the matter would have to be looked into.

The majority of the chief ministers and finance ministers were of the opinion that banks would have to be made to fall into line. They believed that unless banks participated with the government in nation-building, in raising funds and making them available to government to spend, the objective of national development would be derailed. C. Subramaniam, who was finance minister of Madras State at the time, suggested that government should get the banks to behave. He observed that since the economy was split between the private and public sectors, the tendency of private banks owned by industrialists was to invest primarily in the private sector. To end this, he suggested that the government stipulate that at least 20 per cent of credit lent by private banks be invested in the public sector. He also emphasized that the policy needed to be enforced at the highest level.

These fiery debates on the politics of economics and of funding development was interrupted in 1962 by geopolitics and war. India was comprehensively defeated by China, and worse, the country found it tough to meet the costs of the war. More importantly, it was difficult to fund deterrence—the most effective way of preventing further conflict. The government found itself short of money to fund the Third Plan. The political class, by now, was firmly convinced that socialism could not be funded without controlling the banks.

This conviction, spurred on by ideology, was also supported by simple arithmetic. While the government could, in theory, borrow from banks, this was limited by the appetite of banks for government bonds and more importantly, the total savings available with the banks in question. The cache of savings could only be expanded when banks were pushed to open branches in rural and semi-urban areas to tap into public savings, savings that were otherwise being mopped up by companies and by usurious moneylenders in the informal money market.

On 29 March 1963, freedom fighter Subhadra Joshi tabled a non-official resolution in the Lok Sabha. It said: 'In view of the emergency created by the Chinese aggression, this House is of the opinion that banks should be nationalized in order to mobilize the national resources.' Opening the debate, Joshi argued that it wasn't enough for a nation that its soldiers fight on its borders; everyone, including banks, must contribute to any war effort. Joshi observed that the concentration of economic power in the hands of bank owners was 'enormous in relation to the capital they employed' and that banks were netting profits but not contributing to the national cause. She also pointed out that of the combined total of 5,111 branches of all the banks then operating in India, only 657 were in rural India. Joshi was followed by Prabhat Kar, an MP from Hooghly who declared that the All India Bank Employees' Association had been demanding the very same thing for six years. Among those who supported Joshi's initiative were a large number of Congressmen and the Young Turks led by Chandra Shekhar. T. T. Krishnamachari, then minister of finance, was one of the few who argued that nationalization by itself was not likely to provide additional resources.

In her resolution, Joshi proposed wide-ranging changes. In the fifties, it was common for the business houses which owned the banks to direct the grant of unsecured loans to their own companies and to their directors. This was banned by the RBI but the practice of directed credit continued. Banks were cajoled and coerced by directors to grant unsecured loans to companies that they had interests in. Often the quid pro quo was that the companies would promise deposits to banks in return for directorships which came in handy to corner loans. Joshi wanted the prohibition to be extended to all companies in which directors held interests. The idea was to ensure that public savings were not monopolized by those who controlled banks. She also suggested that the voting rights of the owners be restricted so that a majority shareholding was not used to corner public savings for private interests.

Joshi was not indulging in political rhetoric when she demanded that voting rights be restricted. A survey of eighteen banks in 1954 had already established that money power was concentrated in the hands of a few capitalists. In 1960, Hoorav Varadaraja Iyengar, governor of the RBI, commissioned a study on the ownership of sixty-four banks. The findings of the study lent further basis to the fears of government. In twenty-three of the sixty-four banks examined, directors of banks and their associates held shares in excess of 30 per cent in these institutions. What was unstated was that they exercised undue influence on lending. There was a slew of suggestions from within the ministry to curb the influence of owners. V. G. Pendharkar, who was then economic adviser in the RBI, contended that it was undesirable for a bank to lock up a large proportion of its resources for a small group of companies and suggested a ceiling. S. L. N. Simha, an adviser in the ministry of finance, suggested that the RBI should appoint a non-voting director to instil the fear of the sovereign into bank managements.

While there was growing support within government and in Parliament for the nationalization of banks, the perils of such a move, beginning with the legalities that it would entail, thwarted Congress. Bank owners, who were major funders of the Congress, and their lobbies within the party, put up stiff resistance to the idea. There was also intellectual opposition from people like Morarji Desai and C. Rajagopalachari who worried that the rights and independence guaranteed by the Constitution were being whittled down.

The situation reached an impasse and was temporarily shelved, but six months later, when the issue bubbled up again, the government recognized that it needed to be conclusively addressed in some way. On 26 November 1963, after much deliberation within the RBI and much opposition from the Indian Banks' Association, the government introduced the Banking Laws (Miscellaneous Provisions) Bill in the Lok Sabha. Under the proposed amendments, chairmen and chief executive officers of banks could no longer be appointed in perpetuity or for indefinite periods. The bill empowered the RBI to remove from office any director, CEO, or any officer or employee if the removal was in the public interest. The bill also contained a proviso for the appointment of up to five additional directors to curtail the supremacy of owners.

Introducing the bill in Parliament, the government declared that this was proof that it championed the cause of the common man, desired a socialistic pattern of society and supported the freeing up of banks from the influence of big business. The battle in Parliament was fought on ideological lines. Minoo Masani, the founder of the Indian Liberal Group and one of the founding members of the Swatantra Party, declared that the measures were akin to the government taking over the banks. Cherian J. Kappen, the Congress MP from Muvattupuzha in Kerala, the state which had elected the first Communist government, said that banks were being targeted by the leftists in Congress. He said that the bill gave the central bank such powers that 'even God in heaven may become jealous of the Reserve Bank'.

The reality, however, was that the proposed law couldn't prevent the owners and directors of the banks from promoting their business interests. The government was not taking away ownership and the fact of ownership afforded the owners and directors rights which could be deployed to further the interests of big business. Therefore, while the liberals felt the bill was unconstitutional, the political class felt it wasn't strong enough. It could, at best, only trim the perpetuation of monopolistic interests of business. After much sound and fury, the bill was passed in December 1963, paving the way for the eventual control of banking by government.

In the meantime, under persistent pressure to raise resources, the government set up two new institutions to garner savings and provide credit for industry. The Industrial Development Bank of India (IDBI) was to provide long-term capital for industry and the Unit Trust of India (UTI) was to provide a safe haven for small savers. The IDBI was set up with share capital of ₹50 crore and was permitted to raise resources from the market by selling its own bonds and deposits as long as the tenure for the bonds was over a year. The UTI—which was allowed to float a variety of financial instruments, including debt, equity and hybrids—pioneered the aggregation of small savings across India.

THE RISE OF INDIRA

By January 1964, the transition of power began and the political landscape started changing. In May 1964, Shastri took over from Nehru, who had virtually anointed him. The Syndicate had ensured Morarji Desai's defeat and believed it now had its own man in place. At the Durgapur All India Congress Committee (AICC) Session, Kamaraj first paid obeisance to Nehru and said, 'Jawaharlalji was the last of the giants,' and went on to indicate that the affairs of the nation would be run by a collective leadership of workers, the euphemism for the Syndicate. The barb did not escape Shastri. He was nobody's puppet and understood that the Syndicate would be useful to deal with a cabinet stacked with Nehru's acolytes and his daughter Indira.

When Shastri took over, India was at the intersection of competing crises—war, failure of agriculture, food scarcity—coupled with a severe crunch of resources. At the geopolitical level, India's relations with the US under LBJ had begun to sour, affecting aid. The leaders of the Congress and the Americans were agreed that the crises were the consequence of a failing system. Hardly a year into the saddle, Shastri came under attack by party coteries for failing to address the critical issues facing the nation. Indira Gandhi, who was fourth in the hierarchy of the cabinet, desisted from open association with the rant clubs but was happy to give a patient hearing to complainants.

Shastri set up a team to address the problem plaguing the economy. Lenders wanted India to devalue the rupee but the Congress, led by TTK, was dead against it. Shastri replaced him with Sachin Chaudhuri of West Bengal as minister of finance. I. G. Patel and P. C. Bhattacharya were despatched to the US to negotiate with donors. The Syndicate realized that they had not even been consulted. The stage was set for a confrontation.

However, history intervened. Shastri died in Tashkent on 11 January 1966 and even as his body was being flown back to Delhi, the contenders began manoeuvring to become prime minister. Gulzarilal Nanda and Morarji Desai were back in the race. Indira Gandhi kept her counsel, working through Madhya Pradesh Chief Minister D. P. Mishra. Kamaraj saw in the turn of events an opportunity to reinvent the relevance of the Syndicate.

By 12 January it became clear that the real contest was between Morarji Desai and Indira Gandhi. The Syndicate, given their pathological aversion to Desai, decided to back Nehru's daughter. Mishra lined up the support of the chief ministers of Maharashtra, Rajasthan and Bihar and conveyed their choice to Kamaraj. Although the numbers weighed heavily in favour of Indira Gandhi, a contest could not be avoided. Kengal Hanumanthaiah, who was the former chief minister of Mysore State, proposed Desai's name. On the opposing side, Nanda, who was earlier a contender, proposed Indira Gandhi's name and N. Sanjiva

Reddy seconded it. Indira Gandhi won by 355 votes against the 169 bagged by Desai. The Syndicate believed it had resurrected itself.

Indira Gandhi's victory was a defining moment for Indian politics and for Indian women—she was the first Asian woman prime minister. As she left Parliament House after her election was announced, some women members of parliament and Congresswomen showered her with rose petals, the flower always pinned close to her father's heart. Early the next day she went to the Nehru and Gandhi memorials to pay personal and political obeisance to her father and the father of the nation. She was sworn in on 24 January 1966, the second member of her family to become prime minister.

When Indira was born, Nehru received a letter from Sarojini Naidu who sent her blessings and ended the missive saying, 'Love to all and a kiss to the new soul of India.' Nehru prized the letter—later published in *A Bunch of Old Letters*—and genuinely believed that Indira would become the new soul of India. Indira's education began with letters from her father and his writing on India. When she was twelve years old, Indira organized the 'vanar sena' or army of monkeys, the children's wing of the Indian National Congress, which played a small but interesting role in the liberation of India. A career in politics was destined for her.

The rise of Indira really began in 1953, while Nehru was prime minister, when she set up the Congress's women's wing, surprising and impressing almost all Congressmen with her organizational abilities. In 1955, U. N. Dhebar, then president of Congress and a Nehru appointee, approached Indira Gandhi to join the CWC. By 1957 she was elected to the powerful Central Election Committee and by 1958 to the Congress Parliamentary Party (CPP). In an interesting turn of events, Indira strategically distanced herself from both Nehru and the government and attacked the regime for not implementing the policies of the Congress. While Nehru used this tactic to put pressure on his colleagues in the cabinet to push through his own agenda for a socialist society, it helped Indira to create her own brand within the party. In 1959, she was elected president, having superseded several Congressmen. Following the death of Govind Ballabh Pant in

1961—who it is believed Nehru wanted as his successor—many in the Congress speculated that Nehru wished his daughter to succeed him though he was too much of a democrat to publicly express this wish or even orchestrate the moves for such a succession.

In 1966, some thirty-seven years after she created the vanar sena, Indira Gandhi found herself at the head of the country. She knew that her supremacy would be challenged sooner than later by the Syndicate. The games began with the formation of the cabinet. Indira Gandhi retained Nanda as home minister as she wanted someone she could control. C. Subramaniam, who was close to the family, was retained to continue with the programme of agricultural revival. Y. B. Chavan was allowed to retain defence and she continued with Sachin Chaudhuri in finance. Some newcomers like Asoka Mehta, Fakhruddin Ahmed and Gopal Swarup Pathak were also brought in though not in any of the cherished slots. Jagjivan Ram, who was made minister for labour, was upset and so were others. Where it suited her, Indira placated the Syndicate, for instance, by inducting S. K. Patil and keeping Krishna Menon out. Yet the Syndicate, especially Kamaraj, was not entirely happy with the constitution of the cabinet for it felt it had not been consulted enough.

When Indira took over, India was caught up in problems on both the economic and political fronts. Drought had brought down crop yields, prices had shot up 16 per cent in less than a year, American food aid was trapped in geopolitics, a foreign exchange crisis was brewing and the IMF wanted India to devalue the rupee. Identity politics had flared up in different parts of the country. The Sikhs wanted a separate state; Maharashtra and Karnataka were fighting over newly freed Goa and in the Northeast, tribal troubles threatened peace in Assam, Mizoram and Nagaland. And, to complicate matters further, elections were due in February 1967. Indira Gandhi had thirteen months to prove that she had it in her to govern India.

She decided to tackle the insurgents and separatists first. She bought peace—though at a price she would later regret—by creating a Punjabi-speaking Punjab and Hindi-speaking Haryana. She settled Goa as a Union Territory, initiated peace talks in Assam and deployed the might of the State to tackle the Mizos and the Nagas who she believed were being egged on by Pakistan—then ruling East Pakistan (now Bangladesh)—and China. In a sense, the troubles of 1966 led to the 1971 war in which she made Pakistan pay dearly for its perfidy.

The troubled economy, though, took longer to fix and fuelled further political turmoil. Food production had dropped from 80 million tons in 1964 to 63 million tons in 1966. Inflation had spiralled from less than 3 per cent in the first three Plan periods to 13 per cent in 1965 and a post-war high of 16 per cent in 1966. Food prices, most critical from the political perspective, had shot up by 18 per cent. As it had for many years, India needed external aid to fund its development programme. It had already approached the World Bank and a consortium of donor nations. Citing drought in many parts of the country, India had also appealed to the US to provide it with additional food aid in the summer of 1965. India had wanted to sign a new deal for 10 million tons of food aid for two years. LBJ kept the request pending.

In January 1966, when Indira took over, the Americans extended an invitation to her to visit the United States. Indira Gandhi had first met LBJ in April 1964 when she carried a letter from Nehru praising the efforts of the US president who was, at that time, working towards a nuclear accord with Russia. She also told *The New York Times* that the US favoured Pakistan on the Kashmir issue. When she met LBJ in March 1966, he countered her perception and said, 'The Indians should realize that the Pakistanis were far more unhappy about our policy toward India than India seemed to be about our policy toward Pakistan.' It somewhat set the tone for the future.

Despite the bonhomie at a personal level, at the political level it was clear that there was a third party—Pakistan—in this courtship. As we have noted in the chapter 'The Hunger Games', from the fifties onwards, the US had maintained a policy of helping India with food and aid so that it didn't go the communist way. Since President Johnson had taken over, a new factor had begun to influence policy—the president's concern about the increasing quantum of aid India was getting from the US. Acting on his concerns, LBJ put all food shipments on what he called a short tether in spite of the fact that India, at the time, faced a drought and near famine conditions. While LBJ's contention was that he wanted India to do something about its agricultural crisis, it was also true that he was upset over India's views on the US involvement in the Vietnam War.

His administration—principally the Pentagon—then stalled the sale of fighter jets that India wanted. The country had been negotiating for F-104 fighter aircrafts since 1960, especially since the Americans had provided these to Pakistan. Despite claiming that they were even-handed in their treatment of both countries, the Americans finally denied the jets to India. They, however, agreed to a $500 million military-aid programme that funded the creation of mountain divisions critical to counter China, air-defence systems and the like. Rebuffed, India under Prime Minister Shastri had signed a deal with the Soviet Union to buy forty-five MIG-21 fighter jets and a manufacturing agreement to produce 400 MIG aircrafts.

Given India's souring relationship with the US, Indira's 1966 visit took on great significance. Two days prior to her visit, Secretary of State Dean Rusk sent LBJ a memo detailing what India was looking for. The Americans indicated that if India committed to economic reforms, the US would work with the IMF and the World Bank to come up with a suitable aid programme.

Indira Gandhi, though, was not going to be seen to be kowtowing to a superpower. To establish her independence in foreign policy, Indira criticized US involvement in Vietnam again as soon as she landed. Back channels were then activated to control the damage. Indian diplomats defended her and said she didn't say anything different from the Pope or the UN Secretary General. The Americans retorted, 'Well, the Pope and U Thant don't want our wheat.'

Indira Gandhi met with LBJ on 28 March. She had come prepared to charm the Americans and this she did most effectively. The two leaders got on famously and the US president stayed on even after the official function. The day after, LBJ told Ambassador B. K. Nehru on the phone that food aid would be made available. On 30 March, LBJ announced that an emergency tranche of food—3.5 million tons that would take the year's tally to 7 million tons—would be cleared by them soon.

Despite the success of the visit, Indira Gandhi thought it wise to hedge her bets. She wasn't too sure about the level of commitment from the LBJ administration for help. She planned her return to Delhi via Moscow with a brief stopover in London. The British, who wanted to make up for cosying up to Pakistan, wanted her to visit Downing Street. Indira declined, forcing Prime Minister Harold Wilson to drive down to the airport to call on her. In Moscow she connected with the Soviet premier Alexei Kosygin and they discussed aid, arms and non-alignment. A window of opportunity was thus created.

Soon after her visit, Mrs Gandhi sent Asoka Mehta and ministry officials to Washington to negotiate a deal with World Bank President George Woods. The bank insisted on its usual pre-conditions—decontrol of imports, reforms in licensing procedures and the setting up of sectoral targets. The understanding was that India would devalue its currency, follow the other suggestions worked out by the Bank and, in return, receive money to fund its development programmes. In the summer of 1966, Indira Gandhi informally broached the subject of devaluation with her party leaders, particularly the Syndicate and Kamaraj. Not one of the leaders was receptive to the idea.

To be fair, the Indian establishment had always been against devaluation, both in economic and political terms. In economic terms because devaluation, it was feared, would fuel inflation in an economy dependent on aid and politically because the strength of the rupee was associated with national virility. Indira nevertheless went ahead. On 6 June 1966, India devalued the rupee from ₹4.76 to ₹7.50 to the dollar, a drop of 57 per cent, the biggest devaluation ever in its history. Indira Gandhi defended the decision, matter-of-factly stating that if the rupee wasn't devalued, essential aid would be denied.

The cabinet meeting on 5 June 1966 that cleared devaluation set the tone for the showdown to come. Manubhai Shah, who was commerce minister and a known opponent of devaluation, was upset at having been kept in the dark about the decision. Kamaraj was incensed that devaluation had been pushed through despite his views. An effort was made to assuage his sentiments by sending a Tamil-speaking economist to brief him. Kamaraj refused to meet the economist and described the devaluation as India selling out to the US. Morarji Desai chose to fish in troubled waters with a solicitous 'if the three former finance ministers had been consulted this could have been avoided'. The coming together of Desai and Kamaraj on one issue was in itself a political statement. Everyone, from the Left to the right-wing Swatantra Party joined the chorus of dissent. The political reaction was best captured by B. K. Nehru who is quoted to have said, 'It was as if devaluation had castrated India.'

Worse was to follow. The promised aid from the World Bank and the IMF failed to materialize, with only half the money trickling in, and that too after months of delay. The devaluation itself failed to deliver the results it had promised. The US, which was to follow up with an aid package, felt the measures to open up the economy were superficial and not adequate to make a difference, and did not keep its word. In India, worsening drought conditions crippled its exports (India was dependent on agricultural commodities—which made up nearly 50 per cent of its export basket—for earnings). Despite devaluation, the value of exports actually fell from $2,058 million to $1,882 million. India needed food aid desperately. LBJ declined to allow the signing of a long-term contract despite the famine-like situation in India and opposition from within his own government from the State Department and the Department of Agriculture. This marked the breaking point between India and the US, a schism that would last for decades.

The idea of using aid as leverage was not missed in India. While visiting Moscow in July 1966, Indira Gandhi had issued a joint communiqué, calling for the bombings on Vietnam to be halted. This coincided with a rising backlash in the US against the war. The Americans expressed their distress at being called imperialist and made the process to grant food aid harder. In response, in March 1967, Indira Gandhi wished Ho Chi Minh on his birthday, infuriating the Americans. Chester Bowles, then ambassador to India, was told by Washington to let India know that if it wanted to tilt towards the Communists then it should review its expectations of aid from America.

The period between 1962 and 1967 was very tough for India. It had lost two prime ministers, fought two wars, faced a major economic crisis and suffered drought in two out of the five years. The country held together despite the immense stresses, but Congress didn't.

THE CONGRESS SPLIT

Congress rarely ever allows reality to concern it or its utterances. And this has delivered many delicious ironies. The fact that there was a war within the Congress was no secret. Yet, when the party went to polls in 1967, it chose 'One India, One Team' as its slogan. In addition to a failing economy and internal conflict, the Congress was also struggling with the fallout of a memo issued in 1965. A few days before the Republic Day of 1965, the home ministry proposed the use of Hindi at the level of the central government. The proposal was interpreted as an attempt to foist Hindi upon the nation as the national language. Parties opposed to the Congress in South India used this to their advantage and triggered an agitation by students. A grand council comprising members of the Congress Working Committee (CWC), cabinet ministers and chief ministers met and concluded that the guarantee of the use of English issued by Nehru was intact. But by then the fire had spread and was converted into an inflammable issue in the elections.

The consequences were reflected in the election results. In 1962, under Nehru, the Congress secured 44.7 per cent of the votes and, in a house of 520, won 361 seats. In 1967 their tally was down to 283 seats and their share of the vote down to 40 per cent. The worst rout was in Tamil Nadu—Congress lost thirty-six out of the thirty-nine seats it contested. The DMK used the language agitation successfully to win twenty-five seats and power in the state. In ten of the states the Congress's share of the vote was about 35 per cent. The major beneficiaries of Congress's loss were the Swatantra Party which won forty-four seats, the Bharatiya Jan Sangh which won thirty-five seats as a result of its sectarian stance and the leftists who won twenty-three (CPI) and nineteen (CPM) seats respectively.

This setback should have led to introspection within the party but, instead, the leaders chose to flex their political muscle. In 1966, when asked about the differences she had with Kamaraj, Mrs Gandhi said rather directly, 'The question is whom the party wants and whom the people want. My position is uncontested.' Indira knew that mass appeal was her strongest weapon and the lack of charisma among her opponents their greatest weakness. What the Syndicate wanted, more than anything else, was to control the reins of power through the party, à la a politburo. Indira Gandhi, post the 1967 drubbing, began the conversion of the party—one in which, historically, decisions were arrived at after consultation—into an instrument of top down decision making. However, her opponents were not yet giving up. Kamaraj was down but not out and Morarji Desai found enough pull in the CWC to get back into government as deputy prime minister. She understood this as an attempt to clip her wings.

Her retaliation began with the formation of the government. The composition of the 1967 cabinet, in many ways, set the tone for events to come. Indira Gandhi rewarded those who supported her with ministerial berths and used merit, experience and integrity as criteria where convenient. She virtually bypassed the organizational leadership.

She also made it a point to distance herself from the party, offshoring the responsibility of the mess on to Kamaraj and company. Alive to the possibility that the Syndicate could rig the electoral college for the next poll for presidentship, she cornered the party bosses in June 1967 at the Delhi AICC meet and attacked them for fuelling bogus membership. And when Kamaraj sought a third term, she promoted the cause of S. Nijalingappa. In a midnight coup, she called a CWC meeting and persuaded Nijalingappa to accept the nomination for party president. In a sense she did a Kamaraj on Kamaraj who had similarly used his coterie, led by Atulya Ghosh, to hijack the CWC while getting himself nominated in October 1963.

Indira Gandhi's approach reflected an unusual grasp of military strategy. Not only did she take on Kamaraj head on, she also engineered flanking attacks. She created room in the Congress for a group of young, left-oriented leaders. Dubbed the Young Turks, the group included Krishan Kant, Subhadra Joshi, Mohan Dharia, K. D. Malaviya, Chandrajit

Yadav, Nandini Sathpathy, K. R. Ganesh, Chintamani Panigrahi, Bhagwat Azad and Bedbrat Barua. The group worked under the banner of the Congress Forum for Socialist Action and was led by Chandra Shekhar. Their target was Morarji Desai and the party bosses.

The mood among the party cadre and the voters indicated that they were all for radicalization. And in the Young Turks they saw a slice of hope. The alibis the Congress hid behind for its failures were no longer acceptable. In fact, in the run-up to the general elections of 1967, many in the party felt that in the allotment of tickets, preference should be given to those with a zeal for socialism. The CFSA reiterated these sentiments to Congress President Kamaraj as the party prepared its manifesto. Kamaraj was also presented with a memorandum which recommended that the manifesto promise the nationalization of banks, the imposition of ceilings on urban incomes, the execution of land reforms and the imposition of curbs on press monopolies.

Typically, the Congress party articulated these sentiments in its manifesto but deliberately chose to be vague about the course of action. 'The goal was for establishing a Democratic Socialist Society and it was imperative that the state should play an active and dynamic role in planning, guiding and directing...economic development.' It also stated that it supported the growth of the public sector, the expansion of cooperatives, increasing social control on banks and applying restrictions to individual holdings of land. But nationalization was not spelt out, not yet.

Like most manifestos it could have been consigned to the archives but Indira Gandhi decided that she would not let that happen. She backed the Young Turks against the party bosses to gain control over the cadre and shrink the influence of the Syndicate and Desai. She forced the CWC to consider a ten-point charter of demands spelt out by the CFSA. The demands included the nationalization of banks and insurance companies, the transfer of import and export monopolies to the public sector, the setting up of rural and urban land ceiling systems and the abolition of princes' privileges and privy purses. A month later, the AICC adopted the programme for implementation. Chandra Shekhar knew the Congress well enough to not rest at this.

He started a signature campaign which was launched on 6 August 1966, the anniversary of the Quit India Movement.

These developments sent tremors throughout the corridors of business and banking. To pre-empt any radical action, the Indian Banks Association (IBA) acted suo moto. On 22 May 1967, IBA Chairman K. M. D. Thackersey sent a seven-page 1,900-word missive to Indira Gandhi. Arguing against the proposed social control over banks, he wrote: 'The powers bestowed by the Banking Regulation Act to RBI are so extensive and comprehensive that there is hardly any scope for adding to them or for extending further social control over banks.' Thackersey went on to illustrate the conflict between the need to safeguard depositors' interests and the demand to extend credit to small scale industry, agriculture and other sectors of the economy. He defended the banks against the charge that private banks were lending only to owners and their relatives and declared that such loans formed only a small proportion of the monies advanced. He concluded by suggesting that a 'small delegation of IBA may kindly be allowed to wait on your good self and the Honourable Finance Minister to enable it to explain the above considerations more fully'.

Indira Gandhi responded by directing all supplicants to her arch-rival Morarji Desai, then deputy prime minister holding the finance portfolio. Morarji Desai was clearly against the idea of nationalization. His argument was that banks were custodians of public monies and no bank—public or private—could abandon the test of viability while lending. He did, however, promise his party that he would implement the promise of social control, winning the banks a reprieve to prove that they would serve the interests of society. He convened a meeting of bankers on 18 June 1967 in New Delhi. Among those who attended were Thackersey, Kamalnayan Bajaj, A. D. Pai, R. D. Birla and M. P. Birla. Morarji hoped to blunt the edge of the campaign for nationalization and asked banks to facilitate credit to politically sensitive sectors and curb advances for speculative activities.

Within the government, it was not just Desai but many bureaucrats who worried about the push to nationalize banks and its larger implications. It would be safe to say that the majority of officials were inclined to accommodate social control but were against the idea of nationalization. A paper on banking authored by Pai Panandikar, economist and then adviser in the ministry of finance, was circulated within the ministry and sent to the RBI. Panandikar observed that agriculture and small-scale industries were receiving less attention. The paper also stated that there was evidence that a few banks had been unduly exclusive in lending and this had led, to some extent, to the concentration of economic power. Panandikar suggested that the objectives envisaged in the ten-point economic programme adopted by the CWC could be achieved with suitable amendments within existing legislation. The paper also mooted the setting up of special institutions to provide credit to specific sectors. In effect, Panandikar did not think that the nationalization of banks was necessary.

Despite the efforts of those opposed to the idea, it seemed increasingly clear that the government was poised on the brink of nationalizing banks unless a workable system for social control was delivered. The business houses used their funding networks to communicate to the party bosses that they had better deter government from its proposed course of action. They were told that even if the government did decide on nationalizing banks it would need to pay compensation as guaranteed by the Constitution and the resources to pay such compensation were unavailable.

There was resistance within the ministry and the RBI too. On 2 June 1967, RBI Governor P. C. Bhattacharya wrote to Morarji Desai warning about the costs of nationalization and said, 'The nationalization of all the banks is not desirable, and is likely to hinder rather than help our economic growth and progress at the present stage.' He then went on to list a fifteen-point agenda that would make 'social control' workable.

The drama that was being played out was closely followed by the press. The *Economic and Political Weekly* commented in July 1967 that 'the chickens have come home to roost'. It revealed that the move to nationalize banks was not new and there had been such a move during the tenure of TTK in 1963 which had died following pressure from business and his resignation. In its commentary, the *Economic and*

Political Weekly observed that for fifteen years, banks had not moved out of traditional banking practices and had hardly adapted to the needs of a dynamic economy. Whatever change was seen was largely due to compulsion from the government or the RBI. The analysis illustrated the failure with hard facts. The total number of branches were just 6,500 and whatever branch expansion had happened, had come about only under the pressure of the RBI. It went on to reveal that at the end of March 1966, banks had lent only ₹90 crore to the small-scale sector as against ₹1,300 crore to big business and ₹500 crore to trade. The banks had lent just ₹5 crore to agriculture (under 1 per cent of total advances). It concluded that it was unfortunate that 'threats of nationalization or social control should be necessary to induce a sense of social responsibility or of larger economic purpose among bankers'.

In the meantime, exasperated by Morarji Desai's tactics to prevent nationalization, Chandra Shekhar commissioned four economists to undertake a study of banking operations in India. The economists were H. K. Manmohan Singh from Punjab University, V. B. Singh of Lucknow University, S. C. Gupta of Delhi University and S. K. Goyal of the Indian Institute of Public Administration, New Delhi. Their report was scathing. The committee found that bank credit, rather than being utilized for projects, was being used for low-priority sectors and that 'between 1953 and 1965, loans to agriculture declined in absolute and proportionate terms'.

The panel of economists revealed that easy credit to industrial houses had spawned monopolies. They also uncovered the extent of the consanguineous relationship between owners, directors, banks and borrowing companies. The panel reported that 188 persons who served as directors in twenty leading banks held 1,452 directorships of other companies besides controlling 1,100 companies. A more detailed study of five leading banks revealed the intricate web of influence that ruled the banking sector. Through common directors these five banks were connected with thirty-three insurance companies, six financial institutions, twenty-five investment centres, 584 manufacturing companies, twenty-six trading companies and fifteen not-for-profit organizations.

Close on the heels of this report, Chandra Shekhar and his group received support from an unexpected quarter. A committee appointed to look into the industrial licensing policy came up with a startling observation. The report authored by R. K. Hazari, a professor of economics at Bombay University, said: 'I should express my doubts about the viability of suggestions [on industrial licensing] so long as many of the major credit institutions are under the direct control or influence of those who might suffer under the suggested arrangements. It would be difficult to undertake credit planning unless the link to control of industry and banks in the same hands is snapped by the nationalization of banks.'

The banks had nowhere to hide. It was assumed by the Young Turks that nationalization was now a given. At the Jabalpur session of the AICC held in October 1967, Desai rejected the demand for nationalization. The Young Turks targeted Desai and others and issued a clear warning to those who were trying to 'adulterate' the promises made in the Congress manifesto in the run-up to the 1967 polls. In November the CFSA and its fifty-six member group organized a convention on socialism in Delhi on Nehru's birth anniversary with Indira Gandhi and senior ministers in attendance where the Young Turks took a pledge to ensure the adoption of the ten-point charter.

Indira Gandhi could have, had she wanted to, used the momentum of the prevailing sentiment to push through the agenda of nationalization. But she did not. Interestingly, while the Congress manifesto did speak about the State playing an active role in the banking sector, the word nationalization was not uttered. Her own views notwithstanding, Mrs Gandhi's support to the forum was yet to be articulated. Perhaps it was not yet opportune to do so, according to her calculations. Quite in keeping with her strategy of using political convenience as the basis of timing, she let Morarji Desai carry the day at the CWC in mid-October. The deputy prime minister argued against nationalization and promoted the concept of social control in which banks would facilitate credit to socially important sectors.

Meanwhile, officials of the RBI and the ministry of finance ironed out the many creases in the note prepared by Panandikar to ready a draft bill on social control. On 14 December 1967—a month after the CFSA members pledged to push through the nationalization of banks at the Young Turks convention—Morarji Desai told Parliament that the links between banks and industrial houses would be snapped and decisions on credit would be dictated by the deliberations of the National Credit Council. On 23 December 1967, a bill to amend the Banking Regulation Act 1949, the Reserve Bank of India Act 1934 and the State Bank of India Act 1955 ushered in social control over banks.

Banks were asked to reconstitute their boards as the new Act required 51 per cent of members of the board to be experts in diverse fields such as accountancy, agriculture, the rural economy, small scale industry, cooperation and, helpfully, banking. There would be at least two directors to represent agriculture, the rural economy, cooperation and small industries. Foreign banks were also asked to set up advisory boards controlled by specialists. The chairman of every bank would necessarily be a professional banker and not an industrialist and all appointments and terminations would require the approval of the RBI. Banks could continue to be owned by industrialists but their operations would now be controlled by the government. The introduction of social controls brought India one step closer to the nationalization of banks.

Through 1968 and into the first few months of 1969, the RBI and government bickered over branch expansion, battled over credit disbursal and fought over the financing of food procurement operations. Banks were pushed to accept a 2:1 ratio on branch expansion—for every branch opened in a banked centre they were obliged to open two in non-banked centres. Between March 1968 and April 1969, the National Credit Council met thrice to review procedures, processes and progress. They were satisfied; the political class was not.

In October 1968, a study group of bankers, economists and industrialists including T. A. Pai, B. K. Dutt, M. Y. Ghorpade, A. N. Mafatlal, N. M. Choksi, P. Natesan and P. N. Damry was constituted under the leadership of D. R. Gadgil, deputy chairman of the Planning Commission, with B. N. Adarkar as convener, to study various gaps in the geographical expansion of branches as also the sectoral expansion of credit. Its first report was damning. As many as 617 towns out of the

2,700 in the country had not been covered by commercial banks. Of these, 444 did not have cooperative banking facilities either. And, worse still, of about 600,000 villages, hardly 500 had banks. By the beginning of 1969, political leaders across the political spectrum including those from regional parties and, of course, the pro-nationalization group in the Congress, had come to view 'social control' as a placebo rather than a cure.

The consequences visited the NDC. In April, at the 26th NDC meeting, chief ministers yet again targeted the central government and the deputy prime minister over the lack of resources for development. M. Karunanidhi, the chief minister of Tamil Nadu, criticized the planning process saying, 'Three Five-Year Plans have not been able to provide food, clothing, housing or even drinking water to people and the Fourth Plan doesn't give out much hope.' Plans, he said, had become an arithmetical exercise. 'In order to secure adequate resources and as a first step towards the establishment of a socialist society, it is necessary to nationalize the banks.' Deputy Prime Minister Morarji Desai responded with the contention that money deposited in banks could not become government money by merely nationalizing banks and argued that the idea of social control deserved a fair trial. Morarji Desai carried the day but it was clear that 'bank nationalization', the old chestnut, was back in the fire.

For Indira Gandhi the timing couldn't have been better. The party bosses were on the back foot. The performance of the Congress in the general election of 1967 was easily its worst since independence. Its tally in the Lok Sabha dipped below 300 and the party lost power in eight out of the sixteen states it contested in. It was fashionable in the late sixties to say that one could drive from Calcutta to Delhi without encountering a single Congress government on the way. It was also true that the entire Gangetic plain was littered with unstable coalitions. In February 1969, the Election Commission conducted what was then described as a 'mini election' for the states of West Bengal, Uttar Pradesh, Bihar and Punjab.

Everywhere she campaigned for Congress candidates in the 'mini elections', Indira Gandhi preferred to seek votes in her name. The idea was simply to distance herself from the Congress party and present herself as the nucleus of a new, separate, entity. The results were disastrous. The Congress emerged as the single largest party in Bihar and UP but without a majority and suffered outright defeat to the Shiromani Akali Dal in Punjab and the CPI and CPM in West Bengal. It became painfully clear that the power of the Congress party, and especially the Syndicate which had once dominated party politics, was fading. The party's loss in eight states in 1967 shrank the membership of the 'chief ministers' club' which formed the power base for the Syndicate. At a personal level, the rout of the Congress in Tamil Nadu dented Kamaraj's stature. The Syndicate, by now, had recognized that Ram Manohar Lohia's 'goongi gudiya' (dumb doll, as the socialist leader had dubbed Indira Gandhi) was not so dumb after all.

When the party met to analyse the 1969 debacle, the younger members of the CPP accused the veterans of promoting groupism. The Syndicate began to fight back. On 3 May 1969 the President of India, Zakir Hussain, passed away and a new president had to be elected. The Syndicate saw this as an opportunity to reinforce their hold over the party. The Syndicate zeroed in on one of their founder-members, N. Sanjiva Reddy, as the choice for the next president. Indira Gandhi preferred Jagjivan Ram.

During the troubled weeks of the summer of 1969, some of the old Congressmen had a regrouping of sorts. The Syndicate even cosied up to Morarji Desai, a man they had once loathed. It was an alliance of necessity as they were now constantly attacked by a common enemy, the Young Turks. While the Syndicate members were besieged within the party, Desai was targeted openly in Parliament over his son Kanti Desai's alleged links with corporate houses. Morarji Desai knew his days in the cabinet were numbered and the growing chasm between him and the prime minister was now a very public fact. It was thus necessary for him to be part of the group which nominated the next president.

Indira Gandhi realized that if she was to triumph in this battle for survival, she would have to acquire suzerainty over the party. She told the members of her kitchen cabinet that the fight could no longer just be between two factions of the party leadership; she needed the cadres and the masses to support her. A few days before the critical AICC Session at Bangalore in 1969, she penned a document known as the *Stray Thoughts Memorandum*. Far from being stray, the document was a well-thought-through turn to the left to capture the reins of the party. Borrowing heavily from the ten-point charter of the Young Turks, the note prescribed the abolition of privy purses, the nationalization of banks, the installation of a ceiling on urban and rural landholdings, a programme to deliver land to the tiller and a crackdown on monopolies. The objective, clearly, was to paint the Syndicate as anti-people and pro-rich and identify herself as pro-poor to woo the socialists and leftists who campaigned for state control of economic muscle. The tussle for power had now acquired an ideological aura.

All the pieces required to nationalize the banks were now in place. The Young Turks had painted a stark picture of the economy and social conditions at AICC meetings in Faridabad and in Bangalore. Indira Gandhi knew well that her ideas would be accepted by the party cadres and the masses. At the same time, the plan she was proposing would drive a wedge between Morarji Desai, with his distaste for bank nationalization, and the Syndicate which had accepted the idea in the 1967 manifesto and was wedded to socialism.

She had prepared well for the event. Even as she took the stage, copies of the *Stray Thoughts Memorandum* were distributed to AICC delegates. Addressing the delegates she said, 'There is great feeling in the country regarding the nationalization of private commercial banks. We can consider the nationalization of a few top banks or issue directions that the resources of banks should be reserved to a larger extent for public purposes.' By the time she finished the delegates were on their feet and the standing ovation that followed was proof that she had won over the party cadres.

Chandra Shekhar, the leader of the Young Turks, urged the cadres to congratulate the prime minister for providing the right sort of leadership. Mohan Dharia, another Young Turk, thundered that the prime minister had stated exactly what they had been demanding all this while. Predictably, following the applause and the accolades, the AICC drafted the services of Y. B. Chavan to pen a resolution that was unanimously adopted. The daughter of Nehru who never displayed allegiance to any -ism, who always trod the middle path, who agreed on the reforms and devaluation mandated by the IMF in 1966 and who had hitherto resisted radical measures, had shifted her stance enabling her to co-opt the radical elements in the party to wrest control of the Congress.

However, the victory was qualified, to some extent, by the old guard having their way in the nomination of Sanjiva Reddy as the Congress candidate for president. The defeat of her candidate, Jagjivan Ram, in the Congress Parliamentary Board elections was, in some ways, akin to losing a vote of confidence. But what the defeat gave Mrs Gandhi was a clear idea of the arithmetic of power within the party. She knew too that a large group within the CPP and the party would probably take her side if she engineered a move that was perhaps the most radical one she had contemplated this far.

Indira Gandhi understood that the most effective way to wreck the Syndicate would be to take government away from the party—in other words, to split Congress. A split would necessitate her having to prove her majority in the Lok Sabha. The Fourth Lok Sabha elected 283 Congressmen. She realized she would need the support of outside parties if her plan was to succeed. Her best bet were the Left parties who commanded forty-two MPs in the house of 520. She knew they were ecstatic over her proposal at the AICC which was exactly what they had been prescribing since the fifties. But she would need a story to sell, a proposition the Communists would buy.

The answer lay in proving her credentials not just through the articulation of leftist views as she had done in Bangalore but with a bold, decisive move. Shortly after her return from Bangalore she summoned I. G. Patel, who was then heading the Department of Banking, and without any preamble asked him to prepare an ordinance for the nationalization of banks. The move to nationalize banks was her decision alone. Until Patel informed L. K. Jha, then RBI governor, even he did not know about it. And neither did Deputy Prime Minister Morarji Desai. On 16 July she simply sent him a letter divesting him of the finance portfolio, suggesting that since he disagreed with the ideas she was promoting, it would be best if he ceased to be finance minister. It is a measure of Indira Gandhi's ruthlessness that she didn't feel it necessary even to discuss with Desai the minor matter of him being deputy prime minister without a portfolio. Desai was no fool and quit the government shortly thereafter. Meanwhile a small team of officials including I. G. Patel, L. K. Jha and RBI Executive Director R. K. Seshadari, who had worked on a previous draft during the TTK regime, worked on the ordinance for bank nationalization. The cabinet obediently passed the ordinance.

On 19 July 1969, the Banking Companies (Acquisition and Transfer of Undertakings) Ordinance was promulgated by acting President V. V. Giri in exercise of the power conferred by clause (1) of Article 123 of the Constitution. Ordinance 8 of 1969 transferred ownership of fourteen commercial banks to the State. These were the Central Bank of India Limited, the Bank of India Limited, the Punjab National Bank Limited, the Bank of Baroda Limited, the United Commercial Bank of India Limited, Canara Bank Limited, Dena Bank Limited, United Bank Limited, Syndicate Bank Limited, Allahabad Bank Limited, Indian Bank Limited, Bank of Maharashtra Limited, Indian Overseas Bank Limited and Union Bank Limited. These banks together controlled 70 per cent of the nation's deposits. The preamble to the ordinance declared it was, 'An Ordinance to provide for the acquisition and transfer of the undertakings of certain banking companies in order to serve better the needs of development of the economy in conformity with national policy and objectives and for matters connected therewith or incidental thereto', leaving no doubt about the political objectives of the move.

On the evening of the promulgation of the ordinance, Indira Gandhi made a broadcast on All India Radio to explain the rationale behind the step. Her core justification was as follows: 'An institution, such as the banking system, which touches—and should touch—the lives of millions, has necessarily to be inspired by a larger social purpose and has to sub-serve national priorities and objectives. That is why there has been widespread demand that major banks should be not only socially controlled but publicly owned. This is why we nationalized the

Imperial Bank and insurance. This step is a continuation of the process.'

The next day, on 20 July, the Congress Parliamentary Board met to congratulate the prime minister on her bold step. The Young Turks hailed the nationalization of the banks and pressed for further radicalization, including the nationalization of the import-export trade and the abolition of privy purses. Indira Gandhi, on her part, held her counsel. She knew the battle would be long. When she had embarked on the journey, she knew she would be fighting on multiple fronts and decided to take it one battle at a time.

Her decision was first attacked through the media by big business. Every major newspaper condemned the move, some dubbed it unconstitutional and some even ridiculed it. On 22 July, Rustom Cavasjee Cooper, a chartered accountant and a shareholder in four of the banks that had been nationalized, and Minoo Masani, barrister, freedom fighter and MP, filed writ petitions in the Supreme Court. The Court issued an interim stay order directing the government to not appoint new advisers to the boards of the affected banks or remove serving directors; government was also directed not to issue any directions that violated the Banking Regulation Act 1949 concerning the interests of depositors. The petitions questioned the competency of government and the calculation of compensation. While these developments were cause for some jubilation among those who opposed nationalization, in actual fact, the stay didn't materially alter nationalization. On 25 July 1969, the government introduced the Banking Companies (Acquisition and Transfer of Undertakings) Bill 1969 in the Lok Sabha and then subsequently in the Rajya Sabha. Indira Gandhi clarified that the order of the Supreme Court did not affect the nationalization of banks.

She was careful in her articulation as any slip in the political rhetoric could have disrupted the sensitive nuances that govern banking. Radical phraseology could scare industry into pulling back investments; lending banks could have shut the pipe, frustrating the need for working capital. And worst of all, any wrong signal would have disrupted the already fragile economy. She heeded the counsel of Patel and P. N. Haksar, her consigliere, to leave the foreign banks alone to avoid international opprobrium. The explanation given, of course, was that they were too small, accounting for less than 4 per cent of total deposits. She also did not touch smaller community-owned banks to protect her vote banks. Her message was crafted to assuage all concerned—borrowers, lenders, depositors and, of course, owners of foreign banks.

She did realize, though, that the big industrialists who owned the banks, and who had been robbed of their vested interests, could potentially play a role in the battle within Congress by funding her rivals. In a flanking move, she asked officials in the PMO to work with the home ministry on the Companies Act to draft an amendment banning donations by companies to political parties. Till 1969, when Mrs Gandhi banned it, companies were allowed to donate to political parties, officially, from their profits. Ironically, the government had been warned once in a court judgement and again by the Santhanam Committee in 1962 that corporate donations could become an instrument of political destabilization. Neither Nehru nor Shastri or, for that matter, Indira took much notice of this. She finally acted on it in 1969, amending section 293 of the Companies Act (it was codified in April 1970). She could not afford to let money-power form a transactional coalition with the Syndicate.

The ordinance to nationalize banks was a call to war. The swift turn taken by Indira Gandhi and mass fervour in favour of the ordinance rattled the Syndicate. Although Indira Gandhi had participated in the ritual of Sanjiva Reddy's nomination, the Syndicate members knew that she had something up her sleeve. Nijalingappa, the Congress president, suspected so too and wanted her to lay her cards on the table. He asked Indira to declare her support for Reddy as a candidate for the presidentship. On 24 July, the last date for nominations, V. V. Giri, the acting president, threw his hat into the ring. Giri had the support of the left parties. This indirectly hinted at an alliance between Indira and the Communist parties. Indira, though, had not yet shown her cards.

1969 was a busy season, both politically and geopolitically. Even as Indira Gandhi planned her moves with the Syndicate, she had to deal with another budding syndicate between the US and Pakistan. In August 1969, Nixon, who was en route to Pakistan to meet Yahya Khan, visited India. Like his predecessor LBJ, Nixon was no admirer of India. India had from independence taken the high moral ground on many issues, be it sovereignty, intervention in the internal affairs of a nation or on the choice of public policy. Nixon was an atheist, a non-believer when it came to India's claims of 'moral leadership' in world affairs. The visit was an unmitigated disaster. Indira, focused on the big battles ahead, had little patience for Nixon's games and she just went through the motions.

The bugle sounded on 6 August 1969. At the CPP meet, Nijalingappa baited a trap for Indira. He made a public appeal—to MPs and legislators—to elect Reddy. It was indicated to Indira Gandhi that she was expected to follow up with the appeal but she did not. Instead, at the meet, she spoke about the party, its programmes and the nationalization of banks. The rattled Syndicate then made their first big mistake. In trying to up the ante, Nijalingappa wrote to leaders of the Opposition parties, including the Jan Sangh and the Swatantra Party, to back Reddy. Chandra Shekhar and his band of Young Turks immediately charged him with supping with the enemy. The die was cast. The official candidate of the Congress party had been virtually declared a pariah by Indira Gandhi's ginger group.

Giri, in the meantime, had secured the support of many regional parties—from the DMK in Tamil Nadu to the Akali Dal in Punjab and to the Bharatiya Kisan Dal in Uttar Pradesh. Close on the heels of the regional outfits, the CPI and the CPM officially declared their support for Giri. In Parliament, Indira Gandhi used the occasion of the introduction of the bill on nationalization to launch into a campaign speech for Giri, painting her rivals in the Syndicate as anti-poor.

The encirclement of the Syndicate was nearly complete. All she needed was a way to protect her followers from the whip of the party. This was provided by Piloo Mody, a member of the Swatantra Party. Mody suggested that there be no whip for the election of the president, the supreme position in a democracy. He opined that it should be a conscience vote. Indira Gandhi seized on the idea; it went well with the aura of socialism she was trying to project. Indira had not only worked on the politics but also the logistics of her strategy. To further protect her supporters from retribution by satraps owing their loyalty to the Syndicate, MLAs were allowed to vote in Delhi in Parliament House. A gap of four days between voting and counting was ensured so that postal ballots could come in. Finally, all the votes were counted in Delhi to prevent any mischief by members of the Syndicate. The power of the government was deployed to hold the Syndicate at bay.

When the votes were counted, Giri emerged the winner with 401,515 votes. Sanjiva Reddy got 313,548 votes. C. D. Deshmukh, who had been minister of finance in Nehru's first term, and who had quit Congress over the exclusion of Bombay from Maharashtra, came third with 112,769 votes. The rules required that the winner bag at least 418,169 votes. The Election Commission factored in all the second preference votes and weeded out the losers. At final count, Giri had bagged 420,077 votes to 405,427 by Reddy. The margin was thin but the victory was huge—the Syndicate had been conclusively defeated. By 5 p.m. V. V. Giri was declared President of India.

Morarji Desai and the Syndicate made one last attempt to rein in the prime minister. In fact, of all of Indira Gandhi's political opponents, Desai was the only one who still had some fight left in him. He suggested that the CWC, and not the prime minister, should decide on his 19 July resignation from government. Indira Gandhi snubbed him by saying that it was the prime minister who had the last word. The Syndicate triggered a whisper campaign. Rumours spread that the government would be toppled in the winter session as sixty MPs were expected to vote against the government. This was an estimate Indira was comfortable with. She had wooed all the state units, barring those in Kamaraj's Tamil Nadu, Desai's Gujarat, Nijalingappa's Karnataka and S. K. Patil's Bombay.

Till the end of October and the beginning of November, various members of the party tried to heal the rift. All these attempts failed because Indira Gandhi stood firm. The next two months saw a heightened proxy war between the Syndicate and Indira Gandhi. The war escalated, with attacks and counter-attacks. The Syndicate ousted Indira acolytes like C. Subramaniam from the CWC citing technicalities, the Young Turks attacked Syndicate members for hobnobbing with the enemy and for being hand in glove with capitalists. On 12 November, the CWC, which was controlled by the Syndicate, expelled Indira Gandhi from the party. The following day, a meeting of the parallel CPP affirmed their confidence in Indira Gandhi. The Congress party was irrevocably split.

While nobody could be certain of the actual numbers, Indira Gandhi's coterie reported that fifty-four members of parliament had fallen in behind the Syndicate. Indira Gandhi's original calculations turned out to be almost accurate. She had calculated in July, after the Bangalore session, that at least fifty of the 283 Congress MPs elected in 1967 would leave her. To ensure her survival she needed the support of at least 260 members in the house of 520. The ordinance enforcing bank nationalization had ensured that she would receive the support of the left parties who had forty-two MPs. On 17 November the Jana Sangh moved an adjournment motion to test the strength of the Indira Gandhi regime. It survived with the support of the Left, the Akali Dal and the DMK. Indira Gandhi had soundly defeated the most experienced and battle-tested members of the Congress party.

In February 1970, the Supreme Court upheld the legislative competence of Parliament in the acquisition of banks but struck down nationalization. As the Department of Banking explained to banks the same evening in a circular, it was struck down mainly on the grounds that it was discriminatory against fourteen banks and that the compensation was not fair. The government, though, was committed to making nationalization happen. Four days after the judgement, officials drafted a new ordinance that avoided the offending provisions and set out new levels of compensation. The fourteen banks were paid ₹8,740 lakh in all. The Banking Companies (Acquisition and Transfer of Undertakings) Bill was introduced into Parliament on 27 February 1970, passed by both houses without any change, and notified as an Act on 31 March 1970.

THE ECONOMIC DIVIDEND

Bank nationalization may well have been born out of political necessity, but it paid dividends as far as the economy was concerned.

In 1969, after twenty-two years of independence, the Indian banking system had barely 6,900 bank branches. By 1979 India boasted 30,202 branches and by 1989 the number had increased to 57,699 branches. Between 1969 and 1989 the number of branches in rural India, in villages, shot up from 1,833 to 33,014. To ensure that the political quest for reach was enforced, one bank in each region was designated to lead branch expansion. To force the pace, a provision—dubbed 4:1—was employed under which banks were required to open four new branches in areas without coverage for every new branch opened in an area with banks. The average number of customers per branch, which was 63,000 in 1969, was down to 14,000 customers per branch in 1989.

Thanks to branch expansion and the democratization of banking services, the country's gross savings shot up from 11.8 per cent of the GDP to 21.2 per cent in two decades. In a comprehensive study, Robin Burgess and Rohini Pande reveal that between 1969 and 1990, branches were set up in 30,000 rural locations and this led to rural savings rising from 3 per cent to 15 per cent and the share of credit to rural areas from 1.5 per cent to 15 per cent. Burgess and Pande point out that poverty peaked in India in 1967 with 61 per cent of the population living below the poverty line, a statistic that dropped to 31 per cent in 2000. It is their considered argument that branch expansion in rural areas can explain roughly half of this fall in rural poverty. Their contention is that lack of access to finance is an important reason why poor people stay poor.

Looking back, it is tempting to disconnect the political reasons for bank nationalization from the happy economic consequences that resulted. It could be argued that branch expansion, the increase in savings and other dividends could have taken place without nationalization. Critics have even ventured to hazard that the private sector would have done this much more efficiently. The governor of the Reserve Bank of India, D. Subbarao, doesn't quite agree, 'The view that banks would have delivered on rural branch expansion on their own is debatable. I believe it's nationalization that has driven this financial penetration. Note that even today it requires RBI to use a "carrot and stick policy" to encourage banks to venture into the hinterland. The net cost benefit calculus of bank nationalization has undoubtedly been positive.'

Indeed, the hypothesis that private banks would have delivered financial inclusion is seductive but doesn't find validation when the facts are reviewed. It is no secret that the fervour of socialism has ebbed since 1991, especially when it comes to the expansion of bank branches.

For the period from 1991 to 2011, following the liberalization of the economy and the advent of private banks, only 30,000 bank branches were added. Contrast this with the twenty years between 1969 and 1989 when banks added over 50,000 branches across India. Between 1969 and 1989, banks added 31,181 branches in rural India while between 1991 and 2011 less than 1,000 branches have been added in rural India. The difference in the levels of achievement between the two periods—1969 to 1989 and 1991 to 2011—is attributable to the politics of the respective periods. In the seventies and eighties, branch expansion was part of the political agenda, since 1991 it has not been explicitly so.

There are many criticisms of nationalization, too. It was held by many that after 1969, banking was governed by political equations and not by profitability ratios. Banks were asked to lend at pre-determined rates and bear the cost of the subsidy granted by the Government of India. There is no denying the ill effects of state ownership which led to the politicization of bank managements and unions, poor efficiency, corruption, loan waivers and loan melas. As the Narasimham Committee pointed out in 1991, 'management weaknesses and trade union pressures have seriously undermined the efficiency of banks and financial institutions'.

Nationalization also led to the perpetuation of profligacy. The Statutory Liquidity Ratio (SLR), prescribed by the RBI under which banks are directed to invest a percentage of funds in government bonds, allows the government first charge on national savings to fund its programmes. Like all good ideas, the SLR was first used to fund economic development. Soon after, it began to be misused to fund political goals. Debt and deficit were expanded to accommodate political interests and to promote the culture of sops. Indeed, till the late eighties, no real effective monetary policy—to control inflation for instance—was feasible as the government could dip its hand into the till of nationalized banks using instruments like the SLR. It could, at will, borrow by issuing bonds and, at will, monetize debt by printing currency.

The brunt of these measures was borne by consumers and the private sector. In the mid-eighties there were as many as 200 different rates across the banking sector depending on who was borrowing from whom, where and for what. It was only later that the government worked towards a single benchmark rate and allowed the RBI to begin crafting a monetary policy.

The inefficiencies nationalization forced on banks notwithstanding, there is no doubt that it resulted in the democratization of banking, credit and entrepreneurship. The nationalization of banks resulted in the creation of what can only be described as institutionalized public venture capital. National savings could be tapped by entrepreneurs from across the spectrum and not just those connected to industrial houses. If bank ownership had stayed with the industrial houses, many entrepreneurs might have been denied access to loans as several of the businesses they were proposing to set up would have been in direct competition with established industrial houses. It is an accepted fact that new entrepreneurs such as the Ambanis, Ruias, Munjals, Adanis, Mittals and many others, including professionally run entrepreneurial ventures, may not have got access to easy credit. Of course the emergence of new entrepreneurs also created a new base for funding the business model of politics.

One positive effect of nationalization—in hindsight—was that state ownership ushered in conservatism and kept public sector banks away from high-risk ideas that destroyed banks on both sides of the Atlantic in 2008. The Congress party didn't lose time in hailing nationalization and claiming credit for saving Indian banking. Speaking at a public event on 21 November 2008, Congress President Sonia Gandhi said, 'If you allow me the liberty of showing what is to you the proverbial red rag to the bull, let me take you back to Indira Gandhi's much-reviled bank nationalization. Every passing day bears the wisdom of that decision.' In February 2009, in his Budget speech Finance Minister Pranab Mukherjee said it was nationalization that saved India's banks. 'Never before has the bold decision to nationalize our banking system appeared as wise and visionary as it has now.' What defines right and wrong is contextually fluid. What is indisputable is that the game changer that the nationalization of banks proved to be was accidental.

While nationalization had far-reaching economic consequences, its political benefits, though, were short-lived. Despite her embrace of socialism, Indira Gandhi could not avoid incurring the nation's displeasure in the mid-seventies, leading to the imposition of the Emergency in 1975 and her defeat in 1977. Shortly after she was re-elected in 1980 and returned to power, Indira Gandhi was presented with a fait accompli. The RBI governor informed her that a second round of nationalization was required. Some private banks had been converted into fiefdoms. On 15 April 1980 the Government of India nationalized six more banks. These were Andhra Bank, Corporation Bank, New Bank of India, Oriental Bank of Commerce, Punjab and Sind Bank, and Vijaya Bank. Indira Gandhi apparently didn't quite savour the idea but went along with the advice of I. G. Patel, the governor of the RBI.

Historically speaking, the 1980 round of bank nationalization was ironic. The ordinance (Banking Companies Acquisition and Transfer of Undertakings Ordinance 1980) was promulgated by N. Sanjiva Reddy. The man whose candidature had triggered the first round of nationalization and the split in the Congress was, in 1980, the President of India.

India's founding fathers dreamt of a nation flowing with milk. But the country didn't have the resources for it, and the government lacked the imagination to make it happen. As early as 1952, the Kaira farmers' milk cooperative became a success, and Anand a pilgrimage site for economists. Yet India's planners and politicians refused to recognize the template for success until Verghese Kurien forced them to accept a 'Billion Litre Idea' which created...

THE MILKY WAY

13 MAY 1949
ANAND

The train from Bombay pulled into the ramshackle railway station at Anand. A young man, felt hat perched rakishly on his thick mop of curly hair, stepped down with his suitcase. At hand were two people to receive him, Kodandapani, an engineer from the National Dairy Research Institute, and Barot Kaka, a member of the local cooperative. The young man was shocked by what he saw. Newly graduated from Michigan State University, his heart lingering in America, Verghese Kurien knew this was not what he wanted for himself. As he looked around the station, it seemed to him that he had travelled not just across continents but backward in time. From bustling New York to sleepy Anand, the abrupt transition from the developed world to the unpaved developing world was almost too much to take.

Anand may have been just another small town on the edge of rural India but it had a unique attribute that made it important to India's political economy. Located barely 442 kilometres from Bombay as the crow flies, and on the Bombay-Ahmedabad arterial route, it was perfectly placed to be one of the catchment areas to generate agricultural and dairy produce for millions of city-dwellers in Bombay.

Nestled in the deltaic convergence of the Sabarmati and its tributaries, Anand is part of Kaira district's Charotar area, often described in Gujarati folklore as a land of milk and honey. Its people harvested two crops of vegetables, grains, and tobacco per year.

Hardworking and enterprising, the local populace—predominantly land-owning patidars—was socially conservative, yet open to new ideas for income generation. The district was home to the first dairies set up by the British, followed by other Europeans like the Germans.

As early as 1904, the administration of the Bombay Presidency, influenced by the British rulers, had zeroed in on Kaira as the focal point of milk production and ordained the creation of milk cooperatives at the local village level. The government believed a cooperative set-up would enable the pooling of local resources, the delivery of credit and afford some protection from rapacious traders and moneylenders who exploited the farmers. Although this was sound reasoning, the idea of cooperatives didn't quite take off as it didn't have the necessary political ballast and administrative backup. Further, exploitative traders and moneylenders, whom the government was trying to remove from the scene, successfully managed to engineer conflicts among the farmers. And so the experiment languished and by the forties the idea of cooperatives had almost collapsed.

Milk output depends on a host of factors, from the quality of feed to the quality of cattle. The latter was especially poor throughout India. In fact, in 1928, the Royal Commission on Agriculture headed by Lord Linlithgow in its report emphasized the need to upgrade dairy livestock by importing better breeds of bulls and ensuring in situ insemination. As this was a relatively complicated process needing both funds and organizational support, it didn't happen. Another factor essential to the process of dairy farming is that seasonal output needs to be in consonance with demand. Typically, in India, the milk output of cows and buffaloes in winter is twice that in summer. This was true for the buffaloes in Kaira too.

One way to deal with the situation would have been to process perishable milk into powder or some other product with a longer shelf life. The creation of cooperatives was meant to address the politics and economics of the situation. It was meant to create a constituency of dairy farmers and deliver economies of scale so that the villagers could negotiate from a position of strength; better income would lead to better lives. But dishonesty on the part of the contractors to whom the milk was supplied, as well as a general lack of support for the scheme, ensured it never quite achieved lift-off.

The farmers were disillusioned and continued to be exploited. The revolution awaited a spark. This was provided by an order of the government of Bombay Presidency in 1946 which obliged all milk producers in the four talukas of the Kaira district to sell their milk to the Polson Dairy, founded by a Bombay Parsi, Pestonji Edulji Dalal, in 1890. Dalal was a shrewd businessman with a legendary capacity for hard work. He understood that in poverty-stricken India, his biggest consumer would be the rulers, especially British soldiers. Using the brand name Polson, which sounded English enough for his intended customers, he decided to milk the opportunity. His products fed British and American troops on the frontier and even abroad during the wars. Dalal knew the potential of Kaira better than the locals and captured the milk collection market to expand his business. Polson was synonymous with butter to most Bombaywallahs at the time just as Amul is today to most Indians.

Dalal raised the fear of shortage because of fluctuations in milk output to convince the government of Bombay Presidency to grant him monopoly rights over procurement. If he didn't receive the monopoly, he said, supplies to the British would suffer. This monopolistic arrangement drove prices down, triggering anger among members of the many cooperatives. The reason the Bombay Presidency could do this at the behest of Polson was because the cooperatives were disunited.

Faced with the fiat from the Bombay Presidency, the milk producers in Charotar approached Sardar Vallabhbhai Patel for help. Many years earlier, Sardar Patel, considered the patron saint of the cooperative movement in Gujarat, had told the milk producers that if they didn't unite, they would be exploited.

Sardar Patel repeated his earlier advice and asked the milk producers to come together. He explained that the institution of the 'united' cooperative would protect the dairy from exploitation, both by moneylenders and the buyers of their milk. He then directed Morarji Desai, revenue minister of the Bombay Presidency, to address the issue. The milk producers lacked unity because they lacked leadership. Morarji Desai decided to fix this. He called for a meeting and asked who would like to head the cooperative. Many put their hands up. There was one man who did not. Tribhuvandas Patel, known for his integrity and commitment to the cause of cooperatives, had kept silent because he was unwell, having spent time in jail during the Quit India Movement. Desai appointed him the leader.

A veteran Gandhian, Patel went by foot to village after village to create milk cooperatives in each. It wasn't easy; he wasn't a known face and in every village he had to chant the sermon of collective action and the collective good. It took some time for the villagers to recognize the benefits of the scheme Patel was extolling. After months of tireless campaigning, the cooperative could finally boast a critical mass of member cooperatives. In 1946, Patel registered it, christening it the Kaira District Cooperative Milk Producers' Union Limited (KDCMPUL).

It was the birth of an idea. Verghese Kurien was to go on to institutionalize this idea into a national milk grid. But on the morning of 13 May 1949 when he arrived in Anand, he certainly did not know that this would be his destiny. Kodandapani and Barot Kaka introduced Kurien to Anand as they headed from the railway station to the office at the creamery. There wasn't much to tell about a place with a population of barely 10,000 that had little claim to fame except that it supplied milk to Bombay.

When they reached the office, Kodandapani, who was relieved at having obtained his liberty from the dreary place, advised Kurien with more than a touch of sympathy that he should take charge the next day as 'Friday the 13th' was perhaps not the best day to start something new. That set Kurien off. He told Kodandapani, 'Let me take charge today and let things go wrong. I am not interested in staying here too long.'

This episode defines Kurien in many ways. The unmistakable intelligence, the keen ability to assess situations, the honesty to accept a circumstance as it was without attendant varnish, the complete contempt for woolly-headed victimhood and, above all, the courage to not yield and face the consequences—all these were qualities of a consummate leader. Every milestone that Kurien gained was on the back of this unique combination of abilities.

Of course, that Friday in May 1949, none of this figured in his thinking. All Kurien wanted was to get out of this place. In his mind everything that could go wrong had gone wrong. Kurien was born into what is colloquially called a 'well-to-do' family. The son of a respected civil surgeon, Kurien did well in school before heading to Madras to gain a degree in science at Loyola College. Although his father passed away when he was twenty-two, the maternal side of the family—headed by Cherian Mathai—took charge of the young Kurien and sent him off to Guindy Engineering College for a bachelor's degree in engineering.

After completing his degree, Kurien knocked at the doors of Tata Iron and Steel Company. He had a recommendation from his grand uncle, John Mathai, one of the authors of the famous Bombay Plan of 1944 and independent India's minister of finance from 1949 to 1951. Kurien was taken on board as a graduate apprentice. It was a good life at Jamshedpur until John Mathai turned up at the hostel. Mathai was a director at Tata headquarters in Bombay. Overnight, Kurien became the nephew of the boss. His proficiency at his job was subsumed by genetic privilege and he would henceforth be viewed differently.

Kurien loathed the change in attitude towards him and told his uncle he wanted out. John Mathai was sympathetic but warned him about the risks of quitting a plum job. Despite his advice, Kurien applied for a scholarship. The government at that time funded students to travel abroad to study; there was a quota of subjects that they wanted young scholars to gain expertise in. Kurien won a scholarship to study dairy engineering at Michigan State University. But being the maverick that he was, when he got there he chose to study metal casting, metallurgy and nuclear engineering.

Upon graduation, Kurien was recommended by the dean of his university for a job with Union Carbide. There was a hitch, though. When he signed up for the scholarship, he had committed to the

Government of India that on returning he would serve the government in the Department of Dairy Development at the ministry of agriculture for five years. Kurien thought he would be able to sidestep this bond. He approached John Mathai and pointed out that since he didn't study what he was sent for he was not qualified for dairy development. Mathai not only refused to help but said he would ensure that Kurien fulfilled his obligation to the government.

So here he was in Anand, armed with a thesis on the heredity in iron castings, a degree in metallurgy and a fascination for nuclear engineering, stuck with the responsibility of managing a milk creamery. Life on the professional and the personal front looked dismal. A Malayali Syrian Christian and a non-vegetarian, the place he found himself in was conservative, mostly Hindu, Gujarati-speaking and predominantly vegetarian. After taking charge, his first task was to find a place to rent. Of course he didn't find one and ended up living in a garage.

The government research creamery in Anand to which he had been deputed was basic to the extreme. It had engaged in no research to speak of and Kurien's job as the dairy engineer involved nothing more than minor tinkering with whatever machinery existed. Kurien took to smoking, neglected his grooming and generally frittered away his days in his first months at the new job. But his intelligence would not let him stay idle for long. The creamery produced tons of milk powder which was lying unsold and he decided to find a market for it. Typically, nobody in the government had thought of this idea. Kurien found that biscuit makers could use the powder. He made a trip to Bombay, found buyers and sold the powder. This gave him some satisfaction and the viability of the creamery improved. The small triumph, though, did not diminish his desire to leave Anand.

KURIEN REMAINS IN ANAND

For over six months after he joined the creamery, Kurien would write to the ministry of agriculture every month about the waste of his talent and government money. These missives would be accompanied by his letter of resignation. Even as this saga was playing out, Kurien made the acquaintance of Tribhuvandas Patel. Kurien didn't know much about cooperatives but was impressed that a group of farmers was trying so hard to make an idea work. Off and on Patel would approach Kurien for help with the cooperative's machinery. One day, after fixing the dairy's creamer for the umpteenth time, Kurien told Patel the cooperative would be better off buying a new one. Patel agreed but on the condition that Kurien would help them procure the machine and install it for them.

Around February 1950, Kurien's persistent efforts bore fruit. The ministry of agriculture accepted his resignation. It appeared that Kodandapani's warning about Friday the 13th was about to come true. Delighted, Kurien was all set to leave when Patel came to see him and asked if he had found another job. When he discovered that Kurien hadn't, he made him an offer. He asked Kurien to join the KDCMPUL, help them set up the new machine and run it till he found another job. Kurien agreed. To him, this was a minor stopover of six to eight weeks.

What was supposed to be a stopgap arrangement for Kurien led to a major turning point in the history of India's political economy. Soon after he joined the KDCMPUL, Kurien was struck by Patel's passion as well as the method by which he tempered his evangelism. Patel used his position in the Gujarat Pradesh Congress Committee without any reservation to help farmers and the KDCMPUL. However, he didn't let politicians or government interfere or influence the operations of the cooperative. Patel ensured that there was no room to practice quid pro quo politics.

Within weeks it became clear that the pairing of Patel's passion and Kurien's managerial ability was extraordinarily beneficial to the functioning of the cooperative. He was, though, still intent on moving out of Anand. The new machinery was installed; Kurien was all set to leave. At that point, Patel simply told him, 'Don't go, we need you.' Kurien was grounded. He was moved by the faith, the trust reposed in him.

Molly Verghese Kurien, his wife, describes it as a coming together of people and circumstance. 'Kurien came to Anand by accident. He did not like the place at all, it wasn't what he wanted. But he was compelled. In Anand he met with Tribhuvandas and was immensely impressed by his commitment, passion and, above all, his simplicity. It dawned on him that here was an opportunity to help people who were helpless in their circumstance.'

Kurien's rebellious nature had discovered a cause worthy of rebellion. The challenge to do something for the poorest came embedded with the opportunity to take on the mightiest: the powers that be, the establishment and the status quo. He couldn't have asked for more. In an interview with the author, Kurien explained it as the transcending of the distance between pleasure and fulfilment. 'Working for the self may deliver pleasure but it is working for a cause that gives one a deeper sense of fulfilment.'

The alliance between Kurien and Patel, one mercurial and the other calm and blessed with old-world wisdom, worked brilliantly. Patel managed the politics of the cooperative, Kurien the economics of the operations. Kurien had absolute faith in the judgement and vision of Patel and the integrity with which he managed the organizational issues that haunt any collective of people. On the other side of the equation, Patel respected Kurien's skills and knowledge, and completely trusted his advice and the decisions he took.

THE COMPLEXITY OF MILK

Milk is a complex, perishable commodity, vulnerable to heat and time, which means that it has value only for a finite period. Traditionally, most farming households in Kaira kept two or three milch cattle at home. The milk produced during the day was partly consumed and partly sold. But there was always a surplus. In their own way the farmers sought to enhance the value and extend the life of the product by converting it into curd, cottage cheese or ghee. The income thus derived was just enough to cover costs but could not change lives.

The membership in the cooperative brought the economies of scale to the operation and delivered profitability. At the Kaira Cooperative, milk was collected twice a day at collection centres across villages. The milk would first be tested for fat content to ensure it wasn't diluted with water and the quantity collected was recorded. It was then despatched to Anand from where it was sent to Bombay. In 1950, the cooperative collected around 7,250 kilograms of milk every day. The economics of dairy farming dictate that farmers must be paid every day. So payments were made in the evening for milk collected in the morning and the evening quota was paid for the next morning. Regular cash flow was important as the micro-budgets that paid for cattle feed and maintenance would crash without daily inflows. By 1952-53, the cooperative had ramped up collections to over 35,000 kilograms a day or nearly 13 million kilograms a year. For the post-liberalization generation, that is roughly 26 million half-litre poly packets of milk.

The economies of scale were achieved but the cooperative was faced with a bigger problem: dealing with the seasonal fluctuation in milk output. Kurien knew that the Bombay Milk Scheme imported powder from New Zealand to augment the city's milk requirements whenever supplies dropped. He pointed out to the Kaira Cooperative that if the Bombay Milk Scheme were to buy the excess milk Kaira produced in winter and convert it to powder, they could use it in the lean months and obviate the need to import milk from New Zealand. Indeed, Kurien demanded that the authorities stop importing milk powder. It was wrong for the Bombay Milk Scheme to be importing milk powder when milk produced by poor farmers went to waste. Dara Khurody, the milk commissioner of Bombay, rejected Kurien's idea outright.

Eventually, as the demand for milk grew, the issue of surplus milk was resolved—though only partially—when the Bombay Milk Scheme ramped up its purchases. However, the stand-off between Kurien and Khurody continued for years. Kurien recalled one such encounter. Khurody wanted to suspend milk purchases from the cooperative because his officials alleged there were dead flies in the milk. Kurien, never at a loss for repartee, retorted, 'Conduct a post-mortem of the flies. See if the flies have been dropped in the milk or drowned in it.'

The story of the success of the Kaira Cooperative had reached Delhi. In late 1952, C. D. Deshmukh, then minister of finance, along with K. M. Munshi, then minister of agriculture and food, arrived in Anand to inaugurate the Institute of Agriculture—now the Anand Agricultural University. After the function, the visitors went to the Kaira Cooperative. They were shown how the Kaira formula worked; they had a first-hand view of the positive economic and political impact it was having. The economic benefits were limited to lifting the farmers' condition above mere sustenance levels but it was the political impact that impressed the political leaders the most. It was hard to imagine that in the India of the fifties, villagers—irrespective of caste, religion, political affiliation or class—would stand in queue to deliver their milk at the collection centres, or that the pricing of their product was not determined by subsets of social hierarchies.

The visit by Deshmukh and Munshi brought Kaira enormous goodwill and Kurien to the notice of the Centre. During the visit Vishnu Sahay, agriculture secretary, who was part of the entourage quipped, half in self-congratulation, that some good had come of the Government of India scholarship that Kurien had got to study abroad. Kurien didn't find it funny and retorted that he had never studied dairy engineering or management and that the whole process of sending people abroad to study was flawed. Kurien then suggested that if the government really wanted to equip people with the right skill sets and expertise in dairy engineering it should send people to Denmark and the Netherlands. After Sahay left, Kurien forgot about the conversation.

In one of the many accidents of history, India joined the Colombo Plan. The Colombo Plan for Cooperative Economic and Social Development in Asia and the Pacific, to give it its full name, was set up in July 1951 to help with the development of countries in the region. Based on the concept of sharing and self-help, it was set up by Australia, Canada, India, Pakistan, New Zealand, the UK and Sri Lanka, and funded and empowered member nations to implement common programmes.

The Colombo Plan was particularly focused on the development of dairy farming to enable farming households raise their incomes. As part of the Plan, the Dairy Division of the Department of Agriculture in New Zealand offered to train Indian professionals. To his surprise Kurien found himself nominated for a five-month course to study the dairy business in New Zealand, a country which had made a huge success of the idea of cooperatives and emerged as one of the big players in the global dairy business. The conversation with Sahay seemed to have made an impact.

Kurien spent five months in New Zealand and two months in Australia between October 1952 and April 1953. He visited over 100 dairy plants, met with workers in the entire process chain to understand the conversion of milk into different products. It was during this trip that Kurien decided Kaira would replicate what the Kiwi cooperatives had done.

Milk can be converted easily into cream, powder, butter or cheese. It followed then that dairies and cooperatives needed to invest in technology to transform the primary product; they needed machinery to manufacture produce on an assembly line and a marketing strategy to ensure that the products found buyers. The value addition delivered by conversion made the milk economy far more sustainable.

It was clear that unless supply found demand there would be waste and loss. As things stood, the inability to sell enough in winter debilitated the farmer's ability to sustain his business model. This simple logic and the correlation of supply and demand appeared to have escaped the bureaucrats. Instead of investing in machinery to convert milk so it could be stored, governments at the central and state levels left market forces to sort out the mismatch between supply and demand.

The government, perhaps, chose not to intervene because it received cheap milk powder under the PL 480 food aid scheme from the US. This powder was converted into milk and sold to consumers in the summer. Since there was only a one-way conversion—from powder to milk—and because the PL 480 powder was cheap, the conversion delivered profits to the various milk schemes that were in operation at the time. The suffering of poor dairy farmers was a fallout that didn't merit much consideration.

Kurien recognized the debilitating impact of cheap imports and the idiocy of existing government policy. He also saw an opportunity for the farmers of Kaira to extend the life of their product and profit from it. Kurien, who was by then the general manager of KDCMPUL, told Patel that a new plant costing around ₹40 lakh had to be set up. To push his case, Kurien added, 'Unless this is done, I will quit.' Kurien explained that the new plant would ensure the end-to-end processing of milk and maximize its value, transforming the Kaira Cooperative into a modern dairy business. The members of the cooperative agreed. Kurien was supported in this endeavour by Harichand Dalaya, an outstanding dairy technologist, whose family owned a large dairy in Sindh prior to the partition of India. Dalaya was an alumnus of Michigan University, like Kurien, and took immense pride in his lineage and knowledge of the business. The triumvirate worked well together.

By 1954, the KDCMPUL was as well organized as any modern corporation. Patel brought political clout and managed the issues of organization, rather like the chairman of the board. Dalaya brought his technical skills and expertise to the table, and was akin to a chief operating officer. Kurien managed business strategy and operations and was effectively the CEO. Maniben, Sardar Patel's daughter, was in many ways the spiritual compass, philosopher and guide to all.

Apart from milk collection, the cooperative had created a sub-universe of services. It offered—on demand and by rotation—the services of veterinarians to farmers. Mobile units travelled through villages offering farmers specialized services in insemination so that the quality of cattle could be upgraded. The cooperative also funded a technical cell which advised farmers on improving cattle feed. All these efforts brought productivity, efficiency and social cohesion to the cooperative.

At the front end Kurien and Dalaya engineered the extension of value. The expansion project of 1954 was ambitious not just in its scale but also in its approach to a complex issue. Around the world, experts in the dairy business believed that buffalo milk could not be converted into powder. Partly, this had to do with the fact that dairies—at least in the developed world—were sustained by cow's milk. As no one had really attempted the exercise, the easy answer was to say it was not possible. There was also fear. If buffalo milk could indeed be converted into powder, it would rob many economies of market share for their cow's milk and their dairy technology.

The emphasis on using buffalo milk was not just a stubborn Kurien-ism. It was also about history, geography and economics. Historically, Kaira and its neighbouring districts were home to buffaloes. Geographically, the region was not blessed with the sort of picturesque grazing pastures on which pedigreed cows thrived. Buffaloes, however, did just fine on wild fodder. Moreover, buffaloes were easier to maintain, hardier than cows, and delivered more milk despite grazing on fodder of poorer quality. Cow's milk generally has around 4 per cent fat while buffalo milk has nearly 8 per cent fat. This enabled better returns when buffalo milk was converted into powder or was processed to make butter.

The downside was that buffalo milk is prone to rapid curdling while being processed into powder. More critically, Kurien and Dalaya had not figured out how to process it. But they were convinced it could be done. The ambitious plan would cost over half a million dollars. The funding itself was a marvel of cooperation. The money came from UNICEF, the Government of New Zealand, a grant and a loan from the Bombay Presidency and, most importantly, the Kaira Cooperative, which raised nearly $300,000. UNICEF stipulated that in return for their investment, milk worth 1.5 times the cost of the machinery would have to be distributed free of cost to children in Anand district over a period of time. This happily coincided with the socially relevant business model of the Kaira Cooperative.

On 15 November 1954, President Rajendra Prasad arrived by special train to lay the foundation stone for the plant. As he departed Maniben asked Kurien when he planned to complete the work and who would inaugurate it. Kurien said, without batting an eyelid, that the plant would be inaugurated on 31 October 1955, the birth anniversary of Sardar Patel, and that it should be inaugurated by Prime Minister Jawaharlal Nehru. Maniben took on the responsibility of inviting Nehru.

THE BIRTH OF AMUL
The confidence of the team was extraordinary. They were planning to construct the first end-to-end dairy plant in the cooperative sector

within a year in a country notorious for delays. More outrageously, the plant was being set up to convert buffalo milk into powder when every international expert had said it could not be done. There was no dearth of sceptics at home either. Dara Khurody bet ₹5 and told Kurien he wouldn't be able to do it.

Patel, Kurien and Dalaya leveraged every resource and connection they had to get the plant commissioned on schedule. From the collector of Kaira to the chief minister of Bombay State to the Danish experts who were advising the cooperative to the team from Larsen & Toubro which supplied the machinery, everyone was prevailed upon to do their best. The Bombay Port Trust was asked to give preference in berthing to ships delivering boilers, the Railway Board was asked to deliver them via a non-stop, special train. There was no escaping the magnitude of the ambition. A month before the inauguration the machinery was yet to be installed and tested. Khurody doubled his bet to ₹10.

The machinery was put in place barely fifteen days before the inauguration. It was yet to be tested, though. Khurody, the self-appointed monitor who was auditing progress, decided to sound the alarm and inform Morarji Desai. He declared the project a failure and advised Desai to call off the function and avoid all-round embarrassment. A worried Desai reached Anand to find Kurien at the plant. He asked Kurien, 'What if Khurody is right, what if the plant doesn't convert the buffalo milk into powder?' Kurien pointed at a stack of bags with milk powder at the top of the plant and said, 'We will pour the ready powder manually.' Desai glared at him and left without saying anything. Kurien recalled, 'I took his silence as consent.'

There were hardly a few hours left for the inauguration when the trials were conducted. The new plant delivered powder. That the plant was set up in eleven months was ample evidence that when people are bonded together by commitment and conviction, India can deliver.

Fifty-seven years later, sitting in his rocking chair at his home in Anand, Kurien said, 'On the day of the inauguration Morarjibhai called me at five in the morning. He asked if the powder was coming down the line. I said yes. After a pause, Morarjibhai asked, "On its own?"'

Nehru arrived, along with Indira Gandhi, to a warm welcome by the villagers and members of the cooperative. The prime minister and his daughter had breakfast at the Kurien home, dressed for the occasion—with a rose specially preserved for Nehru's buttonhole by Molly Kurien—and took a guided tour of the plant. After the inauguration, Nehru was taken back to the Kurien home. As was his wont, Nehru wove in his ideas of nation-building into the economics, politics and history of milk. He then moved on to the quirks of royalty and turning to Molly Kurien quipped, 'Cleopatra used to bathe in asses' milk, you have buffaloes' milk.'

Morarji Desai, who was escorting the prime minister, told Nehru, 'The achievement of this plant is manifold. It was built by cooperative effort, it was commissioned in record time and most importantly it is the first plant in the world to make milk powder from buffalo milk.' As he was leaving, Nehru embraced Kurien and said, 'I am glad we have people like you in India, who go ahead and achieve what seems unachievable.'

Kurien said, 'It is a moment I will cherish all my life.' He also valued the clock on his mantelpiece, a gift from Khurody who, after losing the bet, visited the Kurien home to congratulate him.

The plant triggered a change in the business paradigm as far as cooperatives were concerned. The Kaira Cooperative now manufactured more than just milk powder. It made butter, baby food—which was much in demand—whole and skimmed milk powder. When it set up operations in 1949, the Kaira Cooperative was collecting, on an average, up to 7,200 kilograms of milk daily. By 1957, the average daily collection had touched 40,000 kilograms, half of which was sold to the Bombay Milk Scheme.

The higher output and sales triggered the need for a larger market and new methods of marketing and distribution. Sometime in 1962, Kurien's brother-in-law K. M. Philip, who ran a successful coffee business, explained to Kurien that scale requires brands and brands will build on scale. Kurien realized that wider marketing would deliver greater market share but it required advertising and branding. The first task was to find a brand name.

After many suggestions and many discussions they hit upon a priceless name, Amul (derived from the Sanskrit word 'amulya' which means 'precious'). It was also an abbreviation of the name Anand Milk Union Limited. Soon thereafter, the Kaira Cooperative had a brand name and an utterly butterly ad line 'Amul: The Taste of India' coined by the legendary Bombay adman, Sylvester da Cunha. Interestingly, when Kurien told Patel about advertising, he wasn't convinced and was actually reluctant to clear the expenditure. The sum Kurien had asked for was ₹2 lakh. Amul's advertising budget today is about ₹100 crore a year. Today, Amul boasts a turnover of over ₹11,000 crore, one of the biggest success stories of post-independence India.

CATCH 22

Kaira was a success by 1954. It had established that a cooperative could not only fulfil demand but also be a viable business. Kaira was also the genesis for Amul which was created in 1962. Yet the success of Kaira in dairy development was an island of achievement in an ocean of despair. Through the fifties and the sixties, India continued to be haunted by milk scarcity because of its Catch 22—it did not produce enough milk and was dependent on the import of milk powder through the PL 480 scheme and other aid programmes to satisfy demand; at the same time cheap imports were killing the viability of the dairy business.

It was clear that India needed to desperately ramp up its production of milk. In the fifties, the per capita availability of milk was barely 4.5 ounces a day when the World Health Organization, UNICEF and other global experts stipulated that the minimum requirement for a balanced nutritional diet was 10 ounces a day. India had to double its milk output from 17 million tons if it had to keep pace with increasing demand.

At independence, the country did not have enough milk to feed even a third of its population. The First Five Year Plan in 1952 devoted over 2,000 words to describe the state of animal husbandry and the many problems that afflicted it but offered little in terms of a plan for enhancing milk production. The Second Five Year Plan admitted that production was poor and could only estimate the scale of the problem but was certain that the output of milk and dairy products had to go up. To address the problem, the plan prescribed homeopathic steps—the establishment of twelve cooperative creameries and seven milk-drying plants.

In 1962, the Third Five Year Plan (1961-66) revealed that 'the average per capita milk consumption had snail-crawled from 4.76 oz per day to 4.9 oz per day'. This was ten years after the obviously replicable success of Kaira. After two Five Year Plans and much pondering, the Planning Commission mystifyingly could not produce a workable plan on the lines of Kaira. The planners did not view the scarcity as a major health issue nor did they see the potential for enhancing milk production as an instrument to raise the income of subsistence farmers.

Indeed, from the First Plan through the Fourth Plan, the scarcity of milk was seen largely as an urban problem and milk schemes were instituted accordingly. The first to be set up was the Delhi Milk Scheme (DMS) in 1959 and was followed by several others in different parts of India. All these milk schemes were ill-conceived, in both the logistics of their supplies and the business model.

Buffaloes and cows were moved from the hinterland to the city. Milk was procured from cattle sheds located in and around the city. Cattle which had stopped lactating were either sent to the slaughterhouse or let loose to fend for themselves. Every year, new animals were moved to cattle sheds in the city. It didn't occur to the planners that just as villages supplied cities with vegetables on a daily basis, milk too could reach cities on wheels instead of on hooves.

The business model was worse than the logistics. Milk was procured from the city sheds at a price, and overheads like collection, transportation, storage, bottling and administrative costs were loaded on to the balance sheets of the schemes. In places like Delhi, milk was then supplied at a subsidy. Unsurprisingly, the schemes ran into losses. The confounding problem of high supply in the winter and low supply in the summer resulted in the economics going awry. The bureaucracy found a solution that was worse than the problem. The milk schemes began importing milk powder to augment supplies but no effort was made to process and store the produce when there was an excess of supply. All the bureaucrats had to do was to visit Anand and copy what was being done at the Kaira Cooperative but of course none of them did.

The country's dependence on milk powder imports grew. During the fifties and the sixties India was importing over 60,000 tons of milk powder every year, paying for it with precious foreign exchange. The cheaply priced imported powder played havoc with the economics of domestic production as there was no incentive for the farmer to invest and produce. India needed to put in place a system that made it viable for the cattle owner to invest money. If a farmer who owned three buffaloes was able to cover his costs and earn a small profit, he would be incentivized to not just invest in inputs to improve yield, but also to buy the fourth buffalo. However, cheap imports kept prices low and prevented this from happening. Meanwhile, loan schemes to enable cattle purchase were hijacked, often by those who didn't pay back the money they had drawn. The honest were thus crippled by the dishonesty of politically sponsored borrowers.

The Planning Commission and the Department of Agriculture chanted endlessly about vaccines, fodder, Jersey semen and other technical issues. A programme called the Intensive Cattle Development Project to upgrade cattle quality through artificial insemination failed because of a unique circumstance. For some strange reason, cattle policy was dictated by the Go-Samvardhan Society, a not-for-profit agency of which the animal husbandry commissioner was secretary. It laid down fatwas which bordered on the ridiculous. Cross-breeding of indigenous cattle with high-yield breeds was banned and the breeding of buffaloes was discouraged. Buffaloes are cheaper to maintain and they give more milk. Preserving indigenous breeds and the need to hike milk output are not competing goals. But that is how it was seen then; the economics didn't matter, irrational politics did. The farmer was denied the opportunity to better his life;, families were being denied milk. Kaira and Amul succeeded because Kurien insulated the cooperative from irrationality; that sort of logic was missing at the national level.

India had to wait till 1967 for an injection of rationality into the national process. B. Sivaraman was made agriculture secretary.

Sivaraman, who later played a role in the Green Revolution, drew the attention of Jagjivan Ram, then the minister for agriculture and food, to the backward policies being enforced by the Go-Samvardhan Society. Ram put an end to the Society's influence and thus began the programme of cattle upgradation nationally.

By 1967, political idiocy and social obscurantism had wrecked the dairy sector. Milk production of 17 million metric tons (MMT) in 1950 rose to just 21.2 MMT after three Five Year Plans. In 1952, 74 per cent of the demand for milk and milk products was met through imports. In 1967, some fifteen years later, as much as 55 per cent of the demand was fulfilled by imports. The proportion of imports may seem to have dropped over time but actually—given the rise in demand—India was importing more and more milk and powder. The dairy development programme of the Government of India was a mess of curdled schemes.

The irony is that the government didn't need to invent a plan, it just needed to follow the successful Kaira model engineered by Kurien. It did not.

The idea of cooperatives was being practised internationally. Major milk-producing countries in the world owed their success to farmers' cooperatives. The dairy industry in New Zealand migrated to the cooperative system as early as 1871. By the start of the 1900s, the majority of dairy factories were owned by cooperatives. As exports grew, the New Zealand government merged over 200 cooperatives making it easier to introduce technology and apply the economies of scale to the business. The New Zealand Dairy Board, as a result, became one of the largest players in the world.

Elsewhere too, cooperatives were the chosen vehicle for higher output and the empowerment of farmers. Belgium, the Netherlands, Ireland, Germany, Finland and Denmark all boasted cooperatives which owned dairies. In Denmark the first cooperatives and creameries were established in the county of Ribe in 1882. Spurred by the success of their Danish neighbours, Dutch farmers adopted the idea. Cooperatives were not uncommon in the US either. The first American cooperative was a creamery built at Goshen in Connecticut in 1810. By 1949, when Kurien reached Anand, there were 2,072 dairy cooperatives in the US which accounted for over 50 per cent of milk and milk products produced.

There is a very vital reason for the success of cooperatives. Cooperatives enable farmers to extract special privileges from governments. Whether in New Zealand, Belgium or France, cooperatives flex their social muscle to dictate policy. By virtue of being a peoples' collective and the fact that they address the issues of the largest constituency—farmers plus consumers—no political formation dares refuse them.

The Kaira Cooperative too commanded clout. Over a period of time Anand became a must-visit pilgrimage site for development economists, proactive bureaucrats and important political figures. Nehru visited Anand twice. Indira Gandhi, Rajendra Prasad, K. M. Munshi, Y. B. Chavan, TTK and C. Subramaniam also came in order to understand the miracle that Kurien had wrought. TTK, scion of a famous business family from Chennai, recognized the value of the enterprise that had been installed at Anand. When he left, TTK gave Kurien an IOU. Any time he needed anything, Kurien could call him and it would be done.

Kurien used the IOU when TTK was minister for commerce and industry. When other countries dumped milk powder and butter on to Indian markets, Kurien requested TTK to cut import quotas first by 25 per cent and then to have it restricted to a total of 33 per cent. In an era of foreign exchange scarcity, the cutting of imports helped the country and Amul. When India went to war in 1965, it was Amul which ensured supplies for the armed forces. And when India banned the import of non-essential commodities, TTK asked Kurien to ensure that Amul produced enough.

In 1964, TTK also sought out Kurien to rescue the collapsing Delhi Milk Scheme which sold milk at ₹2 per litre when it cost ₹5 to procure. TTK, along with Minister of Agriculture C. Subramaniam, empowered Kurien to fix the mess. Indeed, he wanted him to personally take over DMS. Kurien declined. Instead, he suggested that DMS be restructured, beginning at the top. The blueprint included the dismantling of the subsidy regime, the ending of rationing and the re-orienting of procurement to match demand. Kurien brought in his crack team to execute this and once done, exited after handing the DMS over to new management.

TEMPLATE OF SUCCESS

At Anand, Kurien constantly innovated, introducing new technology and mechanization to improve efficiency. The approach had its share of critics but the scale of operations at Amul demanded these measures. In October 1964, when a new cattle feed unit was to be inaugurated, Kurien and his team decided that the prime minister should do the honours. The day was pre-ordained, 31 October, Sardar Patel's birthday. Shastri accepted the invitation and informed the cooperative that he would like to spend the evening before the opening mingling with farmers and even spend the night at a farmer's house.

True to his word, Shastri spent 30 October with the farmers of Anand and the next day, inaugurated the unit. Shastri took a tour of the facilities and met Kurien and his team. The prime minister told Kurien that he had come to Anand looking for an answer to a particular poser but had failed to find it. He hoped to understand why Amul was a success and why government-led dairy development in the rest of the country was such a dismal failure. Shastri observed that Kaira had no special qualities to account for its success. Its feed and fodder were inferior to that found elsewhere. The buffaloes in Uttar Pradesh gave more milk than those in Gujarat. The farmers of Punjab worked harder than the farmers of Gujarat. Many of the ideas that had succeeded in Kaira had been tried nationally without delivering the same results.

Kurien told the prime minister that while his observations were on the dot, there was one crucial point he had missed. Amul had a single focus—the benefit of the farmer. Amul owed its success to the institution of the Kaira Cooperative and the way in which it empowered individual farmers. The Amul dairy was owned by the farmers, their elected representatives managed the cooperative, and Kurien, and everyone else, were employees and accountable to them.

Kurien said, 'I told the prime minister that Amul was unique in India but almost all countries with developed dairy systems had followed the cooperative route.'

Shastri realized that this was the template for success and the template was replicable. He asked Kurien to begin work on creating a national grid of 'Amuls' across the country. Shastri told Kurien: 'Make this your mission and whatever you need for it, the government will provide.' Kurien agreed on two conditions: that he would continue to be employed by Amul and that the National Dairy Development Board (NDDB) should be headquartered at Anand. Shastri agreed to both conditions. On his return to New Delhi, Shastri wrote to his ministers and chief ministers announcing the plan to launch Kaira-type cooperatives all over India.

The saga that followed essentially defines what holds India back. Kurien met with Minister for Agriculture C. Subramaniam, in Delhi. Like Shastri, Subramaniam was all for the idea but his department thought differently. Sardar Patel had achieved the monumental task of dismantling 560 princely states to engineer the Republic of India. His successors, however, could not prevent the emergence of satraps and principalities across government departments. The bureaucrats inferred that the creation of the NDDB would render them powerless. Consequently, they set up all manner of roadblocks.

Even the measly ₹30,000 Kurien asked for to set up an office in Anand was denied. Kurien refused to beg and decided that the NDDB would be set up without central funding and that his office would be funded by the Kaira Cooperative. The NDDB was officially registered on 27 September 1965 as a society and placed under the ministry of agriculture. But that didn't stop petty bureaucrats from trying to impede its progress.

One encounter with the Government of Maharashtra is particularly illustrative. Kurien met with the chief minister who was supportive of the idea. He was then sent to the minister for agriculture who arranged a meeting with the milk commissioner. The commissioner asked what his department would run if the farmers owned the dairies. Kurien gave him a presentation on how Amul had succeeded. He showed him how farmers deposited their milk at collection centres managed by the cooperative which then transported the milk to a centralized unit which pasteurized and processed it for distribution. He told them how the farmers employed him, his associates, seventy-five veterinarians, 900 first-aid workers and how 300,000 inseminations took place at the breeding station every year. He concluded by pointing out a very significant fact: Gujarat had no milk commissioner but had surplus milk; Maharashtra had a milk commissioner but no milk.

Kurien and his associates went from state to state, met chief minister after chief minister, many ministers for agriculture and sundry bureaucrats. The general response was cynical and negative. The idea of self-sufficiency threatened the network of patronage fuelled by imports. Moreover, as cooperatives would promote the cause of small and marginal farmers, politicians who were allied with large land-holding farmers were determined to scuttle the idea. Many in the state governments, while mouthing support for the idea, did their best to stall it, as the creation of a monolith of the size envisaged would challenge their suzerainty in the rural political economy.

Most individuals would have thrown in the towel when faced with such institutional resistance. Was he disheartened, depressed, disillusioned? Kurien chuckled, 'I thought, the hell with you guys!' Then, he said sombrely, 'Their resistance made me more determined.'

Kurien realized that one way to overcome resistance was to reject the idea of state funding. NDDB needed seed capital and it was convenient for the babus to deny funding and derail the idea. Thinking out of the box, Kurien turned the idea on its head. He decided that state governments need not fund NDDB. Instead NDDB would fund the state governments to organize cooperative federations. These would then be provided with technical assistance by experts from the Kaira Cooperative. Kurien, assisted by Dalaya and Michael Halse, a Harvard-trained professor visiting IIM Ahmedabad on a Ford Foundation grant, worked on the new blueprint for the NDDB. The idea was to create a supply chain to feed demand at all urban agglomerations just as Amul had done for Bombay. A network of feeder dairies would feed a mother dairy which would supply the city.

The first cut of the idea seemed workable but there was one critical hurdle—the idea needed funding worth ₹650 crore. Among the first funding ideas considered was the use of proceeds earned from the export of meat and hide of slaughtered strays and calves. In hindsight, the expectation that this idea would be accepted or supported by any government was rather naïve. This was after all the country that defined the cliché 'holy cow'.

Kurien's struggle to find funds coincided with a serendipitous event. In 1967-68, global markets were faced with a glut of milk and milk products. The European Economic Commission (EEC) had indicated at the beginning of 1968 that it had a surplus of over 300,000 tons of butter and butter oil besides a huge stock of skimmed milk powder that it was being forced to feed to calves. The EEC was struggling to meet the costs of storage and was willing to sell its stocks at less than cost price. Indeed, the EEC was prepared to donate its surplus milk products to 'needy nations'.

From experience Kurien knew that such charitable impulses were simply the thin end of the wedge of big business seeking to gain a toehold in the Indian market. There were other concerns as well. To start with, free aid—in this case, donated milk powder—could potentially fuel a demand that would later create a need for further imports. More dangerously, the supply of free aid would suppress domestic prices impacting Amul and other milk producers. The premise was not unfounded. As noted in the chapter 'The Hunger Games', food aid under the PL 480 programme from the United States had made agriculture unviable and the government complacent.

There was no doubt that the government would accept the aid given the scarcity, poverty and malnutrition that existed everywhere in the country. Kurien realized that there was opportunity in the challenge. His idea was simple: accept the aid and convert it into venture capital. The NDDB could process bulk supplies into retail offerings and sell it profitably. The proceeds could be then used to fund the NDDB which would fund farmers' cooperatives and promote dairy development. This was how the 'Billion Litre Idea' came to be.

Kurien put his thoughts down on paper and sent it to the

Government of India. His idea was that India should approach the EEC and make a direct pitch. The idea was stalled in Delhi by the bureaucrats. His plans were also affected by the changing dynamics of politics. In the sixties, political equations had changed and the Congress was in the throes of a split. Shastri, who had mooted the idea of NDDB, had passed away. Morarji Desai, one of the patron saints of Amul, was on the wrong side of the political divide, at war with Indira Gandhi and with waning influence. TTK was out of government. C. Subramaniam, a supporter of the cooperative movement, had lost the elections in 1967 and was out of the cabinet. Kurien had upset Jagjivan Ram who had succeeded Subramaniam as minister for agriculture with his blunt manner of speaking. And although Indira Gandhi, who had witnessed Nehru embracing and praising Kurien, was supportive, she had her own battles to wage.

The political flux aggravated India's milk crisis. The landscape was littered with failed milk schemes, uneconomical subsidies, dysfunctional programmes and delayed projects. Meanwhile, milk production remained almost stagnant, growing at 0.7 per cent between 1951 and 1968. Per capita availability of milk actually fell from 124 grams in 1950 to 114 grams. International experts on nutrition warned India to ramp up the availability of milk if it intended to prevent mass malnutrition. Five years after the NDDB was set up, the Fourth Five Year Plan (1969-74) barely mentioned the idea of cooperatives. Kurien's 'Billion Litre Idea' to transform the dairy sector seemed doomed to forever languish in the files of the government.

OPERATION FLOOD

Kurien said that he had almost given up the idea after chasing it from department to department throughout 1968. Then, serendipity struck. Kurien remembered the providential intervention vividly. 'One morning, my friend Imdad Ali, who was the inspector general of police, called me and said I must help out. A senior official from the home ministry was in Anand. There was a gap in the programme and to fill time Imdad Ali wanted to know if he could bring him to the dairy. I said, sure bring him along.' The official was L. P. Singh, then the home secretary. Impressed with the Amul experiment, Singh asked why it couldn't be replicated to which Kurien replied, 'Does anybody in Delhi want anything positive to be done for the country?'

For all the bureaucrats who stalled Kurien, this was the one who reset the wheels in motion. Known for his ability to influence the high and mighty, L. P. Singh arranged for a meeting in Delhi with Cabinet Secretary Sivaraman and other officers. It was at this informal meeting that the government was galvanized into action.

Finally, in April 1969, India approached the Food and Agriculture Organization-World Food Programme (FAO-WFP) council to pitch for its surplus dairy products in order to undertake a programme that would ensure milk for its people and empower marginalized farmers. The proposal stated that India would accept the aid and deploy the proceeds to set up cooperatives based on the Anand pattern. A new national grid, a three-tier system of cooperatives—at the village, district and state levels, owned and controlled by farmers—would be set up. Kurien, in his presentation, stipulated that the cooperatives would be managed professionally, would be free of government interference, and would have the right to set purchase and selling prices, hire and fire staff and file for bankruptcy.

Interestingly, India almost lost the bid because of delays. Had it not been for a tip-off from FAO-WFP executives, Pakistan, which was also in the fray, would have walked away with the aid. The Pakistani delegate was instructed by his government to oppose everything that Kurien proposed. Kurien remembered meeting him later. 'He told me, I came here to oppose you. After you spoke, I simply could not. I could not vote for it but my silence is my vote for you.'

After a series of consultations and meetings, India bagged the aid. The agreement for the project was signed in March 1970. The FAO-WFP combine had named its project WFP 618. Kurien renamed it Operation Flood or OF-1 and presented it to the government. The deal was that FAO-WFP would donate 125,000 tons of skimmed milk powder and over 40,000 tons of butter oil to India over a period of five years. This, when sold, would translate to nearly ₹100 crore in cash which would be used as venture capital by the NDDB to set up the national grid. Since the transfer of aid was from government to government, an intermediary organization, the Indian Dairy Corporation (IDC), was set up in Baroda to manage the operation. Kurien would head both the NDDB and the IDC to ensure synergy in thought and action.

The first batch of aid for Operation Flood came through only in July 1970. The milk products sent were old, the butter oil had turned rancid and the skimmed milk powder was mouldy—it wasn't an auspicious beginning. Between 1970 and 1973 Kurien waged a running battle with FAO-WFP executives. A slump in the output of milk products globally had turned the aid pipe into a trickle and almost derailed the programme. Kurien was having none of it, and continued to battle with the FAO and the WFP to ensure quality and consistency in supply.

Kurien and his team had meanwhile set about creating the three-tier cooperative set-up across the country. The idea is best understood if one looks at the Gujarat Cooperative Milk Marketing Federation (GCMMF), the mother ship that now hosts Amul, which was set up in 1973. It consists of 3.18 million dairy farmers who are members of 16,117 village societies. These village societies form a part of seventeen district cooperative milk producers' unions like the Kaira Cooperative who operate under the umbrella of GCMMF and sell their products under the Amul brand. The Kaira District Cooperative Milk Producers' Union began with just two village dairy cooperative societies and 247 litres of milk. In 2011-12, just the GCMMF collected 10.6 million litres of milk every day or 3.88 billion litres of milk through the year and posted a turnover of ₹11,668 crore.

Operation Flood has now won accolades globally. What is not sufficiently recognized and needs to be recorded is that in getting government out of dairy development, Kurien virtually inverted the political thinking of the day. This was, after all, the seventies, the era of socialization and nationalization. It was a decade during which Indian politicians believed government had to be in every business. In that raucous clamour for state control, here was a programme that took back a sector from government management, removed price controls from trade and established the suzerainty of economics over politics.

Operation Flood had its share of critics. While Shastri empowered Kurien, who made it a one-man mission to deliver milk to Indians, his opponents saw it as an enterprise fuelled by private ambition which had to be halted. The NDDB was a threat to many entrepreneurs whose business model was based on the extraction of profits enabled by the failure of public policy and rising private demand. Multinationals queuing up to expand market share in a growing market for milk and baby food were hit. In the fifties India barely produced 3,000 tons of baby food a year, or 3,000,000 one-kilogram tins barely enough to feed, perhaps, 300,000 babies for a year. The rest came via imports. Post OF-1, the cooperatives produced 40,000 tons of baby food. The success of the NDDB ended the trade in import licences and put many babus and their partners out of business. Kurien recognized that the outcry of the few could only be countered by spreading awareness about the benefits possible to the masses. Instead of going the usual PR route, NDDB funded film-maker Shyam Benegal to direct *Manthan* to bring home to Indians the revolution in the making.

Kurien had acquired many enemies in the political firmament by snubbing politicians who wanted him to set up private dairies in their constituencies. Rao Birendra Singh, who was minister for agriculture, questioned the very need for the NDDB and used a news report to order an enquiry into its functioning. In response, Indira Gandhi appointed a committee under L. K. Jha, former RBI governor, who cleared Kurien and heaped him with accolades. Opponents even accused experts in the NDDB of espionage. On 16 May 1985 Rajya Sabha member Y. S. B. Rao asked the home minister if the government was aware of an article in an international publication in March 'on the espionage implicating the NDDB Chairman, Ford Foundation and a UK citizen' and enquired what steps were being taken and if a parliamentary committee was proposed to be set up. The government rubbished the charges.

All through the three phases of Operation Flood, the programme was the subject of intense scrutiny in Parliament. Rajya Sabha member Shamim Hashmi once asked the minister for agriculture if government was aware of the misuse of food aid being received from the WFP and EEC as reported in a newspaper, and if an enquiry was being ordered. Equipment bought or sold was another area critics focused on. Even a computer bought for the computation of demand and costing by the NDDB was the subject of a query.

It was not just the politicians who were so keen on tripping Kurien up. Academics wrote papers arguing that Operation Flood should desist from using mechanization for the production of dairy foods and that these foods be produced by women using traditional kitchen technology. Some critics even suggested that if the programme reached its peak, it would strain India's feeding and grazing capacity. The doubts raised by some of the academics resulted in the EEC and other donors sending representatives, including the Queen of the Netherlands, to India to find out the truth behind the accusations and criticism.

A lesser mortal would have surely been felled by the barrage of attacks. Kurien thrived on them. It did help that the idea had public support and that the NDDB was held up as an institution of tremendous integrity. It also helped that there was uncommon goodwill towards Kurien in certain pockets at the very highest levels of government. Indira Gandhi had first visited Anand with her father and knew of his work. When Minister for Agriculture Rao Birendra Singh continued targeting the NDDB despite Mrs Gandhi's support, he soon found himself out of a job. Every prime minister, from Nehru to Rajiv Gandhi held the idea, the institution and the individual in high regard. All of the goodwill, and his messianic commitment to deliver milk to every Indian home, helped India's Milkman steer his Billion Litre dream.

When Kurien came to Anand in 1949, India was producing around 17 million tons of milk every year. Between 1947 and 1968, milk output grew to barely 21.2 million tons at the rate of 0.4 per cent a year. Post OF-1, between 1970 and 1996, India's milk production shot up from 31 million tons in 1981 to 54 million tons in 1991 and to over 66 million tons in 1996 at the culmination of Operation Flood-3.

To see this growth in another perspective consider the following facts. In the two decades between 1947 and 1968, milk production grew by barely 4 million tons whereas it tripled in the next twenty-five years or so from 22 million tons to 66 million tons. Between 1970 and 1996, the per capita availability of milk shot up from 107 grams per person to 196 grams per person.

Numbers apart, Operation Flood is about the real transformation of lives. Every morning 15 million farmer members, of which 4 million are women, begin their day with renewed hope. Thanks to Operation Flood, millions of small and marginal farmers have been able to increase their incomes: women in these households have been able to stop working as daily wage labourers and children have been able to attend school. The World Bank in 1997 applauded Operation Flood as a home-grown, participatory development programme which had been able to achieve multiple objectives with a single commodity. NDDB now boasts 145,000 village-level societies and covers 346 districts. The societies afford direct employment to 15 million people and indirect employment in the livestock sector to over 22 million people. Today, the many brands that compete with Amul owe their presence in the market to the idea that came out of Kaira and to the success of Operation Flood. And to think that the White Revolution could well have been a revolution India missed.

Verghese Kurien was honoured by many institutions with many titles. But nothing compared with the honour of his actual achievement. When he reached Anand, Kurien was barely twenty-eight and India produced barely 17 million tons of milk. In 2011, when he turned ninety, India produced 121 million tons and became the largest producer of milk in the world. All this because of a man who did not drink milk. The father of India's Milk Revolution 'did not like the taste'.

Verghese Kurien passed away on 9 September 2012. The interaction with him for this book took place in May 2012, perhaps the last interview he gave. At the end of the long conversation, which appeared to greatly energize him, he pointed to a photograph in his living room and said, 'That is Mount Everest.' Then he pointed to a signature on the photograph, 'See the autograph of Tenzing Norgay. I first asked Norgay to sign and then requested Sir Edmund Hillary to do so.

Hillary was about to sign above the signature of Norgay and I told him, "Not above, below." Hillary looked at me and I pointed, yes that is the place, below Norgay.' Kurien always put the 'little man' first—be it the farmer, the Sherpa or the consumer of milk. Further, to him, it was India and Indians first. He has been laid to rest in a part of the country he made his own, a place he had initially wanted to leave—Anand.

In 1947, eight out of ten Indians did not know how to read and write. Half the population lived below the poverty line. The poor did not earn enough and hence sent their children out to work. Denied education, children lost out on opportunities to change their lives. It was a vicious cycle of cause and consequence. State intervention was required, yet governments chose to live in denial. Till the Supreme Court in 2001 directed the setting up of the...

SOUP KITCHEN FOR THE SOUL

15 SEPTEMBER 1982
PAPPAKURICHI, TAMIL NADU

The grounds of the Samayapuram Mariyamman Temple High School were decked out for the big event. The excitement among the students was palpable. Officials of the state government, local MLAs and MPs had spent the previous day and the entire morning checking and reviewing arrangements. They could not afford any snafus, not in the presence of the chief minister.

Draped in a white veshti and shirt, the trademark cap perched on his head revealing just a glimpse of a receding hairline, and dark glasses parked firmly on his aquiline nose, M. G. Ramachandran—MGR to the people at large, chief minister of Tamil Nadu and Thalaivar to his followers—arrived a little before noon to a thunderous welcome from the crowds. After greeting local party officials and his ministers, MGR strode into the pandal.

The students awaiting his arrival were looking forward to a double treat—a glimpse of the star and a meal. As planned by his aides, MGR sat in one of the rows with the children exchanging pleasantries and jokes. On their plates and on the plantain leaf on which MGR was served, was a generous helping of sweet shakkarai pongal, a traditional Tamil festival delicacy, sambhar rice, vegetables, pickles and curd rice. The smiles on the faces of the children enjoying the sweet pongal was reward enough for MGR for he had known hunger as a child.

Born in Kandy in Sri Lanka to magistrate M. Gopala Menon and

Satyabhama, MGR lost his father early. The family moved to Tamil Nadu where his mother was forced to find work with a drama company in Kumbakonam. When the drama company folded up, Satyabhama couldn't feed MGR and his brother, M. G. Chakrapani, every day. She would often lock up the two brothers fearing they would take to begging to feed themselves.

Satyabhama was MGR's inspiration. She brought her children up in great hardship and was a strict disciplinarian. Her constant strictures to the two brothers were: don't lie, don't steal and don't be abusive. MGR never forgot them. Throughout his film and political career he made sure that he was seen to be a man who valued these principles above all else. They won him a devoted following. In intensely chauvinistic Tamil Nadu it did not matter that he was not a native son. He drank kanji, sipped chuku-kapi and relished ragi dosai. He was one of their own.

The date MGR had picked for his meal with poor schoolchildren was symbolic. It was the seventy-fifth birthday of C. N. Annadurai, the patron saint of the Anna Dravida Munnetra Kazhagam (ADMK), the political party MGR belonged to. The location, Pappakurichi in Tiruchchirappalli district, was carefully chosen as well—Pappakurichi means 'home of the child' in Tamil. As he sat with the children in Pappakurichi, nearly 300 kilometres away in Madras, J. Jayalalitha (now Jayalalithaa)—the heroine of one of MGR's best-known movies *Annam Itta Kai* (1972) which translates literally as 'the hand that fed', and propaganda secretary of the party—sat down at Gopalapuram Corporation playground with over 100 school girls to launch the programme. Several other ministers across the state did the same. Much like the characters he played in movies, MGR in real life was a devout believer in paternal populism. The meal he shared with the children signalled the launch of the biggest welfare scheme launched by any state in India.

Under the scheme, the state would—with an overall outlay of ₹120 crore—feed, everyday at noon, over 6 million school children between the ages of two and fifteen in over 20,000 child welfare centres and over 35,000 schools across Tamil Nadu. The scheme would not only fund the feeding of millions of poor children, it would also provide employment to over 200,000 people who would cook for and feed the children. It was easily the largest employment-generating idea of its time. It was also the intervention the circumstances of illiteracy and poverty demanded.

The free mid-day meal scheme was not exactly an original idea. It had been tested globally, originating in France where writer Victor Hugo campaigned for free meals to be provided in schools and pioneered its inception in 1865. By 1868, all communities in France were instructed by government edict that they would need to establish a School Fund Committee to provide meals to poor and needy children. Each meal should provide 1,200 calories of nutrition—this translated into one meat dish or eggs, cheese and milk. Getting poor children into schools was a concern in Japan too, where a school lunch scheme was instituted as early as 1899.

In Britain, the institution of free meals was the consequence of that country's quest to universalize education. Britain passed the Education Acts of 1870 and 1880 which made it compulsory for all children to be educated regardless of their parents' wishes or objections. Soon enough, the government discovered that compulsory education made children vulnerable to hunger as they were no longer available to work and add their wages to family incomes. Political parties began to campaign for universal free school meals. In 1904, the Bradford City Council became the first to introduce free school meals. In 1906, the Education (Provision of Meals) Act enabled councils to provide meals to those unable to fend for themselves. Implementation, though, was patchy as it was not obligatory. It wasn't until 1944, when Britain was faced with rising cases of rickets fuelled by malnutrition, that the authorities compelled schools to feed all the children who attended them.

In India, the earliest instance of a formal mid-day meal scheme for children was conceptualized and pioneered in 1923 by the Justice Party which ran the Madras Municipal Corporation. Under the scheme, school children from the weaker sections of society were offered a free cooked meal. The idea was also implemented in the late twenties in schools run by Ram Narayan Singh, the raja of Koriya, one of the thirty-six princely states that made up Chhattisgarh. In 1928, the Keshav Academy of Calcutta provided mid-day tiffin for four annas per child per month. In 1942, some schools in the Bombay Presidency started a mid-day meal scheme for poor students. In 1946, schools in Bangalore provided cooked rice and yoghurt to children and 3 kilograms of wheat every month to students with more than 80 per cent attendance. As in Britain, these early efforts at mitigating hunger were funded through charity and by donations from philanthropists. These efforts didn't last and the schemes were discontinued as new regimes came in and the philanthropic impulse petered out.

The twin problems of hunger and illiteracy persisted. After independence, as the problem of hunger and malnutrition worsened in the country, it was clear that the State would have to step in to deal with the problem. Making the situation even more vexatious was the problem of illiteracy. The first census of independent India, carried out in 1951, revealed that only 18 per cent of Indians knew how to read and write—73 per cent of Indian men and 91 per cent of women were illiterate. In 1951 only four out of ten children of school-going age—six to ten—were enrolled. By the mid-fifties the ratio inched up and gross enrolment was pegged at 50 per cent. However, a large percentage of the students dropped out after Class V. Only 20 per cent of the boys who enrolled in primary school went on to secondary school. With girls, the situation was worse. If 31 out of 100 girls enrolled for primary school, only six stayed on to study after the age of eleven. Essentially, two out of three boys and four out of five girls dropped out of school. A combination of factors was at play. The most important among them was poverty which led to parents pulling their children out of school—girls to hold the fort while their mothers and other adult women of the household went to work, and boys to add value to the family income.

KAMARAJ HAD A DREAM

The man responsible for embedding the idea of the mid-day meal in Tamil Nadu's sociopolitical milieu, which was later effectively used by MGR, was K. Kamaraj. In 1955, shortly after becoming the chief minister, Kamaraj was touring the interiors of the state. As was his style, Kamaraj was travelling alone in his car with no security, no convoy and no flashing beacon. At a small town called Cheranmahadevi in Tirunelveli district, Kamaraj had to halt at a railway crossing. He got out of the car and watched a herd of cows and goats being tended by two young boys. His immediate thought was that if children were tending to adult chores instead of going to school, they would lose their childhood and the opportunity for an education. He said to the younger boy: 'Why are you herding cattle? Why aren't you going to school?' The young boy was quick with his response: 'If I go to school, will you give me food to eat? I can only eat if I do these chores. And I can only learn if I eat!'

The encounter made Kamaraj sad, especially as he had grown up in a family of modest means and understood what it meant to go without food. His father, Kumaraswami Nadar, a trader, enrolled Kamaraj at the local Nayanar Vidyalaya and later shifted him to the Kshatriya Vidyalaya but the young Kamaraj had to drop out of school to work and supplement the family's income. He entered politics through the freedom movement, participating in the Vedaranyam Salt Satyagraha where he was arrested and sent to Alipore Jail in Calcutta. Although a school dropout, Kamaraj had an unusually sharp grasp of the complex issues that haunted the political economy. His first missive to his cabinet after taking over on 13 April 1954 was short and direct: 'Let us face the problem. Don't evade the issue, find a solution. However small your solution, people will be happy that you did something.' It was his dream that every boy and girl in the state should be able to study at least till 'final school' without having to pay fees or worry about food.

On his return to Madras, he got his colleagues and a team of officials to put their minds together. It took the team a while to engineer a solution to address the twin concerns of improving school enrolment and feeding hungry children. In July 1956, Kamaraj launched a mid-day meal scheme in Tamil Nadu. It was deemed a voluntary scheme and launched under the guidance of the then director of public instruction. Initially, the idea was to run it as a public-private partnership whereby schools would garner donations from philanthropists and charitable institutions and use them to fund the scheme. To start with, children from Classes I to VIII were to be fed for 200 days a year.

The idea was beset by troubles from its inception. Contributions were hard to come by and teachers had to run around for donations. In 1957, the government set up a provision so that the scheme could be partially funded. Under the modified scheme, schools were given 6 paise and were expected to raise—mostly from local bodies and communities—4 paise to deliver succour worth 10 paise per student. To start with, a rice meal was provided every day to 200,000 children in elementary schools.

Interestingly, Kamaraj's mission coincided with the escalation of concern in the developed world about the magnitude of hunger and poverty in India. It may be recalled that since independence, India had accepted all manner of foreign aid to deal with the situation. In 1961, the Cooperative for Assistance and Relief Everywhere (CARE), an American charity, pitched in with aid to boost the idea. Other agencies offered skimmed milk powder and free food grains. The Government of Tamil Nadu was then able to combine the resources of the state and charity from abroad to expand the programme to cover 2 million children in 30,000 schools across the state.

After Kamaraj left government in 1963, the state continued with the scheme but modified it in 1967. A centralized system of kitchens was set up and food was packed and delivered to schools. However, the programme was still beset with the problems of logistics, funding and implementation. Teachers had to often step in to raise funds and school principals, who were responsible for the implementation of the programme, wasted much time trying to make the scheme work in their institutions. There was also the issue of matching demand and supply and sundry other problems.

Despite all its flaws, it was undeniable that Kamaraj's scheme had made an impact on student enrolment rates in the state. It had also succeeded in alleviating hunger and malnutrition among school-going children to an extent. But it did not grow into a major initiative nor did it have an impact outside the state. Nationally, India continued to grapple with the problem of enrolment and a high dropout rate. India's founding fathers decided that the State would provide free and compulsory education to all children up to the age of fourteen by 1960. It was not to be. Indeed, in 1961, when the universalization of education was to have been achieved, only 28 per cent of Indians were literate, and 60 per cent of Indian men and 85 per cent of women were illiterate. Most of them were out working and adding to family incomes. A decade later, in 1971, barely three out of ten Indians could read and write; India had a literacy rate of 34.45 per cent. Only four out of ten boys and two out of ten girls reached secondary school.

Worst of all, the country's track record, when it came to health and nutrition, three decades after independence, was at par with the poorest countries of the world. A survey conducted in 1978 by the National Nutrition Monitoring Bureau (NNMB) found that 85 per cent of the children it surveyed, aged between one to five years, weighed lower than the prescribed minimum standards and 68 per cent were stunted in height. Studies by the National Institute of Nutrition, Hyderabad, showed that 63 per cent of Indian children below the age of three and 45 per cent between the ages of three and five suffered from anaemia.

Steps had, of course, been taken to deal with the problem. Beginning with the Fourth Five Year Plan (1969-74), the Government of India had begun initiatives to bridge the nutrition deficit and ramp up school enrolment. In August 1974, a National Policy for Children was released, incorporating the supplementary feeding of preschool children under the Fifth Plan with targets for elementary and adult education. Since then, public feeding programmes had expanded to reach over 20 million children. Aid agencies and civil society pitched in to help. In the late seventies, CARE and the United Nations Children's Fund (UNICEF) funded programmes to feed 13 million children in primary schools.

But the initiatives scarcely made a significant contribution to resolving the problem. There were far too many programmes, they were spread too thin, were badly implemented and often collided with each other. Thanks to the lack of coordination, they didn't have the synergy required to deliver a multiplier effect. Census data reveals that in the seventies, infant mortality in rural areas was as high as 130 per thousand births. In other words, thirteen out of every 100 children born died in infancy, three out of ten deaths were that of an infant and, most tragically, every second death was that of a child between the ages of one and four.

RECLAIMING POLITICAL CAPITAL

In many ways, Tamil Nadu was worse off than many other states. In 1981, over 52 per cent of the population in Tamil Nadu lived below the poverty line. MGR didn't need statistics to recognize the poverty and the suffering. As a politician who drew his strength from the masses, he could, perhaps, sense those things better than most. Moreover, his exposure to hunger and poverty in childhood had made him acutely sensitive to the problem.

MGR was also haunted by his failure to keep a promise he had made to the people. One of the biggest reasons for his victory in the elections of 1977 was the word he had given to the women of Tamil Nadu that he would free their men from the oppression of alcoholism. For MGR there was no distinction between what he said in his films and what he said to people at political rallies. The script was often the same and the mode of delivery just as powerful. After his party split from the DMK in 1972, MGR used his popularity as a movie superstar to good effect in the political arena. He promised he would come down hard on arrack and toddy bootleggers, and while he did his best to deliver, he was fighting a losing battle. Prohibition required action against both bootleggers and drinkers. When their menfolk were arrested, the women often had to borrow money, even pawn family silver, to bail out the principal wage earner of the family. At public meetings, MGR was besieged by women who petitioned him for the release of the men incarcerated under prohibition. MGR realized he was being failed by the system. In June 1981, MGR admitted defeat and allowed the sale of arrack and toddy.

The failure resulted in loss of face and political capital. MGR wondered how he could make good on the promise he had made to women voters, his biggest support base. It struck him that he must compensate the family, give back what seemed to have been taken away. The reparation, he decided, would be made to children through a mid-day meal scheme. He called for a meeting of his officials to discuss the idea some time in the summer of 1982. He told them that he wanted to universalize the mid-day meal scheme, renaming it the Nutritious Mid-day Meal Scheme, and have it funded entirely by the state. The first reaction of his officials was that the scheme was too big, too expensive and not implementable. The heads of the finance, health, education and civil supplies departments concluded that it was impractical.

MGR had called the meeting just before noon to ensure the officials went hungry through the afternoon. Sensing their discomfort, he told them, 'If you can't cope with missing one meal, how can you ignore the plight of starving children?' He won the day.

MGR announced a mid-day meal scheme, formally called the Chief Minister's Nutritious Noon-Meals Programme, on 1 July 1982. It was initially meant to be implemented only in child welfare centres for preschool children between the ages of two to five and primary school children between the ages of five to nine. It then occurred to MGR that the idea had much larger political potential. It was then decided that the scheme would be officially launched on the seventy-fifth birthday of Annadurai; it would cover the entire state and cater to all children between the ages of two and fifteen. Each centre would be manned by a staff of three—a child welfare officer and two assistants. This meant that teachers and principals would be free to teach. Each centre would be equipped with utensils, plates and cutlery worth ₹750 to ensure that food was served hygienically. The staff at the centres would be trained by experts and hygiene would be of paramount importance.

The blueprint specified that the teaching staff of the school would have no role to play in the scheme and the programme would be monitored by parents and local community leaders. The centres would be under the overall supervision of the block development officer. Food grains would be supplied directly by the Civil Supplies Department and the scheme itself would be under the purview of the Social

Welfare Department. The scheme was not without its curiosities. The government directed each centre to grow one drumstick tree, one gooseberry tree, one mango tree, two papaya and two coconut trees—the produce from the trees were to be used to enhance the nutritional content of the meals provided.

Predictably, there was criticism of the scheme. The Opposition alleged that MGR, by naming the programme the Chief Minister's Nutritious Noon-Meals Programme, was using it to promote himself at the government's expense. Economists and sociologists also criticized the scheme dubbing it morally hazardous as it created entitlements without obligation. They also said the plan would be as inflationary as it was unproductive. The Opposition declared that the only beneficiaries of the scheme would be traders of grains and food articles.

A major hurdle was created by the fact that there was no allocation for the programme in the budget. And how could there be? The scheme was born not by design but by chance as MGR struggled for a response to address the loss of face he had suffered. The idea finds no mention in his party's 1977 or 1980 election manifestos or campaigns. Till as late as the beginning of 1982 there was no discussion about it within the party or in the government.

It was estimated the scheme would cost the government over ₹120 crore. MGR devised a stopgap method to finance it by setting up the Chief Minister's Nutritious Noon-Meals Programme Fund—funded by a day's salary from MLAs, government workers and others—to create an initial corpus of ₹20 crore to get the programme started. Soon, though, MGR did not have to worry about funding. After the relaxation on prohibition, revenue from duties on alcohol shot up from ₹8 crore or so in 1981 to over ₹110 crore in 1982 providing enough to get the scheme going.

Initially, like the Opposition, the media scoffed at the idea. Many publications wrote off the scheme as a publicity stunt. Then *The Indian Express*—not known to be a pro-establishment paper—sent reporters from its various editions in Tamil Nadu into villages to assess the impact of the scheme. Interviews conducted with students, teachers and parents established that the mid-day meal scheme was being implemented properly, and it was being received well. Soon enough, cynicism gave way to a sense of celebration and pride. There was no doubt that the scheme was—to use a phrase from the film world—a hit from the moment it was released.

To MGR the programme stood for political penance and a genuine desire to address hunger, which is why he located it in the Social Welfare Department and not in the Department of Education. But there was no disputing the impact it had on education, particularly enrolment. According to studies conducted two months after the scheme was launched, enrolment in primary schools across Tamil Nadu shot up—by one estimate 2 million additional children enrolled in schools—and truancy or absenteeism among students dropped by over 80 per cent.

While there was no assurance that attendance would translate into education, it was clear that a large number of children were being saved from child labour. In a sense, the scheme helped the whole family—every child fed was an additional subsidy to the household. Another interesting facet of the scheme was that every Thursday—health day—children were weighed, measured and given a medical check-up. The government claimed that children had gained weight and that there was a drop in deficiency diseases and anaemia. It cost just 45 paise per day to deliver a child from hunger, offer it hope and a shot at the future.

The mid-day meal scheme successfully combined health, nutrition and education and, perhaps, helped family planning as a collateral benefit. After it took off, a World Bank appraisal report revealed that infant mortality rates for Tamil Nadu were 20 per cent lower than the rest of India, two-thirds of infants in the state had completed the necessary immunizations and the death rate in 1986 for children in the ages 0-4 had come down to 25 per cent. Moreover, in 1987, the birth rate in Tamil Nadu was lower at 23 per 1,000 people against the national average of 32 per 1,000 people.

Four months after the scheme was launched, Jayalalithaa unleashed a blitzkrieg of publicity. In a signed article in the January 1983 issue of *The Illustrated Weekly of India*, she claimed that the scheme, run through 62,852 centres, was feeding 6,627,643 children. The scheme had resulted in an additional 263,000 students enrolling into schools, which was over double the national target set by the Planning Commission. She wrote, 'It is no less noble than the work done by Mother Teresa which won her the Nobel Prize for Peace in 1979. Here, in fact, is the most deserving contender for the Nobel Prize in the same category: MGR, Chief Minister of Tamil Nadu.'

There is no doubt that the scheme bestowed tremendous benefits on the people who engineered it. The political class was quick to realize this. MGR had a troubled relationship with the Congress because of his friendship with Morarji Desai during the Janata Party regime. Soon after Indira Gandhi returned to power in 1980, the MGR regime was dismissed by the Centre. MGR was quick to mend fences with the Congress—Indira Gandhi was the first to be briefed about the successful mid-day meal scheme.

Soon after the scheme was launched, he claimed that the prime minister was among the first people to evince interest in the scheme, its logistics and funding. More than the success of additional enrolment, MGR was keen to project the social engineering that the scheme had achieved. The mid-day meal scheme, he told Indira Gandhi, had remarkable success in narrowing social differences among children. The fact that food cooked by 27,000 women from the scheduled castes was being served to and eaten by children of all castes in a state riven by caste differences naturally found pride of place in the propaganda put out by the government.

Other politicians, too, were quick to take notice of the scheme's success. In neighbouring Andhra Pradesh, another former film star, N. T. Rama Rao, had launched a new party, the Telugu Desam Party (TDP). Most of its leaders were former members of the Swatantra Party, the Janata Party and the Socialist Party. The platform that the TDP used was its opposition to the 'eunuch leadership' of Congress and its failure to deal with the problems of the state.

NTR's election campaign began with a bang. He declared that every inch of India was ruled by the states and that the Centre was a conceptual myth. He alleged that Congress had reduced the states of India to glorified municipalities and regional Congress leaders to eunuchs. He argued for more powers to be given to the state and a restoration of Telugu pride. NTR's speeches, delivered in his trademark theatrical style, found audiences but lacked a solid message and gave TDP no traction.

The resounding success of the mid-day meal scheme in Tamil Nadu and the doctrine of paternal populism made NTR realize that while promoting regional pride was a good idea, the path to electoral success lay in the promise to address hunger. A few weeks before the polls he added two important promises to his manifesto. He promised rice to all at ₹2 per kilogram and, more importantly, announced that he would set up a mid-day meal scheme for all students along the lines of the programme in Tamil Nadu. Andhra Pradesh went to polls on 5 January 1983 and NTR's little recognized party swept the polls. His party polled 46.8 per cent of the votes and won 203 seats. The Congress recorded its worst performance winning only sixty out of the 293 seats.

Meanwhile, the scheme ran into trouble in Tamil Nadu. The threat of drought looming over parts of the country in 1983-84 created a shortfall of food grains. Short of supplies, the ministry of agriculture objected to the mid-day meal scheme and the demand for additional food grain from Tamil Nadu. MGR's government engaged in a series of battles with the Centre. MGR's claim that Indira Gandhi had applauded the idea didn't matter. Rao Birendra Singh, then minister for agriculture, alleged that Tamil Nadu was not serious about food management and had not contributed its surplus to the central pool. And because Madras had committed to the mid-day meal scheme without the clearance of the Centre, Delhi was not obliged to help Tamil Nadu. The Centre threatened to cut supplies unless the scheme was curtailed. Eventually, following public pressure and issues of federalism raised by other chief ministers, Rao Birendra Singh backed off. The Centre relented and the supply of grain continued.

Even though the scheme lost steam in Tamil Nadu, by the mid-eighties, it was clear that it had caught the imagination of the political class. Other states—Karnataka and Gujarat, for instance—too showed interest in the idea. Not surprisingly, the discourse on the need to implement the idea on a national scale found its way on to the agenda of the National Development Council (NDC). In 1985, the thirty-eighth meeting of the NDC was held in Delhi on 8 and 9 November. At the meeting, which was chaired by Rajiv Gandhi, chief minister after chief minister highlighted the twin benefits of the mid-day meal scheme—addressing hunger and improving enrolment, and demanded its implementation at the national level. Assam Chief Minister Hiteshwar Saikia said his state was committed to taking up the mid-day meal scheme and wanted central funding. Chief Minister Amarsinh Chaudhari announced that Gujarat had started the mid-day meal programme and wanted it to be part of the Seventh Five Year Plan (1985-90) so that central funding could be allocated for it. West Bengal Chief Minister Jyoti Basu wanted emphasis to be placed on achieving universal literacy in the shortest time and suggested the use of available food grain stocks for a national mid-day meal programme. The chorus was repeated yet again in 1989 at the NDC meeting. Oddly enough and especially given his mother's interest in MGR's scheme, Rajiv Gandhi and his government didn't seem too keen to push the programme nationally.

Notwithstanding the atheism in Delhi, state governments had begun to implement their own versions of the programme with local funding and modifications that suited their particular needs. Often, the schemes would be restricted to tribal children and students from the scheduled castes. Some states limited it to rural areas, others to students in elementary and primary school. Notwithstanding the restrictions, there was no doubt that the revolution triggered in Madras by the Puratchi Thalaivar—the revolutionary leader—was on the march.

By 1990-91, the number of states implementing the mid-day meal programme in bits and pieces with their own resources had increased to twelve. These included Tamil Nadu, Goa, Gujarat, Kerala, Madhya Pradesh, Maharashtra, Meghalaya, Mizoram, Nagaland, Sikkim, Tripura and Uttar Pradesh. Karnataka, Orissa and West Bengal were implementing the programme by combining the resources of the state with international assistance. Rajasthan and Andhra Pradesh instituted models in which the programme was funded entirely by international agencies. In all these states there was clear evidence that the intervention was delivering results on three counts—increased enrolment in schools, lower dropout rates and improvement in the parameters of nutrition.

As the number of states implementing the scheme increased, the demand for a national mid-day meal scheme reached Parliament. A queue of MPs raised questions about when the Centre was planning to adopt the idea. However, the Centre, it seemed, had no intention of doing so, at least till 1995. On 13 March 1992, Narreddy Thulasi Reddy, an MP from Andhra Pradesh, asked the government if 'there [was] any proposal to introduce a national mid-day meal scheme for elementary schools throughout the country' and sought 'details thereof and if not, reasons therefore'. Answering the question, Minister for Human Resource Development, Arjun Singh, said, 'There is at present no concrete proposal to implement a mid-day meal programme for elementary school children throughout the country.' Worse, the government didn't find it necessary to explain itself. His answer to the supplementary question was that the need for one 'does not arise'.

The refusal of the central government to accept the need for change and restructuring ignored the reality across the country, notwithstanding the fact that government knew all too well how serious the problem was. A study conducted in 1990 by development economist Nirmala Murthy and others for the World Bank titled *How Well Do India's Social Sector Programmes Serve the Poor?* delivered a devastating critique of the existing state of affairs. The figures quoted in the study were horrifying. 'Over 30 per cent of the children have low birth weight (less than 2500 gm), over 80 per cent of the pregnant women suffered from severe anaemia and 70 per cent of the preschool children suffer from growth retardation and nutrition morbidity.' A comparison of two major studies conducted twenty years apart—by the Indian Council of Medical Research in 1956-57 and one by the National Nutrition Monitoring Bureau in 1974-79—showed no change in the growth retardation rates of poor children. The study observed that 'despite the massive expansion of physical facilities, incremental policy reforms and successive programme improvements, the overall performance of the education, health and nutrition services in relation to the poor is low'.

HISTORY OF NEGLECT

In 1992, when Arjun Singh disabused Thulasi Reddy of hope and declared there was no national plan for a mid-day meal scheme, India had been independent for forty-five years. India's population was 850 million. Every second person in the country was illiterate. Over 300 million—or every third person—were living below the poverty line. The sheer scale of India's population is often used as an alibi for failure. Yet it is a stark truth that China, with a much bigger population, had a literacy rate of 78 per cent in 1980.

It is also argued that India is too poor to invest in human development. Thailand and Indonesia, with much smaller economies and lesser resources, shamed India with literacy rates of 94 per cent and 84 per cent in 1980. That this is not a question of resources is proved by the success of Kerala. Every decade, Kerala has outdone not just the rest of India but also China. And the success it has shown is best illustrated by female literacy. In 1981, Kerala boasted literacy figures of 76 per cent for women vis-à-vis 51 per cent for China and 30 per cent for the rest of India. In 1991, literacy among women was 86 per cent in Kerala, 39 per cent in the rest of India and 68 per cent in China.

The value of education as a weapon to eradicate poverty was well acknowledged. A series of committees emphasized the need for universalizing education in India. Sir Charles Wood's Despatch on Education of 1854, the Hunter Commission in 1902, the Sir Philip Hartog Committee in 1929, the Sapru Committee in 1934 and the Abbott Wood Committee in 1936 all studied the landscape of education and made wide-ranging recommendations, ranging from teaching English in schools to introducing vocational courses and colleges to upgrading universities. The concept of free and compulsory education wasn't alien either. The Zakir Hussain Committee, in 1937, emphasized that free and compulsory education should be provided for at least the first seven years to all children. It was this report that led to prolonged debate and discussion before the idea of free and compulsory education could find its way into the Directive Principles of State Policy. The committees that were set up soon after independence also proved that the importance of education was not lost on the founding fathers of the nation. The Radhakrishnan Committee in 1948 and the Lakshmanswami Mudaliar Commission in 1952 suggested an increase in investment and the creation of capacity to implement the promise made by the Constitution. The much-quoted Kothari Commission on Education Reforms in 1986 and the Yashpal Committee in 1993 reviewed education and examined why the promises made by the earlier committees had not been fulfilled.

However, despite the awareness and the noble intentions, education in India fumbled and stumbled from committees to commissions, from schemes to programmes. In 1976, responsibility, too, was shifted wholesale—education was moved to the concurrent list of the Constitution, making the states equally responsible for it along with the Centre. The National Policy on Education, first promulgated in 1986, suggested programmes to help states build teaching capacity. The evocatively titled Operation Blackboard that was started in 1987 was aimed at providing grants for classrooms, hiring teachers and acquiring teaching aids to promote primary education, particularly in rural India. This was followed up with a District Institute of Educational Training Programme set up in 1988 to finance the creation of institutes of education training in rural districts. The Total Literacy Campaign that was overseen by the National Literacy Mission provided grants to districts to push adult literacy.

International agencies, too, pitched in with new programmes between 1980 and 1990. A programme funded by the British Overseas Development Administration conducted the Andhra Pradesh Primary Education Project; the Dutch government funded the Mahila Samakhya in Karnataka, Uttar Pradesh and Gujarat; UNICEF ran the Bihar Education Project and the World Bank funded the UP Basic Education Project. All of these were attempts to redress a failed promise.

India's primary education system was described in a 1996 World Bank report as 'a glass two-thirds full and one-third empty'. Of 105 million children between the ages of six to ten, 67 million went to school and one-third, or 33 million—roughly the population of Argentina in 1990—did not attend school. Worse, about 75 per cent of the children who weren't attending school belonged to the poorest states of Andhra Pradesh, Bihar, Madhya Pradesh, Rajasthan, Uttar Pradesh and West Bengal. Half of all girls between the ages of five and fourteen did not attend school. And where poverty was at its deepest, illiteracy was at its highest—only 18 per cent of the women in Bihar and 21 per cent in Uttar Pradesh were literate.

Lack of money is often cited as a reason for the failure of the education system in India. But the issue isn't so much about availability as it is about allocation. If Kerala is a shining example of success, it is simply because it allocates 6-plus per cent of government spend on education. Even a small country like Sri Lanka found reason to commit over 1 per cent of its GDP on direct nutrition programmes focusing simultaneously on health and education for women. India, in contrast, still spends barely 0.19 per cent of its GDP on direct nutrition programmes.

Leaving aside all talk of ratios or of proportions, it can also be argued that India, simply, ignored the need to spend money on education for its poorest citizens. And what was the cost of feeding and getting one child into school? In 1982, it cost the Government of Tamil Nadu barely 45 paise per child per day. Studies by the World Bank and UNICEF have established that it costs barely $10 per child per year. India in the nineties had nearly 300 million children in the 0–14 age bracket so it wouldn't have cost more than ₹3,000 crore to fund a mid-day meal scheme that would have achieved multiple goals— addressed malnutrition, increased enrolment and curbed dropouts.

When India became a republic and adopted the Constitution, the founding fathers made explicit commitments to the welfare of children. In the Directive Principles of State Policy, Article 45 stated: 'The State shall endeavour to provide, within a period of ten years from the commencement of this Constitution, for free and compulsory education for all children until they complete the age of fourteen years.' Article 24 says: 'No child below the age of fourteen years shall be employed to work…' Article 39 stipulates that the 'State shall, in particular, direct its policy towards securing…that the tender age of children [is] not abused and that citizens are not forced by economic necessity to enter avocations unsuited to their age or strength.' In 1991, one-third of all children in the 6-14 age bracket didn't attend school and nearly 15 million were forced into employment.

Successive judgements by the Supreme Court since as early as 1972 exposed the chasm between the commitment made by the Constitution and the reality that prevailed in India. The apex court made clear that a right is a right only when the State enabled its delivery to the entitled. It said that any theory of freedom of expression must account for justice and equality and 'the right of the public to education [arose] from the affirmative duty cast on the government by the directive principles'. In 1982, the Supreme Court stated explicitly that 'rights which are sought to be created in pursuance of the Directive Principles of State Policy essentially require active intervention of the State'. This was followed by another judgement in 1993 in which the Supreme Court ruled that 'citizens of the country have a fundamental right to education'.

Apart from repeated interventions by the Supreme Court, there had been plenty of legislation to promote free and compulsory education. The Andhra Pradesh Education Act 1982, the Assam Elementary Education Act 1974, the Bihar Primary Education Act 1959, the Goa Compulsory Elementary Education Act 1995, the Gujarat Compulsory Primary Education Act 1961, the Punjab Primary Education Act 1960, the Himachal Pradesh Compulsory Primary Education Act 1954, the Jammu and Kashmir Education Act 1984, the Karnataka Education Act 1983, the Kerala Education Act 1958, the Madhya Pradesh Primary Education Act 1961, the Bombay Primary Education Act 1947, the Rajasthan Primary Education Act 1964, the Sikkim Primary Education Act 2000, the United Provinces Primary Education Act 1919, 1926 and 1950, the West Bengal Primary Education Act 1973 and the Delhi Primary Education Act 1960 were all legislated with a common aim. All legislation failed because of the same reasons—lack of political will and lack of a committed bureaucracy.

In what can only be described as criminal apathy, successive governments at the Centre and the states refused to act despite knowing about the mid-day meal scheme, an instrument which had a proven track record in creating the right conditions for the fulfilment of the twin objectives of the government—curbing malnutrition and enforcing free education. It is the duty of the State to enable a citizen to free himself from hunger and illiteracy but a strange elitism denied him this freedom.

Amartya Sen put this elitism in perspective in 1982. In a piece that reviewed three decades of planning, he wrote: 'India's approach to social services has been sadly unimaginative and breathtakingly conservative. That conservatism happens to fit quite well with the elitist character of Indian society and politics.' Analysing the spectre of hunger and illiteracy he said that 'the strength and weakness of the Indian system are clear. It permits endemic malnutrition and hunger that is not acute as long as these happen quietly. It permits the injustice of keeping a large majority illiterate while the elite enjoy the benefits of higher education'.

The picture of denial and deprivation is best illustrated by this story. Kayipady is a fishing hamlet in Kerala. In April 1995, the village had 250 children between the ages of five and fourteen. None of them went to school even though the nearest primary school was only 3 kilometres away. To reach the school, the children would have to wade across a river, cross a railway line and then cross a busy highway—not once a day but twice. It was only when a school was established in their village that the parents enrolled them. On 1 July 1995, when the school opened, 185 children aged between five and ten joined. All of them enrolled in Class I. The loss suffered by generations of the children of Kayipady indeed represents the tragedy of India's education policy and programmes.

That dividends accrue from investment in education too is no secret to policymakers. World Bank studies on better performing states firmly establish the connection between education and growth. Every year of education of the labour force improves productivity in industry and in agriculture. In India, the level of schooling for the labour force was barely 1.6 years in 1971 and had crawled to 2.4 years in 1990. Current figures put average years of schooling for the adult labour force in India at 5.1 years.

Studies have established that every year of schooling led to an increase of 15 per cent in output. The emergence of the Asian Tigers owed a great deal to the investment in education by those governments. The point holds true for India too. In 1993, Ashok Mathur studied human capital in 306 districts to conclude that it is investment in primary education that delivers conditions conducive for equitable and inclusive growth.

The etymology of India's many failures on multiple fronts—health, population control and poverty alleviation—can be located in the failure of its education policy. India's promise to spend 6 per cent of its GDP on education—made in 1986 and subsequently as a signatory at the UNESCO World Education for All conference at Jomtien in Thailand in 1990—has remained on paper even in 2012.

The mid-day meal scheme had a track record of success in Tamil Nadu. States—notably Gujarat—that adopted the programme and implemented it with integrity found it delivering on three important counts: a reduction in malnutrition, improving the enrolment of children in primary schools and the retention of a higher percentage of students in the secondary section. Indeed, all the research done through the nineties prove that the mid-day meal scheme delivered high enrolment and high retention of the critically important girl child in the secondary schools. Clearly, there was no lack of intellectual support, or evidence on the ground for the idea to be taken seriously. Yet, it needed a crisis, and pressure in the public domain, to spur the political class and policymakers into action.

THE SHAME OF ILLITERACY

In 1995, a curious confluence of circumstances brought the crisis of malnutrition and illiteracy back into focus. One of the unintended consequences of the opening up of the economy and the emergence of the software sector as a beacon of hope (discussed in detail in the chapter 'The Black Swan') was greater media coverage of India. The international community was stunned by the contrast between the world-class tech sector and the deficits in development everywhere else. International coverage focused on the horrifying state of children, education, illiteracy and malnutrition.

Writing for *The New York Times* in February 1994, Edward Gargan succinctly described the real India. India, he observed, ranked 134 out of a total of 173 countries on the UN Human Development Index. 'Half of India's 880 million people live in absolute poverty, more than half are illiterate, fewer than 10 per cent have access to sanitation, and of 1,000 children born, 142 die before the age of five.' Academic studies painted an even worse picture of the prevailing state of affairs in the country.

And the picture was worsening. Thanks to the economic crisis of 1991 the Narasimha Rao government cut back spending on education and also diluted its focus on various programmes. Gross enrolment in primary schools had dropped, shockingly, from 100.1 per cent in 1991 to 81.7 per cent in 1994. Gross enrolment in 1977 had been 81 per cent. In effect, in four short years, India's primary education had regressed seventeen years. The regional disaggregation showed that the situation was worse in Hindi-speaking states and the worst among disadvantaged classes—the scheduled castes and scheduled tribes.

In February 1995, Madhavrao Scindia—titular Maharaja of Gwalior and one of the better administrator-politicians in the Congress Party—took charge of the ministry of human resource development. Soon after, he reviewed the various departments in his ministry. He was scandalized by the precipitous drop in enrolment figures and shocked by the fact that for four years, ministry officials had done nothing to arrest the slide. On 1 April 1995 he chastised the officials in the Department of Primary Education, and on 4 April, called for an emergency meeting of all state education ministers and secretaries.

In fact, less than a year earlier, Arjun Singh who was HRD minister had organized a conference in Delhi of all chief ministers to discuss the follow-up action plan on the Education for All summit. There was also a meeting in Bhopal of the chief ministers of Hindi-speaking states. This, and other similar conferences made it clear that the implementation of Operation Blackboard and other non-formal education schemes was below par.

As always, the government only stirred into action when it was clear that it faced a crisis. And the precipitous drop in enrolment was a serious one. Montek Singh Ahluwalia, then finance secretary, cautioned the states that budgeting at the state level would have to recognize new priorities for allocations. 'Our levels of literacy, female education and provision of basic health services fall considerably short of our expectations and are below levels of other countries,' he said. Ahluwalia also observed that India could not create a credible strategy for growth and modernization if there were large gaps in investment in human capital. Following the meeting with the education ministers of the states, the Government of India chose to adopt the Tamil Nadu mid-day meal model to increase enrolment and curb malnutrition.

On 15 August 1995, thirteen years after Tamil Nadu had implemented its mid-day meal scheme, the Government of India followed suit. Its scheme, grandly christened the National Programme of Nutritional Support to Primary Education, aimed to boost the 'universalization of primary education by increasing student enrolment, retention and attendance and simultaneously reduce malnutrition of students in primary classes'. Unfortunately, unlike the MGR initiative of 1982, the Centre's programme was not ambitious enough as it was limited to students from Classes I-V only.

Kicked off in 2,408 blocks across the country, the scheme was expanded in phases to all blocks across the nation and to children studying under the education guarantee scheme and the alternative and innovative education schemes. The Centre promised to supply 100 grams of food grains per child per school day and a subsidy of ₹50 per quintal for the transportation of food grains. The programme envisaged that cooked meals would be provided to students and the cost of cooking meals and other assorted costs were to be met by the states. The states were given two years to set up systems and were allowed in the interim to provide to all children between Classes I-V, 3 kilograms of grains per student per month.

The ministry also introduced a clause, which specified that students would need a minimum attendance record of 80 per cent in order to be eligible for the grant. It escaped the policymakers that there was no logic in punishing the child when his absenteeism was usually the result of poverty. In any event, monitoring and implementing attendance on that scale was impossible. Indeed, many parents would come to pick up the food grains from school while the child was at work. There were other loopholes too. States diverted funds for other expenditures and schools diverted grains to beneficiaries other than school children. The states then claimed that they didn't have the resources to set up kitchens and hire cooks and helpers. Without putting too fine a point on it, the scheme was a complete disaster.

In 1996, in the fourth session of the twelfth Lok Sabha, members of parliament criticized the government over its disastrous implementation of the mid-day meal scheme. P. J. Kurien, an MP from Kerala, launched a blistering attack on the state of education in the country. He was followed by K. P. Singh Deo, MP from Dhenkanal in Orissa. Singh Deo said: 'I would not go into details but suffice to point out what the 56th Report of the Standing Committee has observed.' What he was referring to was a scathing review of the country's educational system. The 56th Report of the Standing Committee questioned the gaps between target and achievement across programmes, pointed out the lack of commitment, highlighted the increase in school dropouts and went on to say that the District Primary Education Programme was in a shambles. The Standing Committee described the mid-day meal scheme launched in 1995 as 'a hoax'. S. R. Bommai—formerly chief minister of Karnataka and then the minister for human resource development—countered the MPs who were attacking his department with a single statistic. He pointed out that the previous year's budget provided for a sum of ₹1,400 crore for the mid-day meal scheme. After a revision it had been brought down to ₹800 crore. Bommai said: 'It is not that we do not have money. We pay the FCI [Food Corporation of India] but state governments are not able to lift the stocks.' It turned out that the very states which had clamoured for a national mid-day meal scheme at the meeting of the National Development Council had shied away from the responsibility of implementing the scheme when it was awarded.

Invoking the name of M. N. Roy, the legendary revolutionary and political theorist, Bommai said: 'Either we educate or we perish. We need not look for examples from outside. Look at Kerala. It has been able to achieve full literacy. Why haven't other states managed?' Kerala, he pointed out, devoted 6 per cent of the state's domestic product to education. 'It has succeeded because the community is committed, the government is devoted.' He also sounded a note of caution to members who called upon the government to make education a fundamental right. 'It is a serious matter. Once we make it a fundamental right, it becomes justiciable. A citizen can go to the court and seek redress if there is no school or teacher or any shortcoming. The court can direct the State Government and the Central Government to act upon it'. The fact is that education can hardly be promoted by committees, reports and programmes. As Sam Pitroda, the technocrat who later headed the Knowledge Commission, observed: 'The real tragedy is that India does not have any real big champion of education.'

Meanwhile, individual states continued to implement the mid-day meal scheme in fits and starts as it suited them. The enrolment figures did show some improvement, moving up from 81.7 per cent to 88 per cent in three years, but the overall picture was one of depressing failure. It was, to quote a cliché about governance in India, business as usual. In 1998, India accounted for less than 20 per cent of the global population but was home to 40 per cent of the malnourished. Spending on children and nutrition programmes was patchy and poor. Expenditure on children ranged from ₹167 per child in Tamil Nadu to ₹31 per child in Bihar. The poorest states, where intervention was most critically required, spent the least on children. Not surprisingly, in 1998, a World Bank study titled *Wasting Away* declared that 'malnutrition is now a silent emergency which demands greater priority than ever before in independent India'.

Poverty and malnutrition logically impacted the state of education. In 2000, fifty-three years after independence, India was home to 304 million people who couldn't read or write. Nearly 30 million children between six and fourteen years of age were not in school. In rural India three out of ten men and six out of ten women were illiterate. Predictably, the poorest states had the highest number of illiterates.

Bihar was home to 43 million illiterates and Uttar Pradesh to 71 million illiterates. The number of illiterates in the two most populous states was almost twice the population of the UK in 2000.

Neither the shocking spectre of illiteracy nor the haunting image of malnutrition fuelled by poverty forced any change in policy. Once again, an accident of history sorted out the crisis. In April 2001, the People's Union for Civil Liberties (PUCL), Rajasthan, campaigning for the right to food, submitted a writ petition in the Supreme Court. The petitioners pointed out a stark tragedy. On the one hand, there was more food grain in the country than could be stored. On the other, there was perennial starvation in some states. The PUCL petitioned the Court to direct the government to widen the scope of beneficiaries for food and nutrition programmes including the mid-day meal scheme in schools. The writ urged the Court to instruct the government to release the food stocks, arguing that the right to life under Article 21 of the Indian Constitution included the right to food. Predictably, the states protested. State governments said the costs of the scheme made it unfeasible. They argued in the Supreme Court that the mid-day meal schemes were unaffordable. Mercifully, the Supreme Court paid no heed to their whining and instructed the states to cut flab elsewhere.

On 28 November 2001, Justice K. G. Balakrishnan and Justice Bhupinder Nath Kirpal of the Supreme Court directed the government to ensure the full implementation of the mid-day meal scheme by providing every child with prepared lunch with a minimum carbohydrate content of 300 grams and 8-12 grams of protein each day of school for a minimum of 200 days. Those governments providing dry rations instead of cooked meals were directed to start providing, within three months, cooked meals to schools in the poorer districts and then, within six months, to all schools.

Two days before the Supreme Court order, on 26 November, India witnessed a surreal moment of politics. Murli Manohar Joshi, minister for human resource development, introduced in Parliament an amendment to the Constitution to make education a fundamental right. The amendment said 'the State shall provide free and compulsory education to all children of the age of six to fourteen years in such manner as the State may, by law, determine'. The very parties whose governments paraded excuses in the Supreme Court to not implement the mid-day meal scheme, were competing to argue in Parliament in favour of the amendment. The amendment, eventually numbered the Constitution (Eighty-sixth Amendment) Act 2002, received presidential assent in December 2002. Twelve years after India became a signatory to the UN Convention on the Rights of the Child at Jomtien, Thailand, and after a series of interventions by the Supreme Court, Parliament passed a bill that guaranteed a promise specified in the Directive Principles. The children of India, of course, had to wait till 2009 for Parliament to pass the Right of Children to Free and Compulsory Education Act and give effect to the guarantee.

On the ground, though, despite the passage of legislation, there was no change in the attitude of the political parties and the bureaucracy. The Supreme Court order to implement the scheme within six months was observed almost only in breach. State after state found reason to delay and deny the entitlement ordained by the Court.

The same political class that claimed credit for the constitutional amendment, aided and abetted by the bureaucracy, peddled more excuses in the Supreme Court. Neither the spectacle of hunger nor the spectre of illiteracy mattered. In as many as 26 per cent of the rural households there was not a single member in the age group of fifteen and above who could read and write; every adult in these homes was illiterate. Worse, there was no literate woman in every second home in rural India and every fifth home in urban India.

Despite the Supreme Court order of 28 November, state governments dragged their feet on its implementation. Activists declared 1 April 2002 as 'action day on mid-day meals' and held protests in 100 districts in nine states against inaction on the Supreme Court order. In Bangalore, children lined the streets with empty plates; in other places, copies of the Supreme Court order were distributed. Elsewhere, the provision of symbolic 'people's mid-day meals' to school children were organized to shame the government into action. The protests yielded little in terms of results.

The activists went back to Court. The Supreme Court intervened once again and by an order dated 29 October 2002 'it was made clear that in case of persistent default in compliance of the orders of this Court, the concerned Chief Secretaries/Administrators of the States/Union Territories shall be held responsible'. But despite the strict orders, some of the states did nothing of any consequence. The Supreme Court had to step in once again. On 2 May 2003 the Court observed that eighteen months after the judgement, some states—Bihar, Jharkhand and Uttar Pradesh, the poorest and the ones with the largest number of illiterate children—had not even begun to implement its order. Counsel appearing for Uttar Pradesh and Jharkhand could give no satisfactory reasons for their inaction. Some states did not even bother to file an affidavit in response to the Court orders. The Court directed the states to implement the order in the poorest districts first. Copies of the orders were sent to the chief secretaries of all the states and union territories directing them 'to file affidavits showing compliance and the extent thereof' before 8 August 2003. The matter was then slated for hearing on 19 August.

There was some progress but the worst affected states continued to play truant. On 2 April 2004 the Supreme Court was forced to review the situation following complaints of non-compliance. The states which claimed that they had started implementing the scheme provided sketchy accounts of the progress they had made. One of the ploys they resorted to was to just list the number of schools the mid-day meal scheme was being implemented in, conveniently leaving out tangible details of how it was being done and, more importantly, leaving out details of where the scheme was not being implemented. The court asked for full details to be provided. Simultaneously, it applauded the progress being made in some states. Noticing that some states were supplying meals even during vacations in drought-affected areas, the court extended the scope of the scheme to such areas during vacations. It then ordered that all states would need to comply fully with its order when schools across the country reopened—1 September 2004 was set as the last cut-off day.

In May 2004, the BJP-led National Democratic Alliance (NDA)

was voted out and the Congress-led United Progressive Alliance (UPA) came to power with the support of the left parties who had sixty-one MPs. The Left Front and activists pushed the government to include the mid-day meal scheme in the Common Minimum Programme. The move was subsequently endorsed by the National Advisory Council, a body of academics, activists, former bureaucrats and Congressmen led by Congress President Sonia Gandhi. This gave them unprecedented leverage in the formulation of policy.

For the first time since the idea was proposed in the eighties, various arms of government could act in concert. The UPA government integrated many of the centrally sponsored schemes to ensure that the mid-day meal scheme succeeded. Road connectivity was improved with the rural roads programme, water supply and sanitation was enhanced using the Prime Minister's Gramodaya Yojana, infrastructure was created using labour from employment schemes like the Jawahar Rozgar Yojana and Sampoorna Grameen Rozgar Yojana.

New ideas and spinoffs have been introduced to make the plan even more effective. Puducherry, for instance, has introduced a breakfast scheme in addition to mid-day meals under which milk and biscuits are provided to students; in Bihar a Bal Sansad, children's parliament, is involved in the monitoring of the mid-day meal scheme; in Uttaranchal, mothers are supervising its implementation and in Chhattisgarh, Gujarat and Madhya Pradesh, children are provided with micro-nutrients and deworming medicines.

By 2010, the national mid-day meal scheme had led to a substantial increase in enrolment and attendance and a decrease in dropout rates in primary and secondary schools. Initial studies showed that enrolment for all school children had gone up in Rajasthan, Madhya Pradesh and Karnataka. The State of the World's Children 2011 report revealed that the gross enrolment ratio for male children was at 115 per cent in India and that for females at 111 per cent for 2005-09. Attendance for boys stood at 85 per cent and for girls at 81 per cent. However, worryingly, only 66 per cent of students continued to attend classes beyond primary school. Enrolment in secondary school, though, was yet low: 61 per cent for boys and 52 per cent for girls. Despite the improvement in the overall scheme of things, it was clear that poverty-stricken parents still chose to withdraw their children from school so they could go to work to supplement the family income.

However, progress continues to be made. Literacy rate in the 15-24 age group is 88 per cent for men and 74 per cent for women. The Sarva Shiksha Abhiyan is recognized as one of the biggest education initiatives anywhere in the world. Spending on education by the Centre and the states has gone up from ₹83,000 crore in 2004 to ₹2,23,000 crore in 2011. The Right to Education (RTE) Act passed by the UPA government in August 2009, which came into effect from April 2010, is a step forward. It guarantees that all children between the ages of six and fourteen are entitled to education. There are clear markers on funding and the act is justiciable.

But the force of the act is blunted as it can only guarantee schooling and not education. The government, in the RTE Act, has provided for 25 per cent reservation in private schools for disadvantaged children. This is akin to the offshoring of responsibility for quality education to the private sector. The question that begs an answer is: what about the other 75 per cent of children in government schools?

It is not enough to get children into schools. The huge challenge India faces now is to provide children with high-quality education. The Annual Status of Education Report 2011 compiled by Pratham, a non-profit organization, reveals that less than one in two students in Class V can read text from Class II levels. Only one out of three students in Class III can perform simple two-digit subtraction and just half the children in Class IV can recognize a five-digit number.

Schools have been constructed across rural India, yet students of three different grades are routinely bunched together in the same space, either because of the lack of space or lack of teachers. The quality of education cannot improve dramatically without quality teachers. Technology can aid and enable better teaching but over 60 per cent of rural schools have no electricity. Thanks to the lack of electricity, only one out of ten schools in rural India provides computer education.

In 1964, M. C. Chagla, the noted jurist who was then the minister for education, said: 'Our Constitution fathers did not intend that we just set up hovels, put students there, [provide] untrained teachers, give them bad textbooks, no playgrounds and say we have complied with Article 45 and primary education is expanding…they meant that real education should be given to our children.' If India is to capitalize on its so-called demographic dividend, it needs to keep all its children in school with mid-day meal schemes. It also needs to equip them for the future with skills that will enable them to compete in a globalized world.

Or else, there can be no India story.

India's location in the international time zone allows it to provide solutions to clients in Tokyo or New York in time for their next working morning. The skill of its human capital was never in doubt, and by the late seventies, it was clear that Indian software engineers could code their way to success. Yet the idea languished until 1990, when it evolved into...

THE BLACK SWAN

21 OCTOBER 1981
CANCUN, MEXICO

'*Hoh-zay Loh-pehz Pohr-tee-yoh*, for Jose Lopez Portillo, President of Mexico.
'*Frahn-swah Mee-the-rawn*, for Francois Mitterrand, President of France.
'*Ihn-dih-rah Gahn'-dee*, for Indira Gandhi, Prime Minister of India.'

'Exhale the O, inhale, hold that breath, pause mid-air, roll the R's exhale on E...' This was no diction spa. When leaders representing three-fourths of the wealth of nations and four billion people come together, no detail can be too small. This list of the heads of state, 'Participants in Cancun', put out by a news wire was a handy cheat sheet for mandarins, journalists, security personnel and even leaders of nations to rehearse from. And vital, for a minor error in pronunciation, could easily shatter brittle egos.

The North South Conference was a jamboree to beat all jamborees. This was where the richest and the poorest would come together to discuss how they could collaborate and make the world a better place. The heads of state, of Bangladesh with a per capita income of $90, and of the US with a per capita income of over $10,000, would share the same table and breathe the same balmy air of Cancun. Their words of wisdom were being covered by over 2,000 journalists from all over the world. The Government of Mexico even set up a new earth station costing over $3 million as part of the infrastructure dedicated to disseminating news from the conference. The choice of location for the conference was rich with irony. Cancun is a fourteen-mile strip of white sands and azure seas where the rich of the world come to holiday. The beach town is also located in one of the poorest regions of the Americas. It was also perfect from the security point of view. The island is easily secured as it is isolated and connected by just two bridges to the mainland. It is also easily insulated from conscientious dissenters, a comforting thought for the leaders of the rich nations.

President Jose Lopez Portillo had a busy schedule. Every thirty minutes he would be receiving leaders of the world with full military honours. Crown Prince Fahd of Saudi Arabia flew in aboard his personal Boeing 747. As did the president of Algeria. The suave intellectual Julius Nyerere flew commercial; Tanzania couldn't afford to fly its chief by private jet. The Indian prime minister, Indira Gandhi, arrived on an Air India flight and drove off in a motorcade. The next aircraft expected was Air Force One, which would bring US President Ronald Reagan to the conference. It arrived eighteen minutes ahead of schedule. As Reagan disembarked, he noticed that it wasn't the red-blue-white colours of his country that welcomed him to Mexico but buntings of the Indian tricolour. It was a symbolic moment. The US president was scheduled to have talks with the Indian prime minister in the afternoon and their meeting was billed as one of the most important ones at Cancun.

While other leaders were ferried by motorcade, Reagan took a helicopter to the conference venue, the six-storied Hotel Sheraton. The building and the 200-yard beach it opened on to had been sanitized and sealed off. A staff of 540 would attend to the needs of the VVIPs. An ultra-high frequency scrambling system was installed at the debate and conference venues to jam eavesdroppers.

Reagan's schedule was interesting for the way in which it had been prioritized and sequenced: in his first two meetings—set back to back on the first day of the conference—he would have met with the two leaders who represented nearly a third of the world's population. The Great Communicator would need all his legendary skills to deal with the Chinese and the Indians, for his country's relationship with the two couldn't have been more different. It had been nearly ten years since Richard Nixon had made friends with China and a decade since he had managed to alienate India from America.

Reagan's first meeting was a luncheon with Chinese Premier Zhao Ziyang. The Chinese premier was fifteen minutes late. Reagan waved off his apologies, wryly saying that it was fashionable to be late at Cancun. There was no awkwardness between the two although they represented opposing ideologies. Zhao told Reagan that although they had never met, he felt they had known each other for a long time. Reagan picked up his glass of water and said, 'I'll drink to that.'

Indira Gandhi was on time. Draped in a beige-brown silk sari rich with Indian motifs, she arrived on the sixth floor and noticed a metal detector placed in the doorway. Mildly annoyed, she gave the Secret Service agents in attendance her imperious Indira look. They instantly apologized and said the detector wasn't switched on. Indira Gandhi walked through it and on to the terrace carpeted by green polygrass. She was welcomed by a youthful looking Reagan, dressed in a yellow sports shirt and slacks. The seating was informal, with both occupying white lounge chairs. Reagan looked out at the blue waters of the Caribbean washing up on to the white sand. In the distance were four Mexican navy gunboats anchored offshore. Reagan switched on the charm. 'It is a beautiful view,' he said to the Indian prime minister. Indira too had come prepared. Nodding in agreement, she replied, 'I am two floors below you.' That evening both sides declared the meeting 'a hit'.

Indira Gandhi had invested a lot of political capital to make this meeting happen. When Reagan was elected to the White House in 1980, Indira, like other world leaders, wrote him a congratulatory note. Then, as Reagan prepared to take charge, she sent another message and made a public statement urging him to forget the past and renew friendly relations with India. She issued the statement on 6 December 1980, barely seventy-two hours before President Leonid Brezhnev of the Soviet Union was due to arrive in India for bilateral talks. And to destroy the myth that India was a client state of the Soviet Union, she reiterated that the Soviets must leave Afghanistan.

She then sent B. K. Nehru, her cousin who had been ambassador to the US during the presidency of LBJ, with a private message to Reagan. Nehru spent many hours trying to get through the multiple levels of bureaucracy surrounding the president and eventually managed to spend a few minutes with Reagan, thanks to the help of senior statesman John McCloy. This was no mean feat as the only other foreign dignitary Reagan had met at that point was Helmut Schmidt, who had just been re-elected as chancellor of West Germany, an important US ally in Europe. Indira Gandhi's message reiterated the sentiments conveyed in her statement: 'Let's start afresh'. Neither Reagan nor the Department of State could understand this unexpected change of heart on India's part although it was clear that Mrs Gandhi meant business. What was puzzling to the US administration then is still a mystery over three decades later. However, by correlating the events that unfolded, one can arrive at a plausible explanation for the Indian prime minister's actions.

The trigger, clearly, was the invasion of Afghanistan by the Soviet Union in December 1979. Although India's stance in the United Nations was ambivalent, in private it made no secret of its anger at the Soviet occupation. The message sent to the Soviets was unambiguous— the presence of the Red Army at the Khyber Pass was unacceptable; the entry of a superpower into South Asia was simply not in the best interests of India.

Brezhnev's trip to India on 8 December was marked by protests by Afghans, their sympathizers and peaceniks. The diplomatic reception accorded to the Soviet delegation was chilly. India made no statement supporting the Soviet cause; indeed, in a seven-page official declaration, India said it was opposed to the interference by foreign powers in the internal affairs of a country. Brezhnev also had to listen to a sermon from President N. Sanjiva Reddy about the foreign occupation of sovereign national territory and of India's opposition to foreign troops in the region. The two sides spent three days agreeing to disagree.

Geopolitics and economics connect the dots of the emerging picture. The Soviet Union had endangered India's security by occupying

Afghanistan. Also, it was clear that Indira Gandhi no longer wished India to be seen as a Soviet stooge. In terms of utility, Soviet influence in the Gulf region was clearly waning. Also critical was India's economic circumstances at the time. India imported goods in dollars but didn't earn enough foreign exchange to pay for it. Yes, there was trade with the Soviet Union, but there was an inherent disadvantage embedded in the rupee-rouble trade. Indian goods were often resold in dollars in the hard currency market while Indians were left with roubles that could only be used to buy what Moscow offered to sell. Indeed, in 1981, it was America—with a trade of $3 billion—that was India's largest trading partner.

There was also a personal angle to the strategic shift. Indira Gandhi never forgot how she or the country was treated by anyone who mattered—every good turn and rebuff was filed away. The Soviets, who on the advice of local communists—the CPI—backed her and the Emergency, made the mistake of ignoring her party after the electoral defeat of 1977. The assessment of the CPI was that she was a spent force. The Americans, in stark contrast, continued to treat her courteously. Unsurprisingly, when the Soviet president invited Prime Minister Indira Gandhi to Moscow, shortly after she was re-elected in 1980, she did not respond.

The Americans, who do not miss much, noted this. However, the US was not about to forsake its friendship with Pakistan. The Americans continued to arm and aid India's belligerent neighbour. On 15 June 1981, just as Foreign Minister P. V. Narasimha Rao, returning from Pakistan, declared that there was the possibility of reconciliation, the Americans announced a $2.5 billion arms package to Pakistan that included F-16 fighter jets. Indira Gandhi protested and sent senior diplomats to the US to argue India's concerns but at the same time she did not tie it to India's quest for better ties with the Reagan administration. More tellingly, she continued to keep the Soviets at arm's length.

Indira Gandhi had come to understand that the great bear hug with the Soviet Union was not helping India's cause. Her quest may well have been primarily dictated by a strategy for geopolitical realignment but it delivered sound economic outcomes too. The move away from the Soviet Union to a more balanced position of non-alignment, back to what her father Jawaharlal Nehru had instituted, would enable India to benefit from the dividends granted by global economic growth.

When President Brezhnev invited her to Moscow, to celebrate the tenth anniversary of the Indo-Soviet friendship treaty—in August 1981—she declined. *The New York Times*, commenting on India's distancing itself from the USSR while attempting to renew ties with the US, called it 'India's Rope Trick'. Mrs Gandhi's response to the American arming of the Pakistanis was simply to diversify India's arms purchases by talking to the UK and France about the supply of Jaguar and Mirage aircrafts.

One of the more delightful facets of Indira Gandhi and her politics was her innate sense of timing and the ease with which she deployed tactics. The day the conference started in Cancun, her cabinet dismissed the CPI (M) government in Kerala. Such dismissals don't usually make ripples in the mainstream US media. But then this political move had been slated to coincide with Cancun. Then, the next day, on 22 October, the *Washington Post* reported from Paris: 'France and India are pushing ahead with major negotiations over the purchase of 150 advanced Mirage-2000 warplanes for the Indian Air Force', a $2 billion deal that would give India a major source of aircraft other than the Soviet Union and give France's Mirage production lines a new lease on life.

The headlines created the right backdrop for the talks. Reagan was a remarkable politician: astute, candid and blessed with uncommon clarity when it came to parsing complex issues. At home he was against the concept of a nanny state. Abroad, he believed the world would be a better place if countries encouraged enterprise and trade instead of begging for aid. He had declared when he left Washington that he would listen and learn, but was not going to agree to another Marshall Plan to bail out the have-nots. Evidently, he shared these thoughts with Indira Gandhi. She too had come prepared to deal with the sermon on self-help as the redeeming factor in human enterprise.

Her counter to the thesis was well known and often articulated. Indira Gandhi believed that those in a strong economic position were happy to support free trade as long as it suited their own interests. She didn't dispute the need for more trade but believed that rich countries must think not just about an increase in aid but about rebalancing the terms of trade.

The sparring of ideas and words was visible the next day when the conference opened. Reagan lectured the less privileged nations on the merits of free enterprise and hard work. He produced what the American media characterized as a Horatio Alger formula. Alger, a prolific writer of dime novels, was instrumental in glorifying the idea of the struggle of the poor against adversity to achieve great wealth. Reagan said the poor nations and their people needed to pull themselves up by 'their bootstraps' and rise out of their predicament through 'the magic of the marketplace'. Indira Gandhi, who spoke after him, countered him with wry humour: 'Most people forget that there are millions of people in the world who don't own any boots and therefore don't have any straps with which they can pull themselves up.' The interaction between the two at the Cancun summit set the stage for a remarkable new phase in Indo-American relations.

The possibility of a new market opening up for American arms suppliers gave India more leverage with the Reagan administration. India needed the assistance of the US to prevent its economy from going into a tailspin. The Janata Party government had collapsed in July 1979 and Indira Gandhi and the Congress had agreed to support Charan Singh, who had the support of just sixty-four MPs, as prime minister. By December, in the final days of the three-legged Charan Singh regime, India's economy was ailing. Its oil bill—thanks to crude oil prices spiralling from $14 per barrel to $34 per barrel spurred by the second global oil shock after the Iranian Revolution—had shot up from a mere $2 billion to $6.6 billion in just twelve months. The current account deficit—the difference between dollar earnings and dollar spending—was $2.9 billion and accounted for almost a quarter of exports. India needed help. It had already withdrawn $530 million from its special drawing rights in the IMF and $266 million from the compensatory financing facility. It needed more to pay its overseas creditors. Its application with the IMF for a $5.8 billion loan needed the backing of the US. The Americans were opposing it as they felt this money would be used to pay for an arms order that didn't come to them.

That Indira Gandhi had wowed the American president soon became apparent at the IMF deliberations. Secretary of the Treasury Donald Regan and Richard D. Erb, the United States executive director for the IMF, had called India's application for the $5.8 billion loan unjustified. Yet, when the IMF board met to vote on the application on 9 November at 3 p.m., the US abstained, letting the application through. Three weeks after their date at Cancun, it was clear that America and India were ready to do business.

THE RIGHT TURN

To those who followed her career, Indira Gandhi's new avatar was astonishing. Here was a prime minister who had sworn by socialism all through the seventies and signed a treaty with the Soviet Union just a few weeks before India's war with Pakistan. This same leader was engaging with a country whose president, LBJ, in 1967, had humiliated India by imposing the ship-to-mouth policy on food grains; the country which armed Pakistan and tried to intimidate India in 1971 by sending its aircraft carriers into the Indian Ocean; the same super power which, under President Jimmy Carter, had cut off fuel supplies to the Tarapur nuclear plant in 1978; this was the country Indira Gandhi was courting! But as her observers would come to understand, for Indira, politics was not about dogma. Nor was it about past reverses. It was all about self-interest, about the country's interest; the twain merged often. Indira Gandhi never forgot a slight but she could paper it over if there was a larger goal she had in mind.

There were other reasons why the US was important to India and vice versa during Reagan's time. This was the first time that members of the Indian diaspora in the US had reached critical mass. There were over 300,000 relatively affluent and influential Indians in the country and they couldn't be ignored. The US had established a clear edge over the Soviet Union in technological innovation. Technology was a moving force in bilateral relations and Indira knew India couldn't depend too long on one source for technology. Indeed, India needed access to that technology for its nuclear programme and its first hesitant steps into computerization.

This was also the decade in which computer sets were set to catch up with television sets in American homes. Nearly 750,000 households had personal computers. Bill Gates was all set to launch the MS-DOS system that operated 90 per cent of the personal computers made by IBM. By 1980, Ethernet, the local area network, had gone commercial; ARPANET was in vogue, the now famous Domain Name System was about to be born and Tim Berners-Lee was already working on the first template for Hyper Text Markup Language (HTML). It was no secret that American companies saw potential in the Indian market for their wares and also sought Indian minds to help them design and develop new systems. US companies such as Honeywell, ITT, Xerox and Texas Instruments were looking at India as a development and investment destination.

Given the legacy of friendship with the Soviet Union, the immediacy of US arms aid to Pakistan and the threat of the nuclear bomb Islamabad was rumoured to be building, any move to cement ties with the US was fraught with negative implications. It was also true that India needed the assistance of the US on a number of fronts, particularly the refuelling of the Tarapur nuclear plant which the Carter administration had put on hold.

In early 1982, given its newfound friendship with India, the US came up with a formulation to break the Tarapur impasse—it would withdraw and get France to step in and restore the supply of fuel to the plant. Then, in the spring of 1982, the Reagan administration suggested to Indira Gandhi that she visit their country. On her part, Indira Gandhi, ever the shrewd timer of events, had kept a decision on a USSR visit pending. Although Brezhnev had visited India immediately after she returned to power in 1980, Indira had not yet returned the courtesy. Her decision to visit the US before she visited the USSR was again deployed as a fine nuance to alter perceptions.

The visit was slated for 27 July 1982. In the run-up to the visit, she told the *Washington Post*: 'My major aim is to try to convince people in America that you can have friendship even if you do not agree on all matters.' To *The New York Times* she said: 'We are friends with the Soviets but that does not mean that we can't be friends with China or the United States.' She ensured expectations were kept low. The official line was, only so much can be done in two days; however, a new tone can be set.

On 29 July Reagan received Indira Gandhi at the White House with personal warmth and the pomp of a nineteen-gun salute. That afternoon Reagan and Mrs Gandhi met with other officials for two hours. In the evening, at a grand dinner in honour of the visiting Indian delegation, Reagan raised a toast to Indo-US relations and described Indira as the 'distinguished leader of a great sister democracy'. Indira Gandhi reciprocated with equal warmth and reiterated her quest for a new friendship. After dinner, Mrs Gandhi, her son Rajiv Gandhi and the other guests walked to the South Lawn of the White House—decorated with flaming torches and Japanese lanterns—where they were treated to a performance by the New York Philharmonic Orchestra conducted by Bombay boy Zubin Mehta.

Away from the glitter and glamour, officials worked hard on deliverables. On the table were ideas on the exchange of agreements on investment and trade, the opening up of the supply of high technology—military and civilian—besides the formulation of a solution for Tarapur. The discussions took forward ideas discussed in Cancun on the resumption of trade, investments and collaboration. It was at this meeting that the doors were opened to American and Indian companies to invest and collaborate on the design and development of new technologies.

In July 1983, the US and India signed the path-breaking Reagan–Indira Science and Technology Agreement. What the agreement was intended to achieve, in principle, was to allow both countries to collaborate and engage across the entire technological spectrum. While that didn't quite come to pass eventually, the agreement was an extremely important development in bilateral trade and cooperation in the technology sector. Among the first American companies to enter India, following the agreement, was Texas Instruments which arrived in 1984. The choice of India as a location for Texas Instruments, which until then had operations only in the developed world—in the US, the UK, France and Japan—sent a positive signal to other tech giants that India was open for business.

EARLY TECH TEMPLATE

India's desire to acquire a technological edge dates back to the period after independence. Jawaharlal Nehru inculcated into the polity the need for modern technology and thinking. Throughout his tenure, he promoted the creation of institutions across the country that would exemplify the ability of Indian minds to comprehend and analyse complex issues of science. Many of the engineering colleges, the Indian Institutes of Technology, the Indian Institutes of Management and colleges of agriculture that flourish in the country today owe their existence to Nehru's emphasis on the need for the country to have solid technological foundations.

In fact, the first computer arrived in India as early as 1955. It was installed at the Indian Statistical Institute (ISI) in Calcutta. The machine was the HEC-2M of Hollerith India Ltd. It took about two months for the ISI staff to install the computer which boasted all of 1 kilobyte of memory. It was a tube-based system, cost around ₹2 lakh, and occupied 300 square feet. At that time it was reputed to be the only computer in Asia outside of Japan. In 1958, the ISI got a second computer, this one from Russia. By 1960, the Tata Institute of Fundamental Research had designed and assembled an indigenous computer which was christened TIFRAC—the Tata Institute of Fundamental Research Automatic Calculator. Thanks to Nehru's commitment to promote science, by 1964, India had sixteen computers which were spread across government departments, R&D institutions and universities. The first commercial computer was installed in Bombay in 1961 by Esso Eastern.

After the disastrous war with China, the need to acquire technology took on a strategic angle and urgency. A core group under Nehru concluded that acquiring an edge in technology was critical to compensate for the country's lack of resources and scale. It was also felt this would help accelerate economic growth. In 1963 the government appointed a high-level committee to focus on the way forward. The committee, headed by Homi J. Bhabha, submitted its report in 1966 and recommended technological expansion and the strengthening of the country's electronic base. This was followed by the Narasimhan Committee, which in 1968, set a target of ten years for self-sufficiency in the manufacture of computers.

Throughout the sixties—perhaps because the early focus of technology was determined by defence interests—matters relating to policy and licensing were vested in the Department of Defence Supplies in the ministry of defence. Several policies were crafted but not implemented because of inter-departmental squabbles. It was only after 1971 that the Department of Electronics was created. ICL and IBM came into India in the sixties and it was believed that their presence could be leveraged to create a base for computer hardware in India. That did not come to pass.

India could have been the giant that South Korea is in electronics. Dominance in hardware in a highly competitive environment would have required four major inputs: the availability of new technology, foreign investment, a policy that encouraged the building of economies of scale and the availability of capital. The import of technology was curbed in the quest for self-reliance, the economy was closed to foreign investment, and the licence-permit-quota raj precluded the possibility of creating capacity and scale. Even if all this were to be done the Indian way, by the government, it would need massive investments. Capital was scarce and had many claimants, and the reigning political ideology dictated its deployment to maximize employment.

The computer software revolution almost went the same way. Many of the issues—ranging from import restrictions to labour regulations—which shackled the hardware sector, also dogged the software industry. But software, unlike hardware, was not capital intensive and could potentially generate much employment. There was no lack of talent either. Indeed, even though close to half of India's population at the time was illiterate, the higher education system still produced high-quality engineers. These engineers had already proved their mettle in multinational companies located in India and abroad. There was no lack of entrepreneurial desire either. The presence of the positives should have spurred the revolution yet software development in the country progressed haltingly.

India's entrepreneurs had recognized the opportunities in software as early as the sixties. Tata Consultancy Services (TCS), one of the largest players in software services today, was set up in 1968. It started operations as the Tata Computer Centre and was intended to provide services to group companies. Soon the group realized the potential to tap into global business opportunities and hired F. C. Kohli—frequently called the father of Indian software development for his pioneering work—to set up TCS as an independent business entity. TCS's first export assignment was to convert the Hospital Information System from Burroughs Medium Systems COBOL to Burroughs Small Systems COBOL out of TCS Bombay.

TCS was not the only company which understood the variety of business opportunities to be had. Another early entrant was Patni Computers, also located in Bombay. Indeed, Patni Computers is the alma mater of some of the best and brightest names in the software business today, including N. R. Narayana Murthy and Nandan Nilekani. The Patnis originally hailed from Rajasthan and had moved to Agra to set up businesses. Following the collapse of a family-owned textile business in Kishangarh, the family moved to Bombay and set up several enterprises, one of which, Industrial Oxygen, was a market leader. The three Patni brothers were all engineers. G. K. Patni, the oldest, studied engineering in Delhi; Narendra graduated from IIT Delhi and MIT and Ashok took his degree from IIT Bombay. They entered the software business in 1974.

Interestingly, TCS, Patni Computers and the early starters were engaged only in data conversion and exports. The first jobs Patni Computers did were data entry and photo typesetting. The computers were used to file information; data was transferred first on to ticker tapes and in later years on to magnetic tapes to be shipped to clients. Business opportunities were scarce in the domestic market. The policy, as it was in India in 1974, required them to take clearances from the labour department. Incredibly, companies could not take up any job that would displace labour. This ruled out any development in the domestic market, which is why Indian entrepreneurs sought opportunities abroad. However, the development of business overseas was shackled by red tape. Therefore, through the seventies, business plans were built around what government policies allowed companies to do rather than what they could have been doing and, in fact, wanted to do.

India established a record of sorts in squandering a series of early-mover opportunities, especially when it came to software development. In 1973, the government established the Santa Cruz Electronics Export Processing Zone (SEEPZ) in Bombay. SEEPZ was the perfect vehicle to propel software exports. This didn't happen. The policies of SEEPZ were lopsided, unrealistic, and built around the belief that foreign exchange could be earned without spending any. Its primary function should have been promoting exports; instead, it was controlling imports.

The business of software required exporters to import computers. Consider how this was denied. The policy stipulated they could import computers only if the dollars spent were earned back as exports within five years. Later, the requirement was bumped up and a company could import only if it promised exports worth 200 per cent of the cost of the computer. And they couldn't procure what they needed at home for what was required wasn't available.

The scarcity of hardware and the maze of clearances created a huge opportunity for fraudsters who traded in licences which commanded a premium. The ability to acquire a computer—through imports, through timeshare or lease—became the core competency of many entrepreneurs. Often, software companies made more money by importing and leasing hardware than from their software businesses.

The situation worsened following the promulgation of the Foreign Exchange Regulation Act in 1974. Foreigners were disallowed from holding more than 40 per cent equity in any firm in India. A higher stake of 74 per cent was allowed only if the company proved its technology was unique and unavailable in India. Ideally, the policy should have encouraged higher foreign ownership to enable the induction of technology but that was precluded by politics. In fact, IBM offered to split its operations into hardware and software sectors and even promised software exports of over $100 million. The discussions went on till 1977, by which time the Janata Party came to power. The Morarji Desai government—because of the influence of George Fernandes and other socialists—was unimpressed by IBM's promises. The company left India in 1978.

Faced with the lack of progress in the software sector, the government did what it does best—tinker with policy without showing much progress. Every time the policy was tinkered with, a new layer would be added to the already complex maze of clearances. Every relaxation came with conditions and required new clearances.

Infosys founder N. R. Narayana Murthy recalls, 'It would take as many as twelve to eighteen months for clearances to come through.' Infosys was created by Murthy, Nilekani and a band of committed professionals who resolved to be bound by certain ethical policies. This policy, depending on who looked at it, was either brave or naive. The licence-permit-quota raj prevailing at that time demanded that entrepreneurs possess political connections and a team with the skill set to navigate the Byzantine corridors of government for permissions.

The business of software exports required three critical components: computers, telecommunications and a reasonably liberal foreign exchange regime to enable companies to promote and expand their businesses. Every element that the sector required to grow was shackled. The mindset that virtually killed the hardware sector was poised to cripple the fledgling software sector too. The Janata Party government then set up a Review Committee on Electronics headed by Mantosh Sondhi, then the secretary, ministry of steel, coal and mines. The report submitted in September 1979 recommended a drastic dismantling of unnecessary controls, restrictions and regulations and the institution of a single-point clearance.

Anybody importing a computer had to follow a five-step process: apply to the Department of Electronics which would first check if the machine could be bought in India. Following this certification, tenders would be placed and the price evaluated by a committee of experts. The software company would then have to procure a clearance letter from the relevant state government certifying that the interests of labour would not be hurt by the import. After another round of approvals, the letter of clearance would be obtained.

The set of challenges this bureaucratic maze posed for the fast-moving software sector was utterly frustrating. For instance, if Infosys applied for a computer in July 1981, it would receive a licence to import the machine in March 1982. In the nine months that it took for government to clear the application and issue the licence, the computer manufacturer would have released a new model of the same machine. In 1981, a 200 MB disk drive cost $30,000. In 1982, the company would be offering a 300 MB machine at, say, $20,000. Naturally, it made sense to buy the advanced, cheaper model, but government was not about to make things that simple. The licences granted were very specific or, as techies would say, 'case-specific' and Infosys would have to go back to government to get its licence amended. This could take as long as another eight to twelve months during which time yet another model of the same machine would be out in the market. This also meant many trips to Delhi. Murthy remembers, 'I would travel by train to the capital, rent a room at an old hotel near Delhi railway station and then trek all the way to the Department of Electronics which was located at Lok Nayak Bhavan near Khan Market.' Between 1981 and 1982, within eighteen months, he made about forty trips to Delhi.

CRIPPLED CONNECTIVITY

Companies abroad which farmed out work to Indian software developers would naturally want to check on how assignments were progressing. This was easier said than done. India in the eighties faced a shortage of telephones. Clients in Europe or the United States, where telephone connections were a given, could not fathom how companies could operate without a number to call. Companies used what was known as 'care of' numbers or booked calls through public call offices. Getting a phone connection was impossible unless one was willing to work the system.

Murthy recollects: 'In the eighties, the waiting period was twenty-four months. It was easier for a retired government official to get a connection than a software company earning precious foreign exchange.' He narrates an anecdote on how the lack of a telephone almost wrecked a big order. 'In 1984, a client wanted Infosys to undertake a major job for them. Aware of the scarcity of computers and computer share time, the client offered to ship to India an IBM-compatible machine, a 4381-Magnuson, which cost over $300,000, so that Infosys could do the job quicker. The client had a condition—Infosys had to provide a telephone number to call on to check on progress.' Infosys, bound by its ethical policies, would not grease the system and, therefore, could not get a phone. Fortunately, the accommodating client offered to ship the computer to any location in the US if Infosys was willing to relocate its engineers. The project was eventually completed in Grand Rapids, Michigan.

By the beginning of the eighties, companies all over the world were using satellite-linked earth stations to transfer information. For Indian companies the possibility of using 24x7 data links to transmit data in real time represented a huge opportunity—they would be able to use local human resources to compete globally. India by then had the capability to set up earth stations and, in theory, software companies could lease satellite links to enable their operations.

However, there was a huge gulf between theory and reality. Government had a monopoly on the setting up of earth stations. Thus, costs were exorbitant and the process cumbersome. As with telephone connections and computer imports, companies interested in leasing a communication link were required to crawl through the maze. The monopoly also allowed the Department of Telecommunications to add the cost of its inefficiency to that of the equipment and operations. This left little room for viability for any software company who wished to lease its lines. In 1983, it could cost as much as ₹45 lakh to lease a 64kbps line.

This was the backdrop against which the Indo-US technology agreement of 1983 between Indira Gandhi and Ronald Reagan was signed. The United States was willing to gamble on India, although the latter had just a few years previously sent IBM packing because it was confident of the business model of its own companies. This confidence came from the massive costs its companies could save. Highly complex software development could be performed by Indians at such low prices that the chaos accompanying permissions and clearances—and the abysmal infrastructure—were worth putting up with.

The decision by Texas Instruments to set up a design and development unit in Bangalore in 1984 marked the city's global rise to fame as India's Silicon Valley. Bangalore first gained prominence as a technological hub when Prime Minister Nehru chose to house strategic establishments in India. As it was situated in the deep south of the country, it was calculated that it would take enemy aircraft—which essentially meant Pakistan's and China's—at least ninety minutes to get to their targets by which time suitable measures could be taken. Of course, all this took place before the advent of Mach 2 fighters and ballistic missiles. This is why the city is home to establishments like Hindustan Aeronautics Limited, Bharat Electronics Limited, the Indian Institute of Science, the National Aerospace Laboratories, Hindustan Machine Tools, Bharat Heavy Electricals and, subsequently, in the seventies, the Indian Space Research Organization.

Interestingly, the cities that host the six key clusters of IT in India—Bangalore, Chennai, Hyderabad, Pune and the National Capital Region of Delhi (including Gurgaon and Noida)—boast the highest concentration of public sector and defence establishments as also educational institutions. In many ways the Indian experience replicated that of the United States where the clustering of advanced defence and technology programmes created an ecosystem for tech outfits to thrive around Boston, Austin and, of course, Silicon Valley.

Texas Instruments had long been planning a second offshore development centre in Asia, the first being in Japan. The assessment team visited many countries. The choice was between China and India. Srini Rajam, who headed Texas Instruments' operations in India before setting up Ittiam Systems, says, 'Driving India's case was Dr Mohan Rao, the guru to many Indian techies.' Rao, who worked out of offices in Dallas, was in charge of advanced product development. Rao pointed out to Texas Instruments' chief, Mark Shepherd, the high quality of Indian talent within the company campus. Rao flagged the availability of a talent pool, the low costs, the location of India in a favourable time zone and the widespread use of English language among techies. Rao's confidence was not unfounded; when Texas Instruments set up shop it received 10,000 applications for seventeen posts.

India's English-language advantage can be traced back to the mid-sixties. As we have seen in the chapter 'Das Kapital', a directive from the ministry of information and broadcasting on the use of Hindi as the official language triggered a major storm in the south. The language agitation, led by the DMK in Tamil Nadu, led to the defeat of the Congress in the 1967 polls—from which it has never recovered—and brought the DMK to power. This agitation can be credited for the continuation of English as the national language, thereby giving India a vital competitive edge over other Asian countries.

The location of India at precisely GMT +5.5 provides another next-level advantage, that of 'same-day operations'. The time difference enables outfits located in India to service those on the eastern rim of the globe and those on both sides of the 'big pond'. As America goes to sleep, India is awake and a job sourced to it is completed by the time America is awake again. Srini Rajam says, 'Soon after the India centre started, Texas Instruments received many messages of appreciation from customers as they received a response to their questions on the same day.'

On 1 October 1985, when Texas Instruments was ready to go live, Bangalore city's skyline acquired a fashionable new accessory—the antenna dish of an earth station atop Sona Towers on Miller Road. Texas Instruments' ambition was to create a world-class research and development centre in Bangalore for product design. As Texas Instruments' top brass wanted the centre to be as good, if not better, than centres in the US or Japan, they made sure that the centre had world-class infrastructure.

In the business of design and development, client-designer interface is critical, which meant a dedicated, high-speed data communications system was essential. Since the Government of India could not guarantee them one, the management of Texas Instruments offered to bring along their own earth station and set it up for captive use. In 1986, a high-speed data connection meant transmission at 64kbps (in 2012 it takes place at an average of 4.8mbps which is roughly seventy-five times faster; even the data dongle on laptops delivers data at forty times the speed of 1986). In 2011, the top ten connection speeds ranged between 6.4 mbps in Belgium to 8.9 mbps in Japan to 13.8 mbps in South Korea.

The offer to set up its own earth station by Texas Instruments generated a typically quixotic response from the Indian bureaucracy. It specified that an officer from the Department of Electronics would be deputed to monitor the data being exported from the earth station. All data being transmitted was in binary form, in 0s and 1s—unintelligible to most people. A five-minute transmission would translate into over 400 printed pages. Nevertheless, government appointed an officer to print out sheets every few hours, scrutinize them and file them away. What the department did with the data is anybody's guess. Finally, in 1988, Videsh Sanchar Nigam Limited (VSNL), then a public sector unit under the ministry of telecommunications, took over the earth station.

The entry of Texas Instruments should have made it fairly obvious to policymakers that they were staring at a potential winner. The company was willing to rough it out in India with its less-than-satisfactory infrastructure to extract value for itself. The money it stood to make obviated all disadvantages. For a start, its cost of operating in India was substantially lower, especially when it came to wages—the cliché then was that you could hire 100 engineers in India for the price of ten in the US. The twelve-and-a-half-hour time difference between India and the West Coast in the US allowed seamless round-the-clock monitoring, scrutiny and execution of jobs and there was, of course, the huge talent bank to be tapped.

Soon after Texas Instruments set up its design centre, Indian software outfits, including Infosys, TCS and Wipro, queued up to visit the facility. It was clear to them that Indians could deliver the goods and garner market share if they were given the right facilities, beginning with access to advanced systems and round-the-clock data communication facilities. The Indian tech outfits began petitioning the government for access to similar facilities to promote the sector. Access to 24x7 data communication was now at the top of the list of facilities demanded by software developers which also included ease of imports and exemption from duties.

The industry was hopeful that their pleas would be heard because in the mid-eighties, India had in Rajiv Gandhi a prime minister most identified with computers and it was expected that his pro-technology stance would deliver a fillip to the sector. It did and it did not. It was during his management of the Asian Games in 1982 that Rajiv Gandhi had become acquainted with a few technologically savvy bureaucrats who later would be dubbed 'Rajiv's Boys'. Among them was N. Seshagiri, additional secretary at the Department of Electronics and director general of the National Informatics Centre, or nic.in as it is known today. Originally from the Department of Atomic Energy, Seshagiri was a passionate believer in the potential of the software sector. He promoted the concept of off-site services and campaigned for a policy that would enable India to achieve, at least in software, what Asian Tigers like Taiwan and South Korea had achieved in hardware.

Rajiv Gandhi pushed the Indo-US tech engagement initiated by his mother further during his visit to the US in 1985. Like Indira Gandhi, her son hit it off with Reagan although the visit took place at a time when, geopolitically, Indo-US ties were not at their best. The American investment in Pakistan, militarily speaking, had strengthened and the hawks in the Reagan administration continued to look at India as a surrogate state of the USSR. None of this mattered eventually as the young Indian leader and Reagan got on phenomenally well, leading some commentators to describe it as a 'father-son bond'. The proposals for investment discussed in Cancun were taken further.

By 1985, India had begun to tentatively open up its economy. The liberalizing of its imports policy and investment environment was encouraging to American companies. India had declared an interest in acquiring technology for the manufacture of computers, lasers, sensors and other hi-tech products that the US had a clear edge in.

On the other side of the table, India's impressive scientific manpower afforded a cache of human capital for American companies to tap into. Equally energizing was Rajiv Gandhi's can-do attitude. Within weeks of assuming power, Rajiv Gandhi got a team of bureaucrats to draft a new policy for electronics and software which would deliver quality and lift Indian goods into the export market. In response to the demands of the industry, the government unveiled, on 18 December 1986, the Computer Software Export Development and Training Policy with the avowed intention of boosting India's software exports.

Hardware imports were liberalized though costs were still 60 cents per dollar more expensive than abroad. An inter-ministerial committee was empowered to clear applications for the import of hardware. For the first time, a time limit of six weeks was set for clearances. Foreign exchange issues were liberalized and a one-window clearance system introduced. The Exim Bank was brought into the picture to fund and boost software exports. There was also the hope of a better telecom regime and access and connectivity thanks to the entry of Sam Pitroda.

Born in Orissa and educated in Gujarat, Pitroda is the archetypal prodigal who made good in the US. A telecom engineer who worked with General Telephone & Electronics Corporation and Rockwell, Pitroda was on a visit to India when he couldn't get through on the telephone to his wife in Chicago. He now chuckles, 'It was infuriating. I sought an appointment with Indira Gandhi to offer a solution to clear the mess called telecom services.' The meeting resulted in his being introduced to Rajiv Gandhi a little before Indira Gandhi was assassinated. When he took over as prime minister, Rajiv Gandhi asked Pitroda to work out a solution for the telecom sector.

Connectivity required telephone lines and the digitization of exchanges. Until then, India was using technology abandoned by the West, spending precious foreign exchange to buy it. Pitroda suggested that India go digital and this resulted in the creation of C-Dot. Pitroda remembers, 'India needed telecommunications to survive and for the economy to thrive it would need to make the exchanges itself.'

With barely $30 million as capital, Pitroda and his team started out in a run-down hotel in Delhi. Three years later, in 1987, the first digital switching systems—designed to survive the heat and dust of rural and urban India—were deployed. India couldn't afford the principle of ownership as neither the government nor the consumers could pay the last-mile costs of laying cable, but the economy could definitely propel the concept of access to all. The new C-Dot exchanges revolutionized telecom connectivity. For both individuals and businesses, the creation of capacity and better connectivity enabled improved access.

Thanks to the improved connectivity and policy push, the software sector was ready for take-off. By then it had taken on shades of a revolution and sounded almost too good to be true. As expected, the politics of economics and carpetbaggers in the system hit back. Rajiv had underestimated the scale of resistance he would have to deal with. By the time the policy to open up the software sector for foreign investment migrated from the draft stage to its final form, those threatened by it had got to work. Domestic software producers loudly lamented the death of domestic software. Soon, the need to enforce national control over the production of computers, an old obsession, came back into the policy. In February 1987, the policy went into reverse gear and many of its concessions were withdrawn. The duty on the import of software was hiked to over 100 per cent. The naysayers in the economic ministries criticized the wastage of foreign exchange and a travel tax of 15 per cent was imposed. The policy, and the booster shot it would provide the software sector, was effectively stifled.

It didn't seem to matter to the people intent on scuttling the initiative that, if it succeeded, it would achieve a major political objective—employment. In the eighties, the country produced over 150,000 engineers and diploma holders—way above the capacity of the economy to absorb—besides nearly 500,000 science graduates who struggled to put to use the degree they had earned. Just the potential for employment and the prospect of earning the foreign exchange that India badly needed should have prompted the policy to sail through the ranks of policymakers and planners. Yet it didn't. It was no surprise, then, that software exports out of India accounted for just ₹71 crore in 1987.

Contrast this with the approach of the US government under Ronald Reagan. On 3 February 1987, a little after Texas Instruments started operations in India, the US Senate Committee on Finance invited Mark Shepherd Jr, chairman of Texas Instruments, Colby Chandler, chairman and CEO of Eastman Kodak, Robert W. Galvin, chairman of Motorola, James Robinson, chairman and CEO of American Express, as well as chairman of the Task Force on International Trade and Investment, and William Lilley III who headed the American Business Conference—the biggest names in that country's technology and trade sectors—to brief its members. The hearing was titled 'Mastering the World Economy' and was intended to enable the US administration to take appropriate steps to preserve its economic superiority. At the hearing, Senator Bill Bradley of New Jersey told Robinson and Shepherd bluntly, 'You want desperately to get access to Third World markets. You know Brazil and India basically vetoed making services a part of the next round [of the WTO conference]. What do you think could get them to reconsider?' Shepherd didn't mince words and said that some markets were locked out, particularly for the computer and information sectors. He later stressed that, 'India is going to be a big problem for us; China is going to be a big problem for us [as competitors].'

It was not just the private sector or the US government which saw the potential in India. In Washington, in 1988 and 1989, a World Bank study also recognized the promise. In its report on India's electronics industry, the World Bank team underlined industrial electronics, computers, data processing, software development and telecommunications equipment as sunrise areas for the Indian economy. In May 1989, when a loan agreement was signed between the Government of India, financial institutions and the World Bank, its assessors declared that, 'computer software though still a tiny industry is particularly promising because of its high degree of skill intensity'.

A criticism faced by Indian software companies was that they did not create branded software products. Instead, they built their business on body-shopping. Meaning, India-based companies thrived on the arbitrage between the wages they paid and the revenue they earned from sending their engineers to work in companies abroad. This was not entirely untrue but the blame for it should fall squarely on the software policy that was framed. Given the scarcity of resources needed to acquire computers and the issues that hobbled lease and imports, contracts were obtained more easily if the company could send its manpower to the US. Indeed, some policymakers had argued that if India were to become to software what the Asian Tiger economies were to hardware, it would have to first pursue volume through body-shopping after which it could move up the value chain. This required enlightened policymaking.

Pronab Sen, then adviser to the Department of Electronics and currently principal adviser to the Planning Commission, succinctly sums up the situation: 'Until 1991-92 there was virtually no policy support at all for the software sector. Even benign neglect would be too positive a phrase to use in this connection. The primary vehicle of Indian software exports, on-site software development, was pejoratively termed body-shopping and every effort was made to discourage it. There was virtually no effort at understanding why software exporters behaved the way they did. In retrospect, considerable credit has to be given to the software sector for pushing ahead despite the lack of support from the government.'

Software companies were not only denied support, they were also handicapped by hurdles. On-site work obviously required engineers to travel and live overseas. Says Murthy, 'At one time, Nandan Nilekani, N. S. Raghavan and Kris Gopalakrishnan were all working on six projects in the US. This meant that dollars had to be sent to them, at least for maintenance. The world over, fees for services are paid after delivery, but rules in India stipulated that exporters had to first bring dollars into India and only then draw a maximum of 50 per cent of the money brought in. All this, despite Infosys paying for the foreign currency in rupees.' Murthy recalls spending hours in the RBI lobby waiting for clearances, sometimes even with his wife and infant in tow.

The matter didn't end with the currency hassles. Company executives were expected to file travel reports along with vouchers on who they met and where. One executive filed for foreign exchange to travel to Europe, intending to spend two days in Frankfurt and one in Paris. As it happened, he spent two days in Paris and one in Frankfurt. The RBI objected to this deviation and all clearances for the company were put on hold. The absurd restrictions ensured that companies could not hire consultants or set up offices abroad to prospect for business.

HORSES WILL FLY

By the end of 1988, the Rajiv Gandhi regime was politically weakened following the eruption of the Bofors scandal that alleged that pay-offs had been made to secure an arms deal. In a chorus, vested interests in the party and in business successfully labelled his policies as being elitist. The software sector was showcased not as an opportunity for growth and employment but as an elitist business that took away jobs. Rajiv Gandhi had run out of political capital and his government had run out of time. Rajiv Gandhi lost the elections.

In November 1989, V. P. Singh took charge as the prime minister, riding the anti-corruption wave and wearing the mantle of crusader. Those were tumultuous days. The Ram temple movement that was peaking at the time and the conundrum of caste-based quotas were competing for attention. Amid political chaos and identity politics, it appeared that the software revolution was being administered its last rites.

Unbeknownst to anyone, certainly to those in the industry, the software sector was about to acquire an evangelist. In June 1990, Nagaraj Vittal, a Gujarat cadre IAS officer with a formidable track record, integrity and an enlightened sense of economics, took over at the Department of Electronics. Working in Gujarat or Maharashtra enables officers to acquire a pro-growth perspective on economic policy and Vittal possessed it. It is common for Gujarat cadre officers to look at business development as part of governance. It is a state where industrialists are frequently called upon to head public sector units as non-executive chairmen.

Vittal's resumé was studded with stellar achievements by the time he arrived in Delhi. In 1965, the government of India had set up the first free trade zone (FTZ) in Kandla, India's deep water port for the west coast. It was the first FTZ in Asia and a failed idea for nine years until Vittal took charge as development commissioner and turned it around in 1974. The challenge enabled him to understand just how the business of exports worked. As industries commissioner of Gujarat, he freed investments from the bane of red tape. Unlike most IAS officers, Vittal also had hands-on business experience—he had served as managing director of the Gujarat Narmada Fertilizer Corporation.

It is not often recognized that in four short years—between 1990 and 1994—Vittal was able to grandfather two of India's most successful revolutions: software and telecom. Vittal quips, 'Throughout my career and life my approach to all situations has been simple: list out the alibis for non-performance. Once the alibis are removed, performance cannot be avoided.'

When Vittal took over as head of the Department of Electronics, Vinod Pandey, then cabinet secretary, told him to sort out the mess. Vittal recalls, 'I found that the Electronics Department was spread across eight addresses in Lutyens's Delhi. So my first decision was to get them all together into one building—a new one near Lodhi Road—now known as Electronics Niketan.' A fortnight after taking over, he called for a meeting with software exporters and heard them out patiently. 'When they met me,' Vittal says, 'they repeated the wish list they had brought up many times before with government.' They wanted profits on exports to be exempt from taxes as it was for merchandise exports, they wanted sops for the import of computers of the sort that other exporters received for capital goods, they wanted high-speed data connections and, of course, they wanted as much red tape removed as was feasible.

To Vittal it was clear that software developers should be housed in a free trade zone where they would have the infrastructure they needed, including a dedicated 24x7 data link. He could see that they needed to be able to import whatever systems were required as well as enjoy access to credit and tax exemptions on profits. He crafted a policy using elements of the success he achieved in turning around the Kandla FTZ and the demands made by the software developers. He then presented the blueprint to a committee of secretaries at the end of August in 1990. Vittal recalls, 'It was a stormy meeting.' Among those who attended were Finance Secretary Bimal Jalan, Commerce Secretary S. P. Shukla and Cabinet Secretary Pandey. The ire of the senior officials was understandable; Vittal was asking for exemptions and sops when the government was virtually bankrupt and facing one of the worst economic crises in its history.

Bimal Jalan asked Vittal what the volume of software exports that year was. Vittal reported that it was about $100 million. Jalan then asked Vittal, 'If we give all these concessions, will the value of their exports touch $500 million?' The figure he had suggested was an impossible one but Vittal wasn't about to give up. He said exports could possibly soar to $350 million in the next three years. Jalan said if he could raise the figure to $400 million, the group of secretaries could consider the suggestions he had made. The meeting ended on that note with both sides agreeing to meet again.

Soon after, members of the National Association of Software and Services Companies (NASSCOM) met with Vittal on the sidelines of a conference. He told the group, which included Harish Mehta of Onward Technologies, Infosys Chief N. R. Narayana Murthy, Rajendra Pawar of NIIT and other key players of the software industry, that the government had agreed to meet their demands, but there was a condition—software exports had to touch $350 million over the next three years. The members of NASSCOM were shocked as the target was three times the value of current exports. To many it was a 'no' cloaked as a 'yes'.

Vittal then told them a story. A key aide of a king was found to be guilty of misappropriation and was sentenced to death. Magnanimously, the king asked the aide what his last wish was. The man thought for a few moments. He knew that the king loved his horse. So the convict said he would like to teach the king's horse to fly. The king agreed but specified a period of five years within which the horse should be able to fly. The family of the convicted man was furious. They asked him why he hadn't asked for something that was more easily deliverable. Vittal asked the entrepreneurs to focus on the strategy of the man, on the opportunity afforded by buying time. 'Five years is a long time,' he said to the businessmen, 'Who knows what lies in store? I could be out of here. The government could be out. You fellows could be out of business. And, who knows, the horse might fly.'

The horse did fly but it took more than five years. Vittal's special package for the software sector had to wait for two governments to fall and a third one to get elected. It had to wait for India to hang tantalizingly on the brink of a disaster, pledge its gold reserves and recover its breath. The software revolution was put on hold but not everything had to wait. One of the interesting things about the Indian bureaucratic maze is that it can create complementary competencies in departments and those who head them. As the secretary, Department of Electronics, Vittal was also a member of the Telecom Commission. This gave him an insight into the issues surrounding connectivity.

The problem with connectivity was primarily caused by the manner in which telecom policy in India had been framed. To start with, the Indian Telegraph Act 1855, a hangover from the British era, made telecommunication a public sector monopoly. No competition meant higher costs and poor service. This needed to be changed. Secondly, the focus of the policy was rural telephony—an extraordinary decision given the lack of phones in urban areas.

Yes, Pitroda had revolutionized connectivity by digitizing exchanges and making direct dialling possible. So it was easier to call cities in India and abroad. This had improved access but telephony still happened mostly through public call offices. Getting a phone at home or in the office was still a Herculean struggle. In a sense it was a revolution that was incomplete. Indeed, in the eighties, only five out of every 1,000 persons had a telephone connection. Over 700,000 people were on the waiting list for phones by the late eighties. In 1993, the number of people waiting for a telephone connection in just the four biggest metros was over 800,000; all over India 3.1 million were wait-listed for a phone.

Vittal recalls, not without sarcasm, the way the telecom department worked in those days: 'It was doing what can be only called de-marketing. A new telephone exchange could only be established in an area if there was a waiting list of 1,000 people. The system defied the supply-demand logic.' VSNL, a public sector unit then, had total monopoly over data links and international telephony.

The paradigm of cost was inverted. The world over, telecom companies deploy every strategy available to acquire scale. The higher the number of subscribers, the wider fixed costs can be spread thereby bringing down the per-subscriber cost. As costs come down, more subscribers join up, driving revenue. In India, however, every business was run on a simple cost-plus model—the telecom department would simply load all costs, the price of inefficiency and the profit margin on to the nearest consumer.

The inefficiencies of voice telephony visited data communications too. De-marketing, to use Vittal's term, prevailed. Vittal recognized that there was no way data connectivity costs could come down if software developers were to remain dependent on the Department of Telecommunications. Vittal had an idea. The Telegraph Act specified that the government would be the sole player; it didn't say that the Department of Telecommunications would be the sole player. Vittal proposed to the government that the Department of Electronics be allowed to set up earth stations on its premises—the costs of building them would be recovered from the software developers. The benefit to software developers would be that they would not have to pay for the earth stations but only for the use of facilities offered by them.

Questions were raised about the propriety of the Department of Electronics entering the telecom sector. Vittal managed to get past those and then suggested the setting up of a society under the Societies' Act, which would preclude any expectations of profit and would insulate the idea from political compulsions. There was a precedent. In several states, the concept of societies had been successfully used to fund and manage minor irrigation projects. There was, of course, the question of how the Department of Electronics could finance the operation. Vittal discovered that ₹190 crore had been budgeted for the construction of a semi-conductor complex in Mohali. He reviewed the costs and found ₹12 crore could be spared. This was used to set up the first earth stations—in Bangalore, Hyderabad, Noida, Gandhinagar and Bhubaneswar.

In June 1991, around the time Vittal revamped the Department of Electronics, a new arrival stirred up things on the telecom front. B. K. Syngal, a protégé of Rajiv Gandhi and Sam Pitroda's friend, arrived to take charge at VSNL. In an eventful tenure, Syngal transformed the moribund public sector company into a blue chip and enabled the first baby steps of Internet penetration in India.

Syngal's first meeting was with Tom Watson Jr of Texas Instruments in Bangalore. Watson had many complaints. The company needed three new connections for data communications and was told it could take eighteen months and cost as much as ₹45 lakh each for the connections to be provided. At that rate, Watson told Syngal, they would rather shut shop. Syngal heard him out and said that though he didn't have a magic wand he would see what he could do.

Later that afternoon he met with software exporters. They, too, wanted connectivity and at lower prices. Syngal worked out the costs and found they could be brought down. Essentially, there were two parts to the amounts that were charged: the cost of the satellite-linked earth station and the ground cable link that the Department of Telecom would provide. Syngal understood that higher volumes—a larger number of connections—would bring costs down. He worked the math backwards from the point of view of an affordable tariff to arrive at new numbers: the satellite link would cost ₹15 lakh, and the lease line from the earth station to the company would cost ₹4 lakh if local, and ₹9 lakh if not. By doing this—in about eight hours—Syngal brought down the cost of connectivity from ₹45 lakh to around ₹20 lakh.

Soon enough, the Department of Electronics and VSNL were competing for the business of setting up earth stations for software exporters. This was an entirely new situation for the companies—they had gone from no connections whatsoever to competition among service providers and, consequently, better deals. At the Oberoi Hotel in Bombay for a meeting, Syngal bumped into tech tycoon, Kanwal Rekhi. The Rawalpindi-born, IIT Bombay-alumnus, known for his pioneering work on Ethernet, was investing in India. Rekhi told Syngal that he had got a connection from the Software Technology

Park of India (STPI). Syngal offered him a free lease for a year to lure him back to VSNL. The best part about this competitive business model was that it was based on best practices, and the sort of efficient functioning expected in the private sector, as a result of which nobody lost any money.

The special package crafted by Vittal was in the waiting chambers of government. Soon after, P. V. Narasimha Rao dismantled the licence raj, and P. Chidambaram liberalized the trade policy. Vittal decided that the STPI policy was an idea whose time had come. He took the idea to Rao. The policy was everything the software sector wanted. The STPI policy assured software outfits the infrastructure they required—including core computer facilities, reliable power supply, ready-to-use office space, satellite-linked communications and administrative support for exports. It promised income tax benefits, customs duty exemptions, central excise exemptions, sales tax exemptions, the lease and import of equipment and the facility to retain export earnings for operations. There was no shortage of resistance to the plan even then. After all, India's fiscal policy was mortgaged to the IMF and the World Bank. Fortunately for the software sector, Vittal recalls, Rao's principal secretary, A. N. Verma, was convinced by the idea and got the prime minister to support it.

The timing was a happy accident. The dismantling of the licence-permit-quota raj and the introduction of a new currency regime in 1992 created room for the software sector's demands. Imports were easier, investment was opened up, travel was made easier and controls on foreign exchange relaxed. The idea of the STPI was IMF and circumstance-friendly. After all, India was in desperate need of foreign exchange and had no option but to promote exports. The sector offered the potential of high employment which would drive consumption and investment triggering the virtuous cycle of growth.

The new, liberalized regime also made it easy for companies to raise funds as the office of the controller of capital issues was abolished. In 1991, when Infosys first wanted to approach the capital markets, it was told by the controller of capital issues that it could only sell a share of ₹10 for ₹11—at a premium of just ₹1. Infosys wanted to raise

₹11 crore and objected to selling its valued equity cheap. It withdrew its offer and approached the market a second time in 1993. It priced its shares at ₹95—that is, a ₹10 share at a premium of ₹85—and the issue enabled it to take on cash-rich MNCs, fund operations and enable its best talent to benefit from stock options. While the issue was undersubscribed at the time, in due course the scrip became the bellwether stock for the IT sector. It is a measure of the value the company created that one share bought at ₹95 in 1993 was worth over ₹2.75 lakh in June 2012.

India was also in desperate need of investments in dollars. In 1993-94, the government decided to allow, under the STPI umbrella, 100 per cent foreign direct investment (FDI) in the IT sector. The delicious irony was that the 100 per cent FDI policy was being announced by the very same government which had imposed the 40 per cent FERA limit on equity holdings by multinationals, driving out players like IBM and Coke.

Murthy, who was chief of NASSCOM at that time, recalls there was considerable resistance within the association to the idea. The software developers were faced with three options: oppose, surrender to karma or play the MNC game. Many of the players felt this was the end and that their best talent would leave them for the multinationals. Some Indian 'rentrepreneurs' preferred that MNCs be forced into joint ventures so that they could rent their names and price their products at a premium.

The companies run by professionals, though, were up for the challenge. Their take on the situation was straightforward—let the MNCs come, we'll see what they do best and we'll learn from them. What the MNCs were good at was providing their employees with a world-class campus for training in, international working conditions, good infrastructure, competitive salaries and, of course, stock options. Their entry into the Indian market enabled Indian companies to lift their game to the next level. Companies like TCS and Infosys spared no effort to create the right working environment, create brand loyalty and offer attractive stock and career options. In fact, by the late nineties, concern had migrated from India to the boardrooms of multinational companies who found their best Indian professionals—for instance, Srini Rajam left Texas Instruments in December 2000 to found Ittiam Systems—leaving them to set up their own units.

Soon enough, technological giants from around the world were queuing up to invest in India. IBM, which had left in the seventies, was among the first to return with a tie-up with the Tatas to build personal computers. In 1993 and 1994, following the lead of Texas Instruments, Hewlett-Packard, 3M and the Digital Equipment Corporation invested in India to set up design and development centres. One of the prime drivers of the rush was the low cost of skilled manpower. Indian software engineers in the early nineties were available for hire at ₹10,000 to ₹15,000 per month—a lot of money considering that the per capita income of India was less than ₹10,000. However, when viewed by US employers, these wages were strikingly low; in fact, less than the minimum wage in the United States at the time.

The timing of the opening up of the sector was fortuitous. In the eighties and the nineties, China and the other Asian Tigers had chosen to invest capital to build the infrastructure required to promote and capture the market for manufactured goods. Their capital was blocked and their best talent completely engaged in manufacturing. India, which had missed the opportunity to cash in on the boom in computer hardware, now had the resources and manpower to take advantage of the demand for software. The STPIs became the vehicles of choice for luring investors and driving growth. By 1998, India had over twenty-five STPIs across the country. Quite appropriately, Prime Minister Atal Bihari Vajpayee described the STPIs as the new temples of modern India.

These new temples got their vaastu and timing right to benefit from the availability of priests who had the skill sets required to write the new mantras of technology. At the dawn of independence, India produced 2,500 engineers. In the following years there was a slump as competing priorities precluded investment in new technological institutes. By the eighties, education barons from the private sector stepped in. By the nineties, India was churning out 150,000 engineers and diploma holders, besides nearly a million science graduates, creating a huge talent bank for the software companies to tap into. There was another edge. Thanks to the scarcity of computers, Indians trained on computers of varying vintage and on different operating systems. Most had written their first code on UNIX systems which were declared obsolete. Then, in the nineties, UNIX made a comeback with personal computers. This made Indians the ideal choice for Americans looking to contract out jobs.

The software revolution was a culmination of a diverse set of circumstances. The multiple crises in the economy forced the dismantling of the licence-permit-quota raj, led to the opening up of markets and the installation of a policy to facilitate exports for earning foreign exchange. Private investment boosted capacity in education. And, most importantly, global economies at that time ramped up computerization on a scale that required them to source Indian help. And the numbers bear eloquent witness to the phenomenon. India's software exports, which were barely $100 million in 1990, touched $5 billion in 1999.

The role of the telecom revolution in the success of the software industry is often understated. The desire to rid the landscape of the phenomenon of waiting lists and the need for connectivity to attract investments led to the opening up of telecom in 1994. Led again by N. Vittal, now telecom secretary, India opened up both landline and wireless mobile sectors to foreign investment. However, long-distance telephony was kept closed to protect the state monopolies—BSNL and VSNL. In 1999, the Vajpayee regime opened up long-distance telephony to private investors. Today, India boasts over 900 million cellphone users and the cheapest tariffs in the world. The lords of the rings were able to cut costs, thanks to the ongoing IT revolution. As the tariffs of both domestic and international calls came down, a new business opportunity presented itself—call centres.

OF NALINI AND NANCY

The advent of better communications created the market for call centres and business process outsourcing (BPO) operations. Thanks to its geographic advantage, India was best placed for business process outsourcing—offering services to sectors as varied as legal and medical transcription, banking, software, microchip design, even the logistics of potato-chip deliveries. Again, what was crucial was the cost factor. Manpower typically accounts for over half the cost of running a call centre and India's wage bills—a fraction of what they would be in the US—were a persuasive option for many corporations to offshore non-critical services. Enterprises—from utility companies to mail-order catalogue retailers, airlines, computer hardware and software dealers and help desks of financial institutions—outsourced customer services and other functions to cut costs at home. The call centre phenomenon—portrayed in books, films and documentaries like *Nalini by Day, Nancy by Night* (2005)—created a whole new category of employment opportunities for young people just out of college.

The designation of Gurgaon in Haryana as the call centre capital of the country owes its genesis to an accidental encounter between K. P. Singh of DLF Limited, a large real estate developer, and Rajiv Gandhi in 1981. The vehicle Rajiv Gandhi was travelling in broke down close to Singh's office. As he waited for it to be fixed, Rajiv Gandhi and Singh discussed urban development. Singh pointed out the potential for creating urban infrastructure to house not only multinational offices but also people in vertical residences. He lamented the fact that a slew of archaic laws held back development. The meeting helped and Rajiv Gandhi took some of the ideas forward. But it wasn't till India opened up its economy that opportunity drove investment. When India's first call centres and software development centres were looking for homes and offices, Singh and DLF were ready. It helped that K. P. Singh had met with Jack Welch when the latter had come to scope out India in 1989. The first call centre—a captive unit of GE—was set up in Gurgaon.

Many followed thereafter as the outsourcing business caught the imagination of entrepreneurs, corporations and the Government of India. Government recognized the potential for employment and export revenues. It allowed the duty-free import of capital goods and provided tax exemptions to what is now described as Information Technology Enabled Services, or ITES, on the same lines as software developers.

India's software sector thus acquired a hyphenated twin—the IT Enabled Services sector. The ITES sector which kicked off with revenues of a few millions has already crossed the $10 billion milestone and NASSCOM has targeted revenues of $60 billion by 2020.

In hindsight, the IT revolution in India took place in two distinct phases. In the eighties, lift-off was helped by the reopening of engagement with the US and because of the technological skills of India's IT professionals; in the nineties, growth was fuelled by new investments and the quality and efficiency of service as also the scale it was able to deliver. However, it truly came of age due to Y2K.

Y2K was the product of time, literally and metaphorically. Computing infrastructure in the US and Europe had been set up on systems that had not accounted for the year 2000. Very simply, all computations were set in the mm-dd-yy (month-day-year, in two digits) format in the US. The year was rendered in two digits. So, at midnight on 31-12-99, the system could, theoretically, roll on to 01-01-00, wrecking all settings and calculations. This was most critical for the financial sector and others where continuous processes could be derailed. The potential for risk was enormous and the Americans and Europeans were naturally paranoid. Their computer systems required a patch that would move the computing cycle seamlessly to the first day of 2000 or 01-01-2000. The job itself was akin to a denting-painting of the systems but the scale was demanding. Across the world, only Indian companies had the talent pool which could be harnessed for an operation of this scale. The money was not much but the volumes made up for the lack of premium. It is this crucial combination of skill and scale that makes the Indian software industry a force to reckon with.

Success through access to international markets—in Europe and America—was made possible by the crucial right turn at Cancun by Indira Gandhi. Nearly 90 per cent of India's software exports are to the US, the UK and Europe. In money terms, nearly $62 billion of the information technology and enabled services exports comes from these markets. If India had not re-engaged with the US in 1981, it would have got neither contemporary technology nor the global market share that it commands now.

In 1999, global consultants McKinsey had predicted that IT and services exports out of India could touch $50 billion by 2010. The IT majors did so much earlier. The Y2K exposure, another happy accident, enabled Indian software majors such as TCS, Wipro and Infosys to acquire a brilliant resumé. As a result, they could bid for and win bigger contracts requiring higher sophistication. The migration from hourly body-shopping contracts to creating the intellectual property desired by mega corporations has lifted them to a higher orbit. Today, 65 per cent of the world's Carnegie Mellon-certified CMM Level 5 development centres and over 100 firms boasting SEI certification are located in India.

As of March 2012, IT and BPO services aggregated revenues of over $100 billion. At $69 billion, software and services exports accounted for nearly a quarter of India's total exports. Delivering over 7 per cent of the GDP in revenues, the sector employs over 2.5 million people and creates indirect employment for over 8.3 million more.

Even more valuable is the shift in the international perception of India that the IT sector has enabled. Leadership in automobile and consumer electronics altered the image of Japan and South Korea. Indian software engineers have done the same for Brand India.

> Democracy is not a spectator sport. Participation of the people in government is essential for a republic to truly be one. The Constitution guarantees the freedom of speech. But without the right to information, this freedom is hobbled. Freeing governance from the fiefdom of the powerful required unlocking...

THE DA VINCI CODE

2 DECEMBER 1994
KOT KIRANA, PALI, RAJASTHAN

It was, on the face of it, just a gathering of villagers dressed in their traditional finery. Yet the assembly of 200 people in Kot Kirana—most of them poor farmers from the nearby villages of Kot, Samel, Kirana, Rokabaria, Pipla Khera, Sirma, Bagdi, Belapana, Bhundap and a dozen other villages from Pali district in Rajasthan—was in itself a mini revolution.

In rural Rajasthan, life and reality were as harsh as the landscape. Paternal feudalism was practically the only code that mattered. And nobody could gather without the hukum of their overlords. But this was precisely what the villagers had decided to do at Pali's first 'jansunwai'—a hearing of the people. Barely one in three of the villagers gathered could read and write and most of them were poverty-stricken. Mingling with them were social workers Sanjit 'Bunker' Roy, a Doon School alumnus, who was passionate about sustainable development, and was working on an alternate model for village-level development from the Social Work and Research Centre in Tilonia, and civil rights activist Sawai Singh of Samagra Sewa Sangh. Although the villagers had gathered to discuss how the government spent public money, there were no government officials present. Just a few subalterns, officials from the district administration, took notes as speeches were made.

The word sunwai normally means a hearing, be it public or private. But the villagers and the Mazdoor Kisan Shakti Sangathan (MKSS) didn't quite intend it to be a hearing in that particular sense of the word.

They had gathered to exchange information about small development works carried out in the Kot Kirana and Bagdi Kalaliya panchayats in 1993-94 that were meant to benefit them as well as information that was not being provided from official channels. The meeting began with the reading out of the names of villagers who were supposed to have been paid for work they had done. The information on the sheet had been gleaned by activists from official records—without permission, of course.

As the names were read out, many stood up and declared that they had never been given work or wages nor had they even gone to those work sites. The signatures, they said, must have been forged and, what's more, many of the names on the muster rolls belonged to people who had either moved away or were dead. A cabal which included the village teacher, a gram sewak and junior engineer had colluded on the fraud.

The next item on the agenda was the cost of construction of the patwarghar—the office of the Revenue Department. The government had paid money—out of funds allocated to the village—for roofing, doors, windows and building material for a structure that did not exist. Someone joked that at least it existed on paper. 'Laughter,' recalls Nikhil Dey, one of the founding members of the MKSS, 'was followed by outrage and anger. The people forced the government to file an FIR against the culprits.' The jansunwai morphed from being a passive forum for exchanging information into a people's court, an early forerunner to the Right to Information (RTI) Act that would empower the people of the country in unimaginable ways.

Activists in Rajasthan had worked for years to find ways to ensure that the programmes which promised succour to the poorest of the poor actually delivered. The situation on the ground, though, was dismal. While welfare programmes existed on paper, more often than not villagers were coerced into working for employment schemes, made to sign fake papers and conned of their dues. Schemes sponsored by the central and state governments were converted into private enterprises for profit. The villagers, poor and illiterate, were hardly in a position to challenge those in authority. They needed help, and even though the activists stepped in, they could not deliver change without an organized movement.

In 1987, three individuals from disparate backgrounds came together—Aruna Roy, a 1968-batch IAS officer who had quit the service in 1975, Shankar Singh, a grassroots activist, and Nikhil Dey. Roy, who would go on to win the Magsaysay Award for community leadership, was living and working in Tilonia. Singh was their ace communicator who had the great gift of being able to connect with people. Dey worked in the region on the rights and entitlements of the poorest. The three were brought together because of the brutal exploitation the villagers faced. This led to the formation of the MKSS by Roy, Singh and Dey.

The trio chose Devdungri in Rajsamand district of Rajasthan as their base and set about understanding the issues that led to the denial of benefits to the poor. Government policies written in Jaipur, the state capital, stipulated that people were supposed to be informed of poverty-alleviation schemes—public works and other similar employment programmes—so that they could benefit from them. However, no information was shared. Worse, even if the poor managed to get work, they were not paid. The trio focused first on ensuring that workers were not bilked out of their dues.

But, to ensure this, the activists needed access to records to prove that fraud was being perpetrated. They also needed the victims to be involved in the process. These mostly poor farmers and labourers were eager to be part of the initiative but were fearful of the feudal hierarchy. With time and patience, the trio found traction. Hunger strike—the most common and desperate instrument of agitation—was deployed. And like all such instruments, it was vulnerable to the law of diminishing utility. There were also countervailing forces, for instance, the goons of the local MLAs would bust strikes or bribe villagers with feasts and liquor. R. Shankaran, then secretary, rural development, Government of India, suggested at one of the meetings with the MKSS that if the organization changed its focus to demanding the right to access information, other benefits would follow.

The tradition in government was that all information—unless

shared by helpful IAS officers, mostly idealistic probationers—was confidential. So the only way to collect information was to get it from official or legislative records, either from the gram panchayat or the state government in the capital. This was difficult. The activists then came up with the idea to create an informal information system. Nothing could happen in the district without the people knowing about it. A public information exchange would be set up to enable the sharing of information and the auditing of official claims. Thus was born the jansunwai.

The success of the first jansunwai at Kot Kirana was well publicized, thanks to the presence of a reporter from *Navbharat Times* who wrote a moving piece titled '*O Gram Sewak Tho Maro Aakhiyon Mein Dhool Jhonkiyan*' (Gram Sewak, You Have Been Cheating Us). On 7 December, the second jansunwai was organized at Bhim. Well-known Rajasthani poet Harish Bhadani was roped in to participate. As before, the hearing revealed a sorry record of lies and corruption on the part of local officials and government. By the time the third hearing was organized at Jawaja in Ajmer on 17 December, the idea of the jansunwai had caught on. It received media coverage and the idea found great support among intellectuals, not just in Rajasthan but also in Delhi. The initial meetings were followed by public hearings at Vijaypur in Rajsamand on 17 January and Thana in Bhilwara on 25 February.

Nikhil Dey asserts that the movement changed the landscape of denial forever. At first, all officers, from the level of the chief secretary down to junior engineers, and even the MLAs, were upset but they eventually had no option but to reconcile themselves to the idea that people power was here to stay. The MKSS followed up the mass movement with a blizzard of petitions to the Rajasthan government signed by writers, thinkers, journalists and other prominent members of civil society.

The move had its impact on the political class. Bhairon Singh Shekhawat, then chief minister of Rajasthan, announced during the campaign for the panchayat elections of 1995 that the state government would provide information to the people. Shekhawat had the knack to spot a build-up of pressure. And he knew exactly how to release the pressure by the promise of action; expediency would decide whether action would actually be taken or not. In April 1995, he declared on the floor of the house that the people of the state would be granted the right to information on all Panchayati Raj institutions and rural development programmes. This included access to and photocopies of documents, bills and vouchers of expenditure. He promised that the state would institute an enquiry wherever fraud was detected and punish the guilty.

But the promise was really a political dodge, a compromise to arrest the momentum built up by the movement. Nikhil Dey remembers, 'For over a year we couldn't even get a copy of the announcement on the floor of the assembly.'

The change promised by government was never delivered. The MKSS intensified its agitation and decided then that it could not settle for anything less than legislation. A law guaranteeing the right to information would have to be passed.

A BRIEF HISTORY

The right to information was not an alien concept. People have sought information relevant to their lives across democracies and even in some monarchies. But it had to be fought for in every instance across the world. The earliest known battle is from the 1750s.

Sweden was the pioneer. The unwritten but well-established covenant in that country was that all the doings of the State were public unless declared secret. In the early days, those who attended the monarch's court were privy to the process of governance and this could, in principle, be narrated to the public at large. But it could not be published. In 1759, Peter Forsskal, a writer, published *Tankar Om Borgerliga Friheten* (Thoughts on Civil Liberty) advocating the freedom of press and information. The State banned the sale of the book and confiscated copies.

This ill-thought-out action led to the movement for the freedom of information which eventually resulted in the adoption of *Tryckfrihetsförordningen* or the Freedom of the Press Act 1766. The Act stated that official documents—of the courts, Parliament or government—could be printed and disseminated as information to the people. The victory was not without a political slant. The new majority in Parliament wanted to excavate the doings of the previous regime which had ruled for over five decades. Whatever the motive, the principle of public access, or as the Swedish would say, *offentlighetsprincipen,* was established. And although the law was passed in 1766, it only came into operation in 1810 after King Gustav IV was replaced.

The tussle for enforcing the right, though, continued between the people and the monarchy. It was only after World War II that Parliament gained the upper hand. Labour unions which dominated politics ensured that the rights were enshrined in theory and in practice. Indeed, many of the social policies that Swedes enjoy today owe their origin to the influence of the labour unions. But the quest for the freedom of information made its next appearance only in 1951, in Finland, which was clearly influenced by its association with Sweden.

Even the world's second largest democracy, the US, was immune to the idea till as late as the fifties when the campaign for the freedom of information made its debut in public discourse. However, it took almost a decade, till 1966, for the freedom of information to be enshrined in that country when LBJ pushed through legislation as part of his party's efforts to create a Great Society. President Johnson said, 'A democracy works best when the people have all the information that the security of the nation permits. No one should be able to pull curtains of secrecy around decisions which can be revealed without injury to the public interest.' That said, the law was weak and replete with exemptions. Americans, for instance, couldn't ask for information about oil wells.

Legislation in the US was followed by the enactment of similar laws in Denmark (1970), Norway (1971), France and the Netherlands (1978), Australia and New Zealand (1982), Canada (1983), Austria (1987), Italy (1990), Belgium (1994), Ireland (1997) and Japan (1999). Interestingly, while older nations dodged and weaved on delivering what is an embedded right in democracy, newer ones like those in Eastern Europe—including Estonia, Bosnia-Herzegovina, Poland

and Serbia perhaps because they were once part of the Communist bloc—included provisions for the freedom of information in their constitutions. The United Kingdom, however, delivered to its people the right to information only in 2000, nearly twenty-two years after the demand was first made in 1978.

CULTURE OF SECRECY

By the time the MKSS flagged off the movement for the RTI in 1994, over a dozen countries across the world had a law guaranteeing the right to information to their citizens. In 1946, the UN General Assembly adopted Resolution 59(1) stating that the 'freedom of information is a fundamental human right and the touchstone of all the freedoms to which the United Nations is consecrated'. The International Covenant on Civil and Political Rights adopted in December 1966, and in force since March 1976, in Article 19 of the Universal Declaration of Human Rights states: 'Everyone has the right to freedom of opinion and expression; this right includes freedom to hold opinions without interference and to seek, receive and impart information and ideas through any media and regardless of frontiers.' Yet India and many other countries, despite being signatories to such international promissory notes, shirked from delivering on the promise.

The movement for the freedom of information gained impetus from the changing nature of democracy. From the concept of direct participation in decision-making in the early days, democracy had morphed into a representative form of government because of the growth in population and the size of the State. The expanded size of the State threw up questions of quality of governance as also of political morality. Do representatives of the people really represent those who elect them? Does decision-making truly reflect the wish and will of the people? Unless governments were the size of Swiss cantons, it was not possible for them to engage directly with local issues that affected their citizens. It followed, then, that new procedures on ways to bring citizen inputs into the process of governance had to be devised.

Since 1952, when the first post-independence government was elected, people voted a party to power and hoped that those elected would do right by them. Accountability, if at all, was enforced not by public participation but as a result of competitive politics. Willy-nilly, governance continued to be a spectator sport. In the first decade after independence, there existed a contract of trust between people and their rulers. Those who ran the government were the people who had secured the country's freedom. The halo began to dim by the sixties. By the seventies it began to seem that the founding fathers had missed a step in the articulation of a framework for the future. They had not explicitly stated the right of citizens to access information to demand accountability.

Worse, while adopting the administrative frame used by the British, India's rulers retained many restrictive British laws. Many of them—like the Official Secrets Act 1923, which was enacted to prevent spying and punish anyone who disclosed government information—were designed to enable imperial masters to deny natives power. The Indian Evidence Act 1872 says, 'No one shall be permitted to give any evidence from unpublished official records relating to any affairs of the State.' Moreover, rules framed after independence added to the culture of secrecy. The All India Services (Conduct Rules) 1968 that governs civil servants prohibits officials from sharing information with people unless authorized.

And so these provisions were used to deny people information and shield the incompetent or the corrupt. As early as in 1952, the R. A. Gopalaswami report, 'The Machinery of Government: Improvement of Efficiency', which dealt with the restructuring of governance, was declared classified. In 1979, the Morvi dam in Gujarat gave way, flooding the town of Morvi and killing more than 1,800 people. The Ahmedabad-based Consumer Education and Research Centre asked for a copy of the enquiry report; the request was denied under the Official Secrets Act. The provisions of the Official Secrets Act were also used to deny public information on the monetary settlement between Union Carbide and the Government of India after the Bhopal gas tragedy.

Every attempt to question the need for the Official Secrets Act was derailed by governments through the use of working groups and committees. In 1977, following the atrocities committed during the Emergency, the Morarji Desai government appointed a working group to draft amendments to the Official Secrets Act. The working group came to the conclusion that no amendments were needed. Despite the fact that many of its ministers had suffered imprisonment and state oppression, the Desai government concurred. A decade later, V. P. Singh rode to power demanding information on the Bofors scandal. After taking over as prime minister, Singh declared that the veil of secrecy was used to shield the guilty and vested interests and emphasized that an open system of governance was essential for democracy to flower. His government set up a committee, but its recommendations were binned.

In principle, the Constitution recognizes freedom of expression as a right, in practice the statute denied the citizen an explicit instrument—the right to information—to exercise it. In the absence of information and access to the process of decision-making, it was not possible for citizens to participate in the process of governance and question governments. In a way, without the enabling provision for freedom of information, the constitutional right to expression was non est. This was established by the various judgements of the Supreme Court.

Justice K. K. Mathew, in 1975, in the *State of UP vs Raj Narain* case, concerning the accusation of electoral malpractice against Indira Gandhi in which information was withheld under the Evidence Act, held that 'in a government of responsibility like ours, where all the agents of the public must be responsible for their conduct, there can be but few secrets. The people of this country have a right to know… To cover with a veil of secrecy the common routine business, is not in the interest of the public. Such secrecy can seldom be legitimately desired'.

In 1982, in the Supreme Court, in the *S. P. Gupta vs Union of India* case, concerning the independence of the judiciary, the judges held that 'the concept of an open government is the direct emanation from the right to know which seems to be implicit in the right of free speech and expression guaranteed under Article 19(1)(a). Therefore, disclosure of information in regard to the functioning of Government must be the rule and secrecy an exception justified only where the strictest requirement of public interest so demands'.

Notwithstanding the wisdom of the Supreme Court, successive governments evaded the idea of open government. Because citizens were kept out of the process of policymaking, people were robbed of the opportunity to contribute and thus make policies more effective and the delivery of services more efficient. It also led to the hijacking of policy by vested groups, the perpetuation of elitism and denial of accountability which led to the breeding of corruption. The worst sufferers were the completely voiceless, the poorest of the poor. As early as in 1991, in a paper on poverty alleviation, Nikhil Dey observed, 'No matter how good the formulation of a programme for the poor, its implementation is largely dependent on its delivery system. If the delivery system is made answerable to the people it is meant to benefit, there is a better chance of the scheme being implemented.'

The misery and suffering caused by the denial of a fundamental right was what the MKSS focused on throughout the right to information movement. MKSS activists held that 'information is the lifeline of people fighting for rights and justice. Without this information the mere articulation of rights as fundamental had little meaning'. Paradoxically, while the IAS lobby continued to resist change, in October 1995 the Lal Bahadur Shastri Academy in Mussoorie, which trains and retrains IAS officers, invited Aruna Roy and her team to make a presentation on the idea of the right to information and how it could be brought into the system. Despite such developments, the government continued to drag its feet over implementing the idea.

In April 1996, the MKSS organized a protest in the town of Beawar in Rajasthan demanding the implementation of the right to information. Over 200 people began a month-long sit-in. On 1 May, all the labour unions—barring the Bharatiya Mazdoor Sangh, which was aligned to the BJP government in power—joined in. It is not easy for a movement of poor people to carry on without resources but the dharna at Beawar was supported by an unusual coalition of traders, farmers and professionals. The poorest brought grain, local traders supported the protesters with donations and individuals offered free services as a token of their support. By this time the idea of the right to information had caught the imagination of the national media. At the end of a month, the organizers set up agitations in multiple locations, including Jaipur, to put pressure on the government.

While governments continued to resist, intellectuals grew more voluble in their support. Senior journalists like the *Jansatta* editor Prabhash Joshi, *Mainstream* editor Nikhil Chakravarty, Kuldip Nayyar and Ajit Bhattacharjea pitched in along with social activists Medha Patkar, Swami Agnivesh and G. R. Khairnar. Speaking at the dharna, Chakravarty said, 'You are not alone, there is a whole country supporting you and watching this movement.' Incensed by the refusal of the Rajasthan government to deliver on its promise, on 26 May 1996 Prabhash Joshi went on to write a stirring essay '*Jaanna, Jeene Ke Liye Hai*' which essentially means, 'To Know, Is to Live'.

Nayyar and Bhattacharjea asked Roy and Dey to speak at a meeting in Delhi to explain the potential of the RTI. They spoke of how the RTI could expose all manner of ills of governance, including corruption. The point was best illustrated by Sushila, an activist from Rajasthan who had accompanied Aruna Roy. She told the audience, 'At my home and my shop I am answerable to my family for all the kamai and kharcha, that is, all the income and expense. The government is run on public money, how can it deny me hisaab?'

THE FIRST DRAFT

In July 1995, Justice P. B. Sawant, who had retired from the Supreme Court, took over as chairman of the Press Council of India. Heading a three-member bench in the *Union of India vs Cricket Association of Bengal* case, Justice Sawant had ruled that 'the right to impart and receive information is a species of the right to freedom of speech and expression guaranteed by Article 19(1) of the Constitution'. The judgement then went on to rule that while the air waves of the country are public property, it cannot be construed to be a government monopoly, thereby opening the doors for the launch of many TV channels in India. It was only natural that having ruled so clearly on the right to impart and receive information, he would champion the cause of RTI.

Justice Sawant recalls that the issue had been on his mind even before the judgement of 1995. 'All along I have felt that freedom of speech and expression cannot be complete without the right to information. In a democracy, wherever government activities have a bearing on people, this information must be available to the people to strengthen democracy.' This, he felt, would enable the people to question their representatives and make the government accountable. 'If the people are sovereign, then government is the servant and information belongs to the people. How can the servants of people keep or deny information from the masters in a democracy?'

Soon after taking over as chairman of the Press Council, Justice Sawant organized meetings of like-minded people in July-August 1995. The group included senior journalists Nayyar, Joshi, Chakravarty and Bhattacharjea, activists Roy and Dey, lawyer Shanti Bhushan and former Prime Minister V. P. Singh. The group discussed the need to pass a law guaranteeing the right to information.

After the group had met a couple of times, it became clear that the campaign needed a coalition of public interest groups. In mid-1996, the National Campaign for People's Right to Information (NCPRI) was formed. Nikhil Dey explains that the idea was not that the NCPRI would be the voice of the movement; on the contrary, it would be a platform for many voices to come together. The consultative group now included thirty people from different geographies and focus areas, including Justice V. M. Tarkunde, jurist, civil rights activist and humanist often referred to as the father of the civil liberties movement in India. At the third meeting of the group Justice Sawant presented a draft of the proposed Right to Information Act.

The group sought to define the gamut of governmental processes and records that could legitimately be sought by the public. Even as it argued the case for access to information, the expert group recognized the need for government to keep some kinds of information secret. N. C. Saxena, former secretary in the Government of India and now a member of the National Advisory Council, brought clarity to the debate on the definition of what information should be made public. He suggested that any information that was made available to representatives of the people—MPs, MLAs and other elected members in local self-governments—could not be denied to a citizen.

After the group finalized a draft bill titled the Right to Information Bill 1996—a name suggested by the Press Council of India—it said that the 'public should be granted the right to access—including inspection, taking notes and extracts—information and material relating to the affairs, administration or conduct of a public authority in respect of which public has a right to know, and includes any document or record relating to the affairs of the public authority'. Public authority was defined as the government and Parliament of India, and the government and legislature of each of the states and local and other authorities in the territory of India. The definition of public authority included a company, corporation, trust firm, society or a cooperative society, whether owned or controlled by private individuals and institutions whose activities affected the public interest. The bill also specified the various provisions, processes, exemptions, penalties and punishment involved.

The demand for the right to information draws legitimacy from the fact that corruption, which leads to poor governance and denial of entitlements, cannot be viewed purely as an issue of law enforcement. By the end of 1996, Justice Sawant propelled the movement forward. He sent a copy of the bill—with a letter under the aegis of the Press Council of India—to the prime minister, state legislatures, chief ministers, members of parliament, MLAs and ministers in the Government of India.

On 2 January 1997, the United Front government led by H. D. Deve Gowda appointed a Working Group headed by H. D. Shourie, editor of the magazine *Common Cause* which dealt with consumer rights, to examine the feasibility and the need to introduce a full-fledged right to information bill. The move was prompted by the weight of the letter sent by Justice Sawant, the public pressure brought to bear by NCPRI and, of course, the presence of high-profile names as signatories to the letter to Gowda. The fact that one of those who had signed was V. P. Singh, who had anointed Gowda as prime minister, kept up the pressure on government.

Also pushing for it were three influential chief ministers, Chandra Babu Naidu of Andhra Pradesh, Digvijay Singh of Madhya Pradesh and S. M. Krishna of Karnataka. At the forty-seventh meeting of the National Development Council in January 1997, Digvijay Singh observed that the right to information had become inevitable for checking corruption. Naidu pointed out to Deve Gowda the success of the Janmabhoomi programme in Andhra Pradesh, which involved people's participation in decision-making and the accountability of the administration to the people. It was important, he said, that the right to information get due attention, and offered to host a seminar in Hyderabad to discuss it.

To celebrate fifty years of independence, the United Front government organized a conference of chief ministers on 24 May 1997. The conference reviewed the promises made by government and listed its numerous failures. The picture was not pretty. India was home to over 400 million illiterate people, more than any other country in the world. Over 36 per cent of its 900-million-plus population were living below the poverty line, unable to feed themselves twice a day.

This failure was impacting the electoral prospects of the political class, they feared an anti-incumbency vote. The phrase describes both voter dissatisfaction and failed governance. Every election since the eighties has seen nearly 40 per cent of sitting MLAs and MPs vanquished by anti-incumbency. The political class recognized that they were paying the price for bureaucratic sloth. They were accountable to voters every election while the bureaucracy was getting away scot-free.

At the conference, in a resolution titled 'Action Plan for Effective and Responsive Administration', many chief ministers admitted rather candidly that, 'as the country completes fifty years people are assailed by growing doubts about the effectiveness and moral standards of administration.' To many it seemed to be the understatement of the post-independence era, albeit quite an admission for the political class to make. The golden jubilee celebrations afforded the political class an opportunity to realign the compass of political power. The CMs resolved that 'central and state governments should move together to justify the trust of faith of the people'. They drew up an action plan, a wish list, for governance and piously called for the need for 'responsive, accountable, transparent and people friendly administration at all levels'.

The chief ministers then passed a resolution to introduce a Citizen's Charter for citizen-friendly governance. The Charter called for a review of existing systems of public grievance redressal, a review of laws and processes, the simplification of regulations and the repeal of obsolete laws. The political class concluded that lack of openness in government decision-making was largely responsible for corruption and was contrary to the spirit of democracy. It was suggested that legislation be framed for a freedom of information act, and amendments introduced to the Official Secrets Act and the Indian Evidence Act.

The call for legislation was supported by Parliament. Cutting across party lines, members of the Standing Committee on Home Affairs in its 38th Report (on Grants for the Ministry of Personnel, Public Grievances and Pensions) observed that a law to facilitate the right to information for 'the promotion of open and transparent government was a long overdue measure and in the view of the committee quite consistent with...democratic ideals'. The committee asserted that there should be a full-fledged right to information act as it would go a long way in firmly establishing the culture of accountability. It said: 'As the subject "Right to Information" is not specifically provided for in the Seventh Schedule to the Constitution, the Union through the residuary clause (97) of List I, has the right to legislate on the subject. The committee recommends that the Ministry take up this matter urgently to facilitate early enactment of the "Right to Information Act".'

Even as these events were happening in the Centre, many states were preparing to introduce legislation related to the right to information. Indeed, Tamil Nadu had already passed, in April 1997, a bill empowering its citizens to seek information. The Tamil Nadu government, then led by M. Karunanidhi of the DMK, had used the template created by the Justice Sawant draft to produce the Tamil Nadu Right to Information Act 1997. But the law was hastily put together and enacted and as a result was full of loopholes. It had no less than twenty-two exemptions, making it useless. It included a fishing net provision that gave the government carte blanche to deny information. It stated under Section 3(2-g) as a condition for non-disclosure 'any information that would prejudice administration of justice and the enforcement or proper administration of law'. The state could also, under the same Section, withhold information on the grounds of prejudice to the economy and commerce.

Any request for information is based on assumptions and suspicions of maladministration. Hypothetically, the provisions could prevent a person from seeking information, say, on the allocation of funds using the first pretext or the allotment of government land to a private company using the second pretext. Additionally, the government could at any time seek refuge under Sections 123 and 124 of the Indian Evidence Act which was retained as one of the grounds for non-disclosure. And, of course, there was no provision for penalties on the denial of information. Flaws notwithstanding, it was clear that the idea was now firmly rooted, with at least half a dozen states examining the feasibility of passing the law.

Meanwhile, in Delhi, in the summer of 1997, the H. D. Shourie Committee submitted its report along with a reworked bill. The committee had a charmed life. Appointed by Deve Gowda, it had survived the toppling of the Gowda government. The report it presented, however, was far from satisfactory. To start with, the change of the title, from the Right to Information to Freedom of Information, was seen as a dilution. The groups argued that they were not asking for a favour, but for a legal instrument that recognized the right of citizens to demand information and accountability. The government argued that the right was already recognized and what was needed was the freedom to access information. The draft of the Freedom of Information Bill 1997 reflected the chasm between what activists were demanding and what the government was willing to yield.

Citizens' groups, the Press Council and the NCPRI argued that the bill was full of loopholes, enabling the government to deny information. For instance, there was a clause—as in the Tamil Nadu Act of 1997—

which allowed the government to deny 'information which would not serve any public interest'. The definition of what constitutes the public interest is usually contextual and left open to interpretation by officials. This was an invitation to denial. The reworked bill had a clause that enabled bureaucracy to question the purpose of the enquiry and thereby deny citizens information.

The bill also excluded corporates and NGOs from the definition of 'public authority' reflecting the power of private influence. The worst dilution was the deletion of the fundamental principle that 'no information that is provided to elected representatives will be denied to citizens'. This was hardly surprising; eight of the ten members in the committee were bureaucrats who worshipped secrecy in government. The activists rejected the draft.

Individual states, meanwhile, were going ahead with their ideas. On 31 July 1997, the Government of Goa passed the Goa Right to Information Act. Soon after he had written to various state governments in 1996, Justice Sawant visited Goa. His interaction with local activists and journalists gave the movement a boost in the state. Unlike many other states, Goa had a high rate of literacy, a progressive administration and a large middle class, all factors that helped move things along.

In Madhya Pradesh, a Congress government led by Digvijay Singh issued orders to thirty-six departments to share information with the public pending comprehensive legislation. In 1998, the Digvijay Singh regime, weeks before elections were due, tabled and passed a bill on the right to information. Unfortunately, the bill was not enacted into law because it did not get the governor's assent. Apparently, there were quibbles on whether the state had the jurisdiction to pass such a law. This, when two states already had fully functional laws for providing citizens access to information.

In November 1997, the Congress withdrew its support to the United Front ending that reign of regional satraps over Delhi. The BJP, which had been forced to resign after thirteen days in 1996 owing to its lack of a majority, charged the Congress with fuelling political instability and mounted a campaign for a stable coalition at the Centre.

SONIA ENTERS POLITICS

As the Right to Information Bill went on the back-burner, Congress underwent a change of guard. Sonia Gandhi, who had stayed out of active politics, began meeting party leaders. In December 1996, at a dinner hosted by Murli Deora in Mumbai, Sonia Gandhi engaged with party members and other guests on national issues, giving the first sign that she would be entering electoral politics. There was immense pressure on her to join the party as the Congress was in disarray. Many of its stalwarts like G. K. Moopanar, often described as the Kamaraj of the nineties, had left the party and started their own, fed up with the whimsical ways of Congress President Sitaram Kesri. It was in this scenario that Sonia Gandhi was persuaded to attend the 80th Session of the AICC in Calcutta.

On 9 August 1997, in a carefully orchestrated first step, Sonia Gandhi accepted primary membership in the party and spoke as a party member for the first time. She chose her lines from one of Rajiv Gandhi's speeches. She said, 'What has become of our great organization? Instead of a party that fired the imagination of the masses throughout the length and breadth of India, we have shrunk, losing touch with the toiling millions. It is not a question of victories and defeats in elections. For a democratic party, victories and defeats are part of its continuing political existence. But what does matter is whether or not we work among the masses, whether or not we are in tune with their struggles, their hopes and aspirations.' By March 1998, when Congress went to the polls, Sonia Gandhi had taken charge as its president.

Congress had lost ground with Muslims who believed that the party had stood by and watched while the Babri Masjid at Ayodhya was demolished. It had lost a large share of Hindu votes thanks to the aggressive stance the BJP maintained vis-à-vis Hindutva. If it had to regain its relevance, it needed fresh ideas. Sonia Gandhi saw that the poorest of the poor had been neglected by national parties after the liberalization of the economy in 1991, when the gap between the rich and the poor had widened. One idea, borrowed from history and Indira Gandhi, was to turn left, to present the party to the poor as one that spoke for them.

As she prepared herself for her new role—and the party for elections—Sonia Gandhi courted ideologues from the Left. One of them was Mohit Sen, a member of the CPI and a friend of the Gandhi family, who had been on good terms with both Jawaharlal Nehru and Indira Gandhi. It was Sonia's interaction with people like Sen which led to the sentiments she expressed at the Plenary Session of the Congress in Calcutta—where she exhorted Congressmen to revive the 'tradition to fight for the poor and the oppressed. Only by doing so shall we gain the strength to create the India of our dreams'. The force of her commitment to turn left was further reinforced in 1999 when she appointed a committee under the former Kerala chief minister, A. K. Antony, known for his socialist leanings, to enquire if reforms were anti-poor. The appointment of the Antony Committee was mainly symbolic—its findings were never made public, but it did help project the idea that the Congress was pro-poor.

Among the people Sonia Gandhi met in the run-up to the polls were bureaucrats who were agitated over the decreasing relevance of the State, economists who worried about rising inequality and the narrowing of scope for government intervention and civil society groups who occupied the non-Hindutva, secular, left-of-centre space. The Congress Party was looking for an image overhaul when NCPRI activists Aruna Roy and Nikhil Dey met with Sonia Gandhi. Their aim: to get the Congress to support the idea of a right to information act. It helped that Congress governments in Goa and Madhya Pradesh had passed similar laws. The Congress Manifesto of 1998 duly endorsed the idea. It said: 'The Congress party will enact a Freedom of Information Act to end the culture of secrecy and to ensure openness in administration. All exercise of discretionary power by its Ministers will be made open to public scrutiny.'

Sonia Gandhi's interest and commitment to RTI was intense, recall Congressmen who were present at meetings to discuss the idea. As one of them recalls, she seemed more of an evangelist than the activists who were persuading her. The left turn didn't pay an immediate dividend; her party did very poorly in the 1998 polls. The BJP couldn't come to power under its own steam but it played its cards well by tapping into the anti-Congress sentiment that prevailed at the time. The BJP crafted the thirteen-party National Democratic Alliance (NDA) with the help of regional leaders. The alliance was created around Vajpayee's aura and by wooing the constituents of the United Front with the promise of a fair share of power at the Centre. The BJP bagged 21 per cent of the votes and won 179 seats. Along with its allies, who had won seventy-three seats, the party staked its claim to form the government. On 19 March 1998, A. B. Vajpayee was sworn in as prime minister.

In less than thirteen months the NDA ran into trouble when the Jayalalithaa-led AIADMK pulled out of the coalition. The country went to the polls again. Once again, the Congress manifesto promised the people that 'a Bill on Freedom of Information and Right to Information will be introduced soon to give citizens easy access to information at all levels'. Once again the Congress lost the election. But although the NDA and its allies had won, the activists promoting the idea of the right to information were assured that the Congress would back the bill on the right to information when brought into Parliament.

By 1998, regional leaders of the national parties and chiefs of regional parties had come to the conclusion that the provision for the right to information would not only help citizens but ruling establishments across the country too. To them it was clear that the only way to take on the bureaucracy was to empower the people. However, on the ground, there was little movement.

THE BREAKTHROUGH

Just as the movement seemed to have hit a dead end, an astonishing event delivered the breakthrough. Lawyer Ram Jethmalani, who was then the urban development minister, grew frustrated with the level of chicanery in the system and decided to open up the files and documents of his ministry to public access. Normally, a decision like this would need to be debated and considered at the level of the Union Cabinet. But Jethmalani had never bothered with the niceties of hierarchy. Suo moto, he issued an official memorandum that stated that those members of the public who wanted to inspect documents were free to approach the ministry of urban development.

It sent the central government into a tizzy. Many ministerial colleagues of Jethmalani described his declaration as a stunt. Among the conscientious objectors were the ministries of home, defence and finance. On 21 October 1998, Prabhat Kumar, then the cabinet secretary, wrote to S. S. Chattophadhyay, special secretary of urban development, ordering him to not carry out the instructions of his minister.

This was just the window of opportunity the activists needed. In December 1998, the NCPRI and two other organizations filed a Public Interest Litigation (PIL) in the Supreme Court challenging the cabinet secretary's order. The petitioners told the Court that the ministry refused to allow the inspection of files as promised by the memorandum issued by Jethmalani and that the order of the cabinet secretary was bad in law. The petitioners argued that the denial violated their fundamental right to information. On 18 December, a three-judge bench comprising Justice S. P. Bharucha, Justice A. P. Misra and Justice D. P. Mohapatra of the Supreme Court admitted the PIL.

The respondent, the Government of India, was not unduly perturbed. It simply bought time by releasing a public statement that a four-member group of ministers headed by L. K. Advani, then the home minister, was looking into the modalities of a bill towards ensuring the freedom of information.

On 19 February 1999, Prime Minister Vajpayee—who normally weighs when to speak—chose the platform of the National Development Council meeting to read the riot act to the bureaucracy. What he said reflected the frustration of the political class with the intransigence of the civil service. He said that 'people often perceived the bureaucracy as an agent of exploitation rather than a provider of services' and that 'corruption had become a low-risk and high-reward activity'. He also told his ministerial colleagues that they should review their own performance if they wanted to regain credibility in the eyes of the people. Vajpayee's annoyance sprang from the fact that poverty-alleviation programmes were losing efficacy despite the enormous sums of money being poured into them. It was clear that much of the public money was going into private pockets. The public distribution scheme, for instance, was a scandal. Nearly half the rations meant for those living below the poverty line was being siphoned off.

But even Vajpayee's anger did not lend any great urgency to the Right to Information Bill. All through 1999, the NDA refused to be intimidated by the Court or shamed by public pressure or censure. It bears mention here that the BJP and the NDA, in the National Agenda for Governance, had promised to bring the right to information to the people, both in 1998 and in 1999. Indeed, in December 1999, at a public function, Vajpayee once again reiterated the need for a bill guaranteeing the right to information and said his government would 'open people's access to all information barring that deemed crucial to national security'. But once again where it mattered—in government and in Parliament—there was hardly any progress. The government was divided on the issue. There was one group which thought the bill was a good idea and didn't mind, there were those who did mind and then those who didn't know their mind. Of the politicians who thought it was a bad idea, many were clearly alarmed at the possibility of being held accountable by an entitlement that was justiciable in a court of law.

The naysayers were further divided; one section saw this as an impediment to decision-making. They feared that a law that offered retrospective review could be used for blackmail and no one would take risks for fear of being punished which would result in no decisions ever being taken. The other section felt that a law for transparency represented a threat to the business model of politics. Within the NDA the debate was vigorous and both factions had their share of supporters.

It would be relevant to pause here to consider the global context in which the churning for the right to information was taking place in India. By the end of 1989, the Berlin Wall had been pulled down. Social movements across the world were arguing fervently for open, responsive and participative forms of government. The decade that spanned the fall of the Wall and the crash of the Twin Towers was marked by the collapse of secrecy and the rise of transparency and accountability around the world. In Russia, a wholly Communist enterprise, Gorbachev had unleashed perestroika and glasnost. Boris Yeltsin opened up state archives of the Soviet era. Bill Clinton declassified more documents—arguably—than all the previous presidents of the US.

Everywhere, human rights activists were being empowered to expose dictators and chase down the perpetrators of state-sponsored murders. Between 1991 and 2000, over two dozen countries passed laws that enabled citizens to participate in the process of governance. Among those who dismantled the culture of secrecy were Lithuania, Trinidad and Tobago, Ukraine, Belize, Latvia, South Africa, Albania, Georgia, Bulgaria, Czech Republic, Slovakia et al. Yet, in India, the government was struggling to come to terms with its internal contradictions.

In the spring of 2000, the activists pleaded that the Supreme Court direct the State to institutionalize the right to information. Finally caving into the pressure that had been brought to bear on it, the BJP-led NDA government picked up the Shourie Committee's draft, diluted its provisions further and brought it to cabinet for approval. Next, the government presented the Freedom of Information Bill 2000, in Parliament on 25 July 2000 first in the Rajya Sabha, and later in the day, in the Lok Sabha.

As is the practice with complex laws dealing with multiple issues of constitutional propriety, it was expected that the bill would be referred to a Parliamentary Standing Committee. For reasons unknown this didn't happen for over forty-five days. On 14 September 2001, the bill was referred to the Parliamentary Standing Committee by the chairman of the Rajya Sabha and the speaker of the Lok Sabha for examination. It was clear that the ruling front was in no hurry to pass the bill. Neither was the Opposition, it would seem. The first meeting of the committee was held on 23 October 2000 in which the members heard oral evidence from the ministry of personnel, public grievances and pensions. The next meeting did not take place until 24 January 2001.

It was no secret that the RTI activists were very unhappy with the contours and content of the bill drafted by the Shourie Committee. In a meeting held on 24 January 2001, representatives of the Commonwealth Human Rights Initiative (CHRI), Madhav Godbole, former union home secretary, senior advocate A. G. Noorani, Manubhai Shah of the Consumer Education and Research Centre, Aruna Roy and Nikhil Dey of MKSS, Justice P. B. Sawant, Chairman of the Press Council of India and former Cabinet Secretary B. G. Deshmukh highlighted the many flaws in the Freedom of Information Bill.

The experts argued, once again, that the title itself was a dilution of the spirit of the idea and that freedom was not the same as a right. Members of the CHRI, MKSS, Godbole, Noorani and Manubhai Shah impressed on the committee that the right was enshrined in the Constitution and said that the bill should therefore be called the Right to Information and not Freedom of Information. They then expressed disappointment with several other provisions, including the exclusion of private corporate bodies from its purview. The experts pointed out that the provision of the clause 'in public interest' in Section 4(d) could be used as an omnibus override to deny information. They also demanded that government fix a date by which the act would be operational.

Typically, the government had explanations for many of the issues it refused to bend on. It also gave itself plenty of room for manoeuvrability by keeping several provisions vague. The government assured the committee that access to information would not be limited to citizens, that the information provided to MPs and MLAs would not be denied to those who sought it and promised that its various departments would be explicitly obliged to publish organizational information. However, it refused to change the name of the bill or bring private corporate bodies within its purview. It also refused to declare a date by which the act would be operational. The activists were by no means satisfied but the committee held its ground, and on 25 July 2001, submitted its report to Parliament. The government, caught up with many controversies and issues, did not move on it. The bill was not brought up for consideration by Parliament for another sixteen months, till December 2002.

The disappointment of the activists found its echo in Parliament on 3 December 2002 when Vasundhara Raje Scindia, as minister for personnel, moved the bill for passage. Speaker after speaker across party lines questioned the many exemptions and provisions. They argued that they were designed to deny people access to information. Somnath Chatterjee, then MP from Bolpur, said in his inimitable style, 'Nobody can have any grievance or question the objective of the bill. But a close study will show that it is more for public consumption than for public enforcement.' Priyaranjan Das Munshi of the Congress questioned the exclusion of private companies and asked why trade and commercial information had been exempted. Yerram Naidu of the TDP, which was supporting the NDA, said too much had been left out. 'Transparency means transparency. That is why since November the government of Andhra Pradesh is putting notings and recommendations in files on the Internet.' The government, however, defended its position and the bill was passed. In the Rajya Sabha, members agreed with the bill passed by the Lok Sabha without any amendment. Finally, the Freedom of Information Bill was passed and received presidential assent on 6 January 2003.

Even as the Centre passed a toothless legislation, many states pushed through their versions of the right to information laws. Karnataka, Rajasthan, Delhi and Madhya Pradesh joined Goa and Tamil Nadu to facilitate access to information. There was nothing uniform about the acts that were passed—the differences ranged from how each state administered it, what was covered and not covered, fees charged and penalties imposed. The Government of Maharashtra in 2000 had pushed through an ordinance enforcing RTI. Activists in Mumbai and Pune railed against the weak provisions, Anna Hazare went on fast. In 2003, Maharashtra passed a vastly improved version.

The NDA regime, in the meantime, delayed the formulation of guidelines which would make the law operational. To make the law effective the government was required to create a ladder of officials at different levels to deal with queries, appeals within the department and, thereafter, a quasi-judicial body to deal with appeals at the state level and then at the Centre. While all this should have been thought of and deliberated even as the law was being drafted and debated in the Standing Committee, it wasn't. The fact that there was no prescribed date by which the law had to be operational allowed the naysayers in the government to delay it.

Impatient with the pace of the process, the activists asked the Supreme Court to direct the Government of India to notify the rules. The government maintained it needed time to set up the superstructure to implement the law. It added that states which had their own RTI laws had to be consulted. It was only in January 2004 that the Department of Personnel and Training drafted the rules governing the implementation of the Freedom of Information Act. There is no denying the complexity of issues to be settled—from rules about public authority, the powers of public information officers to fee structures and the institution of authorities for appeal. However, the inordinate delay in implementation was inexcusable. The public perception was that the government didn't want to open itself up to scrutiny. Beginning with the *Tehelka* sting operation on defence deals in March 2001, the NDA regime was tormented by political turmoil. This was followed in 2002 by the ghastly riots in Gujarat and some more corruption scandals involving the allotment of land and petrol pumps to party favourites. Preoccupied as it was with firefighting, the NDA leadership had little time or appetite for the right to information.

TRIUMPH OF HOPE OVER HISTORY

On 14 January 2004, Prime Minister Vajpayee wished the nation a Happy Makar Sankranti and added what could have been an innocuous statement. He said it was the day when the sun changed its trajectory. But Vajpayee being Vajpayee, the statement was interpreted politically. Those privy to the inside track in the BJP translated it as a signal for early polls; that the general elections scheduled for October 2004 would be brought forward to capitalize on the feel-good factor in the economy. Fuelled by the buzz in the media, the idea caught on and gathered momentum within the BJP and the NDA. The BJP and its allies called for early polls. The Freedom of Information Act 2002 was buried in the heat and dust of the general elections.

In the next few weeks, the nation was swamped by claims of India Shining, the slogan coined by the BJP to represent the mood of economic optimism sweeping the country at the time. The campaign of the Congress focused on those left in the dark with its slogan:

'*Congress ka haath aam aadmi ke saath*'. The BJP didn't do too badly but its allies—DMK, TDP and the National Conference—had all deserted the NDA. The Congress, which had fashioned a rainbow coalition, the United Progressive Alliance (UPA), of former foes and new friends surprised themselves and the nation with a victory.

For the activists fighting for the right to information this was good news. Sonia Gandhi, at least when the Congress was in Opposition, seemed like a convinced member of their parish. But there were doubts on whether her faith would survive the compulsions of power. Why would a regime endanger itself by opening up to such scrutiny? Indeed, not everyone in Congress was convinced by the idea. But Sonia Gandhi, says Aruna Roy, was unwavering in her support.

It is true that the RTI Act would—and has—created trouble for the ruling regime. But it also defangs the Opposition. The seductive thesis is that while the ruling regime does lose face, the Opposition gains no mileage from it. This is validated, at least in part. Since 2009, the UPA government has been hammered for corruption scandals, many of which were exposed through the RTI Act, but the Opposition has not been able to capitalize on it.

The defeat of the BJP-led NDA did not immediately translate into power for the UPA. The rainbow alliance was short of a majority, the magic mark of 272. In a surprising move, the Left Front which had fifty-nine MPs decided to back the UPA with outside support despite the fact that the Congress was their principal opponent in Kerala, West Bengal and Tripura. A National Common Minimum Programme (NCMP) outlining the minimum objectives of a coalition government was agreed upon between the Congress, its allies and the Left. The NCMP—thanks to the influence of the activists—declared that the right to information would be made more progressive, participative and meaningful. There were other surprises too. Sonia Gandhi, who had renounced the post of prime minister, assumed charge as the chairman of the newly created National Advisory Council (NAC), which would direct the government on policy direction. The NAC was a curious cocktail of activists, academics, former bureaucrats and Congress loyalists. After the Syndicate of the sixties, this was the first time that real power in a Congress government was vested outside the office of the prime minister.

In June 2004, as the Congress-led UPA was settling in, the Supreme Court directed the government to operationalize the Freedom of Information Act 2002. The intervention of the judiciary put the right to information squarely on top of the list of things to do for the Congress. In retrospect, the delay by the NDA regime to notify the Freedom of Information Act proved to be a lucky break. Instead of repairing a law that was weak and diluted, the activists decided it would be better to opt for a mint-fresh bill and campaigned for it at the NAC.

At the first meeting of the NAC, Aruna Roy who was a member, and others including N. C. Saxena, who was involved with the first draft of the bill in 1996, pushed the Right to Information Act to the top of the agenda. The move was forcefully supported by Sonia Gandhi. It was decided that a new draft should be finalized and submitted to the NAC. The draft was ready by the end of July 2004 and was forwarded with a letter from the chairperson of NAC to the government. In her letter of 16 August 2004 to Prime Minister Manmohan Singh, Sonia Gandhi urged him to take up the issue and listed four factors to make the law truly empowering: maximum disclosure, minimum exemptions, independent mechanisms for appeal and penalties, and an effective mechanism for access of information.

The activists' access to the fulcrum of power did not translate into an easier journey for the bill. As was expected, vested interests—in the bureaucracy and in the cabinet—did their best to derail the process. Some sections of the bureaucracy and some ministers saw the old bill as a lesser evil and tried to persuade their political masters to push it through with some minor amendments. The activists held their ground. They were joined in their endeavour by the Left Front—and former Prime Minister V. P. Singh who held a special meeting with Prime Minister Manmohan Singh on the issue—to push the new bill forward.

In December 2004, the government came up with a new Right to Information Bill to replace the Freedom of Information Act 2002. Soon after its introduction on 23 December 2004, the bill was referred by the speaker of the Lok Sabha to the Parliamentary Standing Committee on Personnel, Grievances, Law and Justice.

In theory, the Right to Information Bill 2004 aimed 'to provide for setting out the practical regime of right to information for people to secure access to information under the control of public authorities, in order to promote transparency and accountability in the working of every public authority'. In letter and deed, the bill sought to limit the access of information to people through a series of ill-thought-out provisions or well-thought-out hurdles.

The bureaucracy introduced elements that threatened to dilute the right and render the bill impotent. The NAC draft had been forcefully in favour of openness; the RTI Bill 2004 presented in Parliament had virtually nullified the spirit of openness. In an attempt to protect themselves and please their political masters, the bureaucrats tasked with drafting the bill had instituted countervailing conditions to what the NAC draft bill had stipulated. The NAC draft wanted one bill to cover every level of government. The RTI Bill 2004 limited the applicability to the central government. It also specified that seekers would have to prove citizenship; activists pointed out that the poor usually do not have the required documents. Activists had, since 1996, stressed that levying penalties on officials were a must to prevent delay and the denial of information. The bill was weak on penalties. The worst flaw in the bill was that it didn't provide adequate manpower to deal with queries and didn't have a workable mechanism for processing appeals.

The activists approached Sonia Gandhi again. Once again she wrote to the prime minister listing the flaws in the bill and calling his attention to the need for amendments in at least thirty-five clauses. The prime minister appointed a Group of Ministers to review the bill even as the Standing Committee was examining it. The GoM was chaired by Pranab Mukherjee who had also chaired the Parliamentary Standing Committee which had disappointed the activists. This time, however, the circumstances were different. The pressure of the activists, the NAC and the presence of real political power outside the government made all the difference. Those in government—even if in disagreement—did not want to incur the wrath of the chairperson of the UPA.

Unlike the Standing Committee of 2001 which had taken its time, this committee worked quickly. Led by E. M. Sudarsana Natchiappan, the committee met five times between 1 February and 2 March 2005. On 16 March, the Standing Committee submitted its report to Parliament suggesting many changes to the original bill. Activists, including Aruna Roy, Nikhil Dey and Anna Hazare, veteran journalist Prakash Kardaley, Arvind Kejriwal, Maja Daruwala, economist Jean Dreze, Shailesh Gandhi and Jaiprakash Narayan combined forces and lobbied hard with members of parliament and the Group of Ministers to keep up the pressure on the government to pass a bill that was comprehensive and effective. This time their efforts were rewarded.

The Right to Information Bill was finally passed in the Lok Sabha on 11 May and the Rajya Sabha on 12 May 2005. On 15 June 2005, after the president gave his assent to the bill, India finally had a Right to Information Act and its citizens an instrument to participate in governance. Fifty-five years after India became a republic and thirty years after the Supreme Court upheld the right to information as a fundamental right, the Government of India gave people the right to question it and demand accountability.

The battle between citizens and those in power, including the bureaucracy—the permanent government—continues. Since 2005, activists and citizens have deployed the right to information to enforce accountability. Between 2007-08 and 2010-11, 18,32,181 queries were filed with ministries at the Centre. Out of these, information was supplied in 17,33,620 cases. The exposé on the use of electricity by ministers, frequent flier cabinet ministers, the declaration of the assets of ministers, the allotment of land for the president's retirement home, the allocation of mining rights and the 2G and CWG scams were all the result of RTI queries. This has triggered demands by the political establishment at the Centre and the states to institute new controls on queries under the RTI Act. Interestingly, most political parties today boast a cell or at least fund a proxy specializing in using the RTI to dig up dirt about the Opposition.

Every year since the enactment of the RTI Act in 2005, the system has made attempts to regain control over the flow of information and the power embedded therein. The coalition of politicians and bureaucrats has not quite given up. Indeed, the RTI has been deployed as the alibi for the slowdown in decision-making since 2009. More recently, there have been attempts to curtail the power of the RTI through perverse guidelines. One suggestion, for instance, has been to disallow queries with more than 250 words.

Addressing the Convention of Information Commissioners on 14 October 2011, Prime Minister Manmohan Singh suggested the need 'to take a critical look' at the right to information and to 'strike a balance between the need for disclosure of information and the limited time resources available with the public authorities'. He opined that the right to information 'could end up discouraging honest, well-meaning public servants from giving full expression to their views'. He added that the right to information 'should not adversely affect the deliberative processes in the government'. An alert media and activists immediately flagged the statement as an attempt to dilute the right to information, forcing the prime minister to modify his own statement. He said: 'I never said we are going to change the RTI Act.'

There will no doubt be attempts to whittle down the power of the act, to use bureaucratic legalese to deny and delay information, to pre-empt scandal by releasing information selectively. The burgeoning number of cases of citizens being denied information reveals the level of systemic resistance. As of February 2012, over 26,500 appeals are pending at the apex level with the Chief Information Commissioner. The alarming rise in the number of deaths of RTI activists targeting corruption, particularly in smaller towns, is a reflection of the threat from vested political interests.

Seven years after the enactment, there is yet the fear that the empire will strike back. But there can be no relinquishing from this hard-won victory. Eternal vigilance is the price of democracy.

EPILOGUE

India is poised at the intersection of hope and despair, of individual aspiration and frustrating institutional failure. The positives are reassuring; they promise the tryst with destiny India dreamt of at the dawn of its independence. That democracy itself has survived the doom predicted by many Cassandras and that the country has nurtured diversity is no mean achievement. India's success in complex domains lends faith to the belief that Yes, India Can.

The failures, though, can overwhelm hope. Success in space and nuclear programmes cannot obscure the nation's failure to provide the most basic amenities to a large mass of its populace. India is home to the world's largest number of the poor and illiterate—three out of ten people are unable to read and four out of ten people cannot eat two meals a day. Every year one million children die before they are a month old and another million die before they are five years old.

Every year, over 15,000 farmers commit suicide. A quarter of the populace has no access to electricity but that hasn't stopped political parties from promising free power and laptops. Over 49 per cent of Indians in urban conurbations and 65 per cent in rural areas do not have toilets. India spends nearly $100 billion a year on social-sector programmes yet some of its human development indices are worse than sub-Saharan countries and even the junta-ruled Myanmar.

What India lacks is the kind of political leadership that entertains risks and takes decisions. A leadership that exhibits that elusive quality called imagination, of the kind displayed by Roosevelt, Reagan, Thatcher; by Deng Xiaoping and Lee Kuan Yew. And evangelism, of the kind Mahatma Gandhi practised to rally the masses around the cause of freedom.

The United States found its national cause in the twin concepts of free will and free markets. Germany and Japan inculcated national pride and the quest for technological excellence to regain their superiority after World War II. China built its might around the idea of rapid growth. All of these countries had a plan and they worked on it continuously—chopping, changing and reforming.

India, too, has plans except that they are pitifully executed. The Planning Commission prepares a Five Year Plan which is cleared by the cabinet but has no connection to the tenure of the government which passed it. This means that no leader's or party's reputation is at stake. There is no ownership of targets and no accountability. Further complicating all this is the nature of the Indian political beast, adept as it is at dodging and ducking. No plan can ever hope to succeed if the politicians in power and those in the Opposition evade direct responsibility, if every promise becomes a compromise.

Change in India has also been stranded by structural and systemic flaws. The structural problem, to put it very simply, is not that there is too much democracy, but that there is too little of it. Article 1 of the Constitution says: 'India, that is Bharat, shall be a Union of States.' The authors intended India to be ruled by the states, the ideas for renewal moving upwards from the bottom. Instead, the states have often been reduced to dominions of the Centre in matters of policy. The overlap of powers on fifty-two subjects in the Concurrent List of the Constitution and the apportioning of joint responsibility to the union government and the states by the Directive Principles in the Constitution have been exploited by the political executive to shirk responsibility.

Systemic reforms are required to rescue governance from collapsing in and around the rusting steel frame, the bureaucracy that is meant to complement political leadership. Our civil administration—the permanent government—is not designed for acceleration. While development depends on the quality of administrative capacity and quality comes from specialization, we continue to depend on generalists. The government transfers officers every few years, almost as if afraid that they might get good at something. Lateral entry is frowned upon and lateral entrants from the private sector are targeted, just in case they do manage to perform. Clearly, the civil administration needs to be repurposed, individual performance needs to be rewarded and achievement lauded.

What the situation calls for is reform in the structure of governance. Government must get out of those areas in which the private sector performs more efficiently. Delhi must delegate powers to the states and the states themselves must empower local self-governments. The civil administration has to be made accountable through Citizen's Charters that are not just acts but promise action; Charters that ensure the delivery of public services within fixed time frames. One of the ways in which change can be brought about is though the use of information technology, something India is excellent at. Information technology can resolve many of the issues of complexity and scale; it can speed up processes and deliver transparency.

For democracy to survive and for India to thrive, political leaders must be energized by the public good, not private dividend. What they conveniently ignore today as future shocks—water, energy, poverty, corruption, national security and relations between the Centre and the states—are already the silent crises of today.

WATER: A SILENT THIRST

Psychologist Abraham Maslow, in his 1943 paper 'A Theory of Human Motivation', places water second on the hierarchy of human physiological needs. In India it is difficult to spot water on the list of priorities of the government. The crisis of thirst symbolizes the systemic crisis of India. Water supply, believe it or not, is managed by six ministries—rural development, urban development, agriculture, food, environment and, of course, water resources. All six ministries claim to be responsible for it, yet none is accountable.

These factoids best tell the story.

- According to studies by the ministry of water resources, by 2025, eleven river basins, including the Ganga, will be 'water-deficit.'
- Ground water levels have plunged in 206 districts in the country.

- In six states—Rajasthan, Maharashtra, Gujarat, Haryana, Karnataka and Punjab—demand outstrips supply.
- Every summer, across India, ninety districts are vulnerable to drought and over sixty to floods.
- With over 20 million tube wells, ground water now accounts for over 50 per cent of irrigated area. About 15 per cent of India's food is being produced using non-renewable 'mined' ground water.
- Satellite data shows that between 2002 and 2008 bore wells had drawn 109 cubic kilometres of water, enough to fill Wainganga, India's largest reservoir, twice over.
- Over 65 million people living in 200 districts risk fluoride contamination and 15 million risk arsenic poisoning every time they drink water.
- In as many as 203 of the 401 class-II towns, citizens get less than 100 litres of water per person per day.
- It is estimated that over a million tankers are deployed each year across cities in India to supply water to urban dwellings.
- Over 100 million children across India suffer from diarrhoea each year that kills half a million, thanks to the lack of drinking water.

The crisis in any commodity is about demand and supply, need and availability. In 2050, India's population is expected to touch 1,500 million, at least. Demand for water will double from current levels to touch 1,180 billion cubic metres. Two-thirds of the water used in India is needed for agriculture. India will need to ramp up its food production from the current 250 million tons to over 400 million tons.

It is not as if India is short on natural supplies. India receives an annual precipitation—as snow and rainfall—of around 4,000 billion cubic metres. Of this the runoff—which means accessible water—is 1,869 billion cubic metres. Of this, barely 690 billion cubic metres is used. The rest drains into the sea because we don't have plans in place to store water.

What makes things worse is that much of the precipitation happens during the 100 days or so of monsoon while water is needed for

365 days. This makes planning for storage an imperative, a task at which India has failed miserably. Per-capita water storage in India stands at a measly 190 cubic metres compared to 5,961 in the US, 4,717 in Australia and 2,486 in China.

As always, there has been no shortage of ideas, committees, commissions and reports. Among the most ambitious ideas was the interlinking of rivers to transport water from river basins with a surplus to regions facing scarcity. Using a web of thirty links, it was planned that water would be stored in thirty-two dams to deliver 173 billion cubic metres of water—a fourth of the volume in the mighty Brahmaputra—through a maze of 12,500 kilometres of canals to irrigate 34 million additional hectares, deliver 34,000 MW of power and bring drinking water to 101 thirsty towns. The cost for this ambitious project was estimated at over $25 billion in 2002.

The idea of linking rivers is not new. In the US, water was taken from Texas to New Mexico, and in China the Three Gorges project now supplies water and electricity to millions. Rivers have been linked in India too. In the nineteenth century, water was transferred from the Periyar basin in Kerala to the Vaigai river basin in Tamil Nadu. In 1895, British and Indian engineers built a 47 metre masonry gravity dam across a gorge on the Periyar and a 1.7 kilometre long tunnel was constructed to discharge water into the Vaigai basin. Similarly, in the sixties and the seventies, in a project jointly undertaken by Rajasthan, Punjab, Haryana and the central government, the Ravi river was dammed and water was transported to the Beas river and from the Beas to the Sutlej. Another dam on the Ravi, called Ranjit Sagar, was used to provide water to Beas which was then funnelled to Rajasthan through a system of canals.

The scale of the idea of interlinking rivers was grand and intimidating. Water was to be moved from river basin to river basin, from the Ghagra in Nepal to the Yamuna—a distance of 431 kilometres; from the Mahanadi in Orissa to the Godavari—a distance of 932 kilometres. It was estimated that 56 million tons of cement and 2 million tons of steel would be used. The project promised to create 37 million man years of employment. First mooted in 1972 by then irrigation minister Kanuri Lakshmana Rao, the idea was expanded upon in 1977 by Captain Dinshaw Dastur, an engineer and airline pilot. It was called the Garland Canal.

The idea then languished in the Planning Commission for a couple of decades and was revived in 2001 by the NDA regime. A committee headed by former minister for power Suresh Prabhu reckoned the potential costs and dividend. A typically Indian debate followed and the idea was shelved again. The Congress Party promised to support the idea but later withdrew its consent. The states which had a surplus refused to agree to the transfer of water. Economists found the costs to be prohibitive, environmentalists questioned the efficacy of the idea. As expected, the debates centred more on the negatives than on the positives. It could be argued that the negatives outweighed the positives, but nonetheless the debates threw up nothing as an alternative.

What the government needs to do to prevent a catastrophe is to bring water under the control of one ministry, co-opt states into a national plan, replicate the experiments at local levels which have been successful at recharging groundwater, transfer water management back to communities, introduce mandatory water-harvesting and recycling plants in cities and towns, provide tax incentives and venture capital for water recycling and impose a price on water supply so that costs can be recovered and wastage is avoided.

In agriculture, India must draw up a plan to map and alter cropping patterns. Should water-scarce Maharashtra be growing sugar cane when it is better done in water-surplus states? Should farmers in the Cauvery and Krishna valleys be growing paddy? There is also a need for the introduction of new technology in seeds and in irrigation. Micro and drip irrigation accounts for less than 5 per cent of agriculture in India compared to 49 per cent in Israel. Efficiency measures in agriculture must shift conceptually from yield per acre to yield per litre.

The absence of urgency signals a dangerous sense of complacency. The dire warnings by climate-change scientists on the retreat of glaciers, of a fall in precipitation that could affect millions in the Gangetic belt, the falling levels of ground water and the environmental costs of polluted rivers have all been kept aside for another day.

In a democracy, every decision comes with a cost. There is also a price to not doing anything.

ENERGY SECURITY: HIGH-OCTANE CHAOS

Man discovered fire in the early Stone Age. Thereafter, the quest for energy to fuel and sustain life and livelihood has been a relentless race for nations. Modern economies plan their energy strategy—the ideal mix of gas, crude, coal and electricity generated by a blend of fuels—and constantly alter and modify plans to sustain growth. In India, the presence of such a strategy is conspicuous by its absence. India is trailing in power generation, overly dependent on crude-oil imports, and despite huge reserves, forced to import coal.

India set up its first power plant in 1889 in Calcutta, not too long after the US, so the excuse of being a late-entrant to the sector doesn't really apply. In 1947, India could generate 1,362 MW of electricity; six decades later, it can generate 185,000 MW. Compare this with China for a sobering perspective. China started at the same level as India in the forties; it has a generating capacity of over 900,000 MW in 2012. Between 2000 and 2011 India added 75,000 MW to its capacity; China added 75,000 MW every year to its grid. In effect, China adds in a month what India adds in a year.

India's inability to deal with the most basic issue, fuel linkage for power plants, reflects the chaos in the system. The cumulative reserves of coal in India are estimated to be around 285,862 million tons but production is only 500 million tons a year. A country boasting the fourth largest coal reserve in the world is expected to import over 100 million tons of coal in 2012. This is primarily because guidelines for mine lease, land acquisition and environmental clearances await legislation that has been pending since 2005. Natural gas is a greener alternative and India is estimated to host over 1.5 trillion cubic metres. But investment in gas exploration is hampered by tax policies—oil fields get tax breaks, gas fields don't. Investment is also deterred by controls. Once gas is produced, it is government which decides who will sell which gas to whom, at what price and in which quantities.

India boasts a technical potential of over 89,760 MW in renewable energy—hydro, solar, biomass, wind—of which barely a fifth has been tapped. There has been some progress in wind and solar energy but growth still requires a policy push. The big question is that of economics. Solar power is three times costlier than coal-generated power so state boards have to find the funds to pay for it. Also, solar and wind power need ten times the land required for a coal-powered plant so land acquisition policies need sorting out. The potential for hydro power is frozen because parties skirt the political minefields which dot large projects, ranging from land acquisition to rehabilitation.

As with water, energy security in India is held hostage by a multi-layered governance structure. Power generation depends on six ministries. Coal supplies are controlled by the ministry of coal, gas supplies by the ministry of petroleum, hydro projects depend on clearances from several ministries, wind and solar require clearances for land acquisition.

The problems don't cease with power generation. Once power is produced, it has to be sold to state electricity boards, most of which are in dire financial straits thanks to poor pricing policies. Twice, since the nineties, political parties informally agreed that supplying free power to farmers was wrecking state electricity boards and the water table and that a flat fee must be charged. But no political party dares alter subsidy policies.

Nearly 40 per cent of the power generated has to be sold at rates determined by vote-bank considerations. Worse, nearly 25 to 30 per cent of the power is lost in transmission and distribution—a polite way of saying that power is stolen. Every year, state electricity boards lose over ₹30,000 crore to power theft. The Electricity Act 2003 suggested that the theft of power be made a criminal offence but political parties balk at the thought. In every domain, policy is mired in electoral considerations. In the meantime, the overall peak-hour power deficit stands at 15 per cent and a large number of towns and industries suffer up to twelve-hour power outages.

The performance in the oil sector isn't any better. Crude oil imports are the biggest item on India's import bill. In 2011, India consumed 206 million tons of crude oil of which 164 million tons were imported. At the current rate, the demand for petroleum products could cross 300 million tons in a decade while its production—it is estimated—will grow, at best, by 1 per cent or by around 3 million tons a year. India has recoverable reserves of over 750 million tons and produces 37 million tons a year. Its last major oil discovery was in the Bombay High in the seventies, thereafter, its efforts to prospect and produce have been, at best, sporadic. As we have noted earlier in this book, at least three of the major economic crises faced by India since the fifties have been triggered by high oil prices. Yet there is no apparent hurry to promote domestic exploration.

One out of four Indians doesn't have an electricity connection and 34 per cent of the rural populace lives without the facility of an electric bulb. Over 55,000 Indian villages have no access to electricity. Ditto is the case with fuel consumption. Over 77 per cent of rural households in India continue to depend on firewood for cooking, which means that over 650 million people do not use petroleum fuels. Even in urban India only 62 per cent of the populace uses LPG for cooking. Consider how India compares with others in energy consumption. The average fuel consumption in India is 610 kilograms per person compared to 7,778 kilograms in the US and a world average of 1,818 kilograms. On an average, India uses 813 kilowatt-hour of electricity per capita compared to 1,500 kilowatt-hour by the Chinese and 14,000 kilowatt-hour by the Americans. As of now, poverty and low incomes have kept the demand low but that cannot be a constant. Neither will be the population.

If India is aiming to grow its GDP at 8 per cent a year, it must ramp up its energy supply four times. In the next twenty years, that is, by 2032, India needs to generate close to 1,000 GW to sustain growth. This means India must add 40,000 MW a year. There are plans to boost nuclear power capacity but even when ramped up by twenty times, nuclear power will contribute less than 5 per cent of the total power needed by 2032.

Since India is yet a low-energy consumer it has the luxury of choice, of charting a course that is both economically and environmentally sustainable. The landscape of energy consumption affords it the opportunity to devise a global model. For instance, transport accounts for only 41 per cent of petroleum-based fuel consumption in this country compared to 79 per cent in the US. India could design a mass rapid transport system to curb profligacy in petroleum-based fuel consumption. With over 300 days of sunlight a year and vast, untenanted wastelands, India could engineer a solar grid. It could negotiate with its neighbours Bhutan, Bangladesh, Myanmar and Nepal and create additional generation of both hydroelectric and gas power. Pakistan is power starved and there is clearly an opportunity to let Pakistan deliver gas into India in return for power. The quest for energy could also deliver geopolitical dividends.

The question, as always, is: does the political class have the vision and the gumption to make any of this happen?

POVERTY: HUMAN DEPRIVATION

India ranks sixty-sixth among eighty-eight countries surveyed—behind Cameroon, Kenya, Nigeria and Sudan—when it comes to combating hunger. In twelve of the thirty states of India, the severity of hunger is described by the International Food Policy Research Institute as alarming. Worse, despite its status as one of the leading producers of food grains in the world, India is home to the largest number of malnourished children. Forty three per cent of the children—twice that in sub-Saharan Africa—under the age of five in India are underweight, which means roughly 60 million of the 160 million children under the age of six suffer from malnutrition. Malnutrition manifests most visibly as stunting and six out of ten children are stunted in growth. India loses 218 children to malnutrition and disease—every hour! Life expectancy at birth, UNICEF data tells us, is better for those born in war-torn Iraq and Guatemala.

The problem of human deprivation is located in the circumstance of poverty which is, largely, a result of the neglect of the rural economy. The tragic irony is that those who feed the nation are unable to feed themselves adequately. Nearly 60 per cent of India's population which depends on agriculture is forced to live off one-sixth of the national income. The persistence of poverty stems from this ratio of inequality.

In the post-reform decades between 1991 and 2011, the economy as a whole has grown at over 7.5 per cent while agriculture has straggled along at 2.9 per cent.

Deprivation persists because growth has been asymmetric across sectors, segments and geographies. Rural India, which hosts 75 per cent of the country's population, is growing the slowest. Growth is uneven across geographies too. Of the thirty small and big states, just the four southern states account for 22 per cent of the GDP and 28 per cent of the employment. The most populous states of Uttar Pradesh and Bihar, where the majority of the poor reside, are the worst off—gawkers in a multiplex economy.

For four decades after independence, no matter what government did through its Five Year Plans and programmes, the population below the poverty line stayed constant at around 40 per cent. It was only after the government dismantled the licence-permit-quota raj in 1991 that poverty levels dropped. There is admittedly no reliable evidence showing a correlation between reforms and poverty reduction. But what is evident is that growth came as a result of a segment of the labour force moving out of low-productivity agriculture into industry which boasts a better productivity, thereby lifting some boats off the creek of poverty.

It is not that the State has not intervened to alleviate poverty. A plethora of instruments of intervention exist, schemes for virtually every deficit in the list of human development indicators. For over three decades since 1975, the Integrated Child Development Scheme has been in operation to target infant and maternal mortality. A dole scheme—the Mahatma Gandhi National Rural Employment Guarantee Act—promises 100 days of employment to the rural jobless. Then there is the public distribution scheme under which food is rationed to the poorest at subsidized rates. Yet, the outcomes are poor because implementation of these programmes is pathetic.

Political parties use the vast and unsustainable superstructure of entitlements to evade their true obligations. The tragedy is that governments choose to rely only on tactical sops, subsidies and programmes and refuse to make strategic investments for the long term. Investment in agriculture has declined from 3.4 per cent in the eighties to less than 2 per cent in the past twenty years when it should have been at least 6 per cent of the GDP, given agriculture's share in the GDP and the mass of people who depend on it. Instead of investing in infrastructure, successive governments have preferred to provide higher procurement prices, subsidized fertilizer and free power. Unsurprisingly, two-thirds of farmland has no irrigation and is vulnerable to the vagaries of the monsoon. Credit availability has been boosted from less than ₹75,000 crore to over ₹4 lakh crore. However, mere credit availability cannot boost growth.

Agriculture is the challenge and the opportunity that daunts the Indian economy. India's largest private sector is the most controlled and undernourished, despite the fact that three out of five MPs list themselves as agriculturists and claim to represent farmers. Poverty cannot be eradicated and food security cannot be ensured unless the bulk of the populace dependent on agriculture are empowered to earn better.

China modernized its agriculture only after 1978 but invested in both irrigation and technology. Today its per-hectare yield of paddy is over 6,300 kilograms compared to the 3,300 kilograms per hectare achieved by India's best farmers in Punjab. Farmers in France produce over 5,000 kilograms of wheat per hectare. Compare this with the average yield in India which is less than 2,000 kilograms per hectare and even lower in states like Bihar. The economics is simple. Doubling the yield improves supplies and, therefore, incomes. Yet, politicians have shackled the technology which improves crop yields thereby suppressing incomes. Consecutive governments have abysmally failed to get the economics and the politics of agriculture right.

India is perched precariously on a fast-ticking time bomb. It is vulnerable on three fronts—food production, human deprivation and economic growth. It needs to produce enough to feed 1,500 million people by 2050. And unless yield goes up, India could go back to being an imports-dependent, ship-to-mouth economy.

To rid India of the shame of poverty, its politicians must focus on the rural economy and align their politics to national economics.

CORRUPTION: CATCH ME IF YOU CAN

The country has been wracked by scams in every decade since independence. In the forties, the purchase of Jeeps for the army was tainted by scandal. In the fifties, there was a stock market scam which involved investments by the Life Insurance Corporation in dubious companies owned by businessman Haridas Mundhra. In the sixties, the Pratap Singh Kairon scandal was the first instance of the use of office for personal enrichment. In the seventies, in the Kuo Oil deal scandal, public sector oil companies were duped by a fictitious Hong Kong-based company. In the eighties, in the Antulay Trust scandal, builders were forced to donate money to the Congress for cement quotas. The nineties saw the Bofors commission-for-arms scandal and the Bihar fodder scam. The next decade saw many more starting with the UTI-Ketan Parekh scam to the allotment of petrol pumps to the 2G and CWG scams.

The Jeep scandal set the template on how the post-scam scenario would play out. An enquiry committee would be appointed, their censure would be ignored, and the government and everyone else would blithely go about their business. Indeed, in 2003, my research on twenty-five years of political scams since the Bofors deal revealed that there were barely two convictions in scams, accounting for ₹25,000 crore of public monies. Of course, today, after the 2G spectrum scam, that amount appears miniscule.

A surfeit of recommendations has been filed with successive governments on the causes of corruption, its consequences and the course of action to be taken to tackle it. Starting with the 'Report on the Reorganization of the Machinery of Government' by Gopalaswami Ayyangar in 1949, there has been a parade of recommendations. In 1951, A. D. Gorwala, who chaired the Committee on Public Administration, observed while submitting the Report that, despite grave allegations, 'people holding positions of high authority remain in power without being cleared', leading the public to believe that the influential always get away.

In 1962, the government set up a committee under K. Santhanam to suggest mechanisms and institutions to combat corruption. In 1964, this committee said, 'There is a widespread impression that failure of integrity is not uncommon among ministers and that some ministers who have held office during the last sixteen years have enriched themselves illegitimately, obtained good jobs for their sons and relations through nepotism and have reaped other advantages inconsistent with any notion of purity in public life.' This holds true even more so today.

There has been no dearth of institutions to combat corruption. The report submitted by the Santhanam Committee in 1964 recommended the creation of the Central Vigilance Commission and the setting up of a code of conduct for ministers. The Central Bureau of Investigation, set up in 1963, came out of the Delhi Special Police Establishment Act 1941 (enacted to target corruption in supplier-contracts during World War II). The Administrative Reforms Commission of 1967 suggested the creation of Lokpal and Lokayuktas at the Centre and states to investigate cases of corruption against ministers.

Every decade since the sixties has seen changes in the laws to tackle corruption. The original avatar of the Prevention of Corruption Act was passed in 1947 which, along with the Commission of Enquiry Act, formed the legal instrument for tackling corruption. When the Rajiv Gandhi government was wracked by charges of corruption in the Bofors arms deal, it reconfigured the Prevention of Corruption Act in 1988. In 2003, following a series of scams, the NDA government legislated a law empowering the Central Vigilance Commission.

Theoretically, the statute has enough legal teeth to tackle corruption. Yet, in 2011, public outrage—fuelled by Anna Hazare and Baba Ramdev's activism—forced the political class to accept in Parliament the urgent need for the longstanding Lokpal Bill. A bill was tabled in Parliament, studied by the Standing Committee on Personnel, Public Grievances, Law and Justice and passed in the Lok Sabha in December 2011. However, it fell through in the Rajya Sabha. The Lokpal Bill was recognized as an imperative by the First Administrative Reforms Commission of 1967, the National Commission to Review the Working of the Constitution in 2002 and the Second Administrative Reforms Commission in 2007 besides a host of other committees. Between 1968 and 2011, the bill was introduced before Parliament under seven different prime ministers—in 1968, 1969, 1971, 1977, 1985, 1989, 1996, 1998 and 2001—and failed each time.

Meanwhile, corruption spirals. The crux of the problem rests with the approach to it. The approach to corruption in India has always been from the standpoint of the law enforcement, whereas it is an issue with much wider dimensions. Power dwells in a dominant coalition of interests. The land-owning classes routinely pledge muscle power to politicians to retain assets and control social hierarchies. Big and small businesses fund the revenue model of political parties, using their influence in the clearance regime to thwart competition. Politicians use both social and business models to remain in power. In this they are aided by the bureaucracy which seeks to safeguard its own power and privileges. Thus corruption turns into a cancer.

The reigning cliché about India is that we have a law for every problem and a solution for every law. The Indian State enacts a law just as ritualistically as its people perform pujas to cure ills. Every law is, in essence, a cascade of smartly arranged words, clauses that seem to address the cause and punishments that promise deterrence. But the actual implementation of law is always left for another day as electoral expediency overtakes the logic of governance. Unless implemented in letter and spirit—like former election commissioner T. N. Seshan did for elections in the nineties—laws are essentially dead on arrival.

Corruption in India stems from three quarters—revenue collection, clearances and delivery of citizens' services. The loudest clamour is mostly about corruption in clearances, where the political executive uses its decision-making powers to deliver benefits for a price. The theft in revenue areas, however, has not received equal attention although it is a creeping crisis. The under-reporting of income in business transactions, the over-invoicing of imports by corporates and the under-invoicing of exports are the principal routes of black-money generation. In recent times mergers and acquisitions have been used to transfer ill-gotten assets.

Then, of course, there is the delivery of services. India spends roughly ₹50,000 crore or about $10 billion on food subsidies every year to get food grains to the poor. The government itself admits that every second bag of food grain never reaches the intended beneficiary and is siphoned off. Every year, the Centre and state governments spend over ₹5 lakh crore (about $100 billion) on social-sector programmes. Evaporation of public monies is one of the fallouts of the social percolation theory. Obviously, none of this can transpire without political patronage.

One way to prevent the poor from being robbed and the corrupt from being enriched is the effective implementation of the Unique Identity Scheme (UID). While it is a great way to establish identity, with its simple number-based registration and biometric identification, the UID can also create a national database. This data can form the basis for future reforms—ranging from delivery of services to cash transfers to the poor.

The next big move needed is to halt big-ticket corruption. The annual crop of black money is irrigated by the canals of discretionary powers vested in the system. This explains why politicians are so unwilling to dismantle ad hoc practices, particularly in the allocation of natural resources like telecom spectrum, coal fields or iron ore mines. Legislation to deal with mining, for instance, has been pending since 2006.

It is true that political power is vested in the discretion to decide, but discretion must be backed by reason and the reasoning must be transparent. The government must make its system of processes and clearances transparent; it must provide room for public intervention. The Right to Information (RTI) Act enables citizens to question what the government has done and how it was done. Functional democracy requires the government to take the next few strategic steps. A republic, by definition, demands participative governance. The government must make a self-declaration of intent and objectives. This can be monitored through the RTI Act and public scrutiny will identify the wrongdoers. But little is gained if the corrupt go scot-free. With over thirty-one million cases pending in the courts, it is imperative that the system is empowered with fast-track judicial action so that punishment follows swiftly and an atmosphere of deterrence is established.

However, it isn't enough to tackle the supply side of the political economy of corruption. India has to look hard at the demand side of the political economy. The core of the problem is greed but there is also a deemed need. India needs to find a viable system for political parties to fund their politics. The business model of politics thrives on the cash economy. India has a provision for donations to political parties by cheque, but the bulk of the money is transferred in the form of cash derived from corrupt practices. There is no way to know if a donation is a donation or a bribe. Sometimes bribes are converted into donations and even declared to the Income Tax Department. This model of cash-and-carry politics makes it convenient for the corrupt—on either side of the fence—to freely conduct transactions.

Every five years, 13,986 candidates—assuming three serious candidates per party—fight for seats in the Lok Sabha and state legislative assemblies. Depending on the geography and the party, candidates are known to spend ten times the official limit allowed for election expenses. Assume, for a moment, that the limits on expenditure are being adhered to. This means a Lok Sabha candidate spends ₹40 lakh and a candidate for the assembly spends ₹16 lakh. What is the source of all this money? Candidates do declare their known personal assets, but are not required to explain the source, or how they funded the acquisition of those assets. Lawmakers expected to force change themselves derive legitimacy from a fuzzy system.

Indians must demand a transparent system of political funding, the kind followed in America. It has its downsides, of course, such as the rich cornering the attention of lawmakers. But it is transparent enough for citizens to know who is paying money to parties and what is expected in return. Corruption is robbing the poor and the middle class, enriching criminality and is inflationary. Its perpetuation enables the wrong kind of politicians to be elected. This leads to the subversion of the democratic process.

NATIONAL SECURITY: SOFT SUCKER STATE

In February 2012, terrorists on a bike chased a car belonging to the Israeli Consulate and attached a limpet bomb to its boot. This event happened a few hundred metres from the prime minister's residence in the high-security, CCTV-monitored Lutyens's zone of Delhi. Theoretically, the intelligence agencies monitoring the airwaves should have caught on to the possibility of the attack. Theoretically, after the attack, the police should have been able to use CCTV footage to detect the perpetrators.

However, the intelligence agencies had no clue and pointed out that even Mossad didn't know. The CCTV footage had caught the car but not the bikers. Needless to say, the hapless investigators made very slow progress in the case. Terrorism needs to be countered by a combination of imagination, cognitive intelligence and law enforcement. In Delhi, all three aspects were found wanting. The incident starkly illustrates the possibilities of what could have been.

National security in India is trapped between pious intent and unholy sloth. In July 2011, a series of blasts in the crowded markets of Mumbai killed over twenty-five people and left 150 injured. Panic ensued and phone lines were jammed. For fifteen minutes after the blast, the chief minister of Maharashtra could not reach the police commissioner because a recommendation, passed in July 2007 for a secure emergency network to be put in place, had not been carried out. The victims were rushed to hospital in taxis because a 2006 recommendation for an emergency medical system was yet to be acted upon. The investigators were left groping in the dark because a 2008 recommendation for installing CCTVs in crowded markets had not been implemented. Every terror attack in India follows a predictable pattern of excuses, trying to shift the blame and pathos. National security, it would seem, is a priority only in the immediate aftermath of an event when the party in power finds its political existence threatened and when the Opposition senses an opportunity to score points.

Over 200 districts in India are affected by Naxalism. Of these 200 districts, eighty-three are virtually controlled by Maoists, and in thirty-three the state is a mute spectator to their excesses. Left-wing extremism has been described as the single biggest threat to India but the response to this threat is severely affected by the lack of a credible law and order set-up. India has one of the poorest police-to-people ratio with just 1.5 million policemen for a population of 1,210 million. State governments have promised—in successive conferences involving chief ministers and chiefs of police—to ensure that the sanctioned strength is met, yet half a million posts lie vacant. The strategy to combat this growing threat has been held hostage by inter-party and intra-party politics. For two decades, India's political class has failed to agree on an approach. Meanwhile, every day, more people lose their lives to Naxal violence which plagues one-third of the country's districts and has now begun flexing its might through industrial unions in urban areas.

Internal security is also threatened by deepening schisms between various ethnic groups—particularly in the Northeastern states. That the Armed Forces Special Powers Act is operational in these seven states is itself a testament of the seething unrest in the region. Nearly a million people were displaced in the state of Assam, with a cascading effect across the nation, in July 2012 following violence in Bodo-dominated districts. The inability of the State to enforce the rule of law has fuelled the birth of home-grown terrorists—from self-proclaimed mujahideen to right-wing saffron groups—staging operations across India. The possibility of a Molotov coalition of terror groups is a real and present danger.

India, in the last decade, has witnessed two major attacks on its soil—one on its political leadership when Parliament was attacked in 2001 and the other on its national economy when Mumbai was attacked in 2008. The principal political parties responded and reacted almost similarly whether in opposition or in power—they went high on rhetoric and low on legislative action. It would seem that national security is not an end but a means to another end.

India is today an acknowledged nuclear power and home to one of the largest military forces in the world but the maturity of its response to terrorism on its own soil has not graduated with its status. The state of its military preparedness is a matter of ridicule among military strategists. Its political leadership is tentative in responding to cross-border terror. It couldn't respond effectively to the terrorist strike on Parliament and it didn't dare to mount strategic strikes post 26/11. And despite the shame of the Kandahar hijacking, there is, yet, no explicitly stated policy on negotiating with terrorists.

It is probably true that India cannot do what the US did after 9/11—attack Afghanistan and Iraq, sweep into Abbottabad to kill Osama Bin Laden and detain suspects in Guantanamo Bay. But pleading helplessness is not an effective counter-terror option either. In every terror attack where evidence of culpability has been provided to global powers, India has been unable to secure the custody of the perpetrators. From those who programmed the March 1993 serial bomb blasts in Bombay to those who planned the Kandahar passenger-for-terrorists hijack, from those who sponsored the attack on Parliament to those who trained and commanded the 26/11 attackers by phone, all are privileged guests of Pakistan.

India has failed to counter the infamous terror by 'non-state actors' theory put out by Pakistan. The fact is, every attack on India from Pakistan since independence has been initiated first by 'non-state actors' from the invasion in October 1947 when fighters from tribes sponsored by Pakistan and assisted by Pakistani Army regulars plundered and pillaged their way to Srinagar to the terrorists who waged war on Mumbai in 2008. Since Zia-ul-Haq, Pakistan has fought a war of a thousand cuts to avenge imagined and real slurs. Sikh terrorist groups were given shelter and the services of militants like G. S. Dhillon and J. S. Chauhan deployed to indoctrinate pilgrims visiting Sikh shrines. Pakistan effectively used its networks in the West—in Canada, for example—to tap into the emotions of disgruntled Sikhs. It also established feeder lines to the Northeast, tied up with groups from Nagaland and Mizoram and trained them in Pakistan in the eighties.

None of this was unknown to Indian regimes yet they chose not to respond in full measure. India did create an espionage network and funded assets abroad but the intel that was generated was not used effectively. Indeed, by its unconvincing riposte to terrorist activities, India has lost both credibility and assets internationally. Meanwhile, India continues to confuse Pakistanis with Pakistan. Pakistanis are victims, not Pakistan.

The state of our response is best reflected in the difference between the American response to 9/11 and the Indian response to 26/11. On 11 September 2001, al-Qaeda operatives struck down the Twin Towers in New York. The attack killed hundreds and maimed many for life. The US retaliated within a month and bombed the Taliban out of power in Afghanistan. More dramatic is the story of how the US restructured its security systems. By 7 October 2001, it had passed the Patriot Act, on 24 October it created the Homeland Security Department and by November it had brought twenty-two agencies under one command. In less than ninety days, the US had a security ring.

Now consider India's response. Post 26/11, it was decided that India needed to overhaul internal security systems. The government announced three key pieces to the strategy: the National Intelligence Grid (NatGrid) to bring synergy to intelligence gathering, the National Counter Terrorism Centre (NCTC) to deal with attacks and the National Investigation Agency (NIA) for a speedy probe of terror attacks. The first to be cleared was the NIA. The proposal for NatGrid was stalled from April 2009 to June 2011 by nineteen ministries, all of which had many objections. The plan for the NCTC, which was presented to the prime minister in April 2010, was given a typically Indian stamp of 'in-principle-approval' but is yet on paper. So in 2012 India has an NIA, a half-cleared NatGrid and the idea of NCTC (now being opposed by nine state governments for intruding on their turf). The darkest irony in this sequencing is that while India has an agency in place to investigate an attack, it is ill-prepared to either prevent or counter attacks.

The war against terror demands a total systemic overhaul and the implementation of administrative reforms. To start with, the sanctity of the rule of law, without exception, must be established. It is the failure of the state to establish criminality and enforce justice that has led to the mushrooming of sleeper modules and the emergence of fringe groups.

The quest for national security calls for a clear articulation of what constitutes the national interest. The commission that enquired into America's 9/11 terror attacks said, 'Across the government, there were failures of imagination, policy, capabilities and management.' India lacks on all counts: particularly intelligence and imagination—intelligence to rearrange its policy and imagination to foresee future results.

Till 1962, India did not imagine a threat from the mountains and didn't even plan for mountain divisions. It took two wars and six years before India's external intelligence agency, the Research and Analysis Wing (RAW), came into being in 1968 although the need for such an agency was emphasized immediately after the 1962 debacle. More tellingly, five decades after 1962, the Indian government is still unwilling to open the post-mortem conducted by the Henderson Brooks-Bhagat Operations Review Report to learn the lessons of history.

It is instructive at this point to compare China with India. China focused on growth, augmenting energy and food by acquiring assets and land for cultivation in South America and Africa. Growth helped it find the resources to hike its defence budget by four times in ten years to over $106 billion. A chessboard has sixty-four squares and Indians play the game well. But the Chinese play Weichi on a board with 362 squares. The objective of Weichi is not to checkmate but to encircle the rival. In the past five decades China has planned and executed encirclement by creating room for manoeuvre in Sri Lanka, Myanmar, Bangladesh, Nepal and Bhutan besides its all-weather ally Pakistan. In 2009, on the sixtieth anniversary of the Communist revolution, China unveiled fifty-three new weapons India didn't know about. In Delhi, the issue was raised at a meeting of cabinet ministers in November 2009. The question raised was whether India was adequately prepared with a strategy to counter this very overt display of power. A year later the ministry of defence presented a paper. The question raised was never fully addressed.

National security cannot be an abstract concept free to interpretation by every passing regime. India needs a security doctrine. Yes, there is a righteous halo to the doctrine of peace. And while morality matters in the war of perception, on the ground it is action that is important. Operation Geronimo which nailed Osama Bin Laden could well have gone wrong, like Operation Eagle Claw to rescue fifty-two US hostages in Teheran did in 1980. But Barack Obama dared to act in the interest of America. Nations become superpowers by aligning, negotiating and fighting for their interests. It is important for the country's decision-makers to understand that you are a victim only once; thereafter, you are a volunteer.

CENTRE-STATE RELATIONS: THE FEDERAL FAULT LINE

Can India in the twenty-first century afford a federal system in which powers are centralized and accountability decentralized? The relationship between the Centre and the states can be divided into three broad areas—legislative, administrative and financial powers. In 2011, the government at the centre was challenged and its initiatives vetoed by regional parties in two of the three areas. Regional parties came together to stall the passing of the Lokpal Bill as well as the attempt to open up foreign direct investment in the organized retail sector. Then, nine chief ministers asked the prime minister to rescind the order to create the NCTC.

The chairman of the Constituent Assembly, and India's first president, Dr Rajendra Prasad, following the adoption of the Constitution, prayed that 'the country may be given men of strong character, men of vision, men who would not sacrifice the interests of the country for the sake of smaller groups and areas and who would rise above the prejudices born of these differences'. The prayer has obviously gone unheard. In the battlefield of competitive politics, the idea of a nation is shrinking.

The arithmetic of politics is changing too. India no longer elects a single party to power and coalitions have taken centre stage. As numbers stake out today, the two principal national parties are politically irrelevant in over 150 of the 542 Lok Sabha constituencies. Since 1996, a clutch of regional parties accounts for a major share of the Lok Sabha seats. The strike rate of both parties has plummeted; the Congress's best was 206/542 in 2009 and the BJP secured 181/542 in 1999. Both regularly depend on regional parties to reach the magic figure of 272 seats in the Lok Sabha. It is also a fact that in eight of the most populous states—including Bihar and Uttar Pradesh—regional parties rule the roost. In the era of split mandates, differences rather than unity of purpose dominate Centre-state politics.

The political economy, too, is riddled with problems. Critical policies are held hostage as the Centre and states war over who has the right to formulate policies and who will bear the fiscal consequences. India needs to expand the production of coal, iron ore and minerals to fuel its 9-per-cent growth aspirations. Mining policy is formulated by the Centre while it is the states which have to deal with the consequent disruption and agitations. The states want a better compensation formula while the Centre wants the states to share royalties with the dislocated and affected people on the ground. Individual states have had their own land-acquisition policies since 2006, yet the Centre has been trying to push through model legislation. As a result, investments worth over $100 billion are stuck over land-acquisition issues. This has resulted in crucial projects of the National Highways Authority of India as well as public-sector power projects being stalled. The hold-up of legislation is not a one-way street. Since 2004, over 110 bills passed by state assemblies are pending with the Centre for clearance.

The authors of the Constitution were unambiguous in their espousal of a strong Centre to maintain national unity. The word 'Union' was used to emphasize that the federation of states was forged and not the result of an agreement. Therefore no state could, or would, be allowed to secede from the Union. As a safeguard, provisions were put in place to prevent the arbitrary use of powers. To make constitutional amendments, the Centre has to consult states, get the consent of the Rajya Sabha, which is the house of the states, and obtain the approval of half the states.

The balance was best articulated by B. R. Ambedkar, the father of India's Constitution: 'Though the country and the people may be divided into different states for convenience of administration, the country is one integral whole, its people a single people living under a single imperium derived from a single source.' This lofty idea survived relatively unchallenged two decades after independence thanks to the iconic stature of Jawaharlal Nehru, his persuasive skills, and the brute majority Congress enjoyed in Parliament. The virus of discord first made its appearance in 1967 when Congress lost eight out of sixteen states, triggering the first rush of competitive politics.

Since the sixties, a series of committees and commissions have examined the issue. The Administrative Reforms Commission in 1968 took the position that the three 'Lists' were well crafted and did not 'consider the time ripe or appropriate for a review'. This could have led to dissent from the states and a rethink but, in 1971, the Congress, riding a wave of socialism, recaptured its political ground. The seventies left no room for debate or dissent. As Congressman D. K. Baruah put it most memorably, 'India is Indira and Indira is India!' Congress used its brute majority to force its programmes through.

Centre-state relations came back on to the discussion table in 1983 when N. T. Rama Rao reigned and three out of the four southern states were ruled by non-Congress governments. The Centre, N. T. Rama Rao thundered, was a conceptual myth and every inch of India was ruled by the states. NTR was right, every inch indeed is ruled by the states, but their rule is constrained by the diktats of big brother at the Centre. Theoretically, a government elected in the states can change the complexion of a particular state with visionary leadership and innovative ideas. In practice, though, the states are shackled by a complex maze of laws and fiscal allocations.

In 1983, the Indira Gandhi government appointed the Sarkaria Commission to look into the issues that were raised. The commission held that 'decentralization of real power to local institutions would help defuse the threat of centrifugal forces and increase popular involvement' in governance. The commission which submitted its report in 1988 also held that there has 'been a pervasive trend towards greater centralization of powers over the years' thanks to political pressures. Of the 247 recommendations made by the commission, only 179 were accepted.

Thereafter, the issues have been visited by the National Commission to Review the Working of the Constitution, headed by Justice M. N. Venkatachalliah. Appointed in February 2000, the commission submitted its report in 2002 in which it argued the need for more extensive consultation with the states on issues and the devolution of powers to local governments. More recently, the UPA appointed a Commission for Centre-state Relations chaired by Justice Madan Mohan Punchhi to examine issues. The report, submitted in March

2010, is gathering dust.

Morality in politics is but contextual. While at one level the states argued for greater devolution of powers, at another they denied the same to local self-governments in their own states. Indeed, in 1987, at a meeting of the NDC, Rajiv Gandhi asked chief ministers why they didn't champion decentralization in their own states. In 1992, acknowledging the gaps in governance, the government amended the Constitution to decentralize powers to the level of panchayats and municipalities through the Seventy-third and Seventy-fourth Amendments to the Constitution. Barring Kerala, Madhya Pradesh and Maharashtra, the other states were loath to part with any of their powers.

The Centre shares 32 per cent of its tax revenues with the states. The states believe this is not enough as the bulk of the administrative costs of implementing policy falls on them. The cost of funding this Leviathan, the states argue, is not reflected in the calculus of Centre-state transfers. Today, the gross fiscal deficit of the states—the difference between income and expenditure—has shot up from ₹18,000 crore to over ₹2 lakh crore in twenty years.

Similarly, the states have starved local governments tasked with providing basic amenities to citizens. The states may rule every inch of India, but it is panchayats and municipalities who are the real ruling bodies. Yet, less than 3 per cent of the total revenues sanctioned to the state are passed through to over 240,000 local government institutions. As the late Vilasrao Deshmukh, who rose from sarpanch to CM, put it succinctly, 'The Centre does to states what the states do to local governments!'

When the founding fathers authored the Constitution, they balanced the quest for a strong centre with the aspiration for a federal structure. It is time India assessed whether it needs to host a multiplicity of authorities both at the Centre and states, and why the Centre needs to retain control over so many areas of governance. If the state governments are being voted to power, shouldn't they be allowed the discretion to engineer change? Why should Maharashtra have to ask the Centre to clear new parking charges in the city of

Mumbai just because the Motor Vehicles Act is a central act? Why should the ministry of environment decide on every major clearance in the states—from questions on infrastructure to which cities will be allowed to hold public functions beyond 10 p.m. on specific days? And if the logic is that the Centre knows best, why waste public resources to hold elections to elect state governments?

Governance in India, in 2012, is a sham and a shame. The glaring absence of strategic objectives is ubiquitous. In every crisis listed above, the common thread is the inability of successive governments to think imaginatively and act decisively.

India deserves better.

AUTHOR'S NOTE

OCTOBER 2012

Every chapter of *Accidental India* begins with a date. This is for a reason. It is to show how each change has taken tragically long to bring about accidental transformation. Not just in terms of time, but in terms of the trauma and pain to the people whom the politicians claim to care for. The ongoing crises listed, particularly in the Epilogue, and in the chapters, continue to deny Indians personal, emotional and income security. One thousand two hundred and twelve million Indians must no longer be denied. A nation of over a billion people cannot wait endlessly for accidents. Crisis cannot continue to be the clinching argument for change.

While regular conventions of style and standardization have been followed for most of the proper nouns and acronyms used in the book, in some cases in order to avoid confusing the reader I have chosen to use the popular name of the individual or organization. This is the reason why the initials of some individuals have not been expanded in the text, but these can be found in the index.

Also, in order to distinguish between the various personalities who share the last name Gandhi or Singh, I have not referred to them by their surname alone after the first time they appear in the text but have used variations of their name depending on the context. Likewise, in the case of certain personalities like Lyndon Baines Johnson or C. Rajagopalachari, who were referred to by more than one variant of their name during their lifetime, I have opted not to standardize their names in the narrative. I hope that readers will not be unduly inconvenienced by these decisions.

ACKNOWLEDGEMENTS

Accidental India: A History of the Nation's Passage through Crisis and Change would not have been possible without the blessings of Mr S. Venkitaramanan, Dr C. Rangarajan, Dr Bimal Jalan, Mr Montek Singh Ahluwalia, Dr Vijay Kelkar, Dr Y. V. Reddy, Dr M. S. Swaminathan, Mr Naresh Chandra, Dr Rakesh Mohan, Mr N. Vittal, Mr G. Parthasarathy, Mr Deepak Parekh, Mr K. V. Kamath and the late B. G. Deshmukh, all of whom allowed me access into their sacred space of understanding.

Throughout my study I have had the benefit of guidance from the brightest of minds. I am indebted to Prof. Bibek Debroy, Barun Mitra, Nandan Nilekani, Prof. Mahendra Dev, Dr Indira Rajaraman, Dr Subir Gokarn, Dr Ashima Goyal, Pramath Raj Sinha, Prof. Raghuram Rajan, Pratap Bhanu Mehta, Ashutosh Varshney, Biraj Patnaik, Nikhil Dey and Prof. Rajkamal Iyer for their patience with my many questions.

The distance between idea and implementation is too often a contest between national exigency and political expediency. I have benefitted greatly in my appreciation of this process from interactions with P. Chidambaram, Sharad Pawar, Sushil Kumar Shinde, Arun Shourie, Veerappa Moily, Nitin Gadkari, Arun Jaitley, Manohar Parrikar, R. R. Patil, Rajeev Chandrasekhar, Kamal Morarka and Milind Deora.

I am grateful for the cooperation received for archival and other research from Dorota Wyganowska at the IMF, Vlada Alekankina at World Bank, Dr Jagdish K. Ladha at the International Rice Research Institute, Jennifer Mandel at the Ronald Reagan Library, S. S. Rajasekar at the National Agro Foundation, Jennifer Cuddeback at the Lyndon B. Johnson Library, Jessica Mathewson at the FAO's David Lubin Library, Dr S. K. De Datta at Virginia Tech, Dr Amitendu Palit at the Institute of South Asian Studies, Martina Haefeli at the International

Seed Testing Association and Soma de Silva at the Colombo Plan Secretariat.

David Davidar, *romba nanri*, for all your inputs and for the editing; Anurag Basnet for facilitating the production.

To paraphrase the Beatles, I got by with a little help from my friends. For every step I thank Scherezade Virani, Vimal Bhandari, A. Janakiraman, V. R. Srinivasan, Alpana Killawala, Roshni Jayakar, Rama Lakshmi, Anand Natrajan, Uday Mahurkar, Sandeep Unnithan, Shishir Gupta, Nandini Raghavendra, Priya Sahgal, Indrani Bagchi, Ajit Chaudhari, Anuradha Das Mathur, Milind Khandekar, Rajesh Sharma, Anand Sonar, Shyamlal Yadav, M. V. Ratnam, Sharada Harihar, my dost and host Bimal Parekh.

And Shah, Sharma, Shelgikar…*aabhar*! Jayesh, Shravan and Sanjeev, thank you for always being there.

My mother Mangalam for introducing me to scepticism and my father Venkataramani, to reason.

My wife, Pinki Virani, partner for twenty-five years, grow old with me, the best is yet to be.

SHANKKAR AIYAR
October 2012

SELECTED INTERVIEWS AND SOURCES

THE BONFIRE OF THE VANITIES
S. Venkitaramanan
Chakravarthy Rangarajan
Subramaniam Swamy
Padinjarethalakal Cherian Alexander
Naresh Chandra
B. G. Deshmukh
Montek Singh Ahluwalia
Bimal Jalan
Rakesh Mohan
Yaga Venugopal Reddy
Vijay Kelkar
Subir Gokarn
Bibek Debroy
Indira Rajaraman
Rajkamal Iyer
Yashwant Sinha
Ajit Singh
Kamal Morarka

THE HUNGER GAMES
S. Venkitaramanan
Maankombu Sambasivan Swaminathan
Mahendra Dev
S. S. Rajsekar
G. Ranga Rao
J. Veeraraghavan

SELECTED INTERVIEWS AND SOURCES

DAS KAPITAL
Chakravarthy Rangarajan
S. Venkitaramanan
Yaga Venugopal Reddy
Subir Gokarn
Vijay Kelkar
Indira Rajaraman
Mahendra Dev
Ashima Goyal
Rajkamal Iyer
Ajit Ranade

THE MILKY WAY
Molly Verghese Kurien
Verghese Kurien
S. Venkitaramanan
Montek Singh Ahluwalia

SOUP KITCHEN FOR THE SOUL
Biraj Patnaik
Montek Singh Ahluwalia
A. M. Swaminathan
A. Gopanna

THE BLACK SWAN
Nagaraj Vittal
N. R. Narayana Murthy
Srini Rajam
Nandan Nilekani
G. K. Patni
B. K. Syngal
Jerry Rao

THE DA VINCI CODE
P. B. Sawant

Aruna Roy
Nikhil Dey

EPILOGUE
S. Venkitaramanan
Vijay Kelkar
G. Parthasarathy
M. Damodaran
Mahendra Dev

NOTES

PREFACE

9 **This is a country**; Dominic Wilson and Roopa Purushothaman, 'Global Economics Paper No. 99: Dreaming With BRICs: The Path to 2050', *CEO Confidential* no. 12 (1 October 2003), p. 1.

10 **I scooped the news**; Shankkar Aiyar, 'Secret Sale of Gold by RBI', *The Indian Express* (8 July 1991).

11 **mostly regularities or irregularities**; Philip H. Bagby, 'Culture and the Causes of Culture', *American Anthropologist* vol. 55, Issue 4, (October 1953), pp. 535-554.

11 **'inconstancy and variability'**; Arnold Joseph Toynbee, *A Study of History* (London; Oxford University Press, 1934), p. 109.

12 **discussing the origins**; Francis Fukuyama, *The Origins of Political Order: From Prehuman Times to the French Revolution* (New York; Farrar, Straus & Giroux, 2011).

12 **'India is not one nation'**; As recorded in an interview with journalist Charlie Rose.

12 **The destiny of a country**; Daron Acemoğlu and James Robinson, *Why Nations Fail: The Origins of Power, Prosperity and Poverty* (New York; Crown Business, 2012).

13 **'On 26 January 1950'**; Bhimrao R. Ambedkar, Constituent Assembly of India Debates (Proceedings) vol. 11, (25 November 1949).

14 **In 1951, India's population**; Census, Ministry of Home Affairs, Government of India.

14 **'would have splintered'**; Francine R. Frankel, *India's Political Economy, 1947-2004: The Gradual Revolution* (New Delhi; Oxford University Press, 2006).

15 **'a blessing in disguise'**; Mark Tully, 'Manmohan Singh: Architect of the Modern India', *Cambridge University Alumni Magazine* (October 2005), p. 13.

15 **'liberalize the economy'**; Ibid.

16 **the World Bank ranks India;** The World Bank, *Doing Business in a More Transparent World* (Washington D.C.; The World Bank and the International Finance Corporation, 2012), p. 6.

16 **It is ranked 132/183**; Ibid., p.101.

17 **As early as 1952**; John Kenneth Galbraith, *American Capitalism: The Concept of Countervailing Power* (New Jersey; Transaction Publishers, 1993).

18   'the domination of an organized'; Gaetano Mosca, *The Ruling Class*, Hannah D. Kahn (trans.), (New York and London; McGraw-Hill Book Company, Inc., 1939), p. 53.
19   'Suppressing volatility makes the world'; Nassim Nicholas Taleb and Mark Blyth, 'The Black Swan of Cairo: How Suppressing Volatility Makes the World Less Predictable and More Dangerous', *Foreign Affairs* vol. 90, no. 3, (May/June 2011), pp. 32-39.

THE BONFIRE OF THE VANITIES

23   'What do you think?'; P. C. Alexander, *Through the Corridors of Power: An Insider's Story* (New Delhi; HarperCollins Publishers India, 2004).
25   'was put forward as'; Purushottamdas Thakurdas (ed.), *A Brief Memorandum Outlining a Plan of Economic Development for India* (2 vols.) (London; Penguin, 1945), p. 7.
26   'jobbing shops producing'; Henry F. Grady, Report of the American Mission (1942).
26   **The great economic damage**; As quoted by Manmohan Singh in 'In Acceptance of an Honorary Degree from Oxford University', *The Hindu* (8 July 2005).
27   'no development of the kind'; Purushottamdas Thakurdas (ed.), *A Brief Memorandum Outlining a Plan of Economic Development for India* (London; Penguin, 1945), p. 8.
27   'Every aspect of economic'; Ibid., p. 55.
28   'Inevitably, the trend'; Jawaharlal Nehru, *Independence and After: A Collection of Speeches, 1946-1949* (New Delhi; Ayer Publishing, 1971), p. 175.
30   'statistician devoid of a sense'; Quoted by Amal Sanyal, 'The Curious Case of the Bombay Plan', *Contemporary Issues and Ideas in Social Sciences* 6, no. 1 (July 2010), p. 1.
30   'theoretical shibboleth which'; Ibid., p. 18.
30   'The policies of government': Hans Raj Pasricha, *The Swatantra Party: Victory in Defeat* (The Rajaji Foundation, 2002).
31   **I. G. Patel recalls**; I.G. Patel, *Glimpses of Indian Economy: An Insider's View*, (New Delhi; Oxford University Press, March 2002), pp. 76-77.
32   **was impressed by the idea:** Ibid., p. 31.
32   'Time and again one will hear'; Milton Friedman, 'Indian Economic Planning' (May 1963), as quoted by Parth J. Shah, 'Friedman on India', The Centre for Civil Society, New Delhi, (2000).
32   'The current danger is that India'; Ibid., p. 4.
34   **Rabindra Kishen Hazari pointed out**; Rabindra Kishen Hazari, *Industrial Planning and Licensing Policy: Interim Report to Planning Commission* (New Delhi; Manager of Publications, 1967), p. 8.
36   **Hazari reveals in his report:** Ibid., p. 9.
36   'One gets the impression'; Milton Friedman on the Nehru/Mahalanobis

Plan (15 February 1956), edited by Subroto Roy, India Policy Institute official website.

36 **'There was only modest'**; Bernard R. Bell, *Report to the President of the International Bank for Reconstruction and Development and the International Development Association on India's Economic Development Effort* (14 vols.) (Washington D.C.; The World Bank, 1965).

40 **'failed to fulfil its principal purpose'**; Rabindra Kishen Hazari, *Industrial Planning and Licensing Policy*.

41 **As agricultural production dropped**; Vijay Joshi and I. M. D. Little, *India: Macroeconomics and Political Economy 1964-1991* (Oxford University Press, 1994), p. 53.

41 **In September 1973**; David Henderson, 'Unintended Consequences in Energy Policy', *The Freeman*(March 2009).

42 **its share in global trade**; Jagdish N. Bhagwati and T. N. Srinivasan, 'An Overview: 1950-70', *Foreign Trade Regimes and Economic Development: India* (National Bureau of Economic Research 1975), pp. 1-32.

44 **between 1960 and 1979**; David Morawetz, *Twenty-five Years of Economic Development, 1950-1975* (Baltimore; The Johns Hopkins University Press, 1975).

45 **'A fashionable view'**; Vijay Joshi and I.M.D. Little, *India: Macroeconomics and Political Economy 1964-1991* (New Delhi; Oxford University Press, 1994), p. xiv.

45 **'Our cardinal sin in India'**; I.G. Patel, 'Limits of the Current Consensus on Development' (Washington D. C.; The World Bank, 1994), p. 12.

45 **'In respect of licensing'**; Rakesh Mohan and Vandana Aggarwal, 'Commands and Controls: Planning for Indian Industrial Development, 1951-1990', *Journal of Comparative Economics* vol. 14, no. 4 (1990), pp. 681-712.

48 **'They feel little concern'**; Rajiv Gandhi, 'Inaugural Speech by Congress President Shri Rajiv Gandhi at the Centenary Resolve Session', *Congress Sandesh*, December 1985.

48 **'Millions of ordinary Congress'**; Ibid.

49 **'it would be difficult'**; R. Venkataraman, *My Presidential Years* (New Delhi; HarperCollins Publishers India, 1994), p. 40.

52 **Between 1980-81 and 1990-91**; Ministry of Finance, *Economic Survey 1980-81* and *Economic Survey 1990-91* (New Delhi; Controller of Publications, 1981, 1991).

53 **'The Government's coffers'**; Prabhu Chawla, 'The Prime Minister: Refreshing Openness', *India Today* (December 1989).

54 **The fiscal deficit was double**; Ministry of Finance, *Speech of Prof. Madhu Dandavate Introducing the Budget for the Year 1990-91* (New Delhi; Government of India, 1990).

54 **'risked mortgaging hard won'**; Ibid., p. 2.

55 **V. P. Singh also shot down**; Kelkar produced a template for change that was published by the Asian Development Bank.

55 **Whether V. P. Singh, the reformer**; In fact, many years after India chose the path of liberalization, V. P. Singh met Montek Singh Ahluwalia at a wedding and

discussed reforms at length. At the end he quipped, 'You must be happy your ideas are now in vogue.'

61 **'I told our officials'**; 'India to Seek Big I.M.F. Loan', *The New York Times* (18 December 1990).
61 **'India will not hesitate'**; Ibid.
63 **'India has been confronted'**; International Monetary Fund, Minutes of the Executive Board Meeting 91/7, 18 January 1991, p. 11.
63 **'The industrial policy of May 1990'**; Ibid., p. 41.
63 **'more enduring solutions'**; Ibid., p. 5.
64 **'government intends to implement'**; Ibid., p. 5.
64 **'of the twenty-five specific'**; The World Bank, India-Structural Adjustment Loan/Credit (Washington D. C.; 1995), p. iii.
64 **'a blueprint for the change'**; 'Today's Fiscal Crisis Is More Acute Than in 1991', Deepak Nayyar in conversation with Sanjaya Baru, *The Financial Express* (25 February 2002).
66 **'The burden of servicing'**; Ministry of Finance, *Interim Budget 1991-92: Speech of Shri Yashwant Sinha, Minister of Finance* (New Delhi; Government of India, 1991), p. 1.
67 **it was clear that**; Yashwant Sinha, *Confessions of a Swadeshi Reformer: My Years as Finance Minister* (New Delhi; Penguin Books India, 2007).
69 **A time-bound programme**; 'A Forgotten Revolutionary', Arvind Panagriya, *The Times of India* (28 June 2012).
72 **'Thanks to the efforts'**; Ministry of Finance, *Budget 1991-92: Speech of Shri Manmohan Singh, Minister of Finance* (New Delhi; Government of India, 1991), p. 3.
72 **'No power on earth'**; Ibid., p. 31.

THE HUNGER GAMES
76 **'the cause existed principally'**; Romesh Chunder Dutt, *Famines and Land Assessments in India* (London; Kegan Paul, Trench, Trubner & Co., 1900), p. 2.
76 **A survey conducted by the Congress**; Indian National Congress, *Agrarian Distress in the United Provinces: Being the Report of the Committee Appointed by the Council of the U.P. Provincial Congress Committee to Enquire into the Agrarian Situation in the Province* (Delhi; Prabhu, 1931).
76 **'is born in debt'**; Malcolm Lyall Darling, *The Punjab Peasant in Prosperity and Debt* (London; Oxford University Press, 1928), p. 279.
77 **'India has long been'**; *Royal Commission on Agriculture in India* (Bombay; Government of India, 1928).
77 **'therefore production in India'**; Ibid.
79 **'dependence on food imports'**; Government of India, *Interim Report: Foodgrains Policy Committee (Purushottamdas Thakurdas Committee)* (New Delhi; Manager of Publications, 1948).
81 **'the abolition of zamindari'**; As quoted by Francine R. Frankel in *India's Political Economy, 1947-2004: The Gradual Revolution* (New York; Oxford

University Press, 2005) from *The Kisan Speaks* by N. G. Ranga (Madras; Kisan Publications, 1937).
82   **'cannot endure and an obvious step'**; Jawaharlal Nehru, 'Presidential Address to the Indian National Congress at Faizpur', *The Labour Monthly* vol. 19, no. 2 (February 1937), pp. 98-107.
83   **'a third way which'**; Francine R. Frankel, *India's Political Economy, 1947-2004: The Gradual Revolution* (New York; Oxford University Press), p. 3.
84   **'Ever since the demand'**; Jawaharlal Nehru, *The Discovery of India* (New Delhi; Oxford University Press, 1985), p. 301.
85   **'I am delighted to'**; Harry S. Truman, 'Statement by the President upon Signing the India Emergency Food Aid Act' (15 June 1951). *The American Presidency Project* online, put up by Gerhard Peters and John T. Woolley.
86   **'India has long been'**; The World Bank, *India: First Loan Administration Report* (Washington D.C.; 1952). p. 14.
86   **'only if further financial'**; Ibid., p. 20.
86   **'During the last fifteen'**; Ministry of Law and Justice, The Constitution (First Amendment) Act, 1951.
86   **'insert provisions fully securing'**; Ibid.
89   **these monies amounted**; John H. Perkins, *Geopolitics and the Green Revolution: Wheat, Genes, and the Cold War* (New York; Oxford University Press, 1997).
89   **This creation of money**; B. R. Shenoy, *PL 480 Aid and India's Food Problem* (Delhi; Affiliated East-West Press, 1974).
92   **Mincing no words**; Ford Foundation, 'Report on India's Food Crisis and Steps to Meet It', prepared by the Agricultural Production Team, New Delhi, 1959: Ministry of Food and Agriculture and Ministry of Community Development and Cooperation, Government of India.
92   **'This means that food'**; Ibid.
93   **Rao proved through forensic analysis**; Ibid.
95   **'Wars are fought over'**; Inder Malhotra, 'Defeated, Not Destroyed', *The Indian Express* (31 October 2011).
96   **'If this House thinks'**; Ibid.
97   **Agriculture, the study declared**; R. N. Poduval, 'Agricultural Planning in India', *Agricultural Planning Studies* vol. 3 (1963), pp. 277-287.
97   **'no comparable modernization'**; Bernard R. Bell, 'Report to the President of the International Bank for Reconstruction and Development and the International Development Association on India's Economic Development Effort', vol. 1 (Washington D.C.; The World Bank, 1965).
97   **In 1959-60, the average yield**; Ibid., p. 13.
97   **'If difference in farmland'**; Ibid., p. 38.
98   **'warned of an untoward event'**; C. Subramaniam, *Hand of Destiny: The Green Revolution* (Mumbai; Bharatiya Vidya Bhavan, 1994), pp. 76-77.
103 **the capital cost of producing**; Poduval, 'Agricultural Planning in India', pp. 277-287.

104 **'There is nothing derogatory'**; C. Subramaniam, convocation address delivered at the Indian Agricultural Research Institute, New Delhi, 28 September 1965.
104 **'If the cabinet is not'**; C. Subramaniam, *Hand of Destiny*, p. 113.
107 **'Should we stop industrial development'**; Ibid., p. 138.
107 **took issue with him**; Balaraman Sivaraman, *Bitter Sweet: Governance of India in Transition* (Columbia; South Asia Books, 1991), pp. 302-305.
110 **'Isn't this seed'**; Ibid.
110 **By a strange coincidence**; The sixties and the seventies saw the publication of nearly half a dozen books by disciples of Malthus including William and Paul Paddock, Paul and Anne Ehrlich, Donella Meadows and Garrret Hardin.
111 **Based on a set of**; Paul Paddock and William Paddock, *Hungry Nations* (London; Little, Brown, 1964).
111 **'India is the example'**; Paul Paddock and William Paddock, *Famine 1975! America's Decision: Who Will Survive?* (London; Little, Brown, 1967), p. 217.
111 **'today's trends show'**; Ibid.
111 **'of all the national leaderships'**; Ibid., p. 218.
111 **'If we cut off the food aid'**; Ibid., p. 219.
112 **became 'blood brothers'**; George E. Reedy, Transcript, Oral History Interview XIX(13 June 1985), by Michael L. Gillette, Internet copy, LBJ Library.
113 **'You can't give all this'**; Orville Freeman Oral History Interview III, 7/21/69 by T. H. Baker, LBJ Library.
113 **'I consider self-sufficiency'**; Lal Bahadur Shastri, quoted by Perkins, *Geopolitics and the Green Revolution*, p. 243.
114 **'We had them over a barrel'**; Richard P. Dauer, *A North-South Mind In An East-West World: Chester Bowles And The Making Of United States Cold War Foreign Policy, 1951-1969* (Greenwood Publishing Group, 2005), p. 206.
116 **571 irrigation projects**; Ministry of Water Resources, 'Report of the Working Group on Major & Medium Irrigation and Command Area Development for the XII Five Year Plan (2012-2017)' (New Delhi; Government of India, 2011), p. 21.
116 **Of the 253 projects**; Comptroller and Auditor General of India, Performance Audit of Accelerated Irrigation Benefits Programme (AIBP) 2010-11.
116 **What this means is that**; The working group on agriculture for the Twelfth Five Year Plan says: 'More than three-fifths of India's population draws their livelihood from agriculture that adds just one-fifth to its GDP. There should be obvious and serious concerns about the efficient functioning of this sector both in terms of its output/productivity and its marketing.'

DAS KAPITAL
118 **'should be a leader'**; 'Express News Service', *The Sunday Standard* (6 October 1963) p. 1.
120 **'Socialism is of many kinds'**; Jawaharlal Nehru, *Glimpses of World History: Being Further Letters to His Daughter, Written in Prison, and Containing a Rambling Account of History for Young People* (New Delhi; Penguin Books India, 2004).

120 **'priorities for development'**; Planning Commission, *First Five Year Plan 1951-56* (New Delhi; Government of India, 1951).
120 **'visualized for the economy '**; Ibid.
121 **'the anticipated gap between'**; Planning Commission, *Summary Record of Discussions of the National Development Council Meetings*, vol. 1 (New Delhi; Government of India).
121 **'a vast country like India'**; J. C. Johari, *Indian National Congress Since Independence* (New Delhi; Lotus Press, 2006), p. 119.
122 **'The danger is not'**; Karl Gunnar Myrdal, *Indian Economic Planning in Its Broader Setting: Being an Address to Members of Parliament on 22nd April 1958* (New Delhi; Secretary, Congress Party in Parliament, 1958).
123 **In 1951, there were 566 banks**; Reserve Bank of India official website.
123 **'the resources with'**; Planning Commission, *Summary Record of Discussions of the National Development Council Meetings*, vol. 2 (New Delhi; Government of India), p. 187.
123 **no real reason**; Ibid., p. 198.
124 **'In view of the emergency'**; Ram Singh Awana, *Pressure Politics in Congress Party: A Study of the Congress Forum for Socialist Action* (New Delhi; Northern Book Centre, 1988), p. 97-98.
125 **A survey of eighteen banks**; *The Reserve Bank of India 1951-1967* vol. 2.
127 **'even God in heaven'**; Ibid., p. 125.
129 **When Indira was born**; Jawaharlal Nehru, *A Bunch of Old Letters: Being Mostly Written to Jawaharlal Nehru and Some Written by Him* (Bombay; Asia Publishing House, 1958), p. 1.
131 **'The Indians should realize'**; Dennis Kux, *India and the United States: Estranged Democracies, 1941-1991* (Washington D.C.; National Defense University Press, 1992), p. 228.
132 **'Well, the Pope and U Thant'**; Chester Bowles, *Promises to Keep: My Years in Public Life* (New York; Harper & Row, 1971), p. 526.
134 **'if the three former finance ministers'**; Dwarka Prasad Mishra, *The Post Nehru Era: Political Memoirs* (New Delhi; Har-Anand Publications, 1993), p. 37.
134 **'It was as if devaluation'**; Dennis Kux, *India and the United States: Estranged Democracies*, p. 254.
134 **the value of exports actually fell**; *India: Macroeconomics and Political Economy 1964-1991:* Vijay Joshi and I. M. D. Little, *The Crisis of 1965-67: Antecedents and Consequences*, (Oxford University Press, 1994).
136 **'The question is whom'**; V. Krishna Ananth, *India Since Independence: Making Sense of Indian Politics* (Noida; Pearson Education India, 2011), p. 73.
137 **'The goal was for establishing'**; Ram Singh Awana, *Pressure Politics in Congress Party: A Study of the Congress Forum for Socialist Action*, p. 113.
138 **'The powers bestowed'**; The Reserve Bank of India, *The Reserve Bank of India*, vol. 3 (Mumbai; 2005), p. 787.
138 **'small delegation of IBA'**; Ibid., p. 790.

139 **A paper on banking**; Ibid. p. 19.
139 **'The nationalization of all banks'**; Ibid., p. 791.
139 **'the chickens have come'**; 'Off the Record', *Economic and Political Weekly* (22 July 1967).
140 **'threats of nationalization'**; Ibid.
140 **'between 1953 and 1965'**; As quoted in *The Reserve Bank of India*, vol. 3 (Mumbai; The Reserve Bank of India, 2005), p. 18.
140 **The panel reported**; Ibid., p. 19.
140 **Through common directors**; Ibid., p. 19.
141 **'I should express'**; *The Reserve Bank of India*, vol. 3, p. 20.
142 **Its first report was damning**; *The Reserve Bank of India*, vol. 3, 1967-1981, p. 20 and p. 60.
143 **'had not been able'**; Planning Commission, *Summary Record of Discussions of the National Development Council Meetings*, vol. 3 (New Delhi; Government of India), p. 16.
143 **'in order to secure'**; Ibid., pp. 16-17.
145 **'There is great feeling'**; *The Reserve Bank of India*, vol. 3, 1967-1981, (Mumbai; The Reserve Bank of India, 2005), p. 34.
147 **'An institution, such as the banking system'**; Abhik Ray, A. K. Chakraborty, Suman Das and J. S. Mathai, *The Evolution of the State Bank of India: The Era from 1995 to 1980*, vol. 4 (New Delhi; Penguin Books India, 2009), p. 23.
153 **In 1969, after twenty-two years**; Reserve Bank of India official website.
153 **By 1979 India boasted**; Ibid.
153 **Between 1969 and 1989**; Ibid.
153 **Thanks to branch expansion**; Robin Burgess and Rohini Pande, 'Do Rural Banks Matter? Evidence from the Indian Social Banking Experiment', *The American Economic Review 95*, no. 3 (June 2005), pp. 780-795.
154 **For the period from**; RBI Annual Reports.
154 **Contrast this with**; Ibid.
154 **Between 1969 and 1989**; Ibid.
155 **'If you allow me'**; Rahul Sharma, 'Indira Was Right, Says Sonia, Congress Is Wrong, Says Left', The *HT* Leadership Summit, 21 November 2008.
156 **'Never before the bold decision'**; Ministry of Finance, *Budget 2009-2010: Speech of Pranab Mukherjee, Minister of Finance* (New Delhi; Government of India, 2009).

THE MILKY WAY
160 **'Let me take charge today'**; Verghese Kurien, *I Too Had a Dream* (New Delhi; Roli Books, 2007), p. 19.
161 **It was a good life at Jamshedpur**; Ibid.
165 **By 1952-53, the cooperative**; Ibid.
165 **'Conduct a post-mortem of the flies'**; Ibid.
171 **'The achievement of this plant'**; Ibid.

172 **In the fifties, the per capita**; Planning Commission, 'Dairying and Horticulture', *1st Five Year Plan* (New Delhi; Government of India, 1951).
172 **The First Five Year Plan**; Planning Commission, 'Animal Husbandry', *1st Five Year Plan* (New Delhi; Government of India, 1951).
173 **To address the problem**; Planning Commission, 'Animal Husbandry and Dairying', *2nd Five Year Plan* (New Delhi; Government of India, 1956).
173 **'the average per capita milk consumption'**; Planning Commission, 'Animal Husbandry, Dairying and Fisheries', *3rd Five Year Plan* (New Delhi; Government of India, 1961).
175 **Milk production of 17 million**; Inder Pal Abrol, 'Agriculture in India' (New Delhi; Centre for Advancement of Sustainable Agriculture, 2002).
175 **In 1952, 74 per cent**; Data from Dairy India and Planning Commission.
175 **In 1967, some fifteen years later**; Ibid.
181 **Per capita availability of milk**; Verghese Kurien, 'India's Milk Revolution: Investing in Rural Producer Organizations', *Ending Poverty in South Asia: Ideas That Work*, Deepa Narayan and Elena Glinskaya (eds.) (Washington D.C.; The World Bank, 2007).
183 **In 2011-12, just the GCMMF**; Details available on the Amul website.
184 **In the fifties India barely produced**; Verghese Kurien, *I Too Had a Dream*.
184 **'on the espionage implicating'**; Rajya Sabha Questions to Answers, 16 May 1985.
185 **Between 1947 and 1968, milk output grew**; Planning Commission Data.
185 **Post OF-1, between 1970 and 1996**; Planning Commission Data.
186 **The World Bank in 1997**; Nalini Kumar and Wilfred Candler, *India: The Dairy Revolution* (Washington D.C.; World Bank, 1998).

SOUP KITCHEN FOR THE SOUL

189 **She would often lock up**; Vaasanthi, *Cut-Outs, Caste and Cine Stars: The World of Tamil Politics* (New Delhi; Penguin Books India, January 2006), p. 67.
191 **The first census**; Census data, Government of India, Ministry of Home Affairs.
191 **In 1951 only four**; Planning Commission, 'Gross Enrolment Ratio at Schools Stages (1950-51 to 2007-08)', *Data for Use of Deputy Chairman, Planning Commission* (New Delhi; Government of India, 2012), p. 161.
191 **By the mid-fifties**; Ibid., p. 161.
191 **Essentially, two out of three**; Ibid., p. 161.
194 **Indeed, in 1961**; Ibid., p. 161.
194 **Only four out of ten boys**; Ibid., p 161.
194 **A survey conducted**; As quoted by C. Gopalan, 'Development and Deprivation: The Indian Experience', *Economic and Political Weekly* (13 December 1983).
194 **Studies by the National Institute of Nutrition**; Ibid.
198 **After it took off**; World Bank, *India: Second Tamil Nadu Nutrition Project* (Washington, D.C.; 1990), p. vi.
198 **Moreover, in 1987**; Ibid.

199 **'It is no less noble'**; Jayalalithaa, 'Mid-day Meal Scheme—MGR Deserves the Nobel Prize, *Illustrated Weekly of India* (16-22 January 1983), p. 8.
200 **Not surprisingly, the discourse**; Planning Commission, *Summary Record of Discussions of the National Development Council Meetings*, vol. 4 (New Delhi; Government of India).
202 **'there [was] any proposal'**; Rajya Sabha Archives, 13 March 1992.
202 **'There is at present no'**; Ibid.
202 **'Over 30 per cent of'**; Nirmala Murthy, Indira Hirway, P. R. Panchmukhi and J. K. Satia, *How Well Do India's Social Sector Programmes Serve the Poor* (Washington D. C.; The World Bank, 1990), p. 3.
202 **'despite the massive expansion'**; Ibid., p. 6.
203 **Thailand and Indonesia**: UNDP International Human Development Indicators.
203 **In 1981, Kerala boasted:** Government of Kerala website.
203 **In 1991, literacy among women**:Planning Commission Data.
204 **'a glass two-thirds full'**: The World Bank, *India Primary Education Achievement and Challenges* (Washington D.C.; The World Bank, 1996).
204 **Of 105 million children**; The World Bank, *India Achievements and Challenges in Reducing Poverty* (Washington D.C.; 1997), p. 5.
205 **Worse, about 75 per cent**; Ibid., p. 26.
205 **Even a small country**; Anthony R. Measham and Meera Chatterjee, *Wasting Away: The Crisis of Malnutrition in India* (Washington D.C.; The World Bank, 1999), p. 2.
205 **India, in contrast**; Ibid., p. 25.
205 **'The State shall endeavour'**; Ministry of Law and Justice (Legislative Department), Constitution of India 1949, Article 45.
205 **'No child below'**; Ibid., Article 24.
205 **'State shall, in particular, direct its'**; Ibid., Article 39 (e).
206 **In 1991, one-third**; Planning Commission Gross Enrolment Data.
206 **'the right of the public'**; Supreme Court of India, *Bennett Coleman & Co. and Others vs. Union of India and Others* on 30 October 1972.
206 **'rights which are sought'**; Supreme Court of India, *S. P. Gupta vs. President of India and Others* on 30 December 1981.
206 **'citizens of the country'**; Supreme Court of India, *Unnikrishnan and Others vs. State of Andhra Pradesh and Others* on 4 February 1993.
207 **'India's approach to social services'**; Amartya Sen, 'How Is India Doing?', *The New York Review of Books* (December 1982).
207 **'the strength and weakness'**; Ibid.
207 **In India, the level**; The World Bank, *India Primary Education Achievement and Challenges*.
208 **Studies have established**; Ibid.
208 **In 1993, Ashok Mathur studied**; Ashok Mathur, 'The Human Capital Stock and Regional Economic Development in India', Sheel Chand Nuna (ed.),

Regional Disparities in Educational Development (New Delhi; South Asia Publishers, 1993).
209 **'Half of India's 880 million people'**; Edward A. Gargan, 'Shackled by Past, Racked by Unrest, India Lurches Toward Uncertain Future', *The New York Times* (18 February 1994).
210 **'Our levels of literacy'**; Satya Pal Ruhela, *India's Struggle to Universalize Elementary Education* (New Delhi; M. D. Publications, 1996), p. 142.
210 **'universalization of primary education'**; Ministry of Human Resource Development, National Programme of Nutritional Support to Primary Education, 1996.
211 **'I would not go'**; Parliament of India, Lok Sabha Debates, 11th Lok Sabha, 4th session.
211 **'It is not that we'**; Ibid.
212 **'Either we educate'**; Ibid.
212 **'The real tragedy':** Ibid., p. 209 .
212 **Expenditure on children**; The World Bank, *India—Attaining the Millennium Development Goals in India's Poor States: Reducing Child Mortality in Orissa*, (Washington D. C.; The World Bank, 2007).
212 **'malnutrition is now a silent emergency'**; Measham and Chatterjee, *Wasting Away*, p. 6.
212 **In 2000, fifty-three years after independence**; Derived from Census 2001 and Planning Commission Data.
212 **Nearly 30 million children**; Ibid.
213 **Bihar was home to**; Ibid.
213 **'the State shall provide'**; Ministry of Law and Justice (Legislative Department), The Constitution (Eighty-sixth Amendment) Act 2002 (New Delhi; The Government of India, 2002).
215 **'it was made clear'**; *Supreme Court of India, People's Union for Civil Liberties vs. Union of India and Others* on 29 October 2002.
215 **On 2 May 2003 the Court**; *Supreme Court of India, People's Union for Civil Liberties vs. Union of India and Others* on 2 May 2003.
215 **On 2 April 2004 the Supreme Court**; *Supreme Court of India Record of Proceedings/ Writ Petition (Civil) No. 196/2001/PUCL vs Union of India and Others.*
216 **The State of the World's Children**; United Nations Children's Fund, *The State of the World's Children 2011* (New York: Division of Communication, UNICEF, 2011), p. 115.
216 **Attendance for boys**; Ibid., p. 105.
216 **However, worryingly**; Ibid., p. 105.
216 **Enrolment in secondary school**; Ibid., p. 105.
217 **less than one in two students**; Pratham, 'Annual Status of Education Report (Rural) 2011'(January 2012), p. 57.
217 **Only one out of three students**; Ibid, p. 58.

THE BLACK SWAN

224 **'India's Rope Trick'**; Michael T. Kaufman, 'India's Rope Trick', *The New York Times* (13 September 1981).

224 **'France and India are pushing'**; Edward Cody, 'France and India Bargain Over Sale of 150 Mirage Warplanes', *Washington Post* (23 October 1981).

225 **'their bootstraps'**; Flora Lewis, 'Without Guilt or Shame', *The New York Times* (26 October 1981).

225 **'Most people forget'**; George Gedda, *The Associated Press* (24 October 1981).

226 **Yet, when the IMF board**; James M. Boughton, *Silent Revolution—The International Monetary Fund 1979-1989*, 'Extended and Specialized Lending'.

228 **'My major aim is to'**; Dennis Kux, *India and the United States: Estranged Democracies, 1941-1991*.

228 **'We are friends with the Soviets but'**; Ibid.

230 **The committee, headed**; B. Parthasarathy, 'Globalizing Information Technology: The Domestic Policy Context for India's Software Production and Exports', *Iterations: An Interdisciplinary Journal of Software History* vol. 3 (May 2004).

230 **This was followed by**; Ibid.

233 **The Janata Party government**; Andrew P. Dunne, *International Theory: To the Brink and Beyond* (Connecticut; Greenwood Publishing Group, 1996), p. 147.

241 **It was no surprise**; Pronab Sen, 'Indian Software Exports: An Assessment', *Economic and Political Weekly 30*, no. 7-8 (February 1995).

242 **'You want desperately'**; 'Mastering the World Economy', Hearings before the Committee on Finance, United States Senate, 100th Congress, First Session, 3 and 5 February 1987, p. 98.

242 **'India is going to be'**; Ibid, p. 107.

242 **In its report on India's**; The World Bank Memorandum and Recommendation on proposed loans to IDBI and ICICI for Electronics Industry Development Project (May 1989).

242 **'computer software though still'**; The World Bank, India: Electronics Industry Development Project (Washington D. C.; 1989), p. 6.

243 **'Until 1991-92'**; Pronab Sen, 'Indian Software Exports: An Assessment', *Economic and Political Weekly 30*, no. 7-8 (February 1995).

247 **In 1993, the number of people waiting**; Rajya Sabha Archives, Written Answers to Questions (7 December 1993).

255 **In money terms**; Ibid.

256 **In 1999, global consultants**; NASSCOM, *Perspective 2020: Transform Business, Transform India* (New Delhi; 2009).

256 **At $69 billion, software and services**; Ibid.

256 **Delivering over 7 per cent**; Ibid.

THE DA VINCI CODE

262 **'A democracy works best'**; United States Department of Justice, 'Statement by President Johnson upon Signing Public Law 89-487 on July 4, 1966'.

262 **'freedom of information'**; United Nations General Assembly, First Session, Resolution 59(I), *Calling of an International Conference on Freedom of Information, 1946.*
263 **'Everyone has the right'**; United Nations General Assembly, International Covenant on Civil and Political Rights, 1966.
264 **'No one shall be permitted'**; Ministry of Law and Justice, 'The Indian Evidence Act, 1872'.
265 **'in a government of responsibility'**; Supreme Court of India, *State of UP vs. Raj Narain* and Others, 24 January 1975.
265 **'the concept of an open'**; *Supreme Court of India, S. P. Gupta vs. President of India and Others*, 30 December 1981.
266 **'No matter how good'**; Nikhil Dey and Aruna Roy, 'Report on Delivery systems of Poverty Alleviation Programmes for the Rural Poor: A Study in Bhim and Devgarh Tehsils of Rajsamand and District of Rajasthan', 1991.
267 **Incensed by the refusal**; Prabhash Joshi, *Lutianke Tile ka Bhugol* (New Delhi; Rajkamal Prakashan, 2008), p. 119.
267 **'the right to impart'**; The Supreme Court of India, *Secretary, Ministry of Information and Broadcasting vs. Cricket Association of Bengal and Others*, 9 February 1995.
269 **'public should be granted'**; The Right to Information Bill 1996 (As suggested by the Press Council of India).
270 **Digvijay Singh observed**; Planning Commission, *Summary Record of Discussions of the National Development Council Meetings*, vol. 5 (New Delhi; Government of India), p. 112.
270 **Naidu pointed out**; Ibid., p. 83.
272 **'any information that'**; The Tamil Nadu Right to Information Act 1997.
274 **'What has become'**; Rajiv Gandhi as quoted by Sonia Gandhi at the Proceedings of the 80th Plenary Session, Calcutta.
275 **'tradition to fight'**; Ibid.
275 **'The Congress party will enact'**; Indian National Congress, 'Manifesto 1998'.
276 **'Bill on Freedom of Information'**; Indian National Congress, 'Manifesto 1999'.
277 **'people often perceived'**; Planning Commission, *Summary Record of Discussions of the National Development Council Meetings*, vol. 5 (New Delhi; Government of India), p. 140.
277 **'corruption had become'**; Ibid.
281 **'Nobody can have any'**; Lok Sabha Debates, 'Government Bills: Further discussion on the Freedom of Information Bill on 3 December 2002'.
285 **'to provide for setting'**; The Right to Information Bill 2004.
286 **Between 2007-08 and 2010-11**; Press Information Bureau Government of India Ministry of Personnel, Public Grievances & Pensions 11 August 2011.
287 **As of February 2012**; Press Information Bureau, Government of India, Ministry of Personnel, Public Grievances & Pensions 14 March 2012.

EPILOGUE

288 **India is home**; Derived from Census 2011 and Planning Commission Data.

288 **Every year, over 15,000**; Ministry of Home Affairs\Annual Reports\Data on suicides.

288 **A quarter of the populace**; 'National Sample Survey Report No. 535: Housing Condition and Amenities in India'.

288 **Over 49 per cent of Indians**; 'NSS Report No. 535: Housing Conditions and Amenities in India'. UNICEF in its 2012 Update, 'Progress on Drinking Water and Sanitation' reports 814 million people or 'One third of the 2.5 billion people in the world without improved sanitation live in India'.

288 **India spends nearly $100 billion**; Derived from Ministry of Finance and Planning Commission data.

289 **'India, that is Bharat'**; Ministry of Law and Justice, Constitution of India, Part I, Article 1, 'The Union and Its Territory'.

290 **'second on the hierarchy'**; Abraham H. Maslow, 'A Theory of Human Motivation', *Psychological Review 50*, 1943, pp. 370-396.

290 **According to studies by**; Shankkar Aiyar, 'Thirsty India', *India Today* (9 June 2003).

291 **With over 20 million tube wells**; John Briscoe and R. P. S. Malik, *India's Water Economy: Bracing for A Turbulent Future* (Washington D. C., World Bank, 2006), p. xvii.

291 **Satellite data shows**; 'Satellites Unlock Secret to Northern India's Vanishing Water', *UC Irvine Today* (12 August 2009).

291 **Over 65 million living**; Shankkar Aiyar, 'Thirsty India', *India Today* (9 June 2003).

291 **In as many as 203**; Water Supply & Sanitation, WHO-UNICEF Sponsored Study, Planning Commission.

291 **It is estimated that**; Shankkar Aiyar, 'Thirsty India', *India Today* (9 June 2003).

291 **Over 100 million children**; Water Supply & Sanitation, WHO-UNICEF Sponsored Study, Planning Commission.

291 **India will need to ramp up**; As derived from data issued by the Planning Commission, 'Final Report of Minor Irrigation and Watershed Management for the Twelfth Five Year Plan (2012-2017)' (New Delhi, Government of India, 2012).

291 **India receives an annual**; Ministry of Water Resources, 'Report of the Working Group on Major and Medium Irrigation and Command Area Development for the XII Five Year Plan (2012-2017)' (New Delhi; Government of India, 2011), p. 9.

291 **Of this the runoff**; Ibid., p. 9.

291 **barely 690 billion cubic metres**; Ibid., p. 9.

292 **Per-capita water storage in India**; Ibid, p. 1.

292 **Using a web of thirty links**; Shankkar Aiyar, 'Changing the Course: Interlinking India's Rivers', *India Today* (January 2003).

292 **The cost for this ambitious project**; Ibid.

292 **Water was to be moved from**; Ibid.

NOTES

292 **It was estimated that 56 million**; Ibid.
292 **The project promised to create**; Ibid.
293 **Micro and drip irrigation accounts**; Derived from Planning Commission Data, May 2009.
294 **In 1947, India could generate**; Growth of Electricity Sector in India From 1947-2011, (New Delhi; Ministry of Power, June 2011).
294 **it has a generating capacity**; Ibid.
294 **Between 2000 and 2011**; Ministry of Power & Planning Commission Data.
294 **The cumulative reserves**; Ministry of Statistics and Programme Implementation, *Energy Statistics 2012* (New Delhi; Government of India, 2012), p. 1.
294 **India is estimated to host over**; Ministry of Statistics and Programme Implementation, *Energy Statistics 2012*, p. 5.
294 **India boasts**; Ibid.
295 **state electricity boards lose**; Derived from Lok Sabha Archives, Power Finance Corporation Data quoted by Ministry of Power in August 2012.
295 **In 2011, India consumed**; Ministry of Petroleum and Natural Gas, *Basic Statistics on Indian Petroleum and Natural Gas 2010-2011* (New Delhi; Government of India, 2006), p. 5.
296 **At the current rate**; As derived from data issued by the Planning Commission, 'Integrated Energy Policy: Report of the Expert Committee' (New Delhi; Government of India, 2006) and the Ministry of Petroleum and Natural Gas, *Basic Statistics on Indian Petroleum and Natural Gas 2010-2011*.
296 **India has recoverable**; Ministry of Statistics and Programme Implementation, *Energy Statistics 2012*, p. 1.
296 **One out of four Indians**; Based on data issued by the Ministry of Statistics and Programme Implementation in *Housing Condition and Amenities in India 2008-2009* (New Delhi; Government of India, 2010) and *Household Consumer Expenditure in India 2007-2008* (New Delhi; Government of India, 2010).
296 **Over 55,000 Indian villages**; Report of the Working Group on Power for Twelfth Plan (2012-17), Planning Commission.
296 **Over 77 per cent of the rural**; Household Consumer Expenditure in India, 2007-08 NSS 64th Round
296 **only 62 per cent of the populace**; Ibid.
296 **The average fuel consumption**; World Bank, 'Energy Use (Kg of Oil Equivalent Per Capita)'.
296 **In the next twenty years**; Integrated Energy Policy, Report of the Expert Committee, Planning Commission 2006.
296 **There are plans to boost**; derived from Integrated Energy Policy, Report of the Expert Committee/Planning Commission 2006 and Ministry of Statistics and Programme Implementation, *Energy Statistics 2012*.
297 **transport accounts for only 41**; Uwe Remme, Nathalie Trudeau, Dagmar Graczyk and Peter Taylor, International Energy Agency, Report Technology Development Prospects for the Indian Power Sector.

297 **India ranks sixty-sixth among eighty-eight**; Anjor Bhaskar, Anil Deolalikar, Purnima Menon, *India State Hunger Index: Comparisons of Hunger across States* (Washington D. C.; World Bank, 2009), p. 5.
297 **the severity of the hunger**; Bhaskar, Deolalikar, Menon, *India State Hunger Index*, p. 16.
297 **Forty three per cent**; HUNGaMA for Change, 'HUNGaMA: Fighting Hunger & Malnutrition Survey Report', 2001.
297 **India loses 218 children**; UNICEF 2012 and Planning Commission Data.
297 **Life expectancy at birth**; UNICEF, *The State of the World's Children 2012* (New York; UNICEF, 2012).
298 **In the post-reform decades**; Reserve Bank of India and Planning Commission Data.
299 **Investment in agriculture**; Planning Commission Data.
299 **Credit availability has been boosted**; Ministry of Finance Data.
299 **Today its per-hectare yield of paddy**; Derived from Agricultural Statistics at a Glance 2011, Directorate of Economics and Statistics, Department of Agriculture and Cooperation.
299 **Farmers in France produce**; Ibid.
299 **Compare this with the average**; Ibid.
300 **Indeed, in 2003**; Shankkar Aiyar, 'Smoking Guns', *Writing a Nation: An Anthology of Indian Journalism*, Nirmala Lakshman (ed.) (New Delhi; Rupa Publications, 2007).
300 **'people holding positions'**; Naunihal Singh, *World of Bribery and Corruption: From Ancient Times to Modern Age* (New Delhi; Mittal Publications, 1999), p. 400.
301 **'There is a widespread impression'**; N. Narayanasamy, M. P. Boraian, M. A. Jeyaraju, *Corruption at the Grassroots: The Shades and Shadows* (New Delhi; Concept Publishing Company, 2000), p. 400.
302 **India spends roughly**; Derived from Planning Commission Data.
303 **Every year, the Centre**; Derived from Economic Survey 2011-12 and Ministry of Finance Data.
308 **'Across the government'**; National Commission on Terrorist Attacks upon the United States, 'The 9/11 Commission Report'.
309 **to hike its defence budget**; Mandip Singh and Lalit Kumar, China's Defence Budget 2012: An Analysis, Institute for Defence Studies and Analyses.
310 **'the country may be given'**; Valmiki Choudhary (ed.), *Dr. Rajendra Prasad: Correspondence and Select Documents* (Bombay; Allied Publishers Limited, 1991).
311 **'Though the country'**; 'Report of the Commission on Centre-state Relations' vol. 1, (New Delhi; Government of India, 1988).
312 **'consider the time ripe'**; R. C. S. Sarkar, *Union-state Relations in India* (New Delhi; National Publishing House, 1986).
312 **'decentralization of real power'**; Ministry of Home Affairs, 'General Observations', *Sarkaria Commission and Its Recommendations* (January 1988).
312 **'been a pervasive trend'**; Ibid.

312 **Thereafter, the issues**; Ministry of Law, Justice and Company Affairs, 'Report of the National Commission to Review the Working of the Constitution' (March 2002).
312 **More recently, the UPA:** 'Report of the Commission on Centre-state Relations', (March 2010).
313 **Indeed, in 1987**; 38th Meeting of the National Development Council, Planning Commission Archives.
313 **Gross fiscal deficit of the states**; Derived from Reserve Bank of India data on State Finances and Ministry of Finance.
313 **As the late Vilasrao Deshmukh**; In a conversation with the author in 2011.

Besides the aforementioned specific notes and references, I have relied on numerous articles published in mainstream and specialist business and general interest newspapers and magazines, as well as newsletters, surveys and reports published or circulated by organizations like CII, NASSCOM, numerous UN organizations and Government of India departments for the data found in the book.

INDEX

Abbott Wood Committee, 203
Accelerated Irrigation Benefits Programme, 116
Acemoğlu, Daron, 12
Administrative Reforms Commission, 301, 312
   of 1967, 301, 312
   of 2007, 301
Advani, L. K. (Lal Krishna Advani), 57, 58, 277
   arrested during rath yatra in Bihar, 57, 58
Ahluwalia, Montek Singh, 52, 54, 210
Aid Consortium of Developed Nations, 91
Alexander, P. C. (Padinjarethalakal Cherian Alexander), 22, 23, 47
   Through the Corridors of Power: An Insider's Story, 23
All India Kisan Sabha, 81
All India Services (Conduct Rules) 1968, 264
Ambedkar, B. R. (Bhimrao Ramji Ambedkar), 13, 311
American Mission, 26
   visit to India, 26
Amul, 169, 172, 174-183, 186
   advertising budget of, 172
   birth of, 169, 172
   success story of, 172-177
   turnover of, 172
Anand, 157, 162-166, 169-172, 174, 176-178, 181-182, 185-187
   Government Research Creamery at, 162
   location of, 157

   NDDB headquarters at, 178
Anand Agricultural University, 166
Annadurai, C.N. (Conjeevaram Natarajan Annadurai), 189, 196
Antony Committee, 275
Annual Status of Education Report 2011, 217
Arora, Gopi, 56, 61, 63, 70
Ayyangar, Gopalaswami, 300
   Report on the Reorganization of the Machinery of Government, 300
Azad, Ghulam Nabi, 66

Baba Ramdev, 301
Bagby, Philip, 11
Bangladesh, 11, 41, 131, 219, 297, 309
   creation of, 11, 41, 131
   per capita income of, 219
Bank nationalization, 18, 23, 27, 40, 118, 120, 123-127, 137-143, 145-148, 150, 152-156
   criticism of, 154
   economic dividends of, 153-156
   economists' report on, 140-141
   expansion of banks after, 153
   fifteen-point agenda for, 139
   Indira's justification for, 147-148
   opposition to, 138-140
   positive effects of, 155-156
   promulgation of the ordinance for, 147
   condemnation of the, 148
Banking Companies (Acquisition and Transfer of Undertakings) Bill, 147, 148, 152
Banking Laws (Miscellaneous Provisions) Bill, 126-127

Banking Regulation Act 1949, 142, 148
Bell Mission report, 36, 97
Bell, Bernard, 36
Berlin Wall, 15, 57, 61, 278
    collapse of, 15, 57, 61, 278
Bhagwati, Jagdish, 45 59
Bhakra Nangal complex, 84
Bhattacharya, P. C., 38, 128, 139
Bhave, Acharya Vinoba, 87
    and his Bhoodan Movement, 87
Bihar fodder scam, 300
Bin Laden, Osama, 307, 309
Birla, G. D. (Ghanshyam Das Birla), 25, 30
Bofors scandal, 49, 51, 55, 244, 265, 300, 301
Bombay Plan, 25-28, 120, 161
    objective of, 25-28
    released, 25
Bommai, S. R., 211, 212
Borlaug, Norman, 94
Brahmananda, P. R., 30, 45
Bretton Woods, 22
Brezhnev, Leonid, 221, 222, 224, 227
    trip to India, 221
Burgess, Robin, 153
Business process outsourcing (BPO), 253-256

Call centre phenomenon, 253-255
Camdessus, Michel, 23, 51
    meeting with Rajiv Gandhi, 51
Cancun Conference, 219-221, 224-226, 228, 239, 255
    boost in Indo-American relations during the, 225-226
Capital Issues Control Act 1956, 29
C-DOT (Centre for Development of Telematics), 240
Central Bureau of Investigation, 301
Chagla, M. C. (Mahommedali Currim Chagla), 217
Chalam, G. V. (Guduru Venkata Chalam), 75, 108
    arrival at Palam Airport, 74-75
    experimenting with Taichung Native-1 seeds, 108

Chandra, Naresh, 22
Chaudhuri, Sachin, 37, 128, 130
Chavan, Y. B.(Yashwantrao Balwantrao Chavan), 104, 123, 130, 146, 176
Chidambaram, P. (Palaniappan Chidambaram), 69, 72, 250
Chief Minister's Nutritious Noon-Meals Programme, 196, 197
China, 25, 37, 40, 41, 77, 85, 87, 90, 95, 113, 116, 117, 124, 131, 132, 203, 221, 228, 229, 236, 242, 252, 289, 292, 294, 299, 309
    agriculture in, 299
    attack on India in 1962 by, 37, 95, 124, 229
    friendship with America, 221
    land ownership and revenue collection in, 87
    literacy rate in, 203
    modernization of agriculture in, 299
    power generation in, 294
    progress in farming in, 90, 116, 117
    R. K. Patil's visit to, 90
Cold War, 57, 61, 85, 89
Collective farming, 81, 82, 90
Colombo Plan, 166
Committee on Public Administration, 300
Companies Act 1956, 29, 149
    amended, 149
Computer Software Export Development and Training Policy, 240
Concept of a planned economy, 30-32, 36, 59, 88
    failure of the, 36, 58
Conference of chief ministers, 270
    resolution for a Citizen's Charter passed at the, 271
Congress Forum for Socialist Action (CFSA), 105, 137, 141, 142
    and its ten-point charter of demands, 137
Constitution of India,
    adopted, 28
    Article 1 of the, 289
    Article 19(1)(a) of the, 265, 267
    Article 21 of the, 213

Article 45 of the, 218
Article 123 of the, 147
Constitution (Eighty-sixth Amendment) Act 2002, 214
father of the, 313
review of the working of the, 312
right to property enshrined in the, 86
universal suffrage, 13
Cooper, Rustom Cavasjee, 148
Cooperative for Assistance and Relief Everywhere (CARE), 193, 194
Cummings, Ralph, 106

da Cunha, Sylvester, 172
Dairy farming, 84, 158, 165, 166
Dalal, Ardeshir, 25
Dalal, Pestonji Edulji, 159
Dalaya, Harichand, 168-170, 179
Damodaran, M. (Meleveetil Damodaran), 18
Dandavate, Madhu, 54
Darling, Malcolm, 76
Dastur, Dinshaw, 293
Dawson, Thomas C., 63
Delhi Milk Scheme (DMS), 173, 176
restructuring of the, 177
Delhi Special Police Establishment Act 1941, 301
Depression of the thirties, 15, 83
Desai, Kanti, 144
Desai, Morarji, 43, 44, 97, 99, 118, 126-129, 136-147, 151, 159, 160, 170, 171, 181, 199, 233, 265
as Deputy Prime Minister, 143
opposition to bank nationalization by, 138
as prime minister, 43
patron saint of Amul, 181
visit to the Kaira plant, 171
Deshmukh, B. G. (Bhalchandra G. Deshmukh), 52, 280
Deshmukh, C. D. (Chintaman Dwarakanath Deshmukh), 32, 151, 165
arrival in Anand, 165
Deshmukh, Vilasrao (Vilasrao Dagadojirao Deshmukh), 313

Destructive Insects and Pests Act 1914, 74
Deve Gowda, H. D. (Haradanahalli Doddegowda Deve Gowda), 269, 270, 272
Dey, Nikhil, 258-261, 266, 268, 275, 280, 286, 316, 320
Dhar, D. P. (Durga Prasad Dhar), 41,
Dharia, Mohan, 136, 145
Dhebar, U. N. (Uchharangrai Navalshankar Dhebar), 121, 122, 129
Directive Principles of State Policy, 122, 203, 205, 206
Article 39, 205
Article 45, 205
District Institute of Educational Training, 204
Domar, Evsey, 31
Dubey, Muchkund, 61, 67

East India Company, 26, 76
exploitation of Indian farmers by the, 76-77
Economic and Political Weekly, 139
Economic crisis in India, 22, 24, 69, 135, 209
in 1965, 111-114
of 1979-80, 46
of 1989, 52, 57-63
three lines of thought for, 24-25
of 1991, 10, 15, 16, 67-69, 209
a blessing in disguise, 15, 16
effect on education of the, 209
and pledging of gold, 10, 67-70
effect on Indian agriculture, 77
Education (Provision of Meals) Act, 190
Education system in India, 202-204
international programmes for, 203
legislation to promote, 205-206
progress in, 217
reasons of failure, 205
regression in, 209
Standing Committee report on, 211
UNICEF report on, 205
Eisenhower, Dwight D. (Dwight David Eisenhower), 89
Electricity Act 2003, 295

Energy security, 295
  governance structure for, 295
Ensminger, Douglas, 91, 93
Essential Commodities Act 1955, 29

Famine Emergency Committee, 78
FAO-WFP, 182, 183
Farmers and zamindars, 81
  popular cinema on, 81
  relationship between, 81
Farmers' cooperatives, 175, 180
  demand of, 175-176
  in New Zealand, 175
  success of, 175-176
Fernandes, George, 44, 233
First Five Year Plan, 28, 29, 35, 83-86, 120-122, 172
  revival of agriculture in the, 83-84
Food and Agriculture Organization (FAO), 97, 103, 114, 182-183
Food Grains Enquiry Committee, 91
  suggestion of the, 91
Food Grains Investigation Commission of 1949, 80
Food Grains Policy Commission, 79
  recommendations of the, 79-80
Ford Foundation, 91-93, 108, 179, 184
  report of the, 92-93
Foreign Exchange Regulation Act (FERA), 40, 44, 232, 251
Forsskal, Peter, 261
  Tankar Om Borgerliga Friheten, 261
Fourth Five Year Plan, 105, 110, 143, 181, 194
Frankel, Francine R. 14
  India's Political Economy: 1947-2004, 14
Freedom of Information Bill 1997, 272
Freedom of Information Bill 2000, 279
  debate in Parliament on the, 280-282
  flaws in the, 280
  passed, 280
Freedom of Information Act 2002, 282, 284
Freeman, Orville, 107, 113, 114
  meeting with Subramaniam, 113
Friedman, Milton, 32, 36

criticized planned development thesis, 32, 36
Fuel consumption, 296-297
  in India, 296-297
  in the US and China, 296
Fukuyama, Francis, 12

Galbraith, John Kenneth, 17
  theory of collective bargaining 17
Gandhi, Indira,
  assassinated, 47
  accused of electoral malpractice, 43, 265
  contest for prime ministership, 128-129
  defeated in 1977, 156
  expelled from Congress, 152
  Friendship Treaty with Soviet Union, 41
  imposition of Emergency by, 43, 156
  meeting with Johnson, 38, 131-133
  meeting with Kosygin, 38
  meeting with Ronald Reagan, 221
  new avatar of, 226
  partnering with the Left, 39, 42
  as prime minister, 38
  rise of, 129
  Stray Thoughts Memorandum, 145
  and the Syndicate, proxy war between, 151-152
  visit to Moscow, 134
  visit to the US, 227
Gandhi, Mahatma, 10, 14, 79, 82, 288
  assassination of, 82
  concept of fasting and sacrifice of, 79
Gandhi, Rajiv, 11, 21, 46-55, 57, 58, 65-68, 72, 185, 201, 228, 239, 240, 244, 249, 254, 274, 301, 313
  assassination of, 21, 68
  defeat in 1989 elections, 53, 244
  as prime minister, 49
  process of creative disruption, 49, 59
  speech at the Congress Centenary Session, 48-49
  visit to the US, 228
Gandhi, Sonia, 155, 216, 274-275, 283-285

as NAC chairman, 283
as Congress president, 274
commitment to the RTI, 275, 283
entry into politics, 274-275
meeting with Aruna Roy and Nikhil Dey, 275
turned to the Left, 274-275
Gargan, Edward A., 209
description of India by, 209
Gates, Bill, 227
General Agreement on Tariffs and Trade, 51
Ghosh, Atulya, 118, 119, 136
Giri, V.V. (Varahagiri Venkata Giri), 39, 147, 149-151
as president of India, 151
Goa Right to Information Act, 273
Gorshkov, Sergey, 41
Gorwala, A. D. (Astad Dinshaw Gorwala), 300
Go-Samvardhan Society, 174, 175
Grady, Henry F. (Henry Francis Grady), 26
Green Revolution, 11, 14, 16, 18, 89, 94, 102, 109, 110, 116, 175
Gujarat Cooperative Milk Marketing Federation (GCMMF), 183
Gulf War, 58
and its impact on India, 60

H. D. Shourie Committee report, 272
Haksar, P. N. (Parmeshwar Narayan Haksar), 148
Halse, Michael, 179
Hanumanthaiah, Kengal, 128
Haq, Zia-ul, (Mohammad Zia-ul-Haq), 307
Harrod, Roy F. (Sir Henry Roy Forbes Harrod), 31
Harrod-Domar model, 31
Hazare, Anna, 281, 286, 301
Hazari, Rabindra Kishen, 34, 36, 40, 141
interim report on licensing of, 34
Henderson Brooks-Bhagat Operations Review Report, 309
Homi J. Bhabha Committee, 230

Hoover, Herbert, 78
Horatio Alger formula, 225
Hugo, Victor, 72, 73, 190
campaign for free meals by, 190
Hunter Commission, 203

IBM (International Business Machines Corporation), 44, 55, 227, 230, 233, 235, 236, 251, 252
exit from India, 44, 233
return to India, 252
idea of open government, 265, 266
Imperial Council of Agricultural Research, 78
India,
1962 war with China, 37, 95
1965 war with Pakistan, 113
1971 war with Pakistan, 131
balance-of-payments crisis in, 60, 70, 90
beginning of the aid raj in, 91
centre-state relations in, 310-314
and China, comparisons between, 309
computer software revolution in, 230
concept of a planned economy in, 30, 31, 36
corruption and scams in, 300-303
political economy of, 302-303
statutes for, 300
three quarters of, 302
crude oil imports in, 294-295
culture of secrecy in, 263-267, 275, 279
devaluation of rupee in, 37, 38, 70, 133-134, 146
entry of MNCs in the markets, 251
economic crisis in, 22, 24, 69, 135, 209
economic situation after 1971, 41-43
farmers' suicides in, 116, 288
first computer in, 229
food scarcity after World War II, 78, 86
reasons for, 78, 86
US aid to address, 78, 85
foreign aid requirements of, 24, 37, 52, 83, 112, 120, 193
foreign exchange crisis in 1957, 37-38
health and nutrition status of, 194

history of famines in, 75-76
hybrid seed programme of, 106
impact of Partition on the food security of, 78-79
issue of national language, 135
issue of national security, 304-309
liberalization of the economy in 1991, 16, 18, 64, 70, 72, 73, 116, 154, 274
liberalization of the imports policy in, 239
literacy rates in, 203
milk production in, 172, 175, 181, 185, 186
   business model for, 173-174
need to alter cropping patterns for, 293
new permissions raj of, 16
number of cellphone users in, 253
opposition of America's war in Vietnam by, 112
period between 1962 and 1967, 135
power-generation capacity of, 294
problem of illiteracy in, 191
setting up of agricultural universities, 106
share of world income in 1952, 26
a ship to mouth nation, 74, 114, 226, 299
shortage of telephones, 234-235
situation of software sector in the eighties, 233-235
snail's pace of growth in, 44
software potential of, 242, 250
software sector in 1991-92, 243
state of banking in the sixties, 122-123
state of human deprivation in, 297-299
   schemes for alleviation of the, 298-299
system of primary education in, 203-205
and the US, breaking point between, 134
views on Vietnam War, 132, 134
water crisis in, 290-293
India: Macroeconomics and Political Economy 1964-1991, 45
Indian Banks Association (IBA), 138

Indian Council of Medical Research, 202
Indian Dairy Corporation (IDC), 183
Indian Evidence Act, 264, 271, 272
Indian National Congress (Congress), 25, 129
   manifesto of 1998, 275
   socialism of the, 29
   split in the, 39, 135, 146, 152, 156, 181
Indian Silicon Valley, 236
Indian Telegraph Act 1855, 247
Indo-Soviet friendship treaty, 224
Indo-US technology agreement, 235
Industrial Development Bank of India (IDBI), 127
Industrial Licensing Policy Inquiry Committee 1969, 45
Industrial licensing policy, 40, 45, 47, 141
   Hazari report on, 40, 141
Industrial Policy Resolution of 1956, 28, 29
   Nehru's views on, 28
Industries Development and Regulation Act (IDRA), 28, 33
Integrated Child Development Scheme, 298
Intensive Agricultural District Programme (IADP), 93, 94
Intensive Cattle Development Project, 174
interlinking of rivers, 292
   in China and the US, 292
   estimated cost for the, 292
   in nineteenth-century India, 292
International Covenant on Civil and Political Rights, 263
International Food Policy Research Institute, 297
International Monetary Fund (IMF), 22, 23, 37, 38, 46, 51, 52, 56, 59-65, 67, 90, 112, 130, 132, 134, 146, 225, 226, 250, 316
   aid to India, 46, 63-64, 112, 225, 226
Israeli Consulate car explosion, 304
IT revolution in India, 253-255
   and IT Enabled Services, 255
   two phases of the, 255
Iyengar, Hoorav Varadaraja, 125

Jalan, Bimal, 17, 50, 59, 60, 246
   former governor of the RBI, 17, 59
   as the head of Economic Advisory Council, 60
   Long Term Fiscal Policy of, 50
Janata Dal, 53, 58
   formed, 53
   a hotchpotch of parties, 53
Janata Party, 43-44, 46, 53, 199, 225, 233
   collapse of the government of, 46
   formed, 43
jansunwai, 257, 258, 260
   birth of the, 260
   at Kot Kirana, 257, 260
   success of, 260
   at Pali, 257
Jawahar Rozgar Yojana, 216
Jayalalithaa, J. (Jayalalitha Jayaram), 189, 198, 276
Jethmalani, Ram, 276-277
Jha, L.K, (Lakshmi Kant Jha), 38, 104, 146, 147, 184
Jinnah, Mohammed Ali, 26
Johnson, Lyndon Baines (popularly known as LBJ) 38, 40, 112-114, 128, 131-133, 149, 222, 226, 262
   meeting with Nehru, 112
   ship-to-mouth policy of, 226
Joshi, Subhadra, 124-125, 136
   resolution on bank nationalization tabled by, 124-125
Joshi, Vijay, 45

Kaira Cooperative, 164-179, 183
   collection of milk at the, 165
   expansion project of the, 168-171
   inauguration of the, 171
   funding for the, 169
   new plant at the, 168-170
   services offered by the, 168
   success of the, 165-166
Kaira District Cooperative Milk Producers' Union Limited (KDCMPUL), 160, 163, 168
Kamaraj, K. (Kumaraswami Kamaraj), 39, 96-99, 101, 105, 118, 119, 127-128, 130, 133, 134, 136, 137, 144, 151, 191-193, 274
   as king-maker, 119
   mid-day meal scheme of, 192-194
   impact of, 192-193
   and his Syndicate, 39, 40, 119, 127-130, 133, 136, 137, 144-147, 149-152, 282
Kamaraj Plan, 96, 97, 118
Kameshwar vs State of Bihar, 86
Kandahar hijacking, 307
Kandla free trade zone (FTZ), 244, 245
Karunanidhi, M. (Muthuvel Karunanidhi), 143, 271
Kayipady story, 207
Kelkar, Vijay, 52, 55
Kesri, Sitaram, 22, 274
Khan, Yahya, 40, 149
Khurody, Dara, 165, 170, 171
Kirloskar, S. L. (Shantanurao Laxmanrao Kirloskar), 50
Kisan Credit Card, 116
Kissinger, Henry, 41
   visit to China, 41
Kohli, Faqir Chand, 231
Kosygin, Alexei, 38, 40, 133
Kothari Commission on Education Reforms, 204
Krishnamachari, T. T. (Tiruvellore Thattai Krishnamachari; also known as TTK), 32, 37, 98, 103, 105, 125, 128, 139, 147, 176, 181
Kuo Oil deal scandal, 300
Kurien, Molly Verghese, 163, 171
Kurien, P. J. (Pallath Joseph Kurien), 211
Kurien, Verghese, 157, 160-172, 174-187
   alliance with Tribhuvandas, 163
   arrival at Anand, 157-158, 160
   Billion Litre Idea of, 157, 180, 181, 188
   as dairy engineer in Anand, 162
   joined KDCMPUL, 163
   and Khurody, stand-off between, 165, 170-171
   national mission of, 178-181
   visit to New Zealand, 167
   template for success of, 177-181

Kuwait invasion, 58, 62
  India's response to, 62

Lakshmanswami Mudaliar Commission, 204
Lal, Devi, 53, 58, 66
Lalbhai, Kasturbhai, 25
land reforms, 86-88, 137
Lewis, Arthur, 31
licence-permit-quota raj, 24, 30, 44, 45, 55, 59, 61, 65, 71, 72, 73, 230, 233, 250, 253, 298
  dismantled, 16, 72, 250, 298
  failure of the, 45
  Narasimham Report on the, 47
Licensing, 13
  abolished, 16
  categories of the, 33
  procedure of the, 35-36
Linlithgow, Victor Alexander, 77, 158
Little, Ian Malcolm David, 45
Livestock Importation Act 1898, 74
Lohia, Ram Manohar, 43, 144
Lokpal Bill, 301, 310
  history of, 301

Maddison, Angus, 26
Mahalanobis, P. C. (Prasanta Chandra Mahalanobis), 29, 30, 31, 37, 88
Mahatma Gandhi National Rural Employment Guarantee Act, 298
Malaviya, K. D. (Keshav Dev Malaviya), 104, 136
Mandal Commission, 57
Masani, Minoo (Minocheher Rustom Masani), 126, 148
Maslow, Abraham, 290
  A Theory of Human Motivation, 290
Mathai, John, 25, 161, 162
Mathur, Ashok, 208
Mazdoor Kisan Shakti Sangathan (MKSS), 257-261, 263, 266, 280
  Beawar protest of the, 266
  journalists' support to the, 267
  formation of the, 259
Mehta Committee, 90
Mehta, Asoka, 91, 107, 130, 133

Mehta, Balwant Rai, 90
Menon, V. K. Krishna (Vengalil Krishnan Krishna Menon), 104, 130
Mid-day meal scheme,
  blueprint for the, 196
  in the Common Minimum Programme, 216
  described as a hoax, 211
  earliest instance of in India, 190
  in France and Britain, 190
  funding for the, 197
  impact of the, 197-199
  Kamaraj initiative for the, 191-192
  political implications of the, 196-198
  publicity by Jayalalithaa of the, 198-199
  states implementing the, 201-202
  success of the, 198-199, 215-216
  Supreme Court decision on the, 213-214
  twin benefits of the, 201
  World Bank appraisal report on the, 198
Mini elections of 1969, 143
Mody, Piloo, 150
Mohan, Rakesh, 55, 63, 70
  draft Industrial Policy of 1990 of, 55-56, 63, 70
Monopolies and Restrictive Trade Practices (MRTP) Act, 39, 40
Mookerjee, Syama Prasad, 28
Morarka, Kamal, 58
Mosca, Gaetano, 18
  The Ruling Class, 18
Mukherjee, Pranab, 65, 156, 285
Mumbai,
  attacks in 2008, 307
  blasts in 2011, 305
  26/11 attacks in, 305, 306
Mundhra, Haridas, 300
Munshi, K.M. (Kanaiyalal Maneklal Munshi), 101, 165, 166, 176
Murthy, N. R. Narayana, (Nagavara Ramarao Narayana Murthy), 231, 233, 234, 235, 243, 246, 251
  founder of Infosys, 233
Myrdal, Gunnar, 31, 122

Naidu, Sarojini, 129
Nanda, Gulzarilal, 98, 99, 128, 130
   as interim prime minister, 99
Narain, Raj, 43, 265
   case against Indira Gandhi, 43
Narasimham Committee, 154, 230
Narayan, Jayaprakash, 42
   movement against Indira, 42
NASSCOM (National Association of Software and Services Companies), 246, 251, 255
Natchiappan, E. M. Sudarsana, 286
National Advisory Council, 216, 268, 283
   creation of the, 216, 268, 283
National Campaign for People's Right to Information (NCPRI), 268, 269, 272, 275, 277
   consultative group of, 268
National Common Minimum Programme (NCMP), 283
National Counter Terrorism Centre (NCTC), 308, 310
National Credit Council, 142
National Dairy Development Board (NDDB), 178-186
   funding for the, 179
   success of the, 184
National Development Council (NDC), 91, 92, 121, 123, 143, 201, 270, 313
   meeting at the Hyderabad House, 121
National Intelligence Grid (NatGrid), 308
National Investigation Agency (NIA), 308
National Literacy Mission, 204
National Nutrition Monitoring Bureau (NNMB), 194, 202
National Policy for Children, 194
National Policy on Education, 204
National Programme of Nutritional Support to Primary Education, 210
   aim of the, 210
   expansion of the, 210-211
Naxalism, 305
Nayyar, Deepak, 61, 64, 70
Nehru, Arun, 52

Nehru, B. K. (Braj Kumar Nehru), 132, 134, 222
   talks with Reagan, 222
Nehru, Jawaharlal, 11, 24, 25, 72, 79, 120, 169, 224, 229, 275, 311
   A Bunch of Old Letters, 129
   campaign for food aid, 79, 85
   campaign for 1962 elections, 95
   died, 99
   idea of collective farming of, 82, 90
   idea of socialism of, 120
   model of industrialization of, 83
   visit to Anand by, 171, 176
Nehru-Mahalanobis model, 37
Nehru, Motilal, 26
New Delhi Consensus, 22
New industrial policy, 29, 56, 70, 72
Nijalingappa, S. (Siddavanahalli Nijalingappa), 118, 136, 149-151
   as Congress president, 136
Nilekani, Nandan, 231, 243, 316
Nixon, Richard, 40, 89, 149, 150, 221
   visit to India, 150
Noorani, A. G., 280
Nutritious Mid-day Meal Scheme, 189, 196

Obama, Barack, 15, 309
Official Secrets Act 1923, 264, 265, 271
   working group for, 264
Operation Blackboard, 204, 209
Operation Eagle Claw, 309
Operation Flood, 181-186
   aid for, 182-183
   critics of, 184
   increase in milk production by, 185-186
   success of, 183-184
   World Bank applause for, 186
Operation Geronimo, 309

P. C. Alexander Committee Report, 47
Paddock brothers, 111
   doom-laden prophecy of, 111
   Hungry Nations, 111
Panandikar, Pai, 139, 141
Pande, Rohini, 153

Pant, Pitamber, 99
Pant, Govind Ballabh, 106, 129
Paranjape, Haribhau K., 45
Patel, Chimanbhai, 42
Patel, I.G.(Indraprasad Gordhanbhai Patel), 23, 31, 32, 38, 45, 128, 146, 147, 148, 156
  Glimpses of Indian Economy: An Insider's View, 31
  World Bank lecture of, 45
Patel, Tribhuvandas, 160, 163, 164, 170, 172
  creator of milk cooperatives, 160
Patel, Vallabhbhai, 24, 28, 29, 159, 168, 177, 178
  advice to milk producers, 159
Patni Computers, 231
  first jobs of, 231
  setting up of, 231
Pawar, Sharad, 21, 65
People's Union for Civil Liberties (PUCL), 213
Perkins, John, 89
  Geopolitics and the Green Revolution, 89
Pitroda, Sam, 212, 240, 247, 249
  revolutionized connectivity, 247
  work on telecommunications, 240-241
Planning Commission, 28, 52, 70, 90, 92, 94, 99, 103-105, 107, 110, 120, 121, 142, 173, 174, 199, 243, 289, 293
  constituted, 28
Political economy, 10, 14, 19, 45, 101, 157, 163, 179, 192, 304, 311
Polson Dairy, 159
Portillo, Jose Lopez, 219, 220
Prasad, Rajendra, 24, 169, 176, 310
  prayer for the nation, 310
Pratap Singh Kairon scandal, 300
Prevention of Corruption Act, 301
Public authority, 269, 273, 282, 285
  defined, 269
Public distribution scheme, 298
Public Law 480 (PL 480), 9, 89, 90, 94, 113, 114, 167, 172, 180
  financing of, 89
  impact of, 90

R. A. Gopalaswami report, 264
Radhakrishnan Committee, 204
Rajagopalachari, C. (Chakravarti Rajagopalachari, also known as Rajaji), 30, 102, 126
Rajam, Srini, 236, 237, 252
Ram, Jagjivan, 97, 118, 130, 144, 146, 175, 181
Ram, Lala Shri, 25
Rama Rao, N.T. (Nandamuri Taraka Rama Rao; NTR), 199, 312
  manifesto of, 200
Ramachandran, M.G.(Marudur Gopala Ramachandran; MGR), 188, 189, 191, 195-201, 210
  launching of a mid-day meal scheme by, 196
  at Pappakurichi, 188
  promise for prohibition, 195
Rangarajan, C. (Chakravarthy Rangarajan), 16, 61, 68, 70
Rao, Kanuri Lakshmana, 293
Rao, Mohan, 236
Rao, P.V. Narasimha, (Pamulaparti Venkata Narasimha Rao), 11, 21, 22, 56, 58, 69, 209, 223, 249, 250
  plan to revive the economy, 69-71
  as prime minister, 21-23, 69, 72
  swearing-in ceremony of, 21-22
Rao, V. K. R.V. (Vijayendra Kasturi Ranga Varadaraja Rao), 103, 107
Reagan, Ronald, 220-228, 235, 239, 242, 288
  arrival at Cancun, 220
  meeting with Zhao Ziyang, 221
  meeting with Indira Gandhi, 221-222
  Science and Technology Agreement between, 228
Reddy, N. Sanjiva, (Neelam Sanjiva Reddy), 39, 118, 129, 144, 146, 149-151, 156, 222
Reddy, Narreddy Thulasi, 202, 203
Reddy, Y. Venugopal, (Yaga Venugopal Reddy), 70
Rekhi, Kanwal, 249
Research and Analysis Wing (RAW), 309

Reserve Bank of India (RBI), 243, 244
  managing foreign exchange balance, 70
  shipping of gold to Bank of England, 10, 70-71
Reserve Bank of India Act 1934, 142
Right of Children to Free and Compulsory Education Act, 214
Right to Education (RTE) Act, 217
Right to information, 18, 257, 258 261, 263, 265-287
  a breakthrough in the, 276
  demand for, 269
  history of the, 261-263
  in Sweden, 261-262
Right to Information Bill 1996, 269
  activists support to the, 285
  aim of the, 285
  flaws in the, 285
  impact of the, 286-287
  passed, 286
  presented in Parliament, 285
Robinson, James, 12
Rockefeller Foundation, 94, 105-108
Roy, Aruna, 259, 266-268, 275, 280, 283, 284, 286
  an NCPRI activist, 275
  Magsaysay Award winner, 259
Roy, Sanjit 'Bunker', 257
Royal Commission on Agriculture, 77, 158
  recommendations on agricultural economy, 77
Rusk, Dean, 113, 132

S. P. Gupta vs Union of India, 265
Sahay, Vishnu, 166, 167
Sampoorna Grameen Rozgar Yojana, 216
Santa Cruz Electronics Export Processing Zone (SEEPZ), 232
Santhanam Committee, 149, 300-301
Santhanam, K. (Kasturiranga Santhanam) 300
Sapru Committee, 203
Sarkaria Commission, 312
Sarva Shiksha Abhiyan, 217

Sawant, P. B., 267-269, 271, 273, 280
  as chairman of the Press Council, 267, 280
  visit to Goa, 273
Saxena, N. C. (Naresh C. Saxena), 268, 284
Schultz, Theodore, 97
Scindia, Madhavrao, 209
Scindia, Vasundhara Raje, 280
Second Five Year Plan, 29, 30, 35, 88, 90, 123, 172
  allocation for agriculture in the, 88
  criticism of the, 30
  emphasis on industrialization by the, 88
Sen, Amartya, 207
Sen, Mohit, 275
Sen, Pronab, 243
Sepoy uprising in 1857, 77
Seshagiri, Narasimaiah, 239
Seshan, T. N. (Tirunellai Narayana Seshan), 302
Shah, Manubhai, 133, 280
Shastri, Lal Bahadur, 11, 36, 37, 97-101, 104, 105, 107, 110, 112-114, 119, 127, 128, 132, 149, 177, 178, 181, 184
  died, 114, 128
  induction in Nehru's cabinet, 98
  opposition to, 98
  life and personality, 99-100
  Jai Jawan, Jai Kisan slogan of, 113
  Johnson meeting, 112
  as prime minister, 128
  visit to Anand, 177-178
Shek, Chiang Kai, 85
Shekhar, Chandra, 24, 53, 57-63, 65-67, 125, 137, 140, 141, 145, 150
  end of the regime of, 66
  meeting with industrialists, 58-59
  as prime minister, 58-59
  signature campaign of, 138
Shekhawat, Bhairon Singh, 260
Shenoy, B.R. (Bellikoth Ragunath Shenoy), 30, 89
Shourie Committee's draft, 279
Shroff, Ardeshir Darabshaw, 25

Singh, Arjun, 202, 203, 209
Singh, Ajit, 53, 55-57
Singh, Charan, 46, 55, 225
    fall of, 46
Singh, Digvijay, 270, 273
Singh, K. P. (Kushal Pal Singh), 254
Singh, L. P. (Lallan Prasad Singh), 181, 182
Singh, Manmohan, 15, 23, 58, 64, 67, 69, 70, 72, 284, 287
    as adviser to Chandra Shekhar, 23, 24
    as finance minister, 64, 67, 69
Singh, Rao Birendra, 184, 185, 200
Singh, Shankar, 259
Singh, V. P. (Vishwanath Pratap Singh), 50-60, 62, 244, 265, 268, 270, 284
    demand of information on the Bofors bribes, 265
    fall of, 58
    as finance minister, 50
    first address to the nation by, 53
    movement against corruption, 50, 52
    as Raid Raja, 50
    as seventh prime minister, 53-56, 244
Sinha, Yashwant, 58, 59, 63, 64, 66-68
    Confessions of a Swadeshi Reformer: My Years as Finance Minister, 67
    measures to stave off economic crisis, 59
Sir Charles Wood's Despatch on Education, 203
Sir Philip Hartog Committee, 203
Sivaraman, Balaraman, 105, 107, 108, 110, 174, 175
    as agriculture secretary, 105, 175
    Bitter Sweet, 107
    role in Green Revolution, 175
Software revolution, 230, 244, 247, 253
    role of telecom revolution in, 253
Software Technology Park of India (STPI), 250-252
    new temples of modern India, 252
Sondhi, Mantosh, 233
South Commission, 23
South Korea, 44, 58, 230, 238, 239, 256
    private-sector-led growth in, 44
Soviet invasion of Afghanistan, 222, 223

India's stance on, 222
Srinivasan, T. N. (Thirukodikaval Nilakanta Srinivasan), 45, 59
State Bank of India Act 1955, 142
State-led industrialization in India, 31, 36, 46, 103
    failure of, 36, 46
    thesis of, 46
State of UP vs Raj Narain, 265
Statutory Liquidity Ratio (SLR), 154, 155
Subbarao, Duvvuri, 153
Subramaniam, C. (Chidambaram Subramaniam), 11, 75, 96, 98-110, 114, 115, 124, 130, 151, 176, 178, 181
    father of the Green Revolution, 11, 109-110
    as food and agriculture minister, 101
    Hand of Destiny, 101
    plans for agriculture revival, 102-104
        creation of resources for, 107
        opposition of, 104-107
    as Rajaji's protégé, 102
    success story of, 101-102
    trials of hybrid seeds, 108-109
        success of, 109
Sukhadia, Mohanlal, 123
Swaminathan, M. S. (Monkombu Sambasivan Swaminathan), 93-94, 106, 107, 109, 110, 116
    father of the Green Revolution, 94, 116
Swamy, Subramanian, 50, 51, 58, 62, 63
    conversation with Rajiv Gandhi, 50
Swatantra Party, 30, 103, 126, 134, 135, 150, 199
The Syndicate, 39, 40, 119, 127-130, 133, 136, 137, 144-146, 149-152, 283
Syngal, B. K. (Brijendra Kumar Syngal), 249
    cutting down the cost of connectivity, 249
    meeting with Tom Watson Jr, 249

Taleb, Nassim Nicholas, 19
Tamil Nadu Right to Information Act 1997, 271, 272

Tarkunde, V. M. (Vithal Mahadeo Tarkunde), 268
Tata Consultancy Services (TCS), 231, 238, 251, 256
   first export assignment of, 231
   setting up of, 231
Tata Jamsetji, 26
   setting up of Tata Steel by, 26
Tata, J. R. D. (Jehangir Ratanji Dadabhoy Tata) 25, 39, 49
Tehelka sting on defence deals, 282
telecom department, 247, 248
   inefficiencies in the, 248
Telugu Desam Party (TDP), 199, 200, 281, 283
Tenancy reforms, 86-87
   in China, 87
   impact of, 87
Terrorism, 304-306, 308, 309
   attack on the Indian Parliament, 306
   Indian response to, 306
   and non-state actors theory, 307
   US response to, 308
   war against, 308
Texas Instruments, 227, 229, 236-238, 242, 249, 252
   entry of, 237-238
Thakurdas, Purushottamdas, 25, 79
Third Five Year Plan, 36, 92, 95, 123, 124, 173
Thomas Malthus theory, 110
Tata Institute of Fundamental Research Automatic Calculator (TIFRAC), 229
Total Literacy Campaign, 204
Toynbee, Arnold, 11
   A Study of History, 11
Truman, Harry, 85

UN Convention of Rights of the Child, 214
UN General Assembly Resolution 59(1), 263
UNESCO World Education for All conference, 208
UNICEF, 169, 172, 194, 204, 205, 297

Union of India vs Cricket Association of Bengal, 267
Unique Identity Scheme (UID), 303
Unit Trust of India (UTI), 127
United States,
   arms package to Pakistan, 223
      India's protest against, 223
   campaign for the freedom of information in the, 262
   concepts of free will and free markets, 289
   India Emergency Food Aid Act in, 85
   Marshall Plan, 85, 224
   Mastering the World Economy initiative of the, 242
   and Pakistan syndicate, 149
   warplanes, issue of refuelling in India, 65-66
Universal Declaration of Human Rights, Article 19, 263
UTI-Ketan Parekh scam, 300

Vajpayee, Atal Bihari, 11, 95, 252, 253 276-278, 282
   comments on bureaucracy, 277
   opening of long-distance telephony by, 253
   as prime minister, 276, 277, 282
   speech at the National Development Council meeting, 277
Vakil, C. N. (Chandulal Nagindas Vakil), 30, 45
Venkatachalliah commission, 312
Venkatachalliah, M. N. (Manepalli Nararayana Venkatachalliah), 312
Venkataraman, R. (Ramaswamy Venkataraman), 46, 49, 61, 65
   comments on the Bofors scandal, 49
   as finance minister, 46
   My Presidential Years, 49
   as president of India, 49, 61, 65
Venkitaramanan, S., 52, 55, 67, 68, 70, 75
Verma, A. N. (Amar Nath Verma), 55, 56, 63, 69, 70, 250
Videsh Sanchar Nigam Limited (VSNL), 238, 248, 249, 250, 253
Vira, Dharam, 38

Vittal, Nagaraj, 244-250, 253
  as head of the Department of Electronics, 245, 249
  revamping of the, 249
  work on the software sector, 245-250
Vogel, Orville, 94

Wilson, Harold, 133
World Bank, 16, 22, 23, 37, 45, 60, 64, 67, 86, 90, 91, 97, 131-134, 186, 198, 202, 204, 205, 207, 212, 242, 250, 316
  Project Completion Report of the, 64
  study on India's electronics industry by the, 242
  Wasting Away, study by the, 212
World Children Report 2011, 216
World Health Organization, 172

World War II, 26, 78, 83, 85, 262, 289, 301

Xiaoping, Deng, 57, 116, 288

Yamazaki, K., 52, 63
  views on India's economy, 63
Yashpal Committee, 204
Yew, Lee Kuan, 12, 288
Young Turks, 125, 136-137, 141, 142, 144, 145, 148, 150, 151
  support to Bank nationalization, 141
  ten-point charter of demands of the, 137, 139, 141, 145

Zakir Hussain Committee, 203
Zamindari (Abolition) Act, 86
Zamindari system, 81, 86, 95, 122
  abolition of the, 81, 86, 95, 122